Frozen in Time

The Fagel Collection in the Library of Trinity College Dublin

BIBLIOTHECA FAGELIANA.

A CATALOGUE

of the valuable and extenſive LIBRARY of the

Greffier FAGEL, of the *Hague:*

Comprehending a choice Collection of BOOKS,

in various Languages,

in THEOLOGY and *Eccleſiaſtical Hiſtory*;

in *Claſſical* and *Philological Learning*,

and in moſt Branches of *Polite Literature;*

in *Philoſophy*, *Phyſics*, and *Natural Hiſtory;*

in *Painting*, *Architecture*, *Engraving*,

and the whole Body of *ARTS* and *SCIENCES*:

in Chronology, Egyptian, Greek and Roman Antiquities;

in Antient and Modern Hiſtory and Topography,

including many choice BOOKS of PRINTS:

in Genealogy and Juriſprudence,

and in Geography, Voyages and Travels;

Digeſted by *Sam. Paterſon.*

PART I.

WHICH WILL BE SOLD BY AUCTION,

by Mr. CHRISTIE,

at Number 5, in *Duke Street*, *St. James's*, LONDON,

On Monday, *March* 1, 1802, and the Twenty-nine following Days,

to begin preciſely at 12 o'Clock.

To be viewed on Monday, *February* 22, and to the Time of Sale.

Catalogues, Price THREE SHILLINGS AND SIXPENCE, may be had at Mr. CHRISTIE's, *Pall Mall*, and at the Place of Sale.

Printed by Barker and Son, Gt. Ruſſell-St. Cov. Gar.

Frozen in Time

The Fagel Collection in the Library of Trinity College Dublin

Edited by Timothy R. Jackson

THE LILLIPUT PRESS

First published 2016 by
THE LILLIPUT PRESS LTD
62–63 Sitric Road, Arbour Hill, Dublin 7, Ireland
www.lilliputpress.ie

ISBN 978 1 84351 675 0

A CIP record is available from the British Library.

1 3 5 7 9 10 8 6 4 2

Kingdom of the Netherlands

The Long Room HUB

KINGDOM OF BELGIUM
Federal Public Service
Foreign Affairs, Foreign Trade and Development Cooperation

Set in Garamond and Bureau Grotesque
Design by Niall McCormack
Printed in Spain by Castuera

Contents

BIBLIOTHECA
8120
Q. 3. 1
FAGELIANA
AVEC LE TEMPS
PAVLATIM

Illustrations

FIGURES

PLATES

Foreword

Patrick Prendergast
PROVOST

VISITORS TO the Library of Trinity College Dublin are often amazed when they enter the Long Room of the Old Library. An impressive array of marble busts pays homage to famous scholars of the past, and the room itself has an inspiring barrel-vaulted ceiling very pleasing to the eye. But there is much more to the Library than its architecture, magnificent though that is.

Scholars have the opportunity to be amazed for a second time when they discover just how magnificent the collections in the library are. This volume presents the first book-length scholarly analysis of one of the most treasured: the Fagel Collection. Professor Tim Jackson has succeeded admirably in bringing together a distinguished group of scholars whose contributions range from a history of the Fagel family to examinations of the literature, maps, plans and pamphlets that constitute the collection. A Germanist and Fellow Emeritus of Trinity College, his own contribution deals with Dutch interest in Irish affairs, highlighting material in the collection that is relevant to Irish social and political history.

The Fagel family was one of the foremost political families of the Dutch Golden Age. Effectively exiled in London as a result of the invasion of the Netherlands by French revolutionary forces, the then head of the family, Hendrik, was ultimately forced to sell their vast collection of books, pamphlets and manuscripts. The Library of Trinity College Dublin purchased the collection, whole and intact, in 1802.

The authors of the contributions to this book throw down some challenges to provosts and university librarians. With collections like the Fagel come responsibilities – responsibilities for the preservation of rare and unique material, and for ensuring accessibility through cataloguing and digitization. Also, there is a need to promote study of the collection through scholarships and fellowships. No one underestimates these challenges. In Ireland, as in many other parts of the world, the funding needed is hard to come by. Here in this volume we see the commitment of several scholars to establishing evidence of the collection's importance through their exploration and exhibition of the vast wealth of material that it holds. It is vital that support for the further investigation into the Fagel Collection endures, so that the many resources that lie within it continue to be uncovered.

JUNE 2016

Preface

Tim Jackson
TRINITY COLLEGE DUBLIN

IN 1777 the Revd Thomas Campbell's *Philosophical Survey of the South of Ireland* appeared anonymously. It took the form of a series of letters to one 'John Watkinson', a fictitious Englishman created for the purpose.[1] The author devotes some early pages to a description of the buildings of Trinity College Dublin, in which, alongside some critical remarks about the provost's house and the chapel, he concedes the presence of 'a most superb library, which, being built of very bad stone, is unfortunately mouldering away', but whose interior is 'at once, beautiful, commodious, and magnificent'.[2] He mentions the collections of books that had been left to the library by James Ussher (1581–1656) and Claudius Gilbert (1669/70–1743), but complains that 'Since [Gilbert's] time, which is above forty years, their number has not been much increased, though there are many vacant shelves [...]. Of course the modern publications in this library are very few; yet I am told there is a sufficient fund for purchasing every thing that comes out.'

Campbell was not to know that within a quarter of a century there would be not just the finance but also the opportunity and the will to acquire a private collection that – relative to the existing holdings – was to constitute the largest influx of books and maps in the entire history of that library.

1 [Thomas Campbell] *A Philosophical Survey of the South of Ireland, in a Series of Letters to John Watkinson, M. D.* (London 1777). Campbell (1733–95) received a BA from Dublin University (Trinity College Dublin) in 1756 and was ordained in the Church of Ireland five years later; since 1773 he had been the chancellor of St Macartin's church in Clogher, Co. Fermanagh.

2 *Ibid.*, pp. 10–13.

In the winter of 1794–5 Hendrik Fagel the Younger,[3] 'Greffier' or Chief Minister to the States General of the Netherlands, was stranded in England when French revolutionary forces invaded the Netherlands. Eventually he was able to arrange for his library to be shipped to London, where, because of his reduced financial circumstances, he determined to sell it. However, the auction, for which Christie's had produced an elaborate catalogue (two volumes, containing almost 10,000 lots – see frontispiece),[4] did not take place, because in February/March 1802 the governors of the Erasmus Smith Schools in Dublin put in a successful bid for the entire collection on behalf of Trinity College. In May of that year it began to arrive in Dublin: most of the books were systematically, if slowly, installed in the East Pavilion adjoining the Long Room of the Old Library (see Harris, Thematic shelving, fig. 1), and from March 1809 they were accessible to readers.[5] The map collection is now stored in the West Attic in the Old Library.

In the course of five generations of public service to the States General and Holland, beginning with the appointment of Gaspar as Greffier to the States General in 1670, the Fagel family had built up one of the most important private libraries in early modern Europe. The holdings in history, politics and law were particularly substantial, but virtually every other area of human endeavour was represented too: belles-lettres, philosophy and theology, geography and travels, natural history, the visual arts and much more. As such, the Fagels' collections of books and maps can be compared to, say, their collection of plants: at once a practical resource and a treasure house of aesthetic pleasure. The collection of books was 'not a scholar's library, but the delight of learned gentlemen', not 'the eighteenth-century grand library of men of letters', but as François Fagel the Elder termed it, 'a library of use'.[6]

Through the acquisition of this collection the existing library of the College was transformed. Quantitatively, it is estimated that the total holdings were increased by some 40 per cent: at a time when these consisted of roughly

3 See Thomassen, fig. 2 for the Fagel pedigree.

4 *Bibliotheca Fageliana: a Catalogue of the Valuable and Extensive Library of the Greffier Fagel* [...] *Digested by Sam. Paterson. Part I: which Will Be Sold by Auction, by Mr. Christie* [...] *on March 1, 1802* [...] (London [1802]), accessible via www.digitalcollections.tcd.ie – click on Paterson, Samuel.

5 For brief accounts of the acquisition and contents of the library see Peter Fox, *Trinity College Library Dublin: a History* (Cambridge 2014), chap. 8 (pp. 115–28): 'Fagel: 1798–1809', and the same writer's article in this volume; also Vincent Kinane, 'The Fagel Collection' in Peter Fox (ed.), *Treasures of the Library, Trinity College Dublin* (Dublin 1986), pp. 158–69. As a consequence of the decision of the Board of the College (1966/7) to remodel the interior of the East Pavilion, half of the collection was moved elsewhere: see Fox, *Trinity College Library*, pp. 322f.

6 See pp. 143 and 41 respectively.

50,000 volumes, a further 20,000 were added – and one must realize that a 'volume' can consist of thirty or forty pamphlets bound together, in the same way that twenty-five portfolio boxes contain nearly 3000 sheet maps. Despite the presence of some 1800 lots of religious publications, the volume of other material was such that a university resource that had hitherto been dominated by theological interests became irreversibly secular in orientation. For the intervening two centuries, however, this immense cultural and scholarly storehouse has remained unknown to all but a small number of specialists within Trinity College and elsewhere. As Brummell wrote, 'So completely has it vanished, that it is hardly known that the library of Trinity College houses this collection.'[7]

From 4 to 6 September 2008 the College hosted the Fagel Symposium, organized by Helga Robinson-Hammerstein, Martine Van Berlo, Charles Benson and myself, with the explicit purpose of making the collection more widely known outside the walls. There were some forty-five participants: a mixture of librarians, historians of the book and university academics from a wide range of disciplines, including history, language/literature, history of art, economics and information studies. In addition to Ireland there was substantial representation from the Netherlands, Belgium and Great Britain. Besides sixteen papers treating a wide variety of topics the programme also included opportunities to view the collection *in situ*, a reception in the Long Room of the Library at which an exhibition of Fagel material was opened, and a recital of organ music by the eighteenth-century Dutch composer Unico Willem van Wassenaere in the College Chapel.

This volume contains a selection of the papers presented at the symposium, as well as several new articles. One cannot claim that they provide a comprehensive description of such a large and disparate store of knowledge, but they do constitute the first book-length presentation of the Fagel Collection of books and maps as it stands today in the Library of Trinity College, examined from a number of perspectives. Some of the articles embody the considered results of years of engagement with the family and their accumulations of cultural artefacts; some are the work of relative newcomers to the field.[8]

7 L. Brummel, 'The Fagel Library in Trinity College, Dublin' in *idem*, *Miscellanea libraria: opstellen over boek- en bibliotheekwezen* [...] ('s-Gravenhage 1957), pp. 204–33, here p. 228.

8 The title borrows a phrase, 'frozen in time', that has been used to describe the way in which the collection marks an eighteenth-century change in literary taste: 'the emergence of English as the successful rival of French'; see Jean-Paul Pittion, 'The Fagel Collection', *Hermathena*, 121 (1976), 108–16, here 112.

Following Helga Robinson-Hammerstein's overview of the role of the European university library in the centuries that preceded Trinity College's spectacular acquisition, Theo Thomassen and John Loughman address the background to the collection itself: the administrative activities of the Fagels; the vast archives that relate to them directly or indirectly; their acquisition of books and coins, maps and paintings; the building complex at Noordeinde 140, The Hague, in which they and their archives and collections were housed; and a manuscript tulip catalogue and a planting plan for a bed of tulips that relate to the garden attached to this house. Peter Fox describes the complex processes by which the College acquired the collection and Dr Thomas Elrington, Senior Fellow, arranged for its transportation to Dublin, while Jason Harris deals with the practicalities of shelving it once it had arrived. Four articles investigate the wealth of the holdings across a range of areas: David Brown describes a selection of maps of differing types and provenances found in an immense collection that stretches from the local to the cosmographical; with no less than 30 per cent of the holdings printed in Latin, Jason Harris examines the Neo-Latin material as an expression of the intellectual interests and upward social progression of the family; Clare Guest finds that, with specific regard to the Italian Humanists, who are also well represented in the collections donated to the College by the gift of Gilbert and the bequest of Henry George Quin (1760–1805), the Fagels' interest lay more in the direction of history and art history than literature; and my own article assessing material of Irish interest includes, for example, reference to some sixty pamphlets relating to social and political affairs in seventeenth-century Ireland. The last two articles focus on the future: William Kelly urges that in particular the holdings of legal dissertations be made more widely available as quickly as possible, while Jaap Harskamp argues specifically that it is essential that all relevant holdings be recorded in the Short Title Catalogue Netherlands.

It was frequently observed during the symposium that the Fagel Collection raises questions to which we have – as yet – no answers: every article points to material about which there is much more to be said. Moreover, the collection covers many fields of human activity that the Fagels clearly found important, but which receive no detailed examination below. For example, in relation to legal matters the auction catalogue has more than 600 lots, including over a hundred dissertations – not to mention hundreds of pamphlets relating to municipal ordinances, government proclamations and the like. Of the 1800 auction lots devoted to *Theologia* many relate to religious controversies – deism, atheism, Arminianism, the nature of the soul, resurrection, predestination – some of them gathered by Paterson into subsections like *Tractatus adversus Atheos, Epicureos, Incredulosque* or *Increduli celebriores eorumque refellentes*; and many of these lots offer several titles, multi-volume collections or anthologies, such as the 200 volumes of sermons. At least two areas contain a significant amount of unique material: the map collection holds a number of manuscripts, including battle plans and records of relatively small land holdings or Dutch polder systems; and, based on a chronologically wide-ranging sample of some 300 volumes of pamphlets in the collection, Jaap Harskamp has estimated that perhaps as many as 10 per cent of the titles are not recorded in the STCN. And while Andrew Pettegree calculates that (contrary to Paterson's claim of 'upwards of 10,000') lot 7593 contains some 4500 pamphlets out of a total of approximately 6000, his survey of three volumes relating to the early decades of the seventeenth century confirms this optimistic estimate of the proportion of unrecorded material.[9] Titles that are not to be found in either the STCN or the STC Vlaanderen include: *Nieuwe ordonnancie op tstuck vande navigatie ende toerustinghe van de schepen*, Antwerp: Christoffel Plantijn, 1579 [Fag. H.I.2, no. 34]; *De Religions-vrede: gheaccordeert ende gepubliceert binnen Antwerpen den xiien Junij/* M.D.*lxxix*, Antwerp: Christoffel Plantijn, 1579 [Fag. H.I.2, no. 38]; *Placcaet onss Heeren des Conincr* [*recte*: *Conincx*]. *Inhoudende verbot van egeene waren/ coopmanschappen/ manufactueren oft hantwerck buyten lande vueren/ sonder trecht vanden thienden penninck te betalen* [...], Antwerp: Christoffel Plantijn, 1579 [Fag. H.I.2, no. 13]; *Nyeuwetijdinghe. Van de ancoemst eens Wilden Mans, die in Engelant gebracht is voorleden Jaer/ van den Capiteyn Forbisser* [*recte*: *Frobisher*], Amsterdam: Cornelis Claesz, 1582 [Fag. H.I.17, no. 16]. These relate to subjects as diverse as shipping regulations, confessional relations, tithes on manufactured goods, and the Inuit whom Martin Frobisher brought back to England from his voyage of 1577 (see figs. 1 and 2). It is therefore quite possible that many hundreds of Fagel pamphlets are not to be found in any other library and thus have up to now entirely escaped scholarly attention. Quite apart from socio-historical questions relating to the practice of accumulating collections (what were the complex currents that swept these books and maps into the possession of this family in the Low Countries in the early modern period?),[10]

9 Unpublished manuscript based on a survey carried out in 2012.

10 There is evidence that the Fagels acquired many volumes second-hand: a study of previous ownership might well be rewarding.

De

Religions-vrede:

Gheaccordeert ende gepubliceert binnen Antwerpen den xij^{en} Junij/ M. D. lxxix.

T'ANTWERPEN,
By Christoffel Plantijn / Drucker der Con. Maiesteyt.
M. D. LXXIX.

Fig 1: *De Religions-vrede: gheaccordeert ende gepubliceert binnen Antwerpen den xii^{en} Junij/* M.D.*lxxix*, Antwerp: Christoffel Plantijn, 1579. (Fag. H.I.2, no. 38)

Nyeuwe tijdinghe.

Van de aencoemst eens VVilden Mans, die in Engelant gebracht is voorleden Jaer/ van den Capiteyn Forbisser/ met oock eē Wilde Vrou ende haer Kint/ hoe vreemt sy haer hebben aenghestelt.

Oock mede de vindinghe hares Lants, tvvelck int Noortvvest ghelegen is, al vvaer de Engelschen vvtghebracht hebben, haer Scheepen vol Gouterde gheladen. Met de beschrijuinge van tselue Lant, ende de vreemde manieren van tvolck, die meer Beestachtich dan Menschelijck zijn, seer vvonderlijck om leesen,

In Engels vvtgegaē by Henricy Binneman drucker der Coninginnē.

Nv ghedruckt tot Amstelredam/ by Cornelis Claesz. int Schrijfbouck opt water 1582.

16

Fig 2: *Nyeuwe tijdinghe. Van de ancoemst eens Wilden Mans, die in Engelant gebracht is voorleden Jaer/ van den Capiteyn Forbisser*, Amsterdam: Cornelis Claesz, 1582. (Fag. H.1.17, no. 16)

the Fagel Collection offers an abundance of possibilities for research into material about which we have hitherto had little or no inkling.

A number of institutions and individuals deserve the gratitude of those who attended the symposium and the readers who will benefit from this publication. Firstly, the project could not have gone ahead without substantial financial assistance from the Dutch and Belgian embassies and from Trinity College's research institute for the arts and humanities, the Long Room Hub: we are grateful in particular to Kanta Adhin, Siegfried Peinen and Moray McGowan. Since then there has been further generous support from Trinity Development and Alumni, and from the Provost, Dr Patrick Prendergast.

Many others helped to make the symposium a success: Robin Adams, Jennifer Edmond, Jane Finucane, Elizabeth Fleeton, Andrew Johnstone, Charles Larkin, Eva Muhlhause and Simon Williams. I am grateful to Antony Farrell of Lilliput Press for agreeing to publish this volume, to Djinn von Noorden, Suzy Freeman and Niall McCormack for guiding it through the production process, and to Sharon Sutton of the Digital Resources and Imaging Service in TCD for creating many of the illustrations.

A special word of thanks is due to the staff of the Early Printed Books Department of Trinity College Library, who in the face of dwindling resources (both personnel and finance) continue to demonstrate expertise, commitment and unfailing courtesy towards those who wish to make use of the resources in their charge. Finally, I would like to thank my fellow organizers, Helga Robinson-Hammerstein, Martine Van Berlo and Charles Benson. The motivation for the symposium and this volume lay in our desire to bring the Fagel Collection to the attention of, and in the longer term to make it more accessible to, a wider public, both scholarly and general. As Charles Benson points out in his introduction, the most pressing need is the production of a catalogue of the Fagel Collection based on modern bibliographical principles, which would make redundant the very unsatisfactory means of retrieval provided by the printed catalogue of 1872, even in its electronic form.[11] It is sadly the case that the current level of cataloguing would not enable readers to locate, say, some of the ephemeral and/or unique material, even if they knew

11 This, the product of a labour of love on the part of the late Dr John Byrne, former Professor of Computer Science, and available at https://www.cs.tcd.ie/1872catalogue/index.php, unavoidably has some of the deficiencies of the catalogue itself: in particular the listing of shorter, ephemeral or anonymous publications is incomplete. But – not least due to the facility for searching for keywords from titles, especially those of anonymous pamphlets – this tool represents the greatest improvement to the accessibility of the Fagel Collection in over a century.

to look for it.[12] A programme of digitization is also essential and the website dedicated to the map collection, which David Brown mentions in his article, shows the way forward.[13] Where necessary (though the collection of books and maps is generally in very good condition) measures for the conservation of the holdings must be undertaken.

It is our hope that in due course sufficient funding will be found to realize these aims.

JUNE 2016

12 Of the volumes of pamphlets that have single-sheet items interspersed through them, Fag. H.2.81 is perhaps exceptional in having as many as twenty-seven, including poetic and satirical material. None of them is listed in the 1872 catalogue.

13 See pp. 118–119.

Introduction

Charles Benson
TRINITY COLLEGE DUBLIN

HENDRIK FAGEL the Younger (1765–1838), Greffier or Chief Minister of Holland, had the misfortune of having his property seized by invading French forces in the winter of 1794–5. He did manage to secure the release of his family art collection and library, which were shipped to him in London in 1798. Being in straitened circumstances he decided to sell them and negotiations took place for the purchase of the library for Trinity College; but these broke down, and early in 1802 the library was advertised for sale by auction to commence on 1 March. The catalogue listed almost 10,000 lots. In February 1802 the purchase by Trinity College of the library in its entirety was agreed, with the necessary funds provided by the Erasmus Smith Foundation (the collections of prints and drawings had previously been dispersed in two sales in 1799 and 1801).

The acquisition occurred at a time when the College was modernizing itself. After decades of lethargy the library had, since the early 1790s, enjoyed a surge in funding to redress the deficiencies in the holdings of recent publications. There were signs of increasing intellectual vigour in the academic staff. The library was directed by Dr 'Jacky' Barrett, a librarian possessed of considerable vision and energy. It has been calculated that by 1800 the library possessed about 50,000 volumes. At a stroke the 20,000 volumes of the Fagel Collection increased the stock by 40 per cent. At the same time the library was coming to terms with its recent designation as a legal deposit library for United Kingdom publications. The new accession occupied approximately 1.5 kilometres of shelving, so it is not surprising that it took almost seven years to make the bulk of it available for public use. Housing it involved a major reorganization of library space. Shelf marks had to be allocated and an alphabetical catalogue constructed from the only available listing, the London auction catalogue, which was arranged in broad subject categories. A copy of the auction catalogue was annotated with shelf marks and provides the best subject access to the collection to this day.

As a resource built up by successive generations of a family that was heavily involved in public affairs until 1795, it is not surprising to find that the collection reflects the realities of Dutch political life both within the state and beyond it. The library was primarily a wide-ranging working reference source. It is full of works dealing with the politics, economics and religious controversies of north-western Europe from the late sixteenth until the late eighteenth century. As one would expect, there is extensive coverage of the events of the long war waged to achieve Dutch independence from Spain and the later wars fought with France. There is much other material relating to France, including a large collection of *Mazarinades* published during the *Fronde* in 1648 to 1652, numerous volumes of state entries to cities, and political biographies. Many thousands of pamphlets cover the history and politics of every state in Europe. Much material reflects the early history and civilization of Europe: editions of chronicles, collections of laws, biographies of eminent leaders, editions of the works of writers from classical times onward. The geographical and topographical works include such important compilations as Matthäus Merian's *Topographia* (Frankfurt 1644–57), and numerous histories of cities. Works abound that cover the Dutch colonial and trading experience in the Americas, South Africa, the East Indies, China and Japan. The collection is not limited to matters of Dutch interest: the *Corpus Byzantinæ historiæ* (Paris 1648–1702) published by the *Imprimerie Royale* in twenty-nine volumes points to wider intellectual interests. There are two surprising weaknesses: the paucity of material relating to the disturbances in Austrian Flanders in the late 1780s and to the French Revolution.

The importance and variety of the texts are matched by the immense quantity of illustration in the books. It is obvious that the family had a keen interest in visual material, whether in the superb collection of maps and atlases, in works on natural history, in histories of regions and cities, in architectural works, accounts of archaeology, or histories of state entries and ceremonies. The

Fig 1: Abraham Rademaker, *Hollands Arcadia, Of de vermaarde Rivier den Amstel*, Amsterdam: Leonardus Schenk, 1730 (plates 3 and 4): two of the houses adorning the banks of the Amstel. (Fag. 1.3.20)

auction catalogue gives an indication of the range: *Conterfet Kupfferstich deren jenigen regierenden grossen Herren, so von Käysers Ferdinand dess Andern Geburt, biß zu desselben seeligisten tödtlichen Abschied successivè regiert* (Leipzig 1721–2) in folio is 'embellished with 392 Portraits of sovereign princes'; Dominicus Custos, *Fuggerorum et Fuggerarum* [...] *imagines* (Augsburg 1593) has 'eleven additional Portraits, making together 148'; Abraham Rademaker, *Hollands Arcadia* (Amsterdam 1730) contains one hundred plates (see fig. 1); the elegant first edition of Goethe's *Das römische Carneval* (Berlin 1789) is illustrated with a series of hand-coloured plates by Georg Melchior Kraus printed on fine paper; and an album of fine architectural drawings illustrates the magnificent appearance projected for St Petersburg in the middle of the eighteenth century (see plates 1 and 2).

Some of the most important works are those presenting new discoveries of fauna and plants. Among the early botanical works are Leonhart Fuchs, *De historia stirpium commentarii* (Paris 1543) (see fig. 2); Basilius Besler, *Hortus Eystettensis* ([n.p] 1613); and J.M. Seligmann, *Sammlung verschiedener ausländischer und seltener Vögel* (Nürnberg 1749–64), with 322 plates, is matched for beauty by the brilliant colour of the butterflies in Pierre Cramer, *Papillons exotiques des trois parties du monde l'Asie, l'Afrique et l'Amérique* (Amsterdam 1779–82). A few of these are in spectacular deluxe copies, including Jan Commelin, *Horti medici Amstelodamensis* [...] *descriptio* (Amsterdam 1697) and Abraham Munting, *Naauwkeurige beschryving der aardgewassen* (Leiden and Utrecht 1696). Some of the gorgeous books have bindings to match, but in general bindings are plain, with much use of vellum and dark calf. One of the relatively few incunables in the collection, the two-volume edition of Plutarch's *Vitæ* (Venice 1478) produced by Nicolaus Jenson for the Venetian Agostini family, was printed on fine parchment with a splendid frontispiece to each volume and a wealth of large decorative initials (see plates 3, 4 and 32).

The richness of this remarkable family library remains largely hidden to scholars because the only guides to its contents are the original auction catalogue of 1802 and the Library's Printed Catalogue published between 1864 and 1887. The Printed Catalogue is essentially an author catalogue with some subject grouping, particularly under proper names. The entries are too brief to be useful. Among the alarming, though often unappreciated, defects was the practice of abbreviating titles by the silent omission of preliminary adjectives before the first noun. This makes identification of the edition listed uncertain

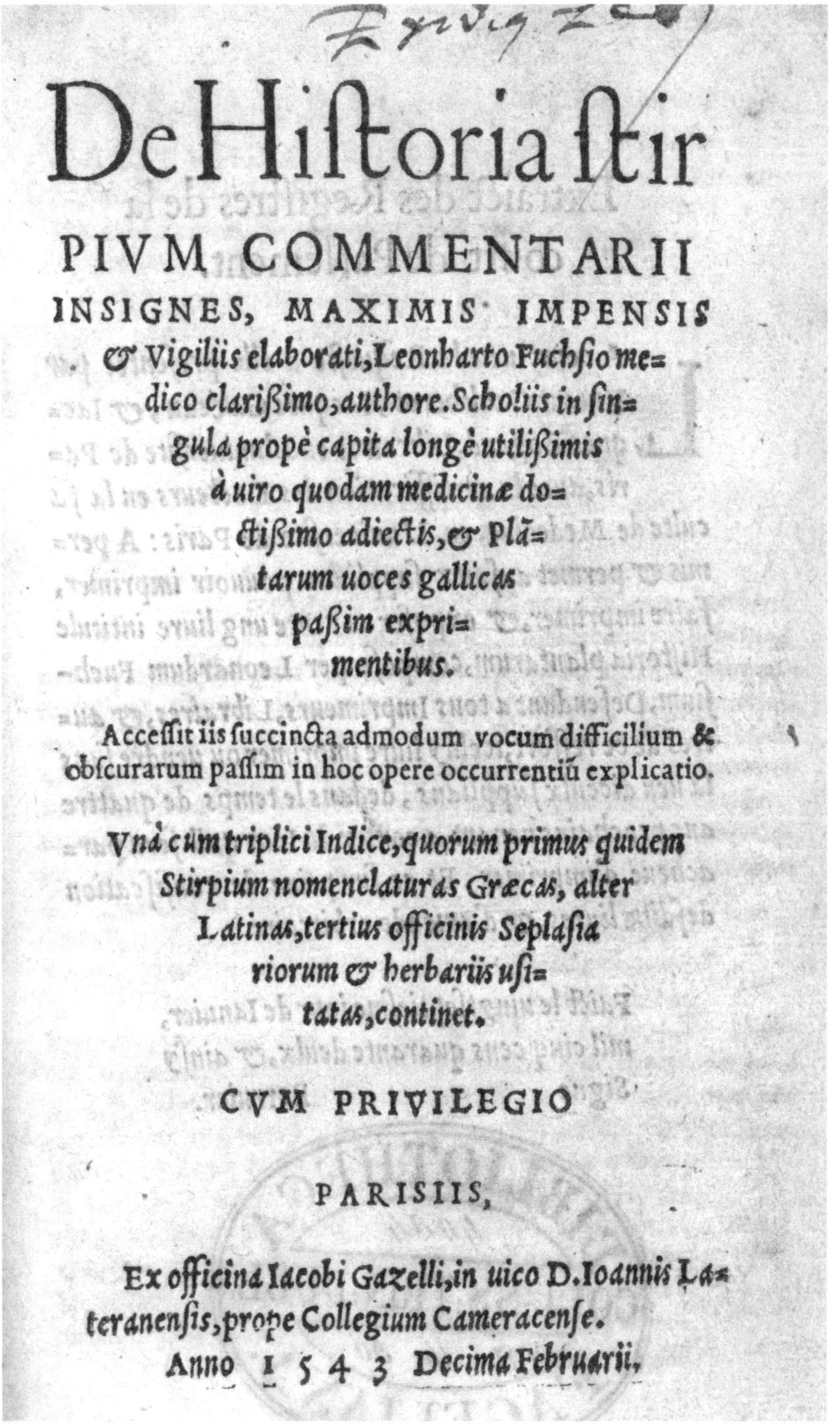

De Historia stir
PIVM COMMENTARII
INSIGNES, MAXIMIS IMPENSIS
& Vigiliis elaborati, Leonharto Fuchsio me-
dico clarißimo, authore. Scholiis in sin-
gula propè capita longè utilißimis
à uiro quodam medicinæ do-
ctißimo adiectis, & Plã-
tarum uoces gallicas
paßim expri-
mentibus.

Accessit iis succincta admodum vocum difficilium &
obscurarum passim in hoc opere occurrentiũ explicatio.

Vnà cum triplici Indice, quorum primus quidem
Stirpium nomenclaturas Græcas, alter
Latinas, tertius officinis Seplasia
riorum & herbariis usi-
tatas, continet.

CVM PRIVILEGIO

PARISIIS,

Ex officina Iacobi Gazelli, in uico D. Ioannis La-
teranensis, prope Collegium Cameracense.
Anno 1 5 4 3 Decima Februarii.

Fig 2: Leonhartus Fuchsius, *De Historia stirpium*, Paris: Iacobus Gazellus, 1543. (Fag. N.10.80)

and difficult. The names of printers/publishers are not supplied, nor is there any statement of pagination. There are 'dump' entries such as the following under 'HOLLANDIA':

> [A collection of ordinances, proclamations [...] relating to Holland, in the Dutch language, dated 1700–1728].
> 's Gravenhage, &c. 14 vols. Fag. H. 9. 19–32.

The uselessness of this description is all the more obvious when one realizes that the fourteen volumes occupy well over a metre of shelving. Another, under the heading 'FRIESLAND', offers

> [Maps, plans, and prospects of Friesland]
> [s. l. v. a.] fol. Fag. B. 2. 3.

This level of description gives no bibliographical control at all.

Even less helpful is the knowledge, gained from experience, that the original Trinity College cataloguers, when dealing with pamphlet volumes, often did not bother to list single-sheet items or indeed pamphlets. Not all the works in the Fagel Collection were catalogued at the time of accession: hundreds of pamphlets were listed in the Accessions Catalogue in the 1950s, and even today some legal treatises remain unlisted. The existence of the Printed Catalogue in a digitized form masks its inadequacy as a tool for 21st-century scholars. It certainly allows better searching of the meagre entries but meagreness remains the primary problem.

The early printed book catalogues in most institutions comprise an inadequate accumulation of records produced over long periods to varying standards. Most libraries have shown a marked reluctance on the part of management to examine the quality of the library catalogue as a working tool for scholars. This has long been the case in Trinity College Library despite a number of inquiries into the functioning of the university and its parts. The Library Working Party Report produced in May 1981 observed that 'to convert catalogue records produced before 1963 [when Trinity first produced a public card catalogue] would involve so many man-years of work that it could only be considered in terms of a national, or indeed international, programme', but did not attempt any assessment of the appropriateness of the records produced in the preceding century. In recent decades there has been a decline in quality control in the general catalogue of modern books and an acceptance of imported low-grade bibliographical records. In the case of the Department of Early Printed Books, high cataloguing standards were elaborated in the early 1970s and followed for the processing of new accessions until the first decade of this century. But sufficient labour was never available to make a retrospective cataloguing programme possible. The failure of the College to provide sufficient skilled library staff has led to a drastic fall in the quantity and quality of information provided in the catalogue – to the extent that very large collections acquired in recent decades have yet to be made available to scholars. And yet – possessing holdings of international importance brings with it the responsibility to make these holdings accessible.

The uses of older printed books have changed. They are no longer read simply for their intellectual content but are examined as physical artefacts and searched for provenances, for evidence provided by illustrations, paper and bindings, and considered as collections of taste. A catalogue must provide accurate information in all these fields to enable best use by scholars of the collections: in respect of both the Fagel holdings and more recently acquired material it is an inefficient use of staff resources to compile catalogue entries that provide inadequate information. Bringing the catalogue up to the best modern standards is an expensive proposition but it will open up new opportunities and areas of research. Such a catalogue is as necessary to scholars in the humanities as a properly equipped laboratory is to scientists. Without it, workers in the humanities – and indeed those researching early science – are doomed to waste time fumbling in relative darkness. The Fagel Collection and the vast bulk of the older printed stock of the library will continue to be little appreciated and underused, even as visitors to the Long Room gasp in awe at the closed volumes on the shelves.

Frozen in Time

The Fagel Collection in the Library of Trinity College Dublin

Libraries, *scholæ* and universities in medieval and early modern Europe: Key stages in their relationship

Helga Robinson-Hammerstein
TRINITY COLLEGE DUBLIN

LIBRARIES HAD existed for a long time before the first universities were founded. The process of western christianization had radiated out from the teachings of one book, the Bible, which was celebrated and preserved, for example, in the exquisitely illuminated manuscripts of Irish monks.[1] Regional rulers of the early Middle Ages began to assert themselves by means of legal pronouncements. Archives of law rolls served to build up a legislative tradition that was essential for the maintenance of order. Within a few decades these archives were extended into libraries. The ambition of the latter to bring together 'all books', however, was inspired less by governmental utility than by the reputation of the fabled library of Alexandria, that had allegedly housed 'all past knowledge'. Cicero, who never missed an opportunity in his writings to praise libraries as vital intellectual tools, possessed possibly the largest private collection of books in Roman antiquity.[2] In retrospect one can argue that the ideal library was conceived as a comprehensive encyclopaedic collection that permitted current issues to be measured against the record of past experiences. Although the ideal was often ignored in the daily political routine the basic insight had been enunciated: libraries are to be cultivated in order to preserve vital memory.

1 Bernard Meehan, *The Book of Kells* (London 2012).

2 See Uwe Jochum, *Geschichte der abendländischen Bibliotheken*, 2nd edn (Darmstadt 2012) and more specifically *idem*, 'The Alexandrian library and its aftermath', *Library History*, 15 (1999), 5–12.

Libraries, *scholæ* and medieval universities

An obvious example of efforts to ensure an effective 'library culture' is the Carolingian Renaissance in the late eighth and early ninth centuries. Charlemagne assembled scholars from all over Europe in his *schola* at the palace school of Aachen. He simultaneously instructed all bishops in his realm to establish cathedral schools that might make use of libraries to halt the educational decline of previous centuries. These libraries collected all available records of Roman philosophy and statecraft in texts that had to some degree absorbed Greek learning. Knowledge of the Roman and Anglo-Saxon legal traditions was complemented by the writings of the church fathers St Augustine and St Jerome. The libraries of the palace, monastic and cathedral schools received from their royal and noble benefactors exemplars of the works of Latin antiquity, Aristotle's logic and such instruction manuals of the late Roman Empire and early Middle Ages as the works of Boethius, Cassiodorus and Isidore of Seville.[3] It is evident that *scholæ* could not exist without libraries.[4] The masters were appreciated as the guarantors of the usefulness of libraries.

The medieval *scholæ* adopted the Roman curriculum of the seven liberal arts contained in the *trivium* (grammar, rhetoric, logic) and the *quadrivium* (arithmetic, geometry, astronomy, music). The compilation of textbooks for students was a central activity of intellectuals. Eleventh-century manuals of grammar, rhetoric, geometry and the *computus* (the correct measurement of time) were widely copied. The masters of the mid twelfth century were responsible for the textbook movement that produced the grammatical, legal and theological works that remained the basis of advanced study until the seventeenth century. The eleventh-century library of the cathedral school of Constance (known from the modern reconstruction by Johanne Autenrieth) offers the earliest evidence of scholars at work. Here students and masters can be seen initiating an early version of 'inter-library loan' in the form of correspondence requesting the loan of books to be copied.[5]

3 See Donald A. Bullough, *Alcuin: Achievement and Reputation* (Leiden and Boston 2004), pp. 252–300.

4 M.L.W. Laistner discusses the connection between libraries and schools in his *Thought and Letters in Western Europe A.D. 500 to 900*, revised edn (Ithaca 1957), especially chapters 8 and 9, pp. 207–50.

5 Johanne Autenrieth, *Die Domschule von Konstanz zur Zeit des Investiturstreits: Die wissenschaftliche Arbeitsweise Bernolds von Konstanz und zweier Kleriker* [...] (Stuttgart 1956). See also Ian S. Robinson, 'Bernold von Konstanz und der gregorianische Reformkreis um Bischof Gebhard III' in Helmus Maurer (ed.), *Die Konstanzer Münsterweihe von 1089* (Freiburg 1989), pp. 155–88, here p. 169.

From *scholæ* and the masters who benefited from the presence of libraries it seems but a small step to the founding of universities for systematic advanced teaching and learning. Universities, however, were not the result of a smooth and inevitable extension of *scholæ*. In the first instance, independent scholars of great renown, who had easy access to famous libraries, attracted students anxious to learn from their lectures and disputations as the means of discovering the truth. The first such gatherings favoured Bologna (specializing in the study of law on the basis of the rediscovery of the *Corpus iuris civilis*), Paris (for the liberal arts and theology) and Montpellier (for medicine, including experimental medicine). In the early thirteenth century one of these previously free scholars, Philippus de Grevia, expressed his bitter anger after he had himself been appointed magister and chancellor of the University of Paris following its formal establishment by royal charter. He complained of the neglect of learning and that 'the time needed to study is wasted in meetings and discussions' about administration. His other grudge was that the students were left to 'organize villainous plots and plan their nocturnal attacks'.[6]

There is indeed much evidence that previously independent scholars did not like the structural constraints that kings and popes imposed when these rulers issued binding university foundation charters from the thirteenth century onwards.[7] The university founders were anxious to supervise the recruitment of 'famous men' who possessed the qualification to teach throughout the entire realm of papal Christendom: *venia ubique legendi*.[8] The sums to be paid for the privilege were substantial and had to be negotiated in each case. The charters describe the purpose and often also the faculties for the teaching of the seven liberal arts, as well as regularizing the inculcation of the higher studies of law, theology and medicine.[9] Migration from one European university to another was the norm. For instance, students might study at the University of Paris but

6 On this topic see the stimulating reflections of Walter Rüegg, 'Themes' in Hilde de Ridder-Symoens (ed.), *A History of the University in Europe*, vol. 1: *Universities in the Middle Ages* (Cambridge 1992), pp. 3–34, here p. 15, and Jacques Verger, 'Patterns', *ibid.* pp. 35–76, here pp. 48–9, including a list of the European universities that had been established up to 1500, with their foundation dates (pp. 62–5).

7 Jos M.M. Hermans and Marc Nelissen (eds), *Charters of Foundation and Early Documents of the Universities of the Coimbra Group*, 2nd revised edn (Leuven 2005).

8 See Rüegg, 'Themes', p. 17.

9 See Gordon Leff, 'The *trivium* and the three philosophies' in de Ridder-Symoens, *Universities in the Middle Ages*, pp. 307–36; John North, 'The *quadrivium*', *ibid.* pp. 337–59. See further Nancy Siraisi, 'The faculty of medicine', *ibid.* 360–87; Antonia García y García, 'The faculties of law', *ibid.* pp. 388–408; Monica Asztalos, 'The faculty of theology', *ibid.* pp. 409–41. – Such research draws on the earlier studies by R.W. Southern in his work *The Making of the Middle Ages* (New Haven 1961).

postulate for their degree at a university where the examination fees and the expenses for the expected entertainments were more affordable.

Despite all the diversity in the operations of European universities, they had one thing in common: no university could survive without a library. Furthermore, university library policy was never narrow-minded, even if the institution itself was sparsely endowed. In order to enhance their reputation university libraries welcomed benefactions of books. The gifts were random and – to emphasize this once more – there was no systematically designed concept of what a university library should contain. In the later medieval period university teaching used only a small set of prescribed scholastic books with a strong emphasis on Latin translations of the works of Aristotle.[10] From a narrowly utilitarian perspective the majority of works in libraries at the disposal of universities were surplus to teaching requirements. With undaunted enthusiasm university libraries continued to champion the Alexandrian ideal of the library as guardian of knowledge and memory.

Humanism and printing

Two signal phenomena of the later fifteenth century combined to create the early modern universities with their libraries: the Italian *studia humanitatis* and Gutenberg's invention of printing with moveable type. The *studia humanitatis* (humanism) percolated through to the universities, replacing the previous emphasis on students' memorizing approved passages of standard works and dictated lecture notes. The printing technology facilitated a change in the method of teaching and learning. With the encouragement of printers to settle in university towns, humanist professors, the champions of the new teaching method of close critical reading of original texts, could acquire the authentic Greek texts and offer new Latin translations, cleansed of scholastic accretions, in rapidly and cheaply produced editions. Rather than mindless memorizing, students were introduced to the analysis of texts as a means to understanding. Since the established syllabus was retained, no 'restructuring' was considered necessary: in fact that would only have led to unproductive confrontations.[11]

10 See Verger, 'Patterns', p. 41.

11 See Agostino Sottili, 'Ehemalige Studenten italienischer Renaissance-Universitäten: Ihre Karriere und ihre soziale Rolle' in Rainer Christoph Schwinges (ed.), *Gelehrte im Reich: Zur Sozial- und Wirkungsgeschichte akademischer Eliten des 14. bis 16. Jahrhunderts* (Berlin 1996), pp. 41–74; Martin Kintzinger, 'Scholaster und Schulmeister. Funktionsfelder im späten Mittelalter', *ibid.* pp. 349–74. On humanism see: Wolfgang Reinhard (ed.), *Humanismus im Bildungswesen des 15. und 16. Jahrhunderts*. Acta Humaniora. Mitteilung XII der Kommission für Humanismusforschung (Weinheim 1984).

Humanist teachers, most of them educated at Italian Renaissance universities, where a quest for authenticity and a new spirit of enquiry had first been asserted, infiltrated the universities north of the Alps before much notice was taken of their presence. The scholastics who adhered to the traditional medieval curriculum were much slower to explore the variety of possibilities offered by printing technology. They rejoiced in the acquisition of large printed Bibles and related works, which could be admired in any library as sumptuously bound volumes continuing the most exquisite scribal tradition. Humanists, on the other hand, concentrated their efforts on searching in libraries for forgotten 'original' manuscripts and used their extended correspondence within an international friendship circle to find the most authentic texts of classical authors and the early church fathers. The collaboration of humanist scholars with printers in the preparation of critical editions of such rediscovered 'original' texts proved of vital benefit. Publishers like Aldus Manutius of Venice (rightly celebrated as the primary rescuer of Greek texts) and Johannes Froben of Basel favoured the clarity of the Roman font. The latter produced Erasmus's new Latin translation of early Greek manuscripts (1516), which he had discovered at Cambridge.[12] In this more legible font humanists and their publishers also released impressively decorated books to enhance the value of the holdings of university and princely as well as municipal libraries. Far from being averse to technological innovation, the humanists welcomed it emphatically. One should be aware, however, that technological innovation was seen as merely a tool to make the content of books more widely available. They insisted that the reading of books, rather than their proud possession, was the key to unlock the libraries and sustain a vibrant book culture.

The activities of Sebastian Brant (1457–1521) best illustrate the 'right attitude' to printing technology.[13] As professor of both laws at the University of Basel and a committed humanist teacher, who never abandoned his deep interest in the poetics (*ars poetica*) of Horace, he appreciated the advantages of printing technology as a medium of communication to enhance university teaching and learning. He published critical editions of lasting influence in both laws and rhetoric. In addition he offered something that in modern usage is called 'outreach'. This kind of outreach was not a university programme,

12 See Elizabeth L. Eisenstein, *The Printing Press as an Agent of Change: Communications and Cultural Transformations in Early-Modern Europe*, two vols (Cambridge 1979), p. 222 *et passim*.

13 Joachim Knape, *Sebastian Brant. Das Narrenschiff. Studienausgabe mit allen 114 Holzschnitten des Drucks Basel 1494* (Stuttgart 2005), pp. 26–51.

but rather the personal decision of a humanist professor, whose primary task it was to introduce university students to critical reading of works in Latin: Brant understood his calling to include the communication of insights in the vernacular to an urban elite who were unfamiliar with Latin. His greatest claim to popular fame is his comprehensive moral satire, *Das Narrenschiff*.[14] Supporting his argument with an abundance of biblical and classical references, Brant shone a clear light on the misguided conduct of teachers. He skilfully circumnavigated the evident failings of institutions. He stressed that their books were useless unless they were read and gave pride of place in his satire to those who called themselves scholars and their students. The scholars' negligence in communicating the content of the 'open books' set a bad example for students, who were only too happy to follow their elders in this foolish conduct in their 'useless studies'. Intellectually incurious young people spent their time socializing and drinking without attending to their studies or drawing on the riches of the libraries. In the first French translation of the *Ship of Fools* (1497) the introductory chapter on the 'book fool' was omitted because the publication was dedicated to the King of France, a great book collector vying with other rulers for the accolade of most powerful ruler in Christendom.[15]

Sebastian Brant's book fool was also used as a point of direct or indirect reference throughout the early modern period when making the case for opening up private libraries to 'the reading public' (meaning learned men). For example, the widely acclaimed scholar Gabriel Naudé (1600–53), reflecting on the varied functions of libraries, warned avid royal collectors that books should not merely be displayed for their beauty and the enhancement of the prestige of the ruler; rather the libraries should admit learned readers who would advance knowledge (*scientia*). Naudé also emphasized that 'a Library which is to be erected for the publick benefit ought to be universal'. He explains that to be universal 'it comprehends all the principal Authors that have written upon the great diversity of particular Subjects, and chiefly upon all the Arts and Sciences'.[16]

14 The original was published at Basel in 1494; the Latin version with more erudite references to classical literature (Basel 1497) became the basis of the translation into other European vernaculars; the most important of these were the French (Paris 1497) and the English (London 1517).

15 *Sébastien Brant, La Nef des Folz 1494–1994* [...] Catalogue d'exposition édité par les bibliothèques universitaires de Bâle et de Fribourg-en-Brisgau *et al.* (Basel 1994), p. 203.

16 See Elizabethanne Boran, 'The function of the library in the early seventeenth century' in Vincent Kinane and Anne Walsh (eds), *Essays on the History of Trinity College Library Dublin* (Dublin 2000), pp. 39–52, here p. 45. Dr Boran quotes from Naudé's *Avis pour dresser une bibliothèque*, trans. John Evelyn (London 1661).

Reformations

There cannot be any doubt that without Wittenberg university and its humanist approach to the new book culture there would not have been a Lutheran Reformation.[17] It is an important fact that Martin Luther (1483–1546) was a university man throughout his career. The University of Wittenberg was founded in 1502, with a medieval charter, by Elector Frederick of Saxony as a vital component of his reform policy. It was housed in the Augustinian monastery with the cooperation of the order. The medieval syllabus was retained, while Philip Melanchthon (1497–1560) conceived the introduction of the humanist method as in a process of transformation from scholasticism to humanism. This, however, instantly revealed dangerous fault lines. On 10 December 1520 in an initial act of reformation Melanchthon incautiously summoned students to burn, together with the papal bull *Exsurge Domine*, pernicious books selected from the library: 'the ungodly papal constitutions, the decretals, the concordances and discordances and the writings of the schoolmen according to an old, apostolic rite'.[18] In their barely concealed barbarity, the book burnings, like iconoclasm, almost inevitably got out of hand: a massive student riot flared up. Martin Luther managed to deflect the destructive energies of the students and regain the good will of the Elector, whose protection was essential to the university and its teachers.

Philip Melanchthon's great reforming act was guided by the humanist rhetorical ideals previously championed by Sebastian Brant and his friendship circle. While designing a detailed study plan for the subjects of the *trivium*, Melanchthon also opened up and cautiously extended the range of the *quadrivium* to initiate something like 'Lutheran sciences'. Johannes Kepler (1571–1630) described himself (somewhat tongue in cheek) as 'a Lutheran astrologer, throwing away the nonsense and keeping the kernel'. It must

17 Helmar Junghans, *Der junge Luther und die Humanisten* (Göttingen 1985). Junghans emphasizes that Luther set great store by the exploration of humanist rhetoric in his works: see pp. 240–73.

18 Reprinted in Ruth Kastner (ed.), *Quellen zur Reformation, 1517–1555* (Darmstadt 1994), p. 110. These are almost verbatim the words of Melanchthon's Wittenberg inaugural address as Professor of Greek, *De corrigendis adolescentiæ studiis* (1518), which elaborates the telling differences between scholastics and humanists in their approaches to study. The relevant passage is reprinted in Michael Beyer *et al.* (eds) *Melanchthon deutsch*, vol. 1: *Schule und Universität, Philosophie, Geschichte und Politik* (Leipzig 1997) p. 48: 'Menschensatzungen, Konstitutionen, Dekrete, Ordensregeln, Dekretalen und erklärende Zusätze von geistigen Kleingeistern'. This address was highly regarded throughout Europe and is basic to any analysis of the history of university libraries at the crucial time of transition.

be admitted, however, that Kepler, while he was educated at the Lutheran University of Tübingen, was not a conventional Lutheran. He never had a university appointment but was one of the most brilliant 'researchers' at the court of Emperor Rudolph II at Prague.[19] Melanchthon oversaw the acquisition of an impressive range of new books and designed a university library policy that was almost immediately introduced in many famous grammar schools in the imperial cities and Lutheran universities in Germany and Scandinavia. In Wittenberg, furthermore, he insisted on the inclusion of authentic editions of all of Luther's occasional writings (*Flugschriften*), a totally new category in any university library collection. This was a necessary measure since Luther's works were frequently published in corrupt, pirated editions that could easily be misinterpreted, leading to further accusations of spreading new heresies.[20]

The Calvinist Reformation also banked on the humanist method of academic study. In this respect it did not differ much from Melanchthon's reforms but it initiated a much more rigorous anti-scholasticism by clearing their libraries of all 'medieval flotsam'. In response to the changed political circumstances, this 'Second Reformation' furthered careful cooperative research in theology. Distinguished refugees from many different parts of Europe met in the specifically created Genevan Academy (1559) to work out 'reformations' that were appropriate to their own churches. The refugees returned to their home countries by the invitation of prominent nobles who controlled their local areas and were favourably inclined to Calvin's thorough reformation of 'true faith'. They tried to avoid confrontation and martyrdom by never going out as missionaries to provoke authorities whose legitimacy they did not recognize.[21] Calvinist reformers were vitally committed to the expansion of university studies, and rulers who championed Calvinism all founded universities with richly endowed libraries. Universities and their libraries defined the shape of Calvinism throughout Europe: without the new generation of universities there would not have been any Calvinist Reformation states. The universities and their libraries became the centres of a prolific range of humanist studies that also furthered the development of natural sciences. The outstanding

19 Heinz Scheible, *Melanchthon und die Reformation. Forschungsbeiträge* (Mainz 1996). More specifically, Sachiko Kusukawa, *The Transformation of Natural Philosophy: The Case of Philip Melanchthon* (Cambridge 1995), p. 188; Heinz Scheible, *Melanchthon. Eine Biographie* (Munich 1997), pp. 49–56. On Kepler and other scientists at the court of Rudolph II see R. Evans, *Rudolph II and his World* (Oxford 1973).

20 Sachiko Kusukawa (ed.), *A Wittenberg Library Catalogue (1536)* (Cambridge 1995).

21 Robert M. Kingdon, *Geneva and the Consolidation of the French Protestant Movement, 1564–1572* (Geneva 1967).

example of a Calvinist academic institution is the University of Leiden.[22] The most prominent spokesman of Leiden scholarship, Justus Lipsius (1547–1606), worked in conflicting religious contexts. Having been educated by Jesuits in Cologne and at the Catholic University of Louvain, he taught at Jena (Lutheran) and Cologne (Catholic). He came to Leiden, where he spent his most productive years at the newly founded university committed to the inculcation of Calvinism. He returned to Catholic Louvain for the final years of his extraordinary career. His political loyalty to the Catholic Habsburg leaders never wavered. What mattered in all the vagaries of his teaching and writing activities was his linguistic, rhetorical humanism that overarched religious barriers and made him attractive to all these universities, even at the height of religious wars.[23]

Historians of the Counter-Reformation agree that, in response to the advance of Protestant university theology, it became necessary to adopt a comparable, combative academic system in Catholic countries. Catholic universities, however, were slower to adopt the humanist 'open book culture' by mounting a consistent and widely influential defence of scholastic (Thomist) content of teaching while adopting humanist techniques of disputation. The Council of Trent laid the foundations for this academic theology. Laurence Brockliss points out that this resulted in the creation of 'critical and often creative commentaries on the Aristotelian œuvre', which eventually furthered rationalism. Of special importance were the *Disputationes metaphysicæ* by Francisco Suarez (1597). Both Catholic and Protestant exegetes could adapt them to suit their purposes.[24] The prominent champions of the Tridentine Counter-Reformation were the new colleges of religious orders, notably the Jesuits. They also furthered the controlled expansion of learning into the natural sciences and secured a special place for the study of medicine and law. Most influential Spanish, Italian and Austrian Habsburg universities had colleges attached to them that were specially designed to attract the many Catholic refugees from other parts of Europe who required education in all subjects. In

22 The University of Leiden (founded 1575) became one of the most influential universities in early modern Europe. The university library reinforced the development of the most inspiring scientific innovations. Cf. Hermans and Nelissen, *Charters*, pp. 62–3, 129–30.

23 G. Oestreich, 'Justus Lipsius als Universalgelehrter zwischen Renaissance und Barock' in T.H. Lunsingh Scheurleer and G.H.M. Posthumus Meyjes (eds), *Leiden University in the Seventeenth Century: An Exchange of Learning* (Leiden 1975), pp. 177–201.

24 Laurence Brockliss, 'Curricula' in Hilde de Ridder-Symoens (ed.), *History of the University*, vol. 2: *Universities in Early Modern Europe (1500–1800)* (Cambridge 1996), pp. 565–620, here p. 580; Wilhelm Schmidt-Biggemann, *ibid.*, 'New Structures of Knowledge', pp. 489–530.

the first instance the Jesuit colleges groomed the students to become priests and to slip back into their home countries to offer what their societies needed to prevent their sliding back into 'barbarism'.[25]

The relationship of libraries and universities on the European continent was one of interdependence. In all instances the library collections far exceeded the teaching programmes of these universities. Political powers promoted this interdependence. For example, the Elector Palatine Ottheinrich, the benefactor of the library of the University of Heidelberg, described the library in his will as a *besonder theurer schatz des churfürstentums* ('an especially precious treasure of the Palatinate') and declared *daß es ein recht fürstlich werck ist, ein stattliche ansehnliche Bibliothek* [...] *zu haben und auf die nachkommen zu erhalten, wie dan viel löbliche verständige könige und fürsten nach außweisung der historien sich deßen vor diser zeit befließen* ('It is a truly princely work [...] to have an imposing and handsome library and to maintain it for future generations, as many praiseworthy and judicious kings and princes in past times made every effort to do, according to the information of the histories [...]'). There is evidence of the general appreciation of the significance of libraries in the conduct of international wars as well as internal conflicts such as civil wars. The invasion of a country often culminated in the destruction or deportation of its most famous university library so as to break the spirit of the enemy. The *cause célèbre* is the fate of the university library of Calvinist Heidelberg at the beginning of the Thirty Years' War.[26]

Universities of Britain and Ireland

There is no substantial difference between the development of the universities and their libraries on the continent and in Britain and Ireland in the age of the Reformation. One has to bear in mind that the Tudor Reformation had been initiated by King Henry VIII as a result of his break with Rome, when he assumed royal supremacy over the church of England as 'only Supreme Head in Earth of the Church of England' (1534). There was no religious reformer in England of the calibre of a Luther, Calvin, or the Jesuit leader Ignatius

25 See Hilde de Ridder-Symoens, 'Mobility', *ibid.* pp. 416–48, here pp. 424–6 and *passim.*

26 The exhibition catalogue of the riches of the library that became the Bibliotheca Vaticana is a treasure trove of research: Elmar Mittler *et al.* (eds), *Bibliotheca Palatina. Ausstellung der Universität Heidelberg in Zusammenarbeit mit der Bibliotheca Vaticana*, 2 vols (Heidelberg 1986), here vol. 1: *Textband*, pp. 3, 13 (Testament of Ottheinrich), pp. 458–93 (deportation of the university library of Heidelberg). For the foundation documents of the university and the integration of the elector's library, see pp. 8–11.

Loyola, who spearheaded the counter-reformation after the Council of Trent. Instead, one could argue that it was only after some agonizing that the Tudor Reformation adopted the vernacular Bible as the instrument of reformation. After the frustration of the efforts of William Tyndale, who translated the New Testament and some books of the Old Testament under Luther's influence in 1534, the version of Miles Coverdale was accepted as 'the King's Bible' in 1535. A Bible in every parish church of the land required learned clergy who could preach the Word of God. King Edward VI, who inherited his father's title of Supreme Head, tried to initiate a proper Reformation policy. His government called upon the universities and their libraries to further this Reformation. The impact of the Reformation is reflected in the fate of Duke Humfrey's Library in Oxford. The Reformation of the English Church under King Edward VI resulted in the cleansing of the library of all 'papal accretions'. The university library in Cambridge had met with a similar fate. The Catholic Mary Tudor failed to reverse it and Queen Elizabeth resumed the policy of her male predecessors with less fanaticism. This Tudor Reformation era seems to have made more vigorous strides towards the expansion or, if necessary, the *ab initio* creation, of libraries for the reformed universities. The outstanding example of the simultaneous foundation of university and library is Trinity College Dublin.

In the brief survey of the relationship of Trinity College Dublin and its library that follows I shall restrict myself to pointing out characteristics that emerged between 1592 and 1613. Here I am relying on the research of others and some earlier studies of my own.[27] The creation of the university and its library in Dublin was a response to the acrimonious struggle between the Tudor Reformation and the European counter-reformation. In the face of the academic rescue operation mounted by Philip II of Spain, Queen Elizabeth could no longer consider the existing English universities of Oxford and Cambridge sufficiently attractive to students from Ireland. The educational migration of Irish students – to Spain, the German Habsburg territories and the Spanish Netherlands, Italy and France – had increased the urgency of a solution to the 'Irish university question'. Indeed the founding of a university in Ireland must

27 On the history of Trinity College Dublin: J.P. Mahaffy, *An Epoch in Irish History: Trinity College, Dublin, its Foundation and Early Fortunes* (London 1903); Constantia Maxwell, *A History of Trinity College, Dublin 1591–1892* (Dublin 1946); R.B. McDowell and D.A. Webb, *Trinity College Dublin, 1592–1952: An Academic History* (Cambridge 1982); J.V. Luce, *The First 400 Years*, Trinity College, Dublin Quatercentenary Series, no. 7 (Dublin 1992). On the development of Trinity College Library: Elizabethanne Boran, 'Libraries and learning. The early history of Trinity College, Dublin, 1592–1641' (unpublished Ph.D. thesis, Trinity College Dublin 1996); Peter Fox, *Trinity College Library Dublin: A History* (Cambridge 2014). I have greatly benefited from Charles Benson's knowledge of the library collections.

be considered an essential instrument of the pacification of her 'rebellious' Irish realm, since those who challenged her claim to rule had adopted the counter-reformation as the expression of their opposition.

Lack of land and ready cash were the apparent reasons for the delay in setting up the academic defence system of Tudor policy. Ultimately Elizabeth's government did not provide any of the necessary start-up funds. This display of the Queen's notorious stinginess could be masked as the tackling of a deeper problem: how to encourage her Irish subjects to make a long-term, sustained commitment to the university project designed to achieve the 'civility' of the rebellious Irish. A public appeal launched throughout the whole of Ireland may have been chosen as the convenient but also most appropriate means to serve the Tudor government's purpose. The royal government, the diocesan bishops and the papacy had only offered early recognition and protection as well as the necessary legal sanction for the coordination of the colleges of Oxford and Cambridge into universities: neither had received an official charter.[28]

There were no medieval foundations of the kind that could have been built on to serve the Tudor reformation policy in Ireland. In the late sixteenth century the Irish university project was championed by less well-endowed sponsors. As early as the 1570s the members of the Dublin Municipal Council had seized the initiative in drawing the attention of the Queen's Council in London to the crucial connection between the need for a local university (with a generously stocked library) and the peaceful governance of her Irish realm.[29] In 1591, with the support of Dublin Corporation and Adam Loftus (1533/4–1605), Archbishop of Dublin, who was to become the first provost of the college, Henry Ussher travelled to London, where he successfully presented the proposal for a university in Dublin to the Privy Council.[30] Their submission spoke of the university as an instrument to ensure the obedience of the Irish subjects; there was no reference to a religious reformation. It was, of course, clear that obedience to the English queen involved recognition of the law of uniformity, without which no good governance could exist, according the conviction of rulers throughout Europe.

28 See Hermans and Nelissen, *Charters*: Oxford, pp. 70–71, 136–7; Cambridge, pp. 36–7, 1068.

29 Helga Robinson-Hammerstein, 'Royal policy and civic pride: Founding a university in Dublin' in David Scott (ed.), *Treasures of the Mind: A Trinity College Dublin Quatercentenary Exhibition, Catalogue* (London 1992), pp. 1–15.

30 Helga Robinson-Hammerstein, 'Archbishop Adam Loftus: The first provost of Trinity College, Dublin' in *idem* (ed.), *European Universities in the Age of Reformation and Counter Reformation* (Dublin 1998), pp. 34–52.

The Royal Charter, dated 3 (13 New Style) March 1592, as a legal document, facilitated the erection of a college-based university in Dublin.[31] As a corporation, it was granted much greater freedom to work out its statutes than that possessed by the English universities. (Students entering college were initially not required to swear the oath of loyalty.) Ireland became an ideal refuge for those who were against the strict enforcement of conformity. The intention was that Trinity College Dublin would stimulate the Elizabethan Reformation of Ireland, without too much attention being drawn to the distinctly Calvinist–Puritan leanings of its first three provosts.[32]

The Charter had also prescribed that the new Irish university should be modelled on Oxford and Cambridge. Trinity College took its cue mostly from Cambridge. The BA degree required four years of study, emphasizing Latin, Greek and Hebrew, rhetoric and logic, as well as philosophy and natural science, by means of lectures and disputations. The contact between lecturers (fellows) and students (scholars) seems to have been very closely monitored. Students had to write weekly Latin synopses of their studies and discuss them in individual tutorials with their teachers. The four years in the university were treated as a progression to perfection in presenting convincing arguments, coherently reasoned, based on logic. Senior students were called upon to demonstrate their ability to speak freely in public academic exercises, including disputations. Following the example of Cambridge, Petrus Ramus's *Dialectica* was adopted as the unassailable guide. Ramus (1515–72), who had studied at Paris, had developed a revolutionary approach to the study of logic, building on Philip Melanchthon's *Dialectices* (1522). Scholars agree that Ramism took Protestant Europe by storm in the second half of the sixteenth century. The *Dialectica* in William Temple's edition of 1584 was warmly welcomed by Trinity College Dublin.[33] Its use enabled the study of theology to be pursued with a confidence to suit the confrontational conditions faced by the new Church

31 See Hermans and Nelissen, *Charters*, pp. 40–41, 109–10.

32 Alan Ford, '"That Bugbear Arminianism": Archbishop Laud and Trinity College, Dublin' in Ciaran Brady and Jane Ohlmeyer (eds), *British Interventions in Early Modern Ireland* (Cambridge 2005), pp. 135–60, here pp. 138–9; *idem*, 'The Church of Ireland 1558–1641: A Puritan church?' in Alan Ford, James McGuire and Kenneth Milne (eds), *As by Law Established: The Church of Ireland since the Reformation* (Dublin 1995), pp. 52–68.

33 Brockliss, 'Curricula', p. 582; Elizabethanne Boran, 'Ramism in Trinity College, Dublin in the early seventeenth century' in Mordechai Feingold, Joseph S. Freedman and Wolfgang Rother (eds), *The Influence of Petrus Ramus: Studies in Sixteenth and Seventeenth Century Philosophy and Sciences* (Basel 2001), pp. 177–99; Mordechai Feingold, 'Aristotle and the English universities in the seventeenth century: A re-evaluation' in Robinson-Hammerstein, *European Universities*, pp. 135–48.

of Ireland. Ramus's determined rejection of the medieval syllogistic method of reasoning and its replacement by a straightforward practical methodology appealed to clergy with Puritan leanings, whom the English Queen preferred to work in Ireland. They were better preachers and, provided they did not insist on a Presbyterian ecclesiastical organization, could prove very effective in helping to build the Church of Ireland. Student numbers and origin are hard to establish accurately for the early years of the university's activities. The composition of the student body for 1605, however, was: 16 Native Irish (21.3 per cent), 10 Anglo-Irish (13.3 per cent), 49 New English or English (65.3 per cent).[34]

Providing the university with a substantial library was not an afterthought, but an integral part of the concept that was well on the way to realization by the mid 1590s, as is evidenced by the payment of bills for woodwork and hinges, nails and glass in 1595 and 1596. A drawing of the layout of the college in 1681 shows how it was to appear when completed.[35] Filling a university library with books was a great deal more difficult than it had been in the case of the colleges in England or on the continent, where the libraries had their medieval antecedents. Trinity College Dublin had to start *ab initio* with private donations of books and to improvise a purchasing policy with irregular sums made available for the *libri in publica Collegii bibliotheca* by the college authorities. Sometimes general funds 'for the benefit of the College' were used for stocking the library. The first extant list of books is to be found in the *Particular Book*, dated 24 February 1601.[36] In this list of roughly forty books ten can be identified as donations. The Ulster King of Arms Christopher Ussher had given three books. There is also evidence of the good will of the non-Irish intelligentsia. Graduates of English colleges supported the project: an early named donor was Richard Latewar, former Fellow of St John's College Oxford. In his will he had donated his private library to his college with the exception of seven books to be sent to the library of Trinity College Dublin. The range covered in the total of forty books says much about the orientation of the university. They included such Classics as Aristotle, Plato and Cicero in critical humanist editions, the atlases of Gerard Mercator and Ptolemy and some standard works to support the higher studies in theology at the new university.

34 Alan Ford, 'Who went to Trinity? The early students of Dublin University' in Robinson-Hammerstein, *European Universities*, pp. 53–74.

35 Cf. TCD MS 2640, and see Fox, *Trinity College Library*, p.7 and fig. 3 on p. 47.

36 *The Particular Book of Trinity College, Dublin*, ed. J.P. Mahaffy (London 1904). Modern researchers have every reason to be grateful for the compilation by J.G. Smyly, 'The Old Library: extracts from the *Particular Book*', *Hermathena*, 49 (1935), 166–83.

There is general agreement among library historians that the relationship between the university and its library began to take shape in the early seventeenth century. Two modes of acquisition had become closely linked: benefactions and acquisitions by purchase. This is clearly evident in the fate of an 'early gift of money'. In 1593 the substantial amount of £623 1*s.* 8½*d.* had been given by 'certain captains toward the building of the College'. The college authorities, made up of academics, had devised a long-term strategy that included the purchasing of books in their concept of building the college. The money became available only in 1601, when it was registered as the gift from 'The Lord Deputie and captins of her majesties armie here in these partes'.[37]

James Ussher, one of the first graduates of the university, and Luke Challoner, one of its three foundation fellows, undertook several book-purchasing trips to England at roughly three-year intervals. Such joint enterprises are verifiable for 1603, 1606, 1609 and 1612. Although there were other prominent book buyers, Challoner and Ussher must be credited with 'creating' the university library in Dublin. Their close link with and intimate knowledge of the needs of the College were crucial.[38] They also compiled several early book lists.[39] By 1613 the library contained 4500 books, a size exceeded in Britain and Ireland by the Bodleian Library alone (about 7000). The collectors intended it to be universal and comprehensive and to reflect recent scholarship, including books to be consulted only for polemical purposes. The scholars, who bought the books for the library, envisaged the eventual development of all the higher faculties, including law and medicine. One should also bear in mind that Ussher and Challoner began to buy books for themselves on the same occasions, building up impressive private libraries that were later integrated into the college collection. Furthermore, these private libraries acted from the start as 'lending libraries', where college dons could borrow books not otherwise available to them.[40]

It may be surprising that Challoner and Ussher had offered no fundamental reflections on the book culture they aimed to realize. They did, however, cultivate contacts with highly active scholar collectors, including Sir

37 J.P. Mahaffy, 'The Library of Trinity College Dublin: The growth of a legend', *Hermathena*, 12 (1903), 68–78, and in general *idem*, *An Epoch in Irish History*. The course of events was disentangled further by Boran, 'The function of the library', p. 44, note 27.

38 Boran, 'Libraries and learning'; Norma MacManaway and Charles Benson, '"A sceliton with taffety hangings": The early College library' in Scott, *Treasures of the Mind*, pp. 143–50.

39 Cf. TCD MS 2160/a 1–17 and Elizabethanne Boran, 'Luke Challoner's library, 1595–1608', *Long Room*, 37 (1992), 17–26.

40 For a more detailed evaluation of the content see Boran, *ibid.*

Thomas Bodley, whose views on building up the new libraries and providing for 'reformed' teaching at Oxford and Cambridge university libraries are fundamental.[41] It is likely that Challoner and Ussher were in agreement with him and other English and Scottish academic collectors. His efforts to 'reconstruct' involved a complete reconceptualization along humanist-reformist lines.[42] Peter Fox places Challoner in the same category as these contemporary collectors when he observes that Challoner's initiative and the favourable response from the Trinity fellows 'demonstrated the importance they attached to developing the Library, even when Trinity was facing serious financial difficulties'.[43]

The relationship between library holdings and teaching at Trinity College is not as difficult to determine as what books were offered for the teaching of the new syllabus for BA and MA degrees. This projected the reformed version of the *trivium* and *quadrivium*, as outlined above. Peter Fox observes that the library organization reflected the demands of teaching requirements, 'with the books arranged in two main categories, theology and humanities'. There was a lower (or outer) library for the humanities, reserved for BA and MA students, who were admitted there to read in the amply provided library reading room: the books were taken off the shelves by a specially appointed keeper. No students were admitted to the upper (inner) library, which contained the books on theology. The inner and outer library collections were separated by a partition. The latter followed the Bodleian arrangement by subject rather than alphabetically and 'as in Oxford, printed books and manuscripts were shelved together'.[44] Indeed from what we know about its 'public nature', referring to the admission of students but not the general public, there can be no doubt that the early university library followed the arrangements of the universities of Oxford and Cambridge.

In a letter to William Camden of 30 October 1606 James Ussher anticipated the fulfilment of the Elizabethan university project. He spoke of a 'most handsome college' that had been granted its academic privileges by the late Queen and was 'recently equipped with a distinguished library'. Moreover,

41 Bodley's intentions are revealed in his correspondence, e.g. with Thomas James, who was employed as librarian of the Bodleian Library. See Boran, 'The function of the library', p. 39 and note. 2.

42 See *Sir Thomas Bodley and his Library: An Exhibition to Mark the Quatercentenary of the Bodleian* (Oxford 2002); *The Autobiography of Sir Thomas Bodley*. With introduction and notes by William Clennell (Oxford 2006).

43 Fox, *Trinity College Library*, p. 11.

44 Ibid., p. 12. See also *The First Printed Catalogue of the Bodleian Library, 1605: A Facsimile* (Oxford 1986), pp. vii–ix.

'it displays the not inconsiderable hope that both religion and all the more cultivated disciplines will come back to Ireland (whither, as if to trade in the good arts, foreigners at one time flocked) as if by right of return to the hospitality of their ancestors'.[45]

45 *Collegium ... pulcherrimum ... Academicis donatum privilegiis, insignique nuper instructum Bibliothecâ, spem ostendit non exiguam, ad Hiberniam (quó veluti ad mercaturam bonarum artium confluxerunt aliquando exteri) et religionem et cultiores omnes disciplinas tanquam ad avitum hospitium postliminio reversuras,* in Elizabethanne Boran (ed.), *The Correspondence of James Ussher, 1600–1656*, 3 vols (Dublin 2015), here vol.1, p. 14. Cf. *idem*, 'The function of the library', p. 39.

'To put in order': How the greffiers Fagel documented themselves as men of politics, men of religion and men of the world

Theo Thomassen
UNIVERSITY OF AMSTERDAM

Documenting professional life, God and the world

MEMBERS OF the Fagel family documented their work, their beliefs and the world in which they and their ancestors lived by gathering together extensive and various documentary collections. The Fagel Library, bought by Trinity College Dublin in 1802 and kept as a discrete collection ever since, comprises less than three-quarters of the library bequeathed in 1790 by Hendrik Fagel the Elder to his heirs. Thousands of his books and manuscripts sold by auction in 1792 and 1803 in The Hague have been lost or are hidden in other libraries, archives or private collections. The original library was only one of the documentary collections of the Fagel family. The Fagel family archives, covering 48 m¹, are preserved in the National Archives in The Hague, as is the supplement to these archives, covering 50 m¹ and consisting of papers re-collected in 1985 from the collections of Hendrik the Elder. To a certain extent, the Fagel collections of coins, medals, prints and drawings sold between 1793 and 1808 can also be considered documentary collections, since they document primarily Dutch and European history. As with the paintings, they are now part of other collections. The Fagel collections of trees and plants are not documentary *per se*, and neither are the Fagel house and garden pavilion on the Noordeinde in The Hague, sold in 1803: what they document is the activities of members of the Fagel family and the culture of their time. There are no clear and sharp distinctions between the Fagel library in Dublin and the Fagel manuscript collections in The Hague, between the Fagel family archives, the supplement to these archives and the archives of the States General, and between the documentary collections of the Fagel family and their other collections. In their relatedness they reflect the lives of the family, their views and ideas on God, the world, nature, the arts, science, history, other nations and the world in which they lived. The contents and structure of these collections cannot be understood without reference to the orders of discourse of which they are both a part and an expression.

Collections to put in order

Around 1754 Hendrik the Elder, Greffier of the Dutch States General, drafted a short description of his collections under the heading, *In ordre te brengen*, 'to put in order' (see fig. 1).[1] This order obviously reflected the relations of the greffier to his work, God and the world. In this rough draft, he distinguished three groups: a collection of documents useful in executing his duties as greffier, a collection of documents useful in relation to religion and a collection of 'objects of curiosity'.

According to the description, the collection of documents that were useful in the execution of his duties as greffier consisted of state resolutions, manuscripts, letters and documents released on a daily basis. The day-to-day documents must have included the edicts and proclamations of ordinances and treaties of the States General, the ordinary resolutions of the States General and the ordinary dispatches to the States General from Dutch envoys abroad. In the eighteenth century all state papers of which five or more copies had to be distributed were printed; the greffier received at least one copy.

Documents useful in relation to religion – an amazing mass of books and treatises on the subject – were established as a separate category. Apparently Hendrik the Elder did not consider this group to be part of his library, which was classified under the third group. This group, comprising the collections of curiosities, is subdivided into collections inside the house – the library, drawings, prints, maps, medals, coins and paintings – and collections outside the house: plantations, trees, plants and crops, and flowers. Family papers are missing from this list, but many papers useful to the discharge of a greffier's duties can be found in the family archives, particularly in the greffiers' archives.

1 N[ational] A[rchives], The Hague, Coll. Fagel, toegang 1.10.29, inv. nr. 682.

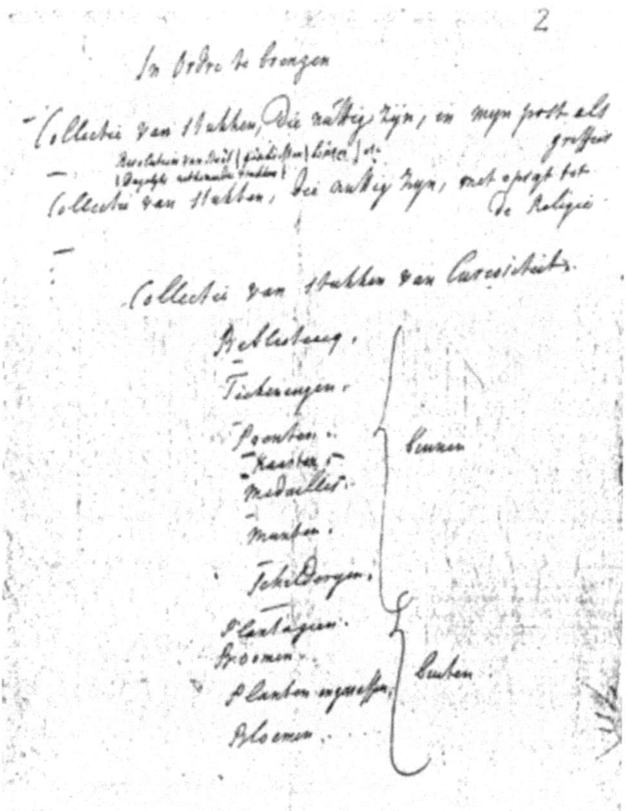

Fig 1: A short description of his collections by Hendrik Fagel the Elder. (Arch. Fagel, familie, inv. nr. 682)

Greffiers and deputy greffiers of the States General

Most of the documents in the Fagel collections were accumulated by members of the Fagel family who held the posts of greffier and deputy greffier of the States General from 1670 to 1795. Gaspar Fagel was greffier from 1670 to 1672, Hendrik the Eldest from 1672 to 1690, François the Elder from 1690 to 1744, Hendrik the Elder from 1744 to 1790 and his grandson Hendrik the Younger from 1790 to 1795. François the Elder was deputy greffier from 1680 to 1690, Hendrik Hz (i.e. son of Hendrik) from 1690 to 1728, Hendrik the Elder from 1728 to 1744, François the Younger from 1762 to 1773, and Hendrik the Younger from 1787 to 1790 (see figs. 2–6).[2] Some understanding of the duties of the greffier is necessary to make sense of the order of their collections.

2 For the pedigree of the Fagel family see W.M.C. Regt, *Genealogie der familie Fagel* ('s-Gravenhage 1906).

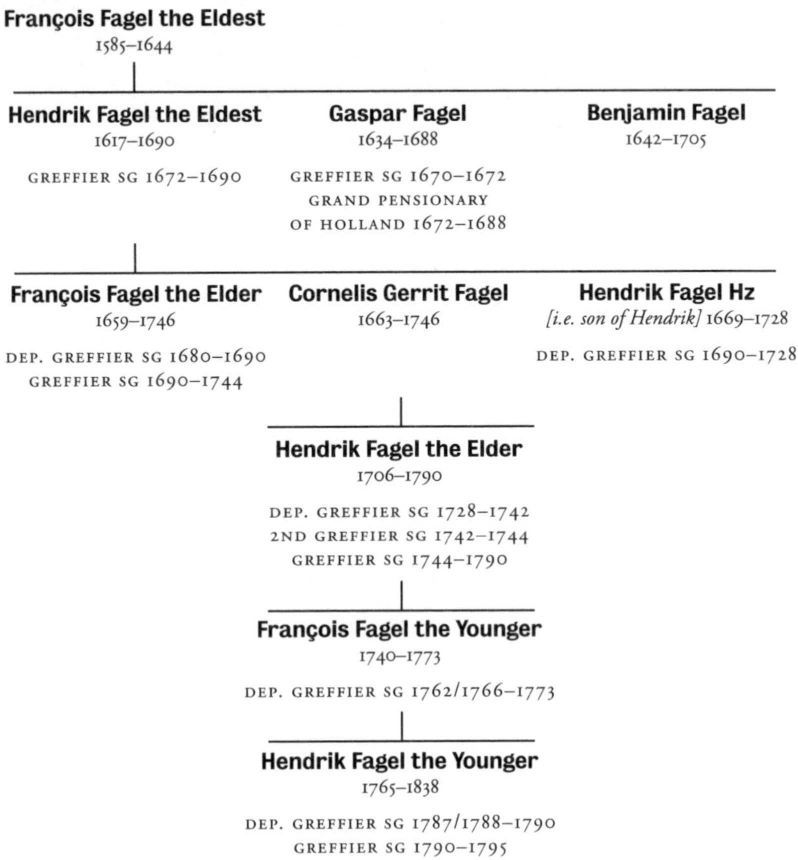

Fig 2: Pedigree of the greffiers Fagel.

The greffier was the chancellor of the States General and secretary of their assemblies. He received their letters, prepared their meetings, was responsible for drafting their resolutions and decrees, issued their outgoing letters, kept their registers up to date and observed the execution of their decisions. In 1690, when François Fagel the Elder was appointed greffier, home affairs issues and the management of the ordinary meetings of the States General were detached from the greffier's duties and assigned to the deputy greffier. From this time on, the greffier could concentrate on secret and foreign affairs of the States General, on managing their secret meetings and committees and on conducting their diplomatic and secret correspondence.[3]

3 A more detailed description of the duties of the greffiers of the States General and the records they created, as well as an extensive account of the identification of their dispersed papers, are included in Theo Thomassen, *Instrumenten van de macht. De Staten-Generaal en hun archieven 1576–1796* (Den Haag 2015).

Fig 3: *Hendrik Fagel the Eldest*, portrayed with seal and document, by an anonymous artist, 1684. (Instituut Collectie Nederland, Amsterdam, inv.nr. c507)

As the highest government official in charge of foreign affairs and the Dutch diplomatic corps the greffier became the unavoidable intermediary between the Dutch and foreign envoys and the assembly of the States General. He conducted his correspondence with the Dutch envoys abroad on behalf of the States General or *in 't particulier* (privately). On behalf of the States General he sent the envoys the resolutions of the States General and other state papers and reprimanded envoys who broke the rules or ignored the orders of their principals. Privately he discussed with them not only archival and secrecy measures, the contents of dispatches to be issued, and their allowances, but also the political situation and foreign policy issues. Sometimes envoys wrote to the greffier privately when they had very secret communications to convey and it was too risky to send secret official letters. The intimacy of the relationship between the greffier and the envoy in question influenced the amount of letters and their contents. Envoys of the Hop family, for instance, also served as intermediaries between François the Elder and his friend – and medal-collector – Philip von Stosch (1691–1757).[4]

4 J. Heringa, 'François Fagel. Portret van een honnête homme' in *Jaarboek Die Haghe* ('s-Gravenhage 1980), pp. 43–126.

Fig 4: *François Fagel the Elder*, copperplate by Pieter Tanje, from the portrait by Gerardus Joseph Xavery, 1747. (Beeldbank Haags Gemeentearchief, identificatienr. kl. B 2418 E 11,15)

As the head of the registry of the States General, which in fact was the chancellery of state, the greffier also became the means of access of the States General to the documented world outside. He was not the records manager of the States General: that duty was assigned to their *agent*. But from the end of the seventeenth century, the greffiers, being responsible for providing the

Fig 5: Francesco Guardi, *Convegno diplomatico* (1753), showing Hendrik Fagel the Elder from the back at the signing of a Treaty of Commerce by the States General and Naples in 1753. (Ca' Rezzonico, nr. Cl. I n. 0766)

Fig 6: *Hendrik Fagel the Younger*, drawn by Benjamin Samuel Bolomey 1782. (RKD-Nederlands Instituut voor Kunstgeschiedenis, IB-nr. 52320)

assembly and their officials at home and abroad with timely, relevant and accurate information, devised finding aids such as indexes to the resolutions and documented state affairs and their precedents, the functions, organization and work processes of the States General, and the complicated form of government of the Dutch Republic. Hendrik the Elder began having his clerks not only write the official registers and dispatches of the States General, but also copies of documents and files from the archives of the States General and other official sources, in order to include them in his information system. These copies were made at the expense of the States General when they could be considered the direct results of formal orders or attributed duties and at the greffier's own expense when this was not the case. When the clerks, who were paid at piecework rates, wrote these copies at the expense of the States General, the greffier earned half of their fees. These writing fees made up the largest part of the greffier's income.

Bringing the collections together

The collections that Hendrik the Elder bequeathed to his grandson Hendrik the Younger in 1790 comprised all his own collections and the collections of his uncle François the Elder, greffier from 1690 to 1744, together with a modest amount of books and papers belonging to other family members.

The contribution deriving from the collections of Gaspar Fagel, Greffier of the States General from 1670 to 1672 and subsequently Grand Pensionary of Holland till 1688, was fairly limited. Though he established a significant library and gathered a considerable collection of plants from Europe and the Dutch colonies in his garden near Leeuwenhorst, close to Noordwijkerhout in the Netherlands, he left no goods and money to his brothers when he died without an heir, as he had squandered everything on the Leeuwenhorst Estate. In 1688 his library and collections had been sold and many of his plants bought by William III, who had them moved to Hampton Court Palace.[5] His papers however – except for the greater part of those resulting from his activities as grand pensionary, which became part of the archives of the States of Holland – were added to those of his stepbrother Hendrik the Eldest and became part of the family archives.[6]

In 1672 Hendrik the Eldest succeeded his stepbrother Gaspar as greffier on the latter's recommendation. When he himself died in 1690, he bequeathed his and Gaspar's papers to his son François the Elder. François's main contribution to the collections was building a house in 1680 and having it redesigned, reconstructed and decorated by Daniel Marot in 1707 (see figs. 7–10). It was situated on the Noordeinde in The Hague on a site occupied by his family from 1672, a few hundred metres from the premises of the States General and the States of Holland at the Inner Court. The garden bordered that of the Prince of Orange and the gallery linking the left wing of the house with the garden pavilion, also designed by Marot, housed François's library and paintings.[7] This was where the family and their collections were united for 132 years; the rooms where the collections were stored and exhibited reflected their functions and influenced their meanings.

5 Elizabeth denHartog and Carla Teune, 'Gaspar Fagel (1633–88): His garden and plant collection at Leeuwenhorst', *Garden History*, 30 (2002), 191–205: http://www.jstor.org.stable/1587252.

6 Liesbeth Strasser, *Inventaris van het archief van Casper Fagel, Raadpensionaris van Holland, 1672–1688* (Den Haag 1990), NA The Hague, arch. Raadpensionaris Fagel, toegang 3.01.18.

7 Now nos. 138–40 Noordeinde. J. van Breen, 'Het Heerenhuis Noordeinde nr. 140' in *Jaarboek Die Haghe* ('s-Gravenhage 1913), pp. 142–54; *id.*, 'De Tuinkoepel van het Huis Noordeinde nr. 140', *ibid.* pp. 155–62. See also below, pp. 59–71.

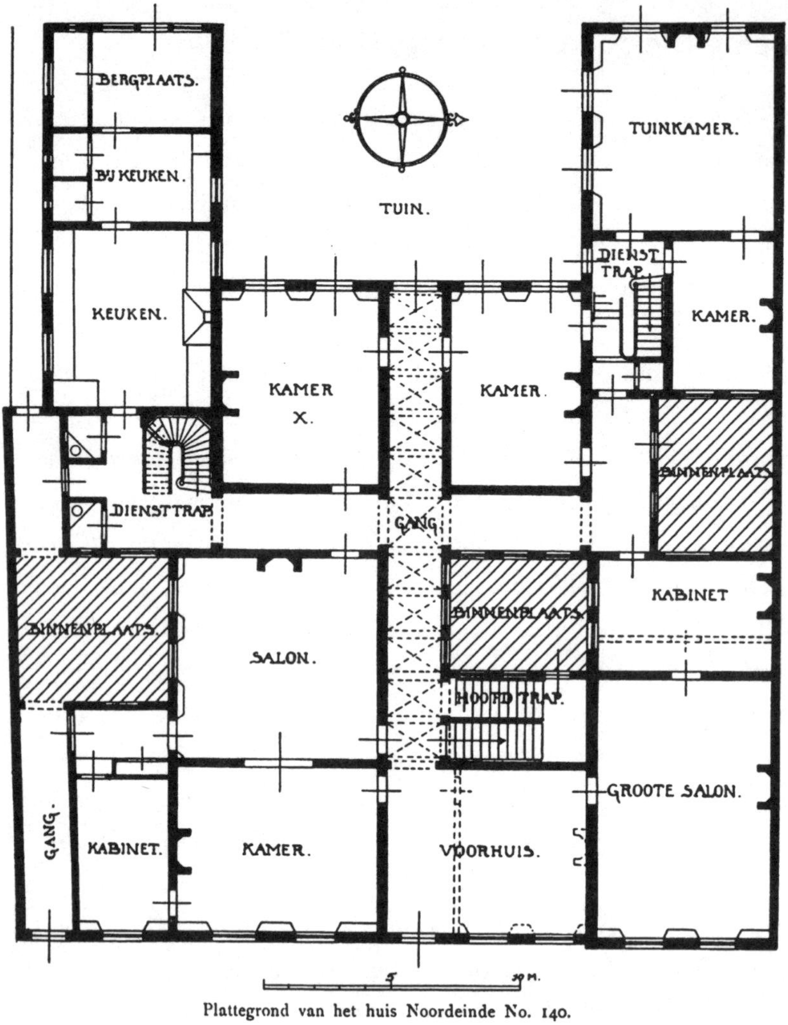

Fig 7: The ground plan of Noordeinde 140. (J. van Breen, 'Het Heerenhuis Noordeinde 140' in *Jaarboek Die Haghe* ['s-Gravenhage 1913], p. 147)

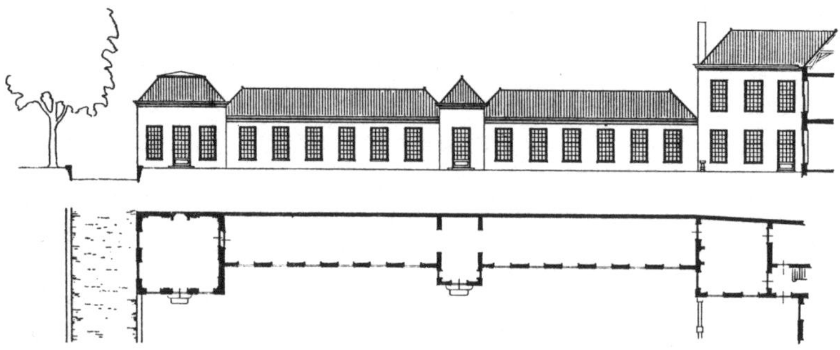

Fig 8: Elevation and ground plan of the gallery between the house and the pavilion that housed the Fagels' library: a reconstruction by the architect Paul den Boer. (The Hague, Royal House Archives, inv.nr. kha-25022010)

Fig 9: The rear façade of Noordeinde 140 in 1906. (Collectie Rijksdienst voor het Cultureel Erfgoed [RCE], Amersfoort, objectnummer 15.037)

François the Elder assembled most of the coins and medals, maps and paintings in the Fagel collections. His collection of coins and medals was, at the time, the largest in the Dutch Republic. He may also be considered the founder of the library, which numbered approximately 5000 volumes in 1723.[8] He also contributed a considerable amount of case files on state affairs and finding aids, in addition to the papers that he inherited from his father, Hendrik the Eldest. In 1728 he was also able to incorporate the collections of his heirless deceased brother Hendrik Hz, who had succeeded him as deputy greffier in 1690. He did not execute his plan for the systematic completion of the library, but when he died in 1746 his book gallery was almost finished.[9] He bequeathed his house and his collections, including a lot of papers on state affairs and letters on private and public affairs, to his nephew Hendrik the Elder, deputy greffier since 1728, who succeeded him as greffier.

Hendrik the Elder was the most active and important collector of books, manuscripts and records of the Fagel family. He added a mass of books, maps, copies of state papers, other documentation on state affairs, letters and finding aids to the collections kept in the house on the Noordeinde. He integrated

8 A catalogue made by François the Elder is in NA The Hague, Coll. Fagel, toegang 1.10.29, inv. nr. 42.

9 Heringa, 'François Fagel', pp. 83–6.

Fig 10: The garden pavilion of Noordeinde 140. (RCE, Amersfoort, objectnummer 74.515)

the documentation on state affairs and his uncle's correspondence with Dutch envoys abroad into his own information system, which included what was later called the greffiers' archives. The contributions of François Fagel the Younger and Hendrik Fagel the Younger to the library and the art collections were relatively small. Their correspondence and other private papers, however, comprise a considerable proportion of the family archives.

The legacy of Hendrik the Elder

In 1790 Hendrik the Elder died at the age of 84. Grandson Hendrik the Younger (1765–1838), who succeeded him as greffier, inherited the house and garden on the Noordeinde, the garden pavilion, stables and coach house, including all ornaments and furniture; the cabinet with the golden, silver and other medals, the paintings and the library; and the country house and farmland near Wassenaar.

Since he had to pay his sisters f 50,000 in compensation – and an office fee of f 30,000 to the States of Holland to take up the post of greffier – he desperately needed cash. He borrowed 100,000 from Willem Boreel, his father-in-law, promising to pay him back from the revenues of the sale of a considerable part of the collections that he had inherited. 'I have a very large and very rich collection of medals, which I have almost decided to get rid of, and the library contains numerous duplicates and several useless books, which could raise a lot of money when sold.'[10]

We do not know when and to whom the collection of coins and medals was sold. But we do know what happened to the so-called 'duplicates and useless books': they were sold by the booksellers Van Cleef en Scheurleer at an auction in The Hague in November 1792. The catalogue listed 2872 lots, which comes to 6000 to 9000 volumes, approximately a quarter of the whole library. Books and manuscripts on the history of the Netherlands and other countries of the world, and resolutions and other state papers accounted for one sixth of the collection; one tenth was dedicated to law and politics. Listed under the heading *Gedrukte Secreete en andere Resolutiën, Staatspapieren &c. in Folio* (Printed secret and other resolutions, state papers etc. in folio) were written *retroacta* (antecedents) of the States of Holland and the States General on every possible subject. Many of these state papers had been part of the greffiers' archives or even the archives of the States General.[11] Systematic research on the subsequent fate of these books and manuscripts has not been undertaken yet; some manuscript volumes ended up in the Royal Library in The Hague and part of the archive of War Commissioner Vegelin van Claerbergen covering the years 1709–13 in the National Archives.[12]

In January 1795, when the Batavian Republic was proclaimed, Hendrik the Younger, removed from his position as Greffier of the States General while on a diplomatic mission in London, was given political asylum in England. His possessions in The Hague, including his house and collections, were seized by the States of Holland. An indignant Charles Bentinck wrote to Lord Grenville:

> Among other real objects of curiosity, the most valuable and complete collections of State Papers in the Republic, transmitted to him [Hendrik the Younger, TT] by his ancestors, a great many of which papers had no immediate connection

10 NA The Hague, Coll. Fagel, toegang 1.10.29, inv. nr. 65.

11 *Catalogue d'une superbe collection de livres,* [...] *étant des ouvrages doubles qui se trouvent dans la bibliothèque de feu Messire H. Fagel, dans son vivant Greffier de LL.HH.PP. etc. etc. etc.* [...] *lequels se sont vendues* [*sic*][...] *le 12 Novembre 1792 & jours suivants, par les Libraires J. van Cleef et B. Scheurleer à La Haye.* KB [Koninklijke Bibliotheek] Veilingcatalogus nr. 4626.

12 Lots 86, 403 and 420 in KB handschriftenverzameling 73 A 39, KB 71 B 6 and KB 70 B 50; the Vegelin documents now in NA The Hague, Coll. Fagel Supplement, toegang 1.10.94, inv. nrs. 105a–105b. There is a list in the Fagel family archives of 107 items that could not be sold: NA The Hague, Coll. Fagel, toegang 1.10.29, inv. nr. 65 nr. 9.

> to the present events, has thus fallen into unknown hands; and together with one of the most complete and considerable libraries, and collection of drawing and prints, to be met with in any part of Europe, formed in the course of above a century by a succession of men distinguished for their taste and their knowledge, as well as for their political talents and character, will most likely be dispersed or lost by the animosity of a few obscure individuals.[13]

Since Hendrik the Younger was considered one of the three leaders of the old régime and now as one of its three most important political delinquents, the States had his political conduct in the years before the change of government investigated by a commission of inquiry. This commission obtained four chests of political records from the house on the Noordeinde and had them transferred to the premises of the States of Holland in order to investigate them. In the years that followed it produced several inventories of the papers and copied some files, but could not arrive at conclusions. In 1797, when the revolutionary spirit was waning, the siege was lifted. Two of the four chests were returned to the family in 1798; the other two could not be traced and remained in the basement of one of the States of Holland buildings at the Inner Court.

In 1798 the Dutch drafted a new constitution facilitating the confiscation of the possessions of all political emigrants. In anticipation, Hendrik the Younger shipped his collections to England in order to sell them. He left behind only the state papers in Dutch, which had no market value in England.[14] In 1799 he sold the cabinet of drawings collected by François Fagel the Elder,[15] in 1801 his remaining drawings and books of drawings[16] and in 1802 the library.[17] The 20,000 books, bought by Trinity College, were for the most

13 H.T. Colenbrander (ed.), *Gedenkstukken der Algemeen Geschiedenis van Nederland van 1795 tot 1840*, vol. 2 ('s-Gravenhage 1906), p. 415.

14 Regarding the sale of the collections and their subsequent fortunes see the correspondence of Jacob Baron Fagel 1799–1802, Coll. Fagel, toegang 1.10.29, inv.nrs. 3353–88.

15 Thomas Philipe, *Catalogue of the Intire Cabinet of Capital Drawings, Collected by the Late Greffier Francois Fagel, [...] To which are Added, some Modern Italian Landschapes, Belonging to the same Family: Which Will Be Sold by Auction, Under the Direction of Mr. Thomas Philipe,* [...] *on Monday, the 20th of May, 1799, and five following days* (London 1797).

16 Thomas Philipe, *Catalogue of the Capital and Entire Collection of Prints, and Books of Prints, of H. Fagel, Esq. Late Greffier of the States General of Holland. Collected by him and his Ancestors during the whole of the last Century,* 4 vols (London 1801). 29 drawings from the collection of François Fagel the Elder sold in London in 1801 are now in the British Museum: http://www.britishmuseum.org/.

17 Samuel Paterson, *Bibliotheca Fageliana. A Catalogue of the Valuable and Extensive Library of the Greffier Fagel, of the Hague: Comprehending a Choice Collection of Books, in Various Languages, in Theology and Ecclesiastical History; in Classical and Philological Learning, and in Most Branches of Polite Literature; in Philosophy, Physics, and Natural History; in Painting, Architecture, Engraving, and the Whole Body of Arts and Sciences* [...] (London 1802).

part written in Latin, English and French, and contained 900 volumes dealing with Dutch history, including twelve volumes of ordinances and decrees, and some 300 volumes with more than 10,000 pamphlets.[18] In 1802 he also sold his collection of paintings. Only forty-five family portraits, tangible evidence of the family's success and identity and reflecting its status and ambitions, stayed in the family's hands.[19] In 1941, a year after the death of the last member of the Fagel family to bear the name, they were bought by the state and added to the state collection of art objects.[20]

On 25 March 1802 France and the United Kingdom signed the Peace Treaty of Amiens, which included provision for an amnesty for émigrés. Confiscations of their goods would be reversed. Hendrik the Younger, who was not intending to return to the Netherlands, took the opportunity to sell his remaining possessions in The Hague.

On 3 May 1803, two weeks before France and England resumed war, he sold the house and garden on the Noordeinde in The Hague. It was bought by the Royal Family in 1853 and sold by Queen Emma to the municipality of The Hague in 1901, although she kept the garden pavilion (see plate 5). The run-down gallery connecting the left wing of the house with the pavilion, where the Fagels had kept the largest part of their library, was demolished. The Queen moved internal fixtures such as wood panelling, door frames and chimney breasts, wall coverings and ceiling linings to her palace at the Lange Voorhout. Her salon was later moved to the Loo Palace. The house on the Noordeinde has since been split into several premises, one of which is now occupied by a Pizza Hut restaurant.

A few months earlier, on 2 February 1803, Van Cleef en Scheurleer auctioned the Fagel manuscripts in Dutch, consisting of 880 volumes of written and printed resolutions and state papers, dating back to the beginning of the Dutch Republic, as well as 166 Dutch maps. These included 'a most excellent' collection of more than 130 river maps, water-board maps, projects, concepts etc. relating to the improvement of coasts and dikes, among them several old manuscript maps, 'unique of their kind, and to be sought in vain elsewhere'. All

18 L. Brummel, 'The Fagel Library in Trinity College, Dublin' in *id.*, *Miscellanea libraria* (The Hague 1957), pp. 204–33. Included were several manuscripts from the two chests returned to the family in 1798. Recent study suggests a figure closer to 6000 pamphlets.

19 Frans Grijzenhout, 'Een statussymbool aan het Noordeinde', *Kunstschrift*, 6 (1992), 28–30.

20 Their images can be retrieved from the database of the Rijksbureau voor Kunsthistorische Documentatie (RKD): http://website.rkd.nl/Databases/RKDimages/default_RKDimages (type: *portret* and *Fagel*).

lots were sold, but the Dutch government prevented many of them from being delivered to their buyers. Shortly after the auction it confiscated 640 volumes of written and printed ordinary and secret resolutions of the States General and the States of Holland from the period 1585–1790, a few collections of resolutions on specific subjects and several indexes to the resolutions and other finding aids, because they allegedly contained state secrets. These volumes were transferred to the archives of the States General.[21]

Hendrik the Younger did not sell all of his family's documentary heritage. He seems to have kept all files and loose items on the Dutch form of government and Dutch state affairs, which were in any case not easy to sell. Moreover, he had left a considerable number of copies of registers, indexes and other administrative tools in the chancellery of the States General at the Inner Court in The Hague after he left his diplomatic mission in 1795.

Papers transferred to the State Archives and rearranged

In 1802 Hendrik van Wijn was appointed archivist of the Netherlands and keeper of the archives of the States General and Holland. At that time these archives were still in their place at the Inner Court in The Hague, but in 1806 they were moved to a special repository. Simultaneously, a considerable amount of Fagel papers was moved, among them the two chests with Fagel State papers that had been left in the basement by the States of Holland in 1797, the resolutions and indexes of the States General and the States of Holland confiscated at the 1803 auction and the papers that had stayed in the chancellery in 1795. The papers from the chancellery consisted of two collections of files on state affairs, finding aids and other administrative papers. The larger one consisted of the case files, bundles of precedents, letters and other State papers collected by Hendrik the Elder between 1750 and 1790, kept in a cupboard in the greffiers' office and accurately catalogued in 1793 by Hendrik Nieuwenhuijsen, custodian of the registry of the States General. The second, much smaller one, held the remains of a larger collection of similar content created earlier by François the Elder and selectively used by Hendrik the Elder to augment his own documentation

21 *Catalogus van eene uitmuntende verzameling van gedrukte en geschreven Staatspapieren van het begin der Republiek, tot 1793, waar onder veele zeldzaame stukken, toebehoorende aan den Heere en Mr. Hendrik Fagel, Oud-Griffier van H.H.M., welke op Woensdag den 2 February 1803 des Namiddags om vier uuren publiek Verkogt zullen worden door de Boekverkopers I. van Cleef en B. Scheurleer in den Haag.* Annotated copies (with the prices and the names of the buyers) in KB veilingcatalogi nr. 4740 and NA The Hague, Arch. Van Wijn, toegang 1.13.20, inv. nr. 137.

system. And finally, the material that was moved included a series of receipts by the clerks for the payment of writing fees over the period 1722–72, supposedly also kept by the greffiers Fagel.

In 1810 and 1812 the most important parts of the archives of the Dutch Republic were moved to Paris by order of Napoleon. On this occasion a collection of clearly legible registers of ordinary and secret resolutions was composed, for the greater part consisting of the volumes seized by the State at the Fagel auction of 1803. In 1815 this collection was recovered from Paris and reunited with the archives of the States General.

During the first half of the nineteenth century the State Archives acquired many government archives and loose papers of government agencies, government officials, families and private persons who had been involved in the administration of the Dutch Republic and Holland in the seventeenth and eighteenth centuries. Together with the archives of the States General and the States of Holland these documents were reshaped as collections pertaining to domains of responsibility in the new constitutional state: foreign affairs, home affairs, finance, war, colonies etc. In this process the Fagel papers were further mixed up with archives of the States General and other archives.

One of the acquisitions was the Goldberg Collection, bought by the State in 1828. Johannes Goldberg (1763–1828) had held important government posts in the province of Holland and the State in the period 1795–1810 and had also been a collector of manuscripts. His collection of state papers included a lot of manuscripts bought by him at the Fagel auction of 1803 and even some files belonging to the Fagel papers seized in 1795.[22] In the second half of the century the State Archives acquired other Fagel manuscripts sold at the 1792 and 1803 auctions, among them the papers of Vegelin van Claerbergen. A substantial amount of Fagel manuscripts was also obtained by the Royal Library in The Hague.[23]

22 H.A.J. van Schie, *Inventaris van de collectie Goldberg*, NA The Hague, Collectie Goldberg, toegang 2.21.006.51. For a description and valuation of the Fagel manuscripts in the Goldberg Collection see R.C. Bakhuizen van den Brink, *Overzigt van het Nederlandsche Rijks-Archief* ('s-Gravenhage 1854), reprint: British Library, Historical Print Editions (London 2011), pp. 120–6. Bakhuizen also depicts the fortunes of the books and manuscripts from the 1795 confiscation to the 1803 manuscript auction.

23 The papers of Vegelin van Claerbergen, acquired by the National Archives in 1882 and 1887, are now in NA The Hague, Coll. Fagel Supplement, toegang 1.10.94, inv. nrs. 105a–105b. Among the manuscripts in the Royal Library coming from the Fagel auctions are copies of outgoing letters of the Council of State (KB 32 H 10–16), indexes to letters and advices of the Council of State KB 71 B 29 and 132 H 17), resolutions of the governing bodies of Gelderland and instructions for their officials (KB 132 H 18, 133 J 1–4, 78 A 3, 78 A 4) and seven manuscripts on various subjects. They are all described in NA The Hague, Coll. Fagel Supplement, toegang 1.10.94.

In the third quarter of the century the holdings of the State Archives increased considerably due to the efforts of R.C. Bakhuizen van den Brink (State Archivist 1851–65). In order to keep all these archives accessible, Bakhuizen had all so-called duplicates moved to the attic of the building, including printed state papers and several series of written resolutions of the States General. Subsequently, series and loose registers and items from this collection of duplicates were transferred to other archives and libraries in the country in order to fill gaps. In this process of heritage redistribution, registers of resolutions from the Fagel collections were transferred to the library of the Dutch Parliament, the archives of the States of Zeeland and Utrecht and the collection of resolutions in the Municipal Archives of Nijmegen.

In the late eighties of the nineteenth century, Th.H.F van Riemsdijk (General State Archivist 1887–1911) started an ambitious programme aimed at rearranging the holdings of the (now General) State Archives according to their provenance. Private papers that had wrongly been added to archives and larger collections were re-established as separate units. One of these units comprised remnants of the collection of files on state affairs created by Hendrik the Elder that remained in the registry of the States General after 1795 – it was renamed the 'Collectie Nieuwenhuijsen'. The other remains of the collection of François the Elder and the papers from the two chests left in the premises of the States of Holland were detached from the States General archives in a 'Collectie Staten-Generaal Vervolg' (supplement), together with other dispersed papers. Many components of the Fagel collections, however, stayed hidden in the archives of the States General, the 'Collectie Staten-Generaal Dubbelen' (duplicates) and other archives and collections in The Hague and elsewhere.

The Fagel family archives stayed in the family's hands and behind closed doors for more than a century. In 1913 the Dutch historian H.T. Colenbrander had the privilege of consulting them. He was impressed and qualified them as – after the archives of the Royal Family – the most valuable collection of historical material in the Netherlands.[24] In 1924 the General State Archives (now the National Archives) succeeded in acquiring them.[25] N.M. Japikse processed them in the early sixties.[26] From the 'Collectie Staten-Generaal Vervolg' he selected

24 H.T. Colenbrander, 'Het Archief Fagel en de geschiedenis van het Oranjehuis van 1806 tot 1813' in F.J.L. Krämer, E.W. Moes and P. Wagner (eds), *'Je maintiendrai'. Een boek over Oranje en Nassau*, vol. 2 (Leiden 1906), pp. 295–311.

25 A few years earlier the letters of William III to Gaspar and Hendrik the Eldest had already been transferred from the family archives to the archives of the Royal Family in The Hague.

26 N.M. Japikse, *Het archief van de familie Fagel* ('s-Gravenhage 1964).

the contents of the two chests and incorporated them into the family papers. His inventory of the archives, covering 48 m¹, was printed in 1964.[27]

In 1982, 767 volumes of resolutions, making almost complete series of ordinary and secret resolutions of the States General and the States of Holland, were transferred to the General State Archives. They were returned by the Second Chamber of the States General, which had received them on loan from Bakhuizen van den Brink in 1854 and 1855. As a junior archivist of the General State Archives I tried to establish the provenance of the various volumes.[28] It turned out that, before being integrated into the collection of so-called duplicates, they had been part of the archives of several governing bodies of the Dutch Republic and the States of Holland and, indeed, of the Fagel collections. Having established the provenance of the volumes of resolutions of the States General in this collection, in the collection of duplicates and in other archives and collections, including the archives of the States General themselves, I finally reconstructed the original series, dispersed over the collection returned from the Second Chamber, the archives of the States General, the collection 'Staten-Generaal Dubbelen', the acquisitions collection of the National Archives, the archives of the States of Zeeland and Utrecht, the resolutions collection in the Municipal Archives of Nijmegen and the manuscript collection of the Royal Library. It turned out that all these volumes of written resolutions had been part of at least seven series belonging to the States General, the Council of State, the General Audit Chamber, the Stadholders, the States of Holland, the Standing Committee of the States of Holland, the grand pensionaries of Holland and the greffiers Fagel.

Between 1982 and 1985 I also identified other components of the Fagel collections: the Collectie Nieuwenhuijsen, the collections incorporated in the Collectie Staten-Generaal Vervolg, the receipts of the clerks (placed unnumbered and unnoticed behind the archives of the States General), the resolutions and indexes confiscated at the 1803 auction, the remaining part of the contents of the two chests that had been combined with the documentation of François the Elder, and, finally, documents bought by collectors at the 1803 auction and later acquired by the General State Archives.

Re-establishing this part of the Fagel collections included, as already mentioned, the reconstruction of the series of ordinary resolutions of the States General, assembled by François the Elder and Hendrik the Elder. This series

27 NA The Hague, Coll. Fagel, toegang 1.10.29.

28 Theo Thomassen, *Beredeneerde plaatsingslijst van de Collectie Tweede Kamer* (Den Haag 1982), NA The Hague, Coll. Tweede Kamer, toegang 1.01.51.

consists of more than 300 volumes, covering many years between 1582 and 1642 and most years between 1642 and 1796. Up to the year 1670 they are handwritten; later volumes are printed, with written supplements for the years 1671–88.

Apparently the resolutions officially received by François the Elder after 1680 had been the core of the series of printed resolutions. Later Hendrik the Elder had obtained the printed resolutions for the preceding years 1670–79, which, according to annotations on pages at the back of several issues, had originally been sent to the Dutch envoys in Hamburg. Fagel finally had his clerks complete the series with written supplements to the volumes for the years 1671–88, the period in which only those resolutions were printed that were considered most relevant to the members of the governing bodies and the Dutch envoys abroad. To these supplements was added an index to both the written and the printed part.

The Fagel series of written and printed ordinary resolutions of the States General was put up for auction in 1803 in seven different lots. The Dutch State confiscated six of them. These lots were mixed with components of other series, sent to Paris in 1812, recovered in 1815, added to the Collection of Duplicates and partly distributed over eight repositories all over the country. The seventh lot, the supplements, was overlooked by the state. These were obtained by a private collector, who apparently was not aware of their function, and resold to the Royal Library, which – to no great purpose – kept them.[29]

The reconstruction of the written part of this series (the part before 1670) was the most complex part of the job. Rather misleading was the fact that a number of volumes appeared to have been copied for Holland by its clerks, but bound in Fagel bindings. Finally it was established that Fagel had obtained these volumes from Holland and had them rebound. The volumes copied by his clerks perfectly filled the gaps.

The reconstruction of the original series was more relevant than had previously been thought. Duplicates of written registers are rarely real duplicates. All series turned out to be different. In most volumes copied by order of government agencies and officials, resolutions of a procedural character and resolutions that were considered irrelevant for that agency or official were left out. The research value of these volumes lies not in their contents, but in their composition, which reflects the character and the intensity of the relationship of the States General with the official in question.

29 KB 131 J 12–20, 132 H 1–9.

The composition of the documentary collections

The documentary collections of the greffiers Fagel are not merely collections of rare and valuable books and manuscripts: they also reflect the functions, objectives, views and social position of their creators, members of the Fagel family. Their library was not the eighteenth-century grand library of men of letters. The qualification 'man of letters' was explicitly denied by François the Elder – nor could it be applied to his nephew Hendrik the Elder. Their library was mainly a library of use, as François put it, or, as we would say now, a reference library. The main reasons for them to collect books, maps and manuscripts was to extend their knowledge in history and other fields in support of the performance of their official, political and social duties and of the lives they would live as men of their rank, influence and beliefs.[30] Being law practitioners rather than scholars and heavily involved in Dutch foreign affairs and diplomacy, they were interested in history and topography, categories that cover more than a third of the titles in the auction catalogue prepared for Christie's by Samuel Paterson (1802), and constitutional and procedural law and jurisprudence, which also comprise a considerable part of the titles in the catalogue. The numerous books on numismatics, botany etc. in their library can easily be associated with the private, family and social life of people of their standing. It is quite interesting that in his 1754 overview Hendrik the Elder regarded his books and treatises on religion, amounting to almost one fifth of the titles in the catalogue, as a separate collection: they probably served contemplative rather than reference purposes.

The reference character of the documentary collections of the Fagel family is even more obvious in the family archives and the supplement to these archives, which contains *i.a.* part of the books, resolutions, state papers and indexes sold in 1792 and 1803. They were not only put at the service of the greffiers themselves, but also at the service of the Stadholders and the States General. It is not a coincidence that the collection of books of the States General themselves easily fitted into one closet in one of their conference rooms and that it consisted mostly of books that were dedicated and presented to them.[31]

The Fagel family archives are an accumulation of the personal archives of members of the Fagel family from the beginning of the sixteenth to the

30 Heringa, 'François Fagel', p. 86.

31 Colleagues and friends of the Fagels were allowed to use the library as well: A.J. van der Aa, *Biografisch woordenboek der Nederlanden* (*s.v.* 'Fagel'), vol. 5 (Haarlem 1862), p. 5.

nineteenth century, inherited from father to son. They consist of papers on private affairs, papers on public affairs (including the so-called greffiers' archives), series of incoming and outgoing letters and deciphered letters from foreign envoys to their governments.

Papers of a strictly personal character are arranged according to their subsequent creators. The papers produced by each look very similar in terms of content and scale. They are relatively few and consist mainly of commissions, doctoral diplomas, deeds of transfer and papers concerning inheritances. In addition to these sorts of documents, the personal papers of François the Elder, Hendrik the Elder, François the Younger and Hendrik the Younger also comprise personal annotations, particularly on books and treatises they had read on politics, law and religion.

The papers on public affairs of the late seventeenth and the eighteenth century, however, have been transformed by Hendrik the Elder into an integrated reference collection on the constitution of the state and on state affairs. More than half of it comprises what is now called the greffiers' archives (25 m[1]). It consists of bundles, files and loose documents drafted by and received by Hendrik the Eldest, François the Elder and Hendrik the Elder, and was extended by Hendrik the Younger with papers from the 1790s. Only a small part of Gaspar's papers, those not moved to the archives of the States of Holland, was included; the rest were kept apart as his own official papers.[32]

Hendrik the Elder treated the private correspondence of the greffiers on state affairs in the same way. He created two series: a series of incoming letters from Dutch envoys abroad, consisting of letters received by François the Elder, Hendrik the Elder and Hendrik the Younger, and a series of outgoing letters written by himself. Hendrik the Younger continued both series from the death of his grandfather until his departure for England in 1794. The series of deciphered letters from foreign envoys to their governments was collected by Hendrik the Elder exclusively.

A divergent part of the greffiers' archives is the sub-collection described by N.M. Japikse in his 1964 inventory under the heading 'Mail and filing'. It does not consist of files on the state and state affairs, like the rest of the greffiers' archives, but of indexes and other finding aids relating to resolutions, incoming and outgoing letters of the States General, copies of letters from the

32 Remarkably, the letters of François Fagel the Elder sent to the Dutch envoys Cornelis Hop, Hendrik Hop, Frans van der Meer and Jacob Jan Hamel Bruijnincx have returned to the Fagel archives: http://www.gahetna.nl/collectie/archief/ead/index/pagina/4/eadid/1.02.00.

States General to the provinces and foreign princes, model books for drafting resolutions and charters issued by the States General, examples of letters of different types and inventories of the archives of the States General. These documents are more complementary to those gathered and systematically described by me in 1989 as the Archief Fagel Supplement than to the other papers in the family archives.[33]

The Archief Fagel Supplement is a little larger than the Fagel family archives: 50 m¹. I have grouped the documents, mainly created and gathered by Hendrik the Elder, into four main sections: correspondence and papers related to mail and filing affairs; documentation on the constitution and on state affairs; similar documents from predecessors and employees of Hendrik the Elder, including receipts of the clerks of the States General; and manuscripts and printed books collected for their usefulness to the greffier in the performance of his duties. The correspondence is only a modest addition to the correspondence of Hendrik the Elder in the family archives. The documentation on the constitution and on state affairs collected by Hendrik the Elder himself in these archives was contained in the closet in his room in the registry of the States General. It complements similar documentation in the family archives. The documentation on diplomatic ceremonies in both collections is a good example of this complementarity. The documentation from Hendrik's predecessors is rather fragmentary. It consists of documents not integrated into the greffiers' archives by Hendrik the Elder, apparently because they could no longer meet current information needs.[34] The section comprising manuscripts and printed books is far and away the largest one. Among them are the almost complete series of written and printed ordinary resolutions and written secret resolutions of the States General, several series of indexes to these resolutions (accumulated or on an annual basis), finding aids to and copies of series of resolutions and letters of the Council of State, a series of printed resolutions of the States of Holland together with the indexes etc. These manuscripts and books, which were among the collection that Hendrik the Younger sold in 1803, are closely related to similar items in the Fagel Collection at Trinity College.

33 T.H.P.M. Thomassen, *Inventaris van het archief Fagel supplement* [...] (Den Haag 1989), NA The Hague, Coll. Fagel Supplement, toegang 1.10.94.

34 Among these predecessors are the *agenten* or archivists of the States General De Heijde (1653–78) and Rooseboom (1688–1720): NA The Hague, Coll. Fagel Supplement, toegang 1.10.94, inv. nrs. 323–4.

Peeling the onion

The collections of the Fagel family as we know them are dispersed among Trinity College in Dublin, the National Archives in The Hague, the Royal Library in The Hague and many other places. There are good reasons for regarding these dispersed collections (and at least the documentary collections) as one collection. The first is that none of these collections is 'complete' and that there are no clear-cut distinctions between the library, the documentary collections and the archives. The Fagel Library at Trinity College is less than three quarters of the library of Hendrik the Elder and many items that are part of it can be considered complementary to similar documents kept in The Hague. The second is that these collections are not only interesting because of the contents of the individual items that form them, but also because of their general composition and their overall structure, which reflect the meaningful contexts within which they have been created, arranged and rearranged.

The documentary collections of the Fagel family are the products of the collecting and record-creating activities of successive greffiers and deputy greffiers of the family for some 125 years and subsequently of the booksellers, collectors, librarians and archivists, who arranged, rearranged, described and re-described them all in their own manner over another 200 years. As a knowledge system ever under construction and later on as the scattered wreckage of this knowledge system, these collections have been processed, inventoried and catalogued in changing configurations, according to the then prevailing methods and techniques, each reflecting the socially constructed conventions on representation of their own times. Hendrik the Elder partly integrated the collections of his ancestors and described them from the point of view of the Greffier of the States General in his relationship to his duties, God and the world. Van Cleef en Scheurleer in their 1792 and 1803 auction catalogues described the books and manuscripts from the Fagel collections according to the then prevailing way of classifying knowledge and arranging books according to format. Paterson in his 1802 catalogue applied a similar universal library classification, but deliberately disregarded format and integrated books on religion with the rest of the library. Dutch collectors and archivists of the nineteenth century described their Fagel papers as Dutch state papers or as parts of the States General archives. In his 1964 inventory of the Fagel family archives, Japikse combined case files on the constitution and state affairs with finding aids to the General State archives. In my own 1985 inventory I created the supplement archives, bringing together documents sold in 1792 with documents sold in 1803, and documents originally kept at the Fagel house on the Noordeinde with documents kept in the premises of the States General at the Inner Court in The Hague.

Disregarded in many of these efforts at arrangement and description was the way in which the Fagels structured their information system. Structure however is meaning. The distinction made by the greffier between his archives and the archives of the States General reflects the boundaries between public and private duties and activities under the *ancien régime*. The categories into which Hendrik the Elder subdivided his collections reflect his approach to Dutch politics, God and the world. The systematic arrangement of his files on the constitution and state affairs reflects the legal thinking that dominated all government processes of the *ancien régime*. The hierarchical classification of documentation on countries according to their place in the all-embracing hierarchy of princes, lords, cities and states reflects the political ideology of that time. To move papers from the Fagel collections to the archives of the States General, mix books on religion with other books, rearrange files on state affairs according to the areas of responsibility of the modern state, or replace a hierarchical with an alphabetical classification is to remodel the structure of the collections in order to let them comply with one's own, anachronistic, representation systems, ideologies and outlooks on life and politics, is to change the meaning of the documents by recontextualizing them.

Eighteenth-century documentary collections can be treated as corpora of knowledge, as objects of theory-free antiquarianism, as sites of memory-construction, but also as sites of meaning-creation. Their composition and arrangement as represented in catalogues and finding aids reflect the contemporaneous order of discourse and form a part of it. Without an analysis of this order of discourse, the order of the books and other documents in these collections cannot be fully understood.[35] Such an analysis is complicated because collections are not static: in the course of their life they are augmented, reduced, split up and otherwise recontextualized. In a continuous process of creation and recreation, they are repeatedly remodelled according to the needs and views of their subsequent creators, who establish new relations between components of the collections and the collections as such and in doing so hide older layers of meaning and older orders of discourse under new ones.

35 Michel Foucault, *L'ordre du discours* (Paris 1971); Jeffrey Garrett, 'Redefining order in the German library, 1775–1825', *Eighteenth-Century Studies*, 33 (1999), 103–23.

The documentary collections of the Fagel family are very rich. Historians, art historians, botanists and scholars of other disciplines are far from having fully exploited the amazing research potential of the numerous rare books and manuscripts in these collections. But these collections offer as least as many research challenges to archivists and library historians who wish to treat them not as sources of knowledge but as objects of research, to analyse them as a coherent system, to reconstruct the various methods of representation, to peel away different and subsequent layers of meaning from this onion and to identify the different orders of discourse that they express.

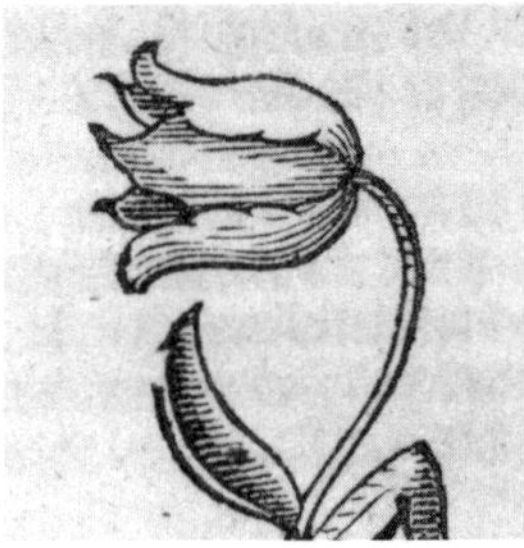

Tulips and building plans: Primary material from the Fagel Collection

John Loughman
UNIVERSITY COLLEGE DUBLIN

BECAUSE OF the enormous number of printed books acquired by Trinity College Dublin from Hendrik Fagel the Younger (1765–1838) in 1802, it is often overlooked that the purchase also included a small but significant amount of manuscript material. Ernst Braches, the Dutch book historian, counted forty-four bound manuscripts when he surveyed the Fagel collection in 1962; some of these had been immediately transferred to the Manuscripts Department when the library arrived in Dublin, while others were catalogued with the printed books and only later removed and treated as manuscripts.[1] The best-known Fagel manuscripts are undoubtedly Simon van der Stel's journal of his expedition to Namaqualand in 1685–6, and a mid fifteenth century missal produced by the Augustinian Canonesses of St Agnes in Delft.[2] There is also a considerable number of manuscripts dealing with numismatics and the historical and political affairs of France.[3] This essay will investigate less familiar primary sources from the Fagel collection: an album of tulip illustrations, which can be dated to around 1637–41, and a set of early eighteenth-century building plans.

1 Ernst Braches, 'Rapport Fagel-Bibliotheek', unpublished report, 1962 (copy, Department of Early Printed Books, TCD), p. 28.

2 See p. 91. A full facsimile of van der Stel's travel record (MS. 984), including the superlative drawings attributed to Hendrik Claudius, has been published, together with a transcription and an English translation. See Gilbert Waterhouse *et al*, *Simon van der Stel's Journey to Namaqualand in 1685* (Cape Town and Pretoria 1979). For the Fagel Missal (MS. 81), see M.L. Colker, *Trinity College Dublin. Descriptive Catalogue of the Mediaeval and Renaissance Latin Manuscripts*, 2 vols (Aldershot 1991), vol. 1, pp. 134–44.

3 T.K. Abbott, *Catalogue of the Manuscripts in the Library of Trinity College, Dublin, to which is Added a List of the Fagel Collection of Maps in the same Library* (Dublin 1900), pp. 155–6, MSS. 893–909, and pp. 168–9, MSS. 987 and 988.

Tulip Book

Among the volumes procured in 1802 was a manuscript depicting sixty-three tulips (see plate 6).[4] It was produced in the immediate aftermath of a phenomenon in Dutch history known as 'tulipmania', when contract prices for certain types of tulip bulbs rocketed to unprecedented levels, fuelling a futures market, and then spectacularly collapsed early in 1637. Only introduced into the Netherlands in the late sixteenth century, the tulip was much sought after by botanists and collectors, particularly its finer, more colourful and scarcer varieties, and admired for its seemingly infinite variability and variety, as well as being a marker of wealth and taste. A recent reassessment of 'tulipmania' has suggested that the scale, impact and nature of this famous speculative bubble have been exaggerated.[5] There was no widespread bankruptcy because the investors were confined to small circles of tulip enthusiasts. The soul-searching that followed, and the demonizing of tulip speculation, was fanned by lampooning pamphlets and reflected a deeper uneasiness about quick material gain during a period of enormous social and economic upheaval, and a devastating outbreak of plague.[6]

The Dublin album is a rare survival. Known as tulip books, fewer than fifty of these manuscripts from the seventeenth and early eighteenth centuries survive.[7] Albums of tulips were either envisaged from the beginning as a series in volume form, or they were bound together at a later stage, sometimes from

4 Abbott, *Catalogue of the Manuscripts*, p. 533, MS. 1706. The manuscript was also catalogued among the printed books held by Trinity College in 1872, with the press-mark Fag. N.3.31. See *Catalogus librorum impressorum qui in Bibliotheca Collegii… Trinitatis…adservantur*, 8 vols plus supplement (Dublin 1864–87), vol. 8, p. 191. It was moved to the Department of Manuscripts in 1962.

5 Anne Goldgar, *Tulipmania: Money, Honour, and Knowledge in the Dutch Golden Age* (Chicago and London 2007).

6 Several of these pamphlets were part of the Fagel purchase in 1802: *Samen-spraeck tusschen Waermondt ende Gaergoedt, nopende de opkomste ende ondergangh van Flora* (Haarlem 1637) [Fag. H.3.23, no. 12]; *Tweede Samen-spraeck tusschen Waermondt ende Gaergoedt, zijnde het vervolgh van den op ende ondergangh van Flora* (Haarlem 1637) [Fag. H.3.23, no. 13]; *Register van de Prijsen der Bloemen, zijnde de derde Samen-spraeck tusschen Gaergoed ende Waermond, Inhoudende het vervolgh van den op ende ondergangh van Flora* (Haarlem 1637) [Fag. H.3.23, no. 14]; and (attributed to) Johannes H. Marshoorn, *Troost-Brief, aen alle bedroefde Bloemmisten/, die treuren over 't sterven oft 't overlijden van Flora, Goddinne der Floristen* (Haarlem 1637) [Fag. H.3.23, no. 15 – see fig. 1]. I am grateful to Tim Jackson for these references.

7 For tulip books, see E.H. Krelage, *Bloemenspeculatie in Nederland* (Amsterdam 1942), pp. 55–9, 101, and 201–2; Sam Segal, 'De Tulp in de Gouden Eeuw' in Sam Segal and Michiel Roding, *De Tulp en de kunst*, exhibition catalogue, Amsterdam (De Nieuwe Kerk) (Zwolle 1994), pp. 74–113, here pp. 81–3; Frans Willemse, *The Mystery of the Tulip Painter* (Lisse 2005), and Goldgar, *Tulipmania*, pp. 98–100. An up-to-date academic survey of all surviving tulip books is urgently required.

Troost-Brief,
AEN ALLE
Bedroefde Bloemmisten/
die treuren over 't sterven oft 't overlijden
VAN
FLORA,
Goddinne der Floristen.

15.

TOT HAERLEM.

Gedruct by Hans Passchiers van Wesbusch, Boeck-
drucker op't Marckt-veldt/ inden beslagen Bybel/ 1637.

Fig 1: *Troost-Brief, aen alle bedroefde Bloemmisten/, die treuren over 't sterven oft 't overlijden van Flora, Goddinne der Floristen*, Haarlem: Hans Passchiers van Wesbusch, 1637, a pamphlet comprising an ironic 'Letter of consolation to all grieving flower-growers, who mourn the death or decease of Flora, goddess of florists'. (Fag. H.3.23, no. 15)

different sources.[8] The artist, or artists, involved began by making a sketch in pencil or graphite and then filling in this outline with watercolour and gouache. They either drew directly from nature or from existing floral images. As with contemporary botanical illustration, the approach of the creators of tulip books is quite economical and entirely focused on carefully delineating the form, texture and colour of the petals rather than in creating any sort of context or background. Even the stem and leaves of the flowers are represented in a cursory manner. The starkly observed and truncated tulips seem almost to float on the page. The Fagel album has inscriptions identifying the names of all but one of the depicted tulips and, in a departure from most of the other surviving tulip books, there is also price information for about one-third of the tulips represented. Bound in red morocco, its edges have been trimmed, with the loss of some inscriptions.

There are two schools of thought as to the motivations for making tulip books.[9] Some believe that they were mostly commissioned by enterprising growers to give buyers an indication of what the bulbs offered for sale would look like when they eventually flowered for a short period in the spring. Thus, according to this view, these collections of tulip portraits were highly elaborate, embryonic bulb catalogues. An alternative suggestion is that these illustrated manuscripts are principally records of ownership, that they were largely ordered by the same small circle of wealthy individuals who could afford to cultivate such expensive flowers. Consequently, any monetary estimates that appear alongside the tulips are not sale prices but a boastful indicator of the type of extravagant sums that certain tulip bulbs could command. In the aftermath of the tulip craze, these prices would also have been regarded as testaments of human folly.

It has previously escaped notice that one of the illustrations in the Fagel album is actually signed by the artist responsible. The final depiction (see plate 7) bears the inscription 'painted by Johan (or Johannes) Barents' (*door Joh. Barents geschildert*). No artist of this name appears to be documented and he may have been an amateur. Most of the painters and draughtsmen who created tulip books, and who can be identified, were not of the first rank. Probably the most accomplished of these artists was Jacob Marrel (1613/14–81), a still-life

8 Judith Leyster's famous representation of a *Vroege Brabantsson* tulip was only bound into a tulip book in the eighteenth century. Some watercolour depictions of tulips on paper were framed and displayed on walls. See Judith Leyster, *A Dutch Master and her World*, exhibition catalogue, Haarlem (Frans Halsmuseum) and Worcester (Worcester Art Museum) (New Haven and London, 1993), pp. 214–19, no. 16.

9 On the function of tulip books, see Goldgar, *Tulipmania*, p. 100.

painter of German birth, who was responsible for several tulip albums, some of them defying convention by depicting more than one flower to a page and by adding insects and shells to enhance visual interest.[10] The illustrations in the Dublin tulip book are of mixed quality. Some have a vividness and artistry that are close to Marrel; others are drably painted and lacking in skill. The possibility that more than one hand was involved should not be excluded.

Who was the original commissioner of the Fagel tulip album? Unfortunately, there is no documented provenance for the manuscript prior to its appearance among the books offered for sale by Hendrik Fagel the Younger in 1802.[11] Some clues to its origins are, however, to be found within its pages. For example, inscribed on the flyleaf is the amount of 43 guilders, 10 stuivers. Was this the artist's fee for producing the tulip illustrations or does it record a later transaction, perhaps the price paid at auction or to a dealer by a subsequent owner of the book? The only comparative information that we have on the cost of making a tulip book is contained in a handwritten notation, dated March 1639, and found on the last page of an album from the 1630s now in the Nederlandsch Economisch-Historisch Archief, Amsterdam.[12] This manuscript was illustrated with tulips and other flowers and insects by Jacob Isaacsz van Swanenburg (1571–1638), a Leiden painter best remembered as the first teacher of Rembrandt, and Adriaen Jansz van Witvelt (c. 1581–1638). Van Swanenburg received 30 guilders and 10 stuivers for painting seventy-six watercolours of tulips and forty-six of other flowers or, in other words, 5 stuivers per image. Van Witvelt's contribution of sixteen illustrated pages was estimated to be worth 8 guilders, or 10 stuivers per page, but he produced more detailed watercolours of flowers, fruit and insects. The entire cost of the painted illustrations was thus 38 guilders, 10 stuivers. However, a note in a later hand informs us that when the album was offered at auction in January 1647 it achieved only 37 guilders, thus failing to recoup even its painting costs. Although we cannot be certain when the sum of 43 guilders, 10 stuivers, was noted on the Fagel tulip book, a price of 13.8 stuivers per illustrated tulip compares very favourably with the outlay for the better-known Amsterdam example.

10 The Rijksmuseum, Amsterdam (RP-T-1950-266), has a tulip book by Jacob Marrel consisting of eighty-five drawn pages with two tulips per page, probably commissioned by the Portuguese grower Francisco Gomes da Costa between 1637 and 1645.

11 The first documented reference to the tulip book is in Christie's auction catalogue of 1802 compiled by Samuel Paterson. See *Bibliotheca Fageliana. A Catalogue of the Valuable and Extensive Library of the Greffier Fagel of The Hague* [...] *Digested by Sam. Paterson* (London 1802), p. 179, no. 4030.

12 For illustrations to this tulip book, see http://www.neha.nl/specialcollections/0254tulp.php.

More revealing is folio 62, towards the end of the Dublin manuscript. Surprisingly no flower is depicted and instead the page is comprised of three circles of roughly the same size, each filled with handwritten text. These circles purport to be the dimensions of flowers measured in the gardens of a certain Jan Joorisz and *Seigneur* Beeresteijn in August 1641.[13] Beeresteijn's garden was located on the Turfmarkt, although no city or town is mentioned. This page is crucial in interpreting the tulip book because it gives us both a probable *terminus ante quem* of 1641 for its production and also a pointer to the milieu in which it originated.

The identity of Jan Joorisz [Jorisz], a common patronymic, cannot be determined, but we can with some confidence trace his fellow garden owner, Beeresteijn. In all probability he is Gijsbert van Beresteyn (1576–1641) (see plate 8), a merchant and governor of the Delft chamber of the East India Company (VOC), who lived in a house on the city's Turfmarkt, from where he was buried in November 1641, just a few months after the bulbs in his garden had been measured.[14] He belonged to a wealthy regent family, who had branches in Delft and Haarlem, and his marriage to Maria Prins (1587–1667) in 1606 brought him connections with a powerful Rotterdam dynasty. His father was Paulus van Beresteyn (1548–1625), an affluent brewer and burgomaster of Delft.[15] We do not know if Gijsbert van Beresteyn was one of the small circle of *bloemisten*, as those who cultivated and traded in tulips were occasionally known, and whose endeavours gave rise to the 'tulipmania' of the 1630s. Certainly at least one of

13 The text in the first circle reads: 'The true size measured by the gardener in Jan Joorisz's garden on 2 August 1641; this was the main flower and larger than the heart of the flower of Seigneur Beeresteijn's gardener' (*De rechte maet vanden boer gemeten inden tuijn van Jan Joorisz ope den 2 augusto anno 1641, dit was de hart blom en ghrooter als de hartblom vanden boer van Sr. Beeresteijn*). To the right is another circle containing the text: 'The true size measured by the gardener at S[eigneu]r. Beeresteijn's on 6 August 1641, was just as large as those measured by the neighbouring gardener of Jan Jooris, and the adjacent flowers were very large' (*De rechte maet vanden boer tot Sr. Beeresteijn gemeeten op den 6 augusto ano. 1641, was noch zoo ghroot geworden als deesen hijer neffenstaenden boer van Jan Jooris en de nae blommen waeren zeer ghroot*). Finally the text of the third circle in the lower left reads: 'The true size of a Dornick Striped plant at Sr. Beeresteijn on the Turfmarket at the end of August 1641, was larger than any drawn by the gardeners above' (*De rechte maet van een Doornickse gestreepte gewassten tot Sr. Beeresteijn aende turreffmart gemeeten int Lestende van Augusto ano 1641, was ghrooter als een vande bovengeteekende boeren*). Presumably it was a tulip that inspired this exceptional bout of competitive measuring, but we cannot be certain. As far as I can ascertain, no tulip with the name 'Dornick Striped' has been recorded. I am grateful to Betsy Wieseman, and especially Claudia Swan, for their help in translating these inscriptions.

14 Gemeentearchief Delft, Begraafboeken Oude en Nieuwe Kerk, DTB, no. 38, 4 November, 1641, fol. 272. For a genealogy of the Van Beresteyn family, see E.A. van Beresteyn and W.F. Del Campo Hartman, *Genealogie van het geslacht Van Beresteyn*, 2 vols (The Hague 1954).

15 In a recent survey of the richest people in the Dutch Republic of the seventeenth century, Paulus van Beresteyn ranked in twenty-first position. See Kees van Zandvliet, *De 250 rijksten van de Gouden Eeuw: Kapitaal, macht, familie en levensstijl* (Amsterdam 2006), pp. 51–3.

his relatives was involved in this trade: his first cousin, Paulus van Beresteyn (1588–1636), a Haarlem lawyer, had shortly before his death in 1636 sold six beds of tulips for a sum of money and a fine atlas from the bookshop of one of the consortium of buyers.[16] The fact that an atlas was part of the deal is significant. Many of the people who bought and sold tulip bulbs also collected paintings, books and curiosities; certain breeds of tulips had long been regarded as exotic collectors' items because of their rarity value and aesthetic qualities.[17] Several generations of the Van Beresteyn family had been interested in art. Gijsbert's grandfather Cornelis van Beresteyn (1517–95) and his uncle Aernout (1556–1612) were both mentioned as collectors and connoisseurs by the artist and writer Karel van Mander.[18] Gijsbert's brother Arnold van Beresteyn (1595–1652) may have taken drawing lessons from the Haarlem still-life painter Willem Heda in 1637.[19] Heda, like many artists, was an active participant in the tulip trade.[20] The renowned portraitist Frans Hals had portrayed his aforementioned cousin, Paulus van Beresteyn, and his third wife Catharina Both van der Eem (1589–1666).[21] The children of this cousin also moved in artistic circles: his son Nicolaes (or Claes) (1629–84) was an amateur painter and engraver who had studied with Salomon de Bray and his daughter Elisabeth (1620–72) married Pieter Cornelisz Verbeeck (1610/15–52/54), a painter mostly of equestrian landscapes.[22]

The reference to Gijsbert van Beresteyn in the Fagel tulip book is important for two reasons. In the first place it is evidence that the manuscript may have been produced in Delft. Secondly, it throws up the possibility that Van Beresteyn could have been its patron and that the book is a visual testament to some of the tulips growing in his garden.

16 Beresteyn and Hartman, *Genealogie*, vol. 1, p. 221.

17 On the relationship between the collecting of art and tulips, see Goldgar, *Tulipmania*, pp. 62–130.

18 Karel van Mander, *Het Leven der Doorluchtighe Nederlandtsche en Hooghduytsche Schilders* (Alkmaar 1604), fols. 208v, 245r, 246v and 285r. See also M.J. Bok, 'Art-lovers and their paintings: Van Mander's *Schilder-boeck* as a source for the history of the art market in the northern Netherlands' in the Rijksmuseum exhibition catalogue *Dawn of the Golden Age, 1580–1620* (Amsterdam 1993), p. 135, and H. Miedema (ed.), *Karel van Mander. The Lives of the Illustrious Netherlandish and German Painters*, 6 vols (Dornspijk 1994–9), vol. 2, pp. 304–5, and vol. 4, p. 73.

19 M.E.W. Goosens, 'Schilders en de markt, Haarlem 1605–1635'(Unpublished Ph.D. dissertation, University of Leiden 2001), p. 103.

20 Goldgar, *Tulipmania*, pp. 127, 247 and 319–20.

21 The pendant portraits by Hals are now in the Louvre. See the exhibition catalogue published by the National Gallery of Art (Washington), the Royal Academy of Art (London), and the Frans Halsmuseum (Haarlem): Seymour Slive, *Frans Hals* (Washington, London and Haarlem 1989–90), pp. 144–7, nos. 6 and 7.

22 Goosens, 'Schilders en de markt', pp. 416 and 435.

The album is explicitly connected to a famous auction of tulips that took place in Alkmaar in 1637. Indeed the title page reads: 'Alkmaar pleasure garden of tulips or [the] sale of a consignment of tulips in Alkmaar on 5 February 1637'.[23] These tulips were sold by the municipal Orphans Court for the benefit of the orphans of Wouter Bartholomeusz Winckel, a local innkeeper and dealer in bulbs. Although the bulbs were still in the ground and could not be removed until the plants flowered in April, May or June (depending on the variety), the buyers at this sale were prepared to pay extravagant sums and almost 90,000 guilders was raised. It is important to point out, however, that these prices were only promises of reimbursement rather than cash transactions, since by the time the bulbs were dug from the ground the following summer and delivered to the purchasers and payment expected, the tulip market had collapsed and few would have been willing or able to honour commitments made in February.

As news of the Winckel auction spread, it quickly became a byword throughout the Dutch Republic for speculative lunacy and a broadside was published carefully itemizing the names of the tulips, the weight of their bulbs, and the incredible hammer prices. The opening folio of the Dublin manuscript lists almost exactly the same information as the broadside, albeit in an abbreviated format, and must have been based upon it.[24] Most of the bulb weights and prices that appear on the individual tulip representations are also taken from this source.[25] Despite this focus on the Alkmaar auction, only about sixteen of

23 *Alckmaarse Lusthoff van Tulpaanen, ofte Verkooping van een Parteij Tulpaanen, binnen Alckmaar den 5 February 1637*. On the Alkmaar auction, see Mike Dash, *Tulipomania: The Story of the World's most Coveted Flower and the Extraordinary Passions it Aroused* (New York 1999), pp. 146–61.

24 The broadside is entitled *Lijste van Eenige Tulpaen, verkocht aen de meest-biedende op den 5en Februarij 1637* and appears to have had a wide circulation. It can be found among the Fagel pamphlets at TCD, glued into *Register van de Prijsen der Bloemen*; there is also a transcription of it in the pamphlet attributed to Johannes H. Marshoorn, *Troost-Brief, aen alle bedroefde Bloemmisten*, pp. 22–4 (see note 6). Anne Goldgar is sceptical about these reported prices and can only find documentary evidence to substantiate the sum for which one bulb was sold at the Winckel auction (*Tulipmania*, p. 203). One tulip book (sale Christie's, Amsterdam, 13 November, 1995, lot 185) purportedly was compiled in order to advertise the bulbs offered for sale at Alkmaar in February 1637.

25 To judge from differences in the ink, information about the prices was added later to some of the pages, but evidently in the same hand as the person who inscribed the names of the flowers. There are some discrepancies between the prices given on the broadside and those in the tulip book. Tulips were sold according to their weight, which was measured in *assen* or aces. One ace is equal to 0.048 grammes. The tulip book suggests that an *Admirael Liefckens* bulb was sold at Alkmaar in February 1637 for 17 guilders 15 stuivers an ace. However, the bulb, weighing 59 aces, achieved 1015 guilders, not 1047 guilders 5 stuivers. Not all prices that appear on the Fagel album are taken from the published results of the Alkmaar auction. An *Admirael Gouda* (fol. 12), sold for 10 guilders 2 stuivers per ace, was not among the lots. A number of bulbs, with prices, are specifically described as having been 'sold by another'. Among these are a *Root en geel van Leijden* (fol. 16; 550 guilders), a *Ghevlugelde van Koorenart* (fol. 20; 1000 aces for 450 guilders), a *Croon* (fol. 25; 1200 guilders), an *Ottho de Man* (fol. 26; 1000 aces for 800 guilders), a *Rijswijcker* (fol. 47; 1000 aces for 800 guilders), and a *Generael de Man* (fol. 61; 1000 aces for 800 guilders).

the tulips illustrated in the Trinity College manuscript were included in this sale. There is no illustration of Winckel's most expensive tulip, an *Admirael van Enckhuijzen*; one of its bulbs complete with an offset was sold by private treaty prior to the auction for 5200 guilders. There are, however, images of the tulip that attracted the highest bids – two bulbs of the *Viceroy* (see plate 9) were sold respectively for 3000 and 4000 guilders – and of the *Admirael Liefkens*, the most valuable cultivar in terms of price per weight. To put these prices into a broader context, the annual household income of successful craftsmen, tradesmen and shopkeepers averaged between 600 and 1000 guilders, while a prosperous burger in Delft could purchase a substantial house for around 2000 guilders.[26]

The first tulip that we encounter in the album had almost mythical status and even Winckel did not own an example. This is the *Semper Augustus* (see plate 10), which was renowned for its extreme rarity and beauty. It belonged to the *rosen* category of cultivated tulips, the petals of which were distinguished by their flamed patterns against a white ground. Very few people in the seventeenth century could possibly have laid eyes on the *Semper Augustus*. According to one source, there were only twelve specimens of this plant in existence in the 1620s and they all belonged to one man, who resisted offers of 2000 or 3000 guilders for a single bulb.[27] Understandably, given its scarcity, it was also the tulip least frequently depicted in tulip books.[28] It is also perhaps relevant that there is a close correspondence between the way that the *Semper Augustus* is represented in the Dublin tulip album and its depiction in at least two other manuscripts, raising the likelihood that the artists involved were copying each other or working from a common source.[29]

With flower collectors' insistence on novelty, and the lack of any classification system or a central regulating body, there was a profusion of tulip names in circulation. Matters were further complicated by the rapid emergence of new 'broken' varieties of tulips, distinguished by their vivid flamed patterns, which we now know were caused by a viral infection. Over 500 names for

26 Jan de Vries and Ad van der Woude, *The First Modern Economy: Success, Failure, and Perseverance of the Dutch Economy, 1500–1815* (Cambridge and New York 1997), pp. 563–4; J.M. Montias, *Artists and Artisans in Delft: A Socio-economic Study of the Seventeenth Century* (Princeton, New Jersey 1982), p. 222.

27 Goldgar, *Tulipmania*, p. 200. Goldgar quotes from the Amsterdam doctor and chronicler Nicolaes van Wassenaer. A copy of the latter's famous *Historisch Verhael* (Amsterdam 1622–30) was in the Fagel library (Fag. H.5.1–6).

28 Willemse, *The Mystery*, p. 51.

29 The manuscripts in question are the so-called 'Great tulip book' (Norton Simon Museum, Pasadena, California, inv. no. M.1974.08.123.D) and Special Collections 254 in the Nederlandsch Economisch-Historisch Archief, Amsterdam.

the seventeenth century are known, which led to considerable confusion and duplication.[30] Since growers were responsible for naming tulips, not surprisingly many of the names they chose were self-referential. In the Dublin album appellations that consist of surnames prefixed by the grandiose titles 'admiral' and 'general' (*Admirael Bogert, Admirael Katolijn, Admirael Fabri, Generael vander Eijck, Generael de Man*, etc.) are not those of Dutch military heroes but of the breeders themselves or the town where they lived (*Admirael Gouda*). Other tulip names are simply the names of those responsible for cultivating them (*Jan Gerritse, Otto de Man*). Distinction was also conferred on the blooms by calling them after classical worthies (*Alexander Magnus, Marcus Aurelius, Scipio Africanus*). Some names extend from the analogy that was often drawn between tulips and veined and streaked stones such as marble (*Ghemarmerde van Kaer*) and agate (*Agaet Blanse*); others simply from their colour (*Bruijn Purper, Purperen Wit van Jeroen, Root en Geel van Leijden)* or their flamed pattern (*Gevlamde Guillaume, Vroeghe* [early] *Gevlamde van Bosschaert*) or their shape (*Gevleugelde* [winged] *van Coornhert, Croon* [crown]).

One of the most intriguing names in the Fagel album is that of the last depicted tulip, *De Paus van Roomen* [the Pope of Rome] (see plate 7), and also significantly the only illustration that is signed with the artist's name. This purple streaked and speckled tulip is entirely unrecorded, at least in any published source, and there is no other example of a tulip being given such a blatantly Catholic title. Such evidence would suggest a Roman Catholic environment for its creation. We do not know the religious persuasion of Gijsbert van Beresteyn. While his immediate family, who held positions in the town government of Delft, swore allegiance to the Reformed Church, the Haarlem branch of the Van Beresteyns remained firmly Catholic. Crucially Gijsbert never achieved political or civic office in Delft, as would have been expected of the eldest son from a regent family. Instead his younger brother Cornelis van Beresteyn (1586–1638) followed his father onto the town council and like him ultimately became burgomaster. Might Gijsbert's reluctance to serve, or his ineligibility, indicate that he was less than committed to Calvinism, the official religion of the Dutch Republic?

Rather than a manuscript to be admired and preserved, or perhaps to be marvelled at in terms of the recorded prices, the Fagel tulip album seems to have been constantly in use and was possibly accessible to the family's gardeners.

30 The most extensive published list of tulip names can be found in Krelage, *Bloemenspeculatie*, pp. 126–41.

Inserted within its pages were various handwritten and printed documents, dating from the opening decades of the eighteenth century, and mostly consisting of receipts for tulips, hyacinths and other flowers purchased by the Fagels or their gardeners, as well as records of bulb auctions.[31] The prices recorded are a lot more modest than those from the 1630s. Much of this material is unique and its worth was recognized by the nurseryman and historian, E.H. Krelage, who published various excerpts from these inserts in the TCD album.[32] Among these documents is a planting plan for a bed of tulips sown in the garden of the family's palatial house in The Hague on 16 October 1718 (see fig. 2). Consisting of four rows, with fourteen flowers per row, this bed was located in the north corner 'behind the office' (*achter het Comptoir*). The plan illustrates the extent to which tulip fashions and nomenclature had changed by the early decades of the eighteenth century. Most of the tulips belong to the *baguetten* (red and purple hues against white) and *bizarden* (various colour combinations against yellow) categories, that were developed in Flanders and Northern France, and provided round flowers on long stems. The *bizarden* were the most sought after, and while prices would never rival those of the 1630s, the bulb of one type called *frère* had achieved between 140 and 336 guilders at auction in 1708. This tulip is found in the Fagel planting plan.

Building plans

The planting plan is not the only document surviving in the collection of Trinity College Dublin that can throw light on the Fagels' residence on the Noordeinde, The Hague, and its appearance and activities in the early eighteenth century (see fig. 3). It comes as something of a surprise to find among the printed maps collected by the Fagel family, and now housed in the Department of Early Printed Books, a set of building plans for this house, dating to around 1706.[33] Original designs for domestic buildings are very rare for seventeenth- and eighteenth-century Holland. It must have been for strategic reasons that the family established their main base on the Noordeinde (now Noordeinde 138–40), one of the most prestigious streets in the city and

31 These loose items are now filed separately from the tulip book at MS. 1706/2/1–10. Only one document remains in the album, pasted to fol. 62.

32 Krelage, *Bloemenspeculatie*, pp. 107–9, and *idem*, *Drie Eeuwen Bloembollenexport* (The Hague 1946), p. 540.

33 Abbott, *Catalogue of the Manuscripts*, p. 491, portfolio XIV, no. 920 (63/1–3).

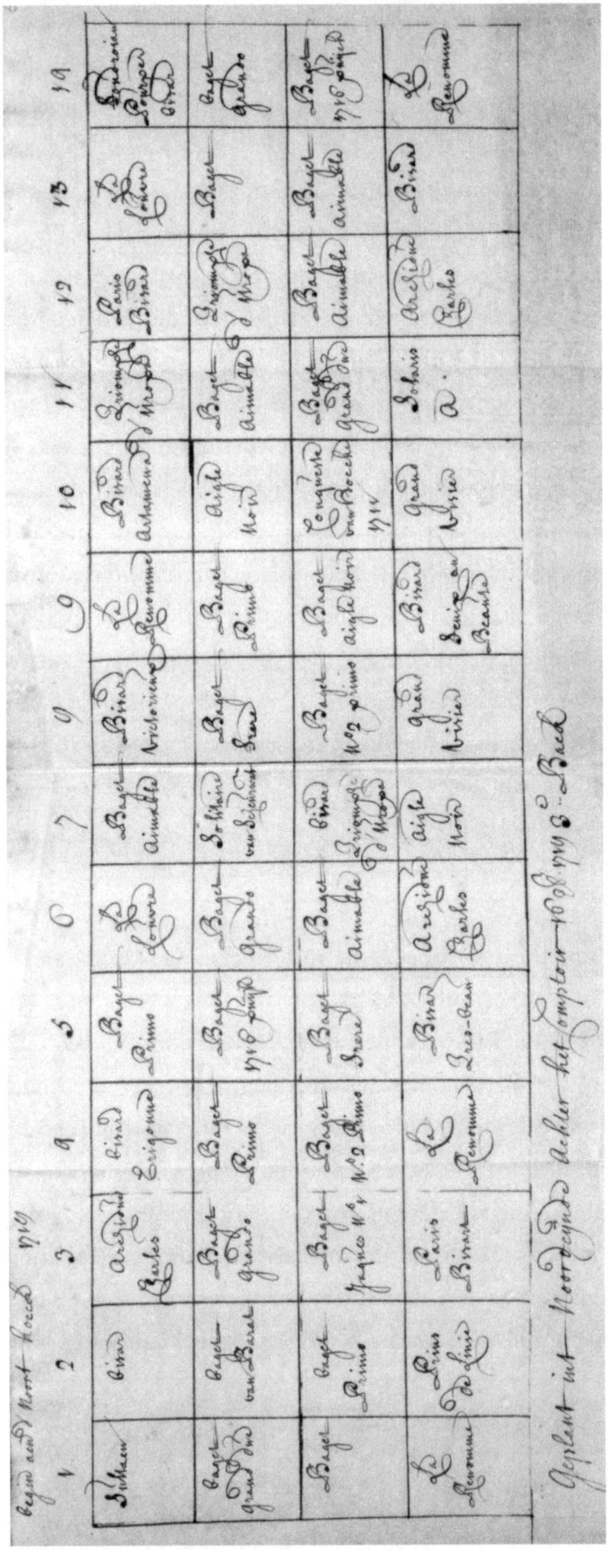

Fig 2: Planting plan for a tulip bed at the Fagel House on the Noordeinde, The Hague (1718). (TCD MS 1706/2/6)

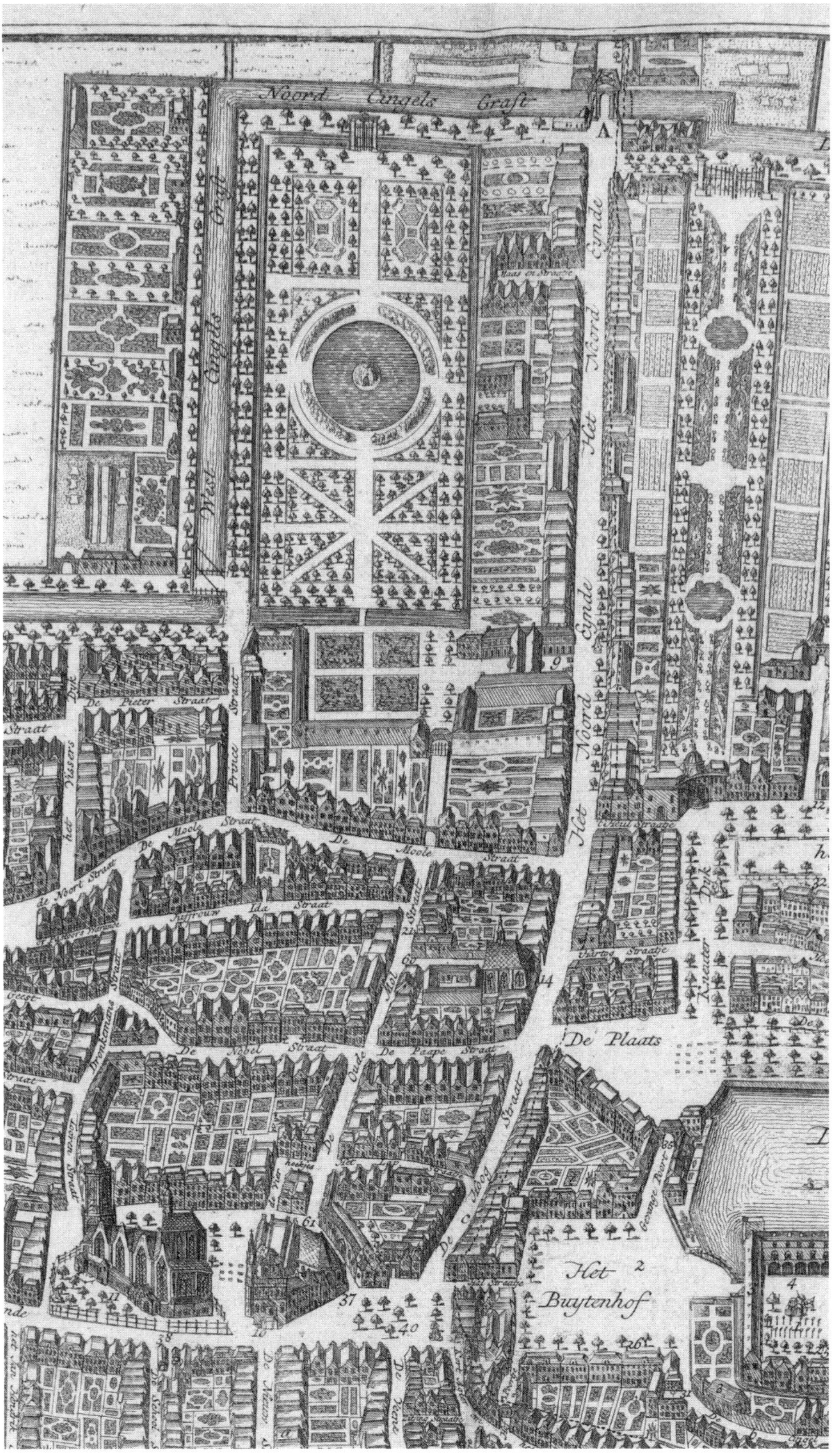

Fig 3: Detail from a street plan of The Hague from 1745, showing the Noordeinde. (Fagel Portfolio 14:015/1; Abbott 872)

within walking distance of the Binnenhof, where the States General met and where successive members of the Fagel family who held the position of greffier had offices. Although this imposing dwelling, which became known as the Fagel House, has a rich architectural heritage, mostly because of its association with the French Huguenot architect and designer, Daniel Marot (1661–1752), these plans are entirely unknown; the most recent monographic study of Marot's work in the Netherlands stated that the earliest surviving plans for the house date to only 1851.[34]

The history of the Fagel House begins in 1680 when Hendrik Fagel the Eldest (1617–90) purchased three parcels of real estate on the Noordeinde.[35] In April 1707 his son François Fagel the Elder (1659–1746) extended this site by acquiring an adjoining house and garden. Shortly thereafter the house was extensively remodelled to create what Gysbert de Cretser, the historian of The Hague, called in 1711 'a very distinguished and substantial new residence which could well pass for a Palace'.[36] Despite an impressive street façade of twenty-six metres, the exterior was relatively sober and unadorned, probably constructed from brick rather than more expensive sandstone. It was a two-storey building with attics above and basement rooms below. Two garden wings projected from a central block, and one of these was connected via a single-storey gallery to a small pavilion, now commonly known as the *Cupola van Fagel* on account of its domed ceiling. The gallery, which ran the entire length of the garden, was the site of François the Elder's library and his other collecting activities, especially in the areas of coins and the graphic arts.[37] It and the pavilion provided a tranquil

34 Rob van Zoest and Xander van Eck, 'Zeer voorname woonhuizen, die voor paleizen niet behoeven te wijken' in K. Ottenheym, W. Terlouw and R. van Zoest (eds), *Daniel Marot: Vormgever van een deftig bestaan* (Amsterdam 1988), p. 31. Trinity College Dublin also has a bound set of engravings by Daniel Marot of designs for a tomb for the Duke of Portland at Rhoon. There are four pages with two engravings per page (Portfolio XXIV, 1629, no. 76 [only marking Fagel HH, 7284]).

35 The most extensive building history of the Fagel House remains J. van Breen, 'Het Heerenhuis Noordeinde nr. 140' in *Jaarboek Die Haghe* (1913), pp. 133–54. See also M.D. Ozinga, *Daniel Marot: De schepper van den Hollandschen Lodewijk XIV-stijl* (Amsterdam 1938), pp. 140–42, and Van Zoest and Van Eck, 'Zeer voorname woonhuizen', pp. 31–2. The three houses purchased in 1680 belonged to Justus van Egmont van der Nieuburch. Also part of the Fagel map collection at TCD is a ground plan, which shows the three houses and the gardens prior to this sale. This plan, drawn up by the surveyor Pieter Floris van der Sallem in November 1658, initially only represented Van Egmont van der Nieuburch's original house on the Noordeinde but was extended in March 1669 to include two other houses that he had purchased in 1662 and 1667. See Abbott, *Catalogue of the Manuscripts*, p. 496, portfolio XIV, no. 1013 (156/2). – For the Fagel pedigree see Thomassen, fig. 2.

36 '[…] een zeer deftige en aanziennelyke nieuwgeboude huizinge […] de welke mede wel voor een Paleys doorgaan kon': Gysbert de Cretser, *Beschryvinge van 's Gravenhage, Behelsende Desselfs eerste opkomste, stichtinge en vermakelyke situatie* […] (Amsterdam 1711), p. 64.

37 See Thomassen, figs. 8 and 10. On François the Elder's collecting activities, see J. Heringa, 'François Fagel: Portret van een honnête homme', *Jaarboek Die Haghe* (1980), pp. 43-126, here pp. 83–94.

haven, a refuge from the affairs of state and public life, and looked out on a well-tended garden. The setting was particularly fortuitous since the rear of the Fagel property bordered the enormous gardens of the Oude Hof, known as the Prinsessetuin or Princess's garden, which had been laid out in fashionable geometrical formations in the early seventeenth century. First used as royal residence in 1591, when Louise de Coligny and her young son Frederik Hendrik, the future stadholder, moved there, the Oude Hof subsequently evolved into the Noordeinde Palace and continues in use by the Dutch royal family to this day.[38] François Fagel the Elder was given privileged access to the Princess's garden by the construction of a footbridge over a canal that separated his garden from that of the Oude Hof.

The Fagel House on the Noordeinde has witnessed considerable change in the intervening centuries. According to J. van Breen, who published a history of the house in 1913, Hendrik Fagel the Elder (1706–90), nephew of François the Elder, radically altered the house c. 1750 to allow for the reconstruction of three reception rooms in the Rococo style.[39] When the fortunes of the family declined after the invasion of the Netherlands by French forces in 1795 and the flight of William V to England, the building was sold in 1803 by Hendrik Fagel the Younger, who was then living in London. In 1853 it was purchased by King Willem III and subsequently divided into two rental dwellings before being occupied by the Crown Estates Department and later still, the Royal Archives. It was at this juncture too that the garden gallery was demolished and the so-called 'Dome of Fagel', which now became a free-standing structure, was incorporated with part of the garden into the grounds of the Noordeinde Palace.[40] Royal ownership of the Fagel House ended in 1901 (see Thomassen, fig. 7 for a ground plan of the house in that year), when the building was purchased by the municipality of The Hague, with the intention of knocking it down to make way for a street. Fortunately this plan was never carried out, but much of the interior was lost in 1899–1900 when marble chimney pieces, overmantle and overdoor paintings, wainscoting, ceilings, cornices and silk damask wall

38 For a recent history of Noordeinde Palace, see Eymert-Jan Goosens, *Noordeinde Palace: Four Centuries of the 'Court of the House of Orange'* (Zwolle 2008).

39 Van Breen, 'Het Heerenhuis', p. 144.

40 Two bays of the original gallery survive and are today integrated with the garden pavilion and serve as its entrance vestibule. For the 'Dome of Fagel' see above, pp. 29–32; Marten Loonstra, 'Taking a royal view: The Fagel pavilion in the Noordeinde Palace, The Hague', *Country Life* (22 August, 1985), 493–5; *idem*, 'De Koepel van Fagel' in Ottenheym *et al.*, *Daniel Marot,* pp. 67–71; and Frans van Burkom *et al.*, *Leven in toen: Vier eeuwen Nederlands interieur in beeld* (Zwolle 2001), pp. 84–5.

coverings were transferred to the Lange Voorhout Palace.[41] Since then, the exterior and the layout of the Fagel House have endured further transformation; today it is occupied by three commercial outlets – including ironically an Irish pub, and a snooker club (see fig. 4). All that remains of the original eighteenth-century interior of the main house are three stuccoed ceilings. The recently restored garden pavilion, the 'Dome of Fagel', has fortunately survived intact and is widely regarded as a gem of eighteenth-century Dutch architecture, but is nowadays hidden behind the walls of the Noordeinde Palace and almost never accessible to the general public. Its sumptuous mixture of gilded stuccowork, dark, richly-veined marble, and ceiling frescoes is unique for the northern Netherlands at this date (see plate 5).

In the absence of building specifications, contracts, bills, receipts, letters or other documentation relating to the construction of the house, we are uncertain about the date of Daniel Marot's involvement and the extent of his contribution. Arriving in the Netherlands in 1686, Marot worked first for William III in designing aspects of royal residences, including the interiors and the garden at Het Loo. It must have been his design for the Treveszaal, the meeting room of the States General in the Binnenhof, The Hague, that first brought him to the attention of François Fagel. After William's death in 1702, and the beginning of the Second Stadholderless period (1702–47), the French architect-designer had to look outside of court circles for commissions. Apart from the 'Dome of Fagel', which is universally accepted as an integrated design by Marot, evidence for his involvement in the architecture of the main house is limited, though two surviving stuccoed ceilings have been attributed to him. One of these can be linked directly to a print engraved and published by the Frenchman, while the other has features in common with his work at Het Loo.[42] In addition, there is a design for an illusionistic painted ceiling by Marot that is inscribed *placfond fait pour Mr. le grefier Fagel* and represents the Four Seasons.[43] Van Zoest and Van Eck have suggested that Marot's contribution was mostly restricted to some of the room interiors, and to the garden side of the house, with

41 For the dismantling of the interior and its integration in the Palace Lange Voorhout, see René Cleverens, *Paleis Lange Voorhout* (Amsterdam, 1994), pp. 40–41.

42 Willem Terlouw, 'Rijke interieurs als spiegel voor bewoner en bezoeker' in Ottenheym *et al.*, *Daniel Marot*, pp. 56–9. Freling suggests that a Louis XIV-style ceiling from a first-floor room in the Fagel House was removed and reinstalled in the dining room of the Noordeinde Palace. See W.V.J. Freling, *Stucwerk in het Nederlandse woonhuis, uit de 17e en 18e eeuw*, 2nd edn (Leeuwarden/Mechelen 1996), p. 294.

43 The design in pen and ink, with watercolour washes, is signed by Marot and is in the Kunstbibliothek, Staatliche Museen zu Berlin. See C. Willemijn Fock (ed.), *Het Nederlandse interieur in beeld 1600–1900* (Zwolle 2001), p. 212.

Fig 4: The Fagel House in 2008 (photograph by J.L.)

its entrance doorway, gallery and garden pavilion. Most architectural historians date the house and the 'Dome of Fagel' to 1707–8; Marten Loonstra appears to be alone in suggesting that the pavilion was begun in 1701. The plans that I discuss below indicate that modifications to the seventeenth-century structure had either begun or were fully envisaged early in 1706. Johan van Gool, the painter and writer, confirmed an earlier dating when he wrote in the *De Nieuwe Schouburg* (1750) that Fagel built his house on the Noordeinde in 1706 and that the artists Gaspar Peter Verbruggen and Mattheus Terwesten provided frescoes and decorative work in that year.[44] However, he also mentions that Richard van Bleeck had provided an overmantel painting for Fagel in 1705, and thus some of the renovation work may have begun even earlier.[45]

Another house in The Hague, for which there is documentary evidence of Marot's design input, gives us insight into how the relationship between the French designer-architect, other professionals involved in the project, and the

44 J. van Gool, *De Nieuwe Schouburg der Nederlantsche kunstschilders en schilderessen* [...] (The Hague 1750), vol. 1, pp. 267 and 326. Van Gool must have been particularly well informed about the Fagel House since he lived on the Noordeinde. See Heringa, 'François Fagel', p. 89. Terwesten inscribed the date 1708 on the ceiling of the 'Dome of Fagel'. See C.J.A. Wansink, 'De decoratieve schilderkunst van Mattheus Terwesten, een Haagse meester uit de achttiende eeuw', *Oud Holland*, 104 (1990), 270–92, here 272, 276 and 287.

45 Van Gool, *De Nieuwe Schouburg*, vol. 1, p. 376.

patron might have worked. Like the Fagel House, the residence built for Cornelis van Schuylenburch on the Lange Vijverberg between 1715 and 1717 involved the incorporation of existing dwellings into a new building.[46] Not only do we have construction plans for this house, but also designs for elements of the interior and the façade, as well as the building specifications, and correspondence. The latter cites Felix du Sart (d. 1735), another French Huguenot refugee who was a master carpenter and bricklayer, as the supervising architect, while the Italian stuccodore Giovanni Baptista Luraghi (c. 1675–1736) played an important part in designing the layout and various decorative features. Van Schuylenburch also had an active role in determining the finished design. One can imagine a similar situation prevailing with the house of François Fagel, particularly since Marot had departed for Amsterdam in 1706 and could not have maintained a hands-on approach with the construction work. François the Elder was a well-informed patron. His library contained standard architectural tracts by Vitruvius, Palladio, Isaac Ware, William Kent, Jacques Androuet du Cerceau, François and Jacques-François Blondel, as well as the collections of engraved views and plans of Parisian buildings by Daniel Marot's father, Jean.

There are three construction drawings for the Fagel house in the possession of Trinity College.[47] Two of them are inscribed with the date 26 March 1706; the third has no date. The dated drawings are titled 'No. 2 Plan of the second floor of the house of the *Heer Greffier* Fagel'[48] (see plate 11) and 'No. 3 Plan of a construction for the *Heer Greffier* Fagel that could be altered from the drawing no. 1' (see plate 12).[49] In all probability the undated plan (see plate 13),[50] which has few inscriptions beyond some room names and no title, is the drawing referred to as number one, and the first in the sequence. It is also the most unfinished of the three and gives no dimensions, although

46 For the Schuylenburch House, see Van Zoest and Van Eck, 'Zeer voorname woonhuizen', pp. 24–8 and 32–6.

47 There is also a fourth plan of the Fagel House and garden drawn up at around the same time. It is a more finished drawing than the other three, but there are few dimensions, room names are different, and there is no date or identifying inscription. Only the central portion of the house is shown; there are no garden wings. However, the plan does contain a new grand staircase and a wide corridor on the central axis. See Abbott, *Catalogue of the Manuscripts*, p. 496, portfolio XIV, no. 1013 (156/1).

48 Abbott, *Catalogue of the Manuscripts*, p. 491, portfolio XIV, no. 920 (63/3): *No. 2 Gront vande tweede verdieping vant huys vande Heer Greffier Fagel 1706 3/26.*

49 Abbott, *Catalogue of the Manuscripts*, p. 491, portfolio XIV, no. 920 (63/2): *No. 3 Gront tot een timmeragie voor de Heer Greffier Fagel soo als die soude verandert kenne werden na de tekening no. 1, 1706 3/26.*

50 Abbott, *Catalogue of the Manuscripts*, p. 491, portfolio XIV, no. 920 (63/1): *Plan van t Huys van d'Heer Griffier Fagel.*

the scale of the plan is indicated. A bar scale marked in Rhineland feet and inches (one Rhineland foot is equal to 0.314 metres) appears in the lower right corner on the base of a depiction of a marbled plinth or table. This structure is inscribed 'Plan of the House of the *Heer Griffier* Fagel' and alongside it stands a bewigged man wearing a broad-brimmed hat and a purple coat with lace cuffs (see plate 14). He would appear to be François Fagel the Elder poring over the plans of his existing home and perhaps considering alterations. Portraits of this nature are extremely unusual in architectural drawings. The fact that the figure is competently handled and that an attempt has been made to apply painterly washes of colour to the plan in places might suggest that the person responsible for its execution was not primarily trained as an architectural draughtsman.

This plan would seem to represent the Fagel home on the Noordeinde at the turn of the eighteenth century when it was still largely a conglomeration of three separate houses that had been purchased and united by Hendrik Fagel the Eldest in 1680. This merging of pre-existing dwellings is reflected in the somewhat haphazard and asymmetrical plan. The façade fronting the street must have been of relatively cramped proportions. There were three rooms looking onto the street: the *voorhuijs* (entrance vestibule), a *salet* (parlour) and a *voorcamer* (front room). The entrance was anything but imposing, with a narrow off-centre doorway giving access to a constricted *voorhuijs*, that was lit by a small window. Indeed natural light must have been in short supply in a long narrow house of this type despite the presence of inner courtyards, that supplied some illumination to adjacent rooms. Adjoining the house to the left was a coach house and a passageway, that provided access to the garden. A long corridor connected the *voorhuijs* with the remaining parts of the house and with the rear garden. Directly behind the coach house, and with access from it, were rooms concerned with the service and maintenance of the household: a *Wasch-Huijs* (wash house), and a *Koock Keucken* ('cooking kitchen'), linked by some sort of covered passageway to the *Binnen Keucken* ('inner kitchen'). In the absence of detailed inventories, that would have itemized the contents and furnishings, it is impossible to be certain about the function of rooms. However, it is likely that one kitchen was used for the preparation of food and that the other was more for the display of porcelain, glassware and other utilitarian objects, as well as for the consumption of informal meals. Next to the 'inner kitchen' was the *Eet-Saal* (dining room), that had two windows overlooking the gardens. It was perhaps used for more formal occasions.

The house to the right of the major corridor is the most summarily indicated, with no room names, and it is difficult to see how some of the spaces connect or relate with each other. An interesting feature of this part of the building is that one block already juts out into the garden, presaging the subsequently constructed garden wings. With its spiral staircases, discordant layout, unplanned character and profusion of small dank spaces, this building belongs firmly in the seventeenth century. The individual responsible for drawing up this plan also devoted a surprising amount of attention to the garden, which appears to be considerably longer than the house. It was a much more symmetrical arrangement, with four parterres separated by an avenue 2.7 metres wide, the only dimension given on the plan. At the bottom of the garden were stables, a bleaching field, and a rubbish and ash pit (*mis-put* and *asput*). Also indicated is the bridge over 'his majesty's garden canal' (*syne Hoogheyts Hof-Sloot*). In the top right-hand corner, abutting the canal, is a structure identified as a summerhouse or arbour (*Prieel*). This is in exactly the same position as, and of similar proportions and size to, the famous 'Dome of Fagel'. Apart from openings on all three sides, the appearance and design of the *Prieel* is uncertain.

More complete in its detail, and containing extensive dimensions, is plate 12, a proposal for modifications to the house drawn up in April 1706. Like the previous drawing it shows the ground floor, where the principal reception rooms were located in Dutch residences. This plan is not a radical departure; many of the original walls were retained and the designer had to work with the existing constraints on space. Despite these limitations, there is a greater emphasis on symmetry and on integrating the rooms with each other. Doorways, for example, are generally aligned with each other, to create, where possible, an enfilade of rooms. The major structural change in the street side of the dwelling is that the coach house is replaced by an *Eet Kamer.* It would appear that the former was relocated across the street; in the inventory of Hendrik Fagel the Elder (the nephew of François) from 1791, the coach house was located on the east side of the Noordeinde, directly opposite the Fagel House.[51] An interesting feature of this new dining room is that it contains a built-in buffet in one corner, an idea derived from France, which became very popular in the houses of the

51 The Hague, Nationaal Archief, Collectie Fagel, Inventory of Hendrik Fagel, 20 January, 1791, fols. 6v–7r: 'A splendid house, yard, and gardens, situated on the west side of the Noordeinde here in The Hague, with the attendant stables and coach houses opposite the forementioned house and thus on the east side of the same Noordeinde' (*Een capital huis, erve, en thuynen, staande en geleegen aan de west zijde van het Noordeinde alhier in Den Hage, met de stallinge en koets huisen daer toe gehoorende staande en geleegen tegens over de voor selveere huizinge en dus aan de oost zyde van het zelve Noordeinde*).

Dutch elite in the eighteenth century. Essentially buffets were sideboards for the display of silver and cut-glass, from which food and drink were served. Some of them could be very decorative and were protected by doors when not in use.[52]

Another major change from the previous plan is that the spiral case behind the front hall is here replaced with a much grander and more imposing staircase; the adjoining courtyard had to be reduced in size to accommodate it. Monumental staircases became a feature of houses during this period and were often decorated with stuccowork and crowned with a dome and lantern. The loss of natural light in the interior through the shrinking of the courtyard was compensated somewhat in the southern part of the building through the enlargement of its courtyard.

There is also evidence of French planning in the creation of an apartment or formal sequence of rooms in the rear part of the house. The long corridor – which seems to have been widened from its predecessor – terminates in a semicircular antechamber, which leads to a bedroom, a cabinet and a garderobe. The French architect Charles Augustin D'Aviler had published a treatise in the 1690s – two editions of which were in the Fagel library – where he stated that these rooms were essential to form an apartment of any size. Presumably this apartment was intended as the domain of François Fagel. The cabinet possibly served as a study or office: it was unheated and could only really have been used during the summer months, but was well lit from the adjoining large courtyard. The bedroom was a much larger space with a fireplace. It may also have been used to receive visitors. Finally, there was a garderobe used to store clothes and as a dressing room. It also contained a water closet or privy.

During this period there was an increased concern with privacy within the home. The new plan, for example, would have made it easier for servants to move through the house without being seen. We know that the Fagels had a domestic staff of six in the 1740s. There is a narrow corridor to the right, which links the front and back parts of the house. The partially concealed spiral staircase would have allowed service personnel to move between floors. Private family activities were largely relegated to the rear. The dining room facing the garden has been retained but appears to have been reduced in size and was perhaps intended for smaller, more intimate groups or, more likely, for exclusive family use.

This plan also makes it clear that by early 1706 the eventual design for the garden façade of the house was already well established. The two wings

52 For a particularly elaborate buffet design by Daniel Marot, which involved water being directed through fountain jets, satyr heads, and a putto, see Fock, *Het Nederlandse interieur*, p. 211.

are in place, one containing a wash-house and 'garden room' and the other the *Groote Sael Tot Biblioteek*, which can mean either a large room or salon leading to the library, or which can be used as a library. However, the former interpretation seems more likely since the walls of the long gallery, where the library was eventually located and which led to the garden pavilion, are sketchily indicated. Unfortunately there are no detailed plans or designs for this portion of the building, where Marot's impact was probably greatest. A large reception room looking onto the gardens was a common feature of Dutch houses in the eighteenth century.[53] Guests dined in this well-appointed room and could also make use of the garden for walks, for the consumption of tea and coffee or for entertainment. This close relationship between interior and exterior space was also seen in the increased popularity for garden houses, like the 'Dome of Fagel', where refreshments could be served and parlour games played.

There is an additional plan for the first floor of the building, also dating from early in 1706 (see plate 11). Most of the rooms on this level were presumably bedrooms; the trend in the houses of the wealthy at this time was towards relocating bedrooms from the ground floor to the first. Although a widower with only one daughter, François Fagel the Elder accommodated a large number of his extended family in his house on the Noordeinde.[54] At one time or another his widowed older sister Maria Doublet (1649–1739) and her son, as well as his younger brother Cornelis Gerrit (1663–1746), his wife and five children, all lived with him. In 1725 the widow of his nephew François Doublet (1688–1725) joined the household together with her three children.

There are two aspects of the proposed first-floor plan that deserve further comment. Firstly, a large lantern or skylight illuminated the intended salon in the right-hand garden wing below and this room extended through two storeys and had very high ceilings. Secondly, one of the existing rooms in this wing was used as an orangery or greenhouse, where more exotic plants could be cultivated and maintained throughout the winter months. Gaspar Fagel (1634–88), François the Elder's uncle, rented a country estate named Leeuwenhorst from 1676, where he started a famous collection of rare exotic plants from the Dutch colonies, and where orangeries and hothouses were an important component.[55]

53 Jet Pijzel-Dommisse, '1700–1750' in Fock, *Het Nederlandse interieur*, pp. 181–202, here p. 185.

54 Heringa, 'François Fagel', p. 68.

55 Elizabeth den Hartog and Carla Teune, 'Gaspar Fagel (1633–88): His garden and plant collection at Leeuwenhorst', *Garden History*, 30 (2002), 191–205, and Elizabeth den Hartog, 'Leeuwenhorst, een tuin van wereldformaat gezien door de ogen van Pieter Teding van Hartog', *De Zeventiende Eeuw*, 24 (2008), 227-37.

It is difficult to determine the extent to which the proposed plans from 1706 were implemented. Certainly revisions were necessary in April 1707 when François Fagel the Elder purchased the adjoining house to the north (on the right on the plans) from the sisters Geertruid and Anna Hallingh.[56] However, this must have been a fortuitous acquisition and allowed for a considerable number of improvements to the plans. The façade could be extended from around 20 to 26 metres. This meant that the entrance doorway was now situated in the centre of the building and that the main corridor stretched uninterrupted from the front door to the garden door, which was moved to the central axis of the rear façade. Interior space was considerably increased and a more balanced and symmetrical arrangement achieved.

Despite alterations to the building in the mid eighteenth century, a comparison between the 1706 plan for the ground floor and an 1851 plan, now in the Municipal Archives, The Hague, shows that much of the internal layout had already been established at the earlier date.[57] The shape and proportions of three front rooms (*Voor Kamer, Voor Huys,* and *Klyne Voor Kamer*) remain unchanged, and while there are some modifications to the elements directly behind (*Binne Kamer*, main staircase, and courtyard), they are fixed in the same position. Greatest change is found in the back of the building, although the concept of two garden wings is retained.

While little remains of the original early eighteenth century house and gardens, these plans give us some indication of François Fagel's ambition to build a house worthy of his family's status as prominent statesmen and his eagerness to adapt to contemporary architectural trends within the restrictions of the site. However, these drawings are also limited in that they can only provide some account of how space was organized; we have to look elsewhere for vestiges of the splendour that the interior once radiated. Fortunately the library of François the Elder and his successors survives relatively intact at Trinity College Dublin and we can reconstruct their collecting activities in other fields from the auction catalogues of 1799–1824. It was probably this François Fagel who purchased the tulip album. Just as his library was primarily a reference tool that informed his professional pursuits, the tulip book also had a practical function and served as a repository of information on the acquisition of this still coveted flower in his own time.

56 Van Breen, 'Het Heerenhuis Noordeinde No. 140', p. 142.

57 For the 1851 ground plan, see Van Zoest and Van Eck, 'Zeer voorname woonhuizen', p. 31, fig. 20.

The Fagel Collection: From Den Haag to Dublin[1]

Peter Fox
UNIVERSITY OF CAMBRIDGE

ON THURSDAY, 31 May 1798 ten men sat down in the Committee Room of the Irish House of Lords and made a decision that turned out to be one of the most momentous in the 400-year history of Trinity College Library. Those men were the governors of the Erasmus Smith Schools, and the decision they made was 'that the surplus money now in hand belonging to the Charity may be well applied in purchasing the library of the Greffier Faghel of The Hague, for the use of Trinity College'.[2]

In almost all respects the decision was an extraordinary one. Here we have the governors of an Irish charity, which had been established just over a century earlier with the aim of supporting schools, providing scholarships and, more recently, lectureships, deciding to spend the equivalent of well over a million euro at today's values on buying a collection of books, mostly of continental origin and belonging to a Dutch statesman, and giving it to Ireland's university, which had no link with the collection – nor, indeed, any apparent interest in it. What made the decision more extraordinary was that it was taken in the midst of civic unrest, when the city of Dublin was practically under siege from the rebels of '98, *and* when the collection appears (a) still to have been in Holland and (b) not even to have been placed on the market.

1 An abbreviated version of this article appears as chapter 8 of Peter Fox, *Trinity College Library Dublin: A History* (Cambridge 2014), pp. 115–28.

2 Registry Book of the Governors of the Erasmus Smith Schools, No. 3, 31 May 1798, Dublin, High School, Erasmus Smith Trust Archives, BG/1008.

These are some of the issues surrounding the acquisition of the Fagel Collection that this article will explore. A number of them remain unresolved and to some extent this should be seen as a work in progress.

From the second half of the seventeenth century to the end of the eighteenth several generations of the Fagel family served their country, the Netherlands, successively holding the office of Greffier der Staaten-Generaal, or Secretary to the States General. The first member of the family to bear the title was Gaspar, a confidant of William of Orange, appointed in 1671. In 1787 Hendrik Fagel the Younger (1765–1838) was appointed as second greffier alongside his grandfather, Hendrik the Elder. Three years later the grandfather died, leaving the younger Hendrik as the sole office-bearer.[3] Simon Schama described the office of Greffier to the States General as one 'whose pivotal diplomatic importance was belied by the humdrum title of, literally, "Clerk"'; and he notes that it was held by the Fagel family 'virtually from the foundation to the liquidation of the Republic'.[4]

The Fagels were an affluent and cultivated family, and each generation collected extensively, bringing together not just an important library but also paintings, prints and state papers. Charles Bentinck (the brother of one of the prominent members of the Dutch prince William V's entourage) wrote in 1795 to Lord Grenville, the British Foreign Secretary, describing the contents of the Fagel home as

> the most valuable and complete collection of State Papers in the Republic [...] together with one of the most complete and considerable libraries, and collection of drawings and prints, to be met with in any part of Europe, formed in the course of above a century by a succession of men distinguished for their taste and their knowledge.[5]

Among the pictures sold in London in 1801 were paintings by many of the Dutch and Flemish masters, including Rubens, Frans Hals, Teniers and Jan Steen. All of these, however, as well as the library, were still in the Netherlands when the French forces began to invade in 1794.

3 G. Waterhouse, 'The family of Fagel', *Hermathena*, 46 (1931), 80–85. For the Fagel pedigree see Thomassen, fig. 2.

4 Simon Schama, *Patriots and Liberators: Revolution in the Netherlands 1780–1813* (London 1977), p. 50.

5 Historical Manuscripts Commission, *Report on the Manuscripts of J.B. Fortescue, Esq., Preserved at Dropmore*, vol. 3 (London 1899), p. 80.

As the French pushed forward throughout the latter part of 1794, the situation in the Dutch Republic became ever more desperate. In October, Hendrik Fagel, as secretary to the States General, was sent to England to explain to the allies that the Dutch could no longer continue fighting and were minded to sue for peace. By January 1795 the Republic had capitulated and many of the nobility had fled to England, though Fagel's wife and family remained in their house in The Hague.

The following month Fagel left England for Hamburg with Bentinck and instructions to try to initiate a revolt against the French. In the same month the new government that had been installed in The Hague, the 'Provisional Representatives of the People of Holland', dismissed Fagel as greffier and appointed one of their own to that office.

In May Fagel wrote to Lord Grenville from Hamburg to report that the new government had sequestered his property with such speed that his wife and family, who were still living in the house, had been denied the use even of the furniture needed for daily life:

> They [the government] have compiled an inventory of all that I possess in the form of lands, furniture, precious objects of all types, such as my library, paintings, prints and drawings [...] It appears that the seizure of my property will be followed by its confiscation if I do not return to Holland; but, however, my entire family all advise me against going back there.[6]

Fagel remained on the continent (though not the Netherlands) until 1798, when he returned to settle in London, and he remained there for much of the rest of his life. In January of that year a new constitution in the Netherlands directed the confiscation of property belonging to Dutch *émigrés*. Fagel wrote on 10 April to Lord Grenville to say that, although his absence from Holland at the time of the revolution in 1795 had 'been the means of protecting me from many perils and personal insults, which I should probably have incurred had I been on the spot', that very absence and the reasons for it had 'made it impossible for me to take the necessary precautions in order to save the whole or at least some part of my property [...]. In consequence of the 35th article of the new constitution [...] I am in daily expectation of seeing my property confiscated and of being deprived of those resources that were still left me'. He asked Grenville, as Foreign Secretary, to intercede with the King, George

6 *Ibid.*, p. 72.

III, 'to adopt some measures for insuring my future subsistence'.[7] His appeal did not fall on deaf ears, and a month later, after his return to England, he was granted a pension by the British government of £1000 a year for life.

This, however, did not solve his financial problems and he soon put in train the sale of his library and the rest of the family collections. It must be assumed that the threat to confiscate his property, or at least part of it, was not put into effect, as in 1800 and 1801 his brother Jacob was in the Netherlands making arrangements for the transfer of Hendrik's pictures and books to England.

The collections started to arrive in London in the summer of 1800 and caused him the sorts of problems familiar to librarians and book collectors throughout the ages. In a letter of 3 October he wrote: 'I am in a state of great embarrassment with regard to the books, etc. I need to take a house with two or three large rooms for them and am having no little trouble finding what is required.'[8] Mounting expenses were also causing him concern. In December he wrote complaining that he was having to pay for the rent of the house, the cost of cataloguing the collection, storage (at more than a guinea a week), fire insurance and the fact that he had had to install a servant to live in the house.

He lost little time putting the works of art on the market. By the beginning of the following year advertisements began to appear in the London papers. In January 1801 *The Morning Chronicle* carried a series of notices from Coxe, Burrell and Foster announcing 'the sale of the very valuable assemblage of cabinet pictures, in the most perfect state of preservation, and of undoubted originality, the property of and collected from the beginning of the last century, by the Greffier's [*sic*] Fagel'.[9] In May the same year Thomas Philipe allocated no less than twelve days to the sale of Fagel's prints and books of prints 'comprising the Masters of the German, Flemish, Dutch and Italian Schools'.[10]

By February 1801 Fagel had also unpacked more than 160 cases of his books. Initially he decided that the Dutch books should be returned, as he believed that they would fetch a better price in Holland than in London. He wrote to his brother Jacob:

7 Quoted in L. Brummel, 'The Fagel Library in Trinity College, Dublin' in L. Brummel, *Miscellanea libraria: opstellen over boek- en bibliotheekwezen* [...] ('s-Gravenhage 1957), pp. 204–33, here pp. 216–7.

8 Quoted *ibid.*, pp.220–21.

9 *The Morning Chronicle*, 9 January 1801 *et seq.*; *The Morning Chronicle* and *The Times*, 2 May 1801 *et seq.*

10 *The Morning Chronicle*, 11 May 1801.

> The number of Dutch books is enormous, and there is also a miscellany of law and ancient theology which will sell badly here. I have decided to send back all the Dutch books. Despite the expense, I am sure that it would be better than to sell them here, where many of them would fetch absolutely nothing, whereas in Holland I am sure that this collection, especially insofar as it covers our ancient history and antiquities, is very valuable.[11]

In the end, as we know, he decided to abandon this plan, to the great benefit of Trinity College Library.

Fagel employed Samuel Paterson to prepare the catalogue of books for the sale, and the plan was for them to be sold at auction by James Christie. Though a man of enormous bibliographical knowledge, Paterson was also renowned for being easily distracted from the task in hand by a book that attracted his attention. His contemporary John Nichols wrote of him: 'His talent at cataloguizing [*sic*] was unrivalled [...]. Few men of this country had so much bibliographical knowledge.' However, his interest in books was also his failing as a bookseller:

> If, in his employment of taking catalogues, he met with a book he had not seen before, which excited his curiosity, or interested his feelings, they must be gratified, and his attendant might amuse himself as he chose. The consequence was, that, on many occasions, catalogues could be procured only a few hours before the sale commenced.[12]

Paterson's lack of progress with the catalogue frustrated Fagel, who wrote to his brother in November 1801 that 'Paterson is driving me to despair with his slowness, and the amount of money this is costing me is enormous.'[13] Shortly after he issued Paterson with an ultimatum, that the catalogue must be completed and printed by the beginning of December or he would not get paid. This seems to have had the desired effect, as advertisements started to appear in the London papers from 14 December, indicating that catalogues for the first part of the sale would be available from 1 February 1802. On that day an amended version of the advertisement appeared, stating that catalogues were now available 'at 3*s*. 6*d*. each, at the place of sale and of Mr. Christie, in Pall-mall'.[14]

11 Quoted in Brummel, 'The Fagel Library', p.221.

12 John Nichols, *Literary Anecdotes of the Eighteenth Century* (London 1812–15), vol. 3, p. 439.

13 Quoted in Brummel, 'The Fagel Library', p.223.

14 *The Morning Chronicle*, 1 February 1802. – See frontispiece.

In the preface to the catalogue Paterson pulls no punches about the importance of the collection. It is, he says

> [...] one genuine library; which has been accumulating in the family of Fagel, a name of the first respectability, and which has born, in succession, the highest civil offices in the United States of the Netherlands upwards of one hundred and twenty years [...] as an historical, geographical, genealogical and statistical library, it may justly rank among the most distinguished. To which may be added, that the books, in general, are in fine condition, and many of them, even of the most estimable, printed upon large paper.[15]

Paterson's approach to the construction of sale catalogues 'established him as a pioneer in the book auction trade'.[16] The novelty of his technique was that his catalogues were classified by subject, not arranged by book format, as was usual at the time. At the beginning of part one he lists the sections into which he has divided the collection, starting with Latin terminology in '*Literæ humaniores*', followed by '*Theologia*', '*Auctores classici*', '*Philologia*', '*Libri italiani*', and '*Auctores hispanici*', but then, perhaps under Fagel's influence, switching to the vernacular with '*Livres français: poesies et melanges* [*sic*]', 'English poetry and miscellanies [...]', '*Teutsch poetische Werke und Mischmasch*', '*Hollandsche Poezy en Mengelwerken*', and then back to Latin for '*Philosophia*', '*Artes et Scientiæ*' and so on.

The sale was to be divided into two parts. The first was set to begin on 1 March 1802 and was scheduled to last until 3 April. The catalogue for the first part of the sale lists 5246 lots, to be sold at the rate of between about 160 and 200 a day, with the lot numbers indicated against each day's sale. It is not clear when the catalogue for the second part appeared. It lists the remaining 4598 lots, bringing the total to 9844. No dates are marked against the lots and the number of copies of the catalogue that were distributed was very much less than for the first part, judging by its comparative scarceness in libraries today and the fact that, when the Fagel books were shipped to Trinity, there were 629 remaining copies of the catalogue for part two of the sale, but only 301 of part one. The reasons for this are obvious, given the way that events unfolded in the early months of 1802.

15 *Bibliotheca Fageliana: a Catalogue of the Valuable and Extensive Library of the Greffier Fagel* [...] *Digested by Sam. Paterson. Part I: which Will Be Sold by Auction, by Mr. Christie* [...] *on March 1, 1802* [...] (London [1802]), p. iii.

16 Richard Landon, 'Paterson, Samuel (1728–1802)' in *Oxford Dictionary of National Biography*.

Let us now leave Messrs Fagel, Paterson and Christie in London preparing for the March sale and return to where we started, Dublin, and that meeting of the governors of the Erasmus Smith Schools four years earlier.

Erasmus Smith was a Leicestershire merchant, born around 1611, who had acted as contractor to the parliamentarian armies, particularly during Oliver Cromwell's campaigns in Scotland and Ireland and in return had acquired large tracts of land in various parts of Ireland. In 1657 he established the trust that bears his name, with the intention that the revenue from his estates should be used to educate children 'in the fear of God and good literature and to speak the English tongue'.[17] This was achieved by establishing five grammar schools, by supporting over 200 so-called 'English schools' throughout Ireland, by providing scholarships at Trinity College and other, similar 'charitable uses'.

During the eighteenth century growing prosperity in Ireland led to increases in rents, which greatly benefited the trust as a major landowner. Its thirty-two governors included several Church of Ireland bishops and archbishops as well as the Provost of Trinity, whose influence seems to have been disproportionately significant, especially when the governors were addressing the issue of how to dispose of the growing surplus for which they were responsible. The value of scholarships was increased and new schools were established, but Trinity College was particularly favoured. Money was granted in the first couple of decades of the century towards the cost of building new chambers for students, increases in the payments for exhibitioners, as well as grants for chairs in Mathematics, Oriental Tongues, History and Oratory. In 1776 the Provost, John Hely Hutchinson, who was also treasurer of the trust, tried the patience of his fellow governors to the limit by proposing a grant of £2500 for the building of the College's public theatre, the building now known as the Examination Hall. There was opposition and a decision was delayed, but in the end the Provost won the day and the plan was approved.[18] In this context, the proposal to buy the Fagel Collection is perhaps not quite so extraordinary, but it too was far from plain sailing.

The resolution of the governors at their meeting on 31 May 1798 remains something of a mystery. Why was such a proposal made and by whom? How had word reached the governors that the collection was likely to

17 Deed of Foundation, 1 December 1657, Erasmus Smith Trust Archives, BG/1021.

18 W.J.R. Wallace, *Faithful to our Trust: A History of the Erasmus Smith Trust and the High School, Dublin* (Blackrock, County Dublin 2004), pp. 63–77.

come on the market? What happened after the resolution had been approved? There is no further mention of the purchase of the collection in either the minutes of the Erasmus Smith governors or of the Board of Trinity College until four years later, March 1802.

The driving force seems undoubtedly to have been John Foster, Speaker of the Irish House of Commons, a graduate of Trinity College and one of the Erasmus Smith governors. His role in promoting the purchase is specifically mentioned in the minutes of the College Board after the collection had been acquired,[19] and his position as Speaker and a member of the British Privy Council would have given him access to discussions that may have been going on in London. It was Foster who caused the offer for the collection to be conveyed to Fagel in February 1802. On the fifth of that month Fagel reported the offer in a letter to his brother: 'The catalogue for the first part, having now been published, has caused a great sensation and this morning I have received a proposal to sell all of it in one lot. I have asked for two days to think about it.'[20]

In making this offer, Foster was certainly acting in accordance with the resolution of the Erasmus Smith governors from four years earlier, even though the matter had not been formally discussed by them since then, but it is clear that some of the governors had been having second thoughts in the meantime. The church party in particular were far from unanimous in their support for the proposal, perhaps because, as suggested by Anthony Malcomson, the acquisition of the collection would tilt 'the balance of the TCD library in a secular direction'.[21]

Charles Agar, the Archbishop of Dublin, opposed the plan but Lord Pelham, the Home Secretary, applied pressure. On 26 February Pelham wrote to Agar from London:

> I am so thoroughly convinced of the advantages to the University of Dublin to be derived from the purchase of the Fagel Library, that I cannot help submitting to your Grace an earnest wish that you would reconsider the subject. It is universally considered one of the best private collections in Europe, perhaps the most perfect in History and diplomatic information, & a collection of

19 Board Register, 13 March 1802, Dublin, Trinity College Library (hereafterTCD), MUN/V/5/5.

20 Brummel, 'The Fagel Library', p. 227.

21 A.P.W. Malcomson, *Archbishop Charles Agar: Churchmanship and Politics in Ireland, 1760–1810* (Dublin 2002), p. 250.

> Maps not to be obtained at present without great difficulty & expense. Lord Spencer (who is unquestionably a very good Judge) thinks it a most valuable acquisition for any Public Body [...] I have requested Mr Fagel to postpone the Auction for a fortnight, in order to admit of a reconsideration of his offer.[22]

The governors met on 6 March, and the supporters of the proposal prevailed. The minute of the meeting noted 'that a sum not exceeding ten thousand pounds British be applied to the purchase of the Fagellian Library in augmentation of the present Library of Trinity College Dublin'. A ten-man committee was established to carry out the resolution, its members including Foster, the Provost of Trinity, the unenthusiastic Agar and his equally unenthusiastic Armagh counterpart, William Stuart.[23] The Primate, Stuart (a governor who had not been present at the meeting) and Charles Brodrick, Archbishop of Cashel (one who had), remained less than convinced about the wisdom of using the Trust's surplus funds in this way. Stuart wrote to Brodrick on the day after the meeting saying that 'the education of the people is a matter of so much more importance than an additional library for Trinity College.'[24]

But the decision was now made and things began to move quickly. Fagel consulted James Edwards, a well-known London bookseller and an expert on continental private libraries, who advised him to agree to sell the collection as one lot and to ask for £5000. Paterson felt that this was far too little and recommended £10,000. In the end Fagel settled on £8000. On 16 March advertisements appeared in *The Times* and *The Morning Chronicle* to the effect that the public sale, that ought to have started two weeks previously, would not now take place, and that 'Mr Christie is further happy to make it known, that this collection will henceforth be preserved entire, and that it will form a part of the very valuable Library of Trinity College, Dublin.'[25]

Dr Thomas Elrington, Senior Fellow of Trinity College and an Erasmus Smith governor, was dispatched to London to organize the packing and shipping of the collection. He started work on 16 March and kept a detailed diary, recording each day's work.[26] This is a typical entry for just one day:

22 Pelham to Agar, 26 February 1802, Belfast, Public Record Office of Northern Ireland, Normanton Papers: T/3719/C/36/7.

23 Registry Book, 6 March 1802, Erasmus Smith Trust Archives, BG/1008.

24 Stuart to Brodrick, 7 March 1802, Dublin, National Library of Ireland, MS 8869 (1).

25 *The Times* and *The Morning Chronicle*, 16 March 1802.

26 TCD MUN/LIB/12/1.

Tuesday March 16th 1802

Put the loose maps into 25 portfolios – packed nineteen of them in rough deal case square.
N° 1 with some loose maps rolled

A rheam of paper	7*s*
Nails &c.	9.6

N° 2. Small box – six portfolios maps. Also from N^{r}. 1. to 51 octavos. from 111 to 112. Quartos. Also some between 58 & 94 [?] octavo.
Paid Mr Joye for valuing the Library 20*g*^{s}

N° 3 Folios. 29. to part of 79.
Q^{to}. 787. 56.
D. 58 to 93.

N° 4 Folios. Rem^{r} of N^{r}. 79, 101, 132, 129, 110, 133, 134, 157, 188
Duod. 225. 11 of the vols – packed with pamphlets

The payment of twenty guineas to Mr Joye for 'valuing the Library' was presumably for insurance purposes, as Elrington later noted the insurance valuation for each case as it was prepared for shipping. By the end of the first week he had filled fifty packing cases, most of them newly purchased, but some bought secondhand from Fagel. He recorded briefly the contents of each case as it was packed. The full cases were strapped and sent off on 24 March to Newenden in Kent for transport to Dublin on the *Linenhall*. Elrington also noted that Foster, who was obviously retaining a close interest in the process, called on 23 March with 'a broker who sent two men to cord the cases'.

Once he had cleared some space by the removal of the first fifty cases, Elrington began to calculate the implications for housing the collection when it arrived in Trinity and came to the conclusion that it would require 5200 feet of shelving – almost a mile (see fig. 1):

Thursday March 25

Measured shelves in parlour. 10 feet high 38 feet round the room.
D° back parlour – 10 feet high 27 round.
Each 10 shelves high – the first floor is eleven shelves high – the second 10 – the third [no figure]

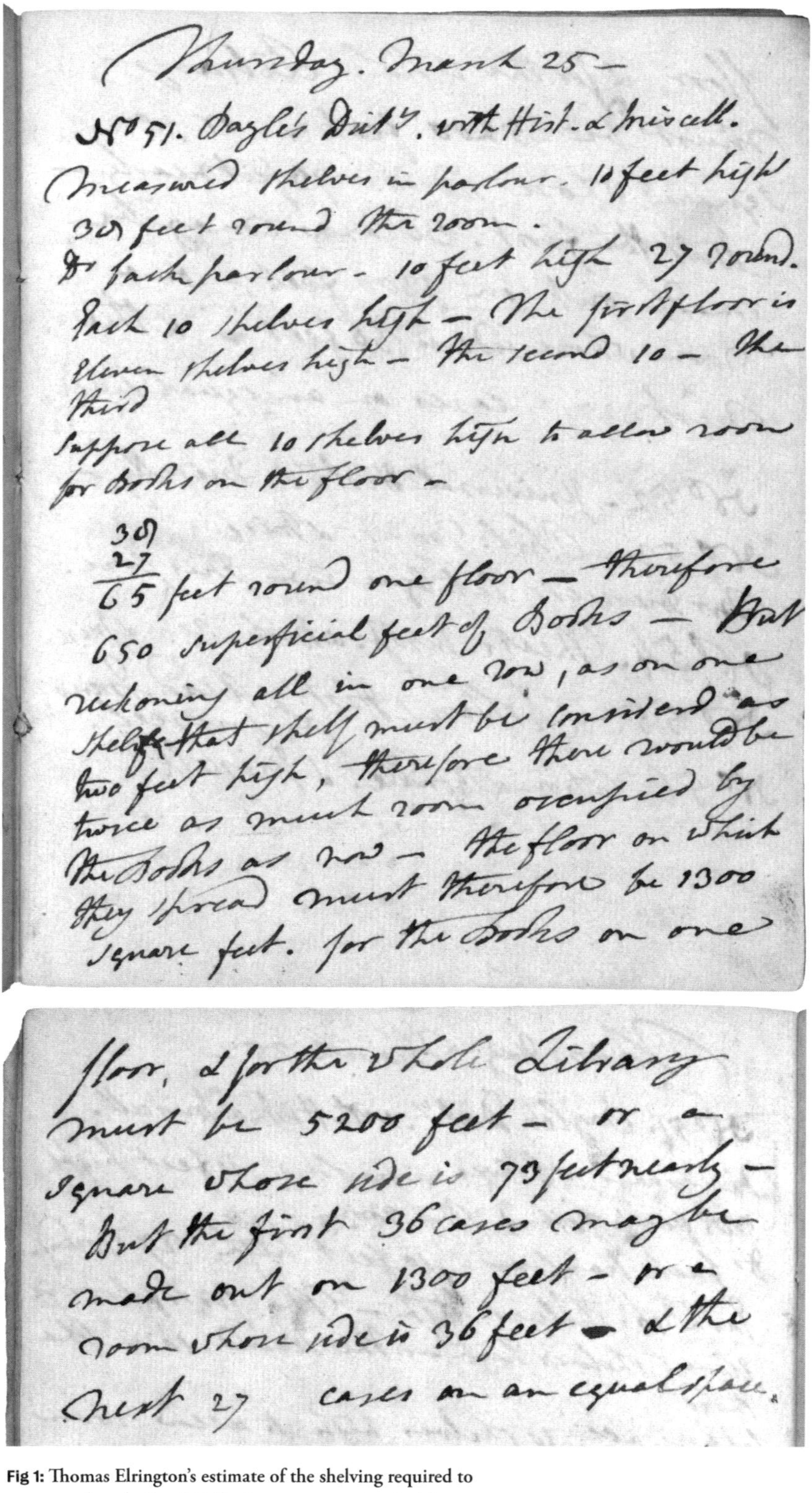

Fig 1: Thomas Elrington's estimate of the shelving required to accommodate the Fagel Collection. (TCD MUN/LIB/12/1)

Suppose all 10 shelves high to allow room for books on the floor –

38

27

65 feet round one floor – therefore 650 superficial feet of Books – But reckoning all in one row, as on one shelf, that shelf must be considered as two feet high, therefore there would be twice as much room occupied by the Books as now – the floor on which they spread must therefore be 1300 square feet. for the books on one floor, & for the whole Library must be 5200 feet – or a square whose side is 73 feet nearly – But the first 36 cases may be made out on 1300 feet – or a room whose side is 36 feet – and the next 27 cases on an equal space.

The work of packing resumed the following day, and on 14 April he 'paid M[r] Fagel £7500 at the Bank of Mess[rs] Coutts & C[o]'. It is not clear when the other £500 was paid but since Elrington recorded interest charged by Coutts on £7500 it might be assumed that the £500 had already been paid as a deposit. The recording, packing and dispatch continued for five weeks in all, with the final batch of cases (taking the total to 115) being sent off to Newenden on 21 April. The following day, Elrington paid his various bills. They came to a total of £388 12*s.* 10*d.* of which the main elements were:

Insurance	£121	16*s*	8*d*
Packing cases	£91	13*s*	4*d*
Shipping London to Dublin	£83	17*s*	0*d*
Labourers	£56	8*s*	1*d*
Valuation	£21	0*s*	0*d*
Interest on £7500	£13	17*s*	9*d*
Elrington's total bill	**£388**	**12s**	**10*d***

With this, Elrington's work in London was completed and he returned to Trinity to attend a Board meeting on 1 May.

In the meantime, on 29 March, during Elrington's stay in London, the committee established by the Erasmus Smith governors had met and had drawn down £9000 sterling, from which they subsequently paid Elrington's expenses and reimbursed the £8000 that he had paid Fagel. Some months later, on 19 November, they met again to agree their report to the governors, which was presented at the meeting on 11 February 1803. In it they noted the payments that they had made and recommended that Elrington should be paid an honorarium of 200 guineas 'in consideration of his great trouble, loss of time and expense in going to London to transact the business of the said purchase'.[27] This payment was approved and was additional to the sum of 100 guineas that the Board of Trinity College had agreed to pay Elrington the previous December 'for his trouble in purchasing the Fagel Lib. in England'.[28] These payments, totalling over £300, were substantial, considering that the College Librarian's annual salary at the time was only £100 and that of the Assistant Librarian just £30.[29]

The books arrived in the Library between 11 and 14 May 1802 and the College was faced with the not inconsiderable problem of where to house them and how to process them. It is estimated that the Fagel Collection contains about 20,000 volumes. That may not sound much given the size of Trinity's Library now, but as the College Library before the acquisition of the Fagel Collection probably contained about 50,000 volumes this represented an increase of no less than 40 per cent. It is as if today's College librarian were to be presented with a collection of around two million volumes for which she had to find space and processing capacity. In 1802 the staff of the Library consisted of the librarian, the assistant librarian and a couple of porters, so there was no spare manpower to deal with the new collection.

In many ways the timing could not have been worse as the Library was about to start feeling the effects of the Copyright Act of 1801, which entitled Trinity to receive free copies of books that had been registered at Stationers' Hall in London. That legislation changed the nature of Trinity's Library for ever. The first consignment of legal deposit books from Stationers' Hall arrived in August 1802, just three months after the Fagel Collection.[30]

The College Board decided that it would clearly be pointless to unpack the collection until they had somewhere to store it. The only case that was opened – on 2 July – was the last, number 115, which contained copies of the sale catalogue. These were distributed by order of the Board to each fellow and professor in the College. Five copies of both parts were sent to the College binder, Richard Mercier, four to be bound for the Provost, and one to be 'elegantly bound in Morocco for the Lord Lieutenant'.[31]

27 Registry Book, 11 February 1803, Erasmus Smith Trust Archives, BG/1008.

28 Board Register, 4 December 1802, TCD MUN/V/5/5.

29 Lydia Ferguson, '*Custodes librorum*: Service, staff and salaries, 1601–1855' in Vincent Kinane and Anne Walsh (eds), *Essays on the History of Trinity College Library Dublin* (Dublin 2000), pp. 25–38, here p. 29.

30 Library Minutes Book, 10 August 1802, TCD MUN/LIB/2/1.

31 Board Register, 19 July 1802, TCD MUN/V/5/5; Library Minutes Book, 16 August 1802, TCD MUN/LIB/2/1.

The location selected for the Fagel Library was the east pavilion of what we now call the Old Library, at the Long Room level, which meant that a new home had to be found for the Library's manuscripts. On 8 May, just before the books arrived, the Bursar was asked to obtain costs for fitting out a new manuscripts room on the floor above (where the Early Printed Books Reading Room now is). By the end of July the following year William Chapman produced a bill for £1090 for carpentry work in what he described as 'the additional Room to the Library' (see fig. 2).[32] The bill recorded work to produce 'oak fluted pilasters' and 'Corinthian Capitals'. In 1986 Vincent Kinane assumed from this that the work was for the new Fagel Library, as seen in Taylor's *History of the University of Dublin*, but Ernst Braches, writing in 1991, maintained that it was for the new manuscripts room on the floor above and that the Fagel Collection was simply unpacked onto the existing shelves in the old manuscripts room, which became the Fagel Library.[33] Whichever explanation is correct (and other evidence supports Kinane's view), building work on the new Fagel Library continued until 1809. Throughout 1807 and 1808 students were employed by the librarian to help arrange the collection.

Space was not the only problem. The collection also had to be organized and catalogued. Elrington noted in his diary that on 7 August 1802 the College Board decided that at their next meeting they would consider arrangements for cataloguing the Fagel Collection, though neither his notes nor the Board minutes record anything further on this.[34] In the following May the Provost reported to the Board that the Librarian, Dr John Barrett, was preparing a catalogue of the Fagel Collection. This catalogue, in six manuscript volumes, was delivered to Barrett's successor as Librarian, Dr Richard Graves, on 7 November 1807.[35] For that '& for his putting up the Books in said Lib. the Board agreed to allow him [Barrett] the Sum of One Hundred Pounds'.[36]

32 TCD MUN/P/2/187/3.

33 Vincent Kinane, 'The Fagel Collection' in Peter Fox (ed.), *Treasures of the Library: Trinity College Dublin* (Dublin 1986), pp. 158–69, here p. 161; W.B.S.Taylor, *History of the University of Dublin* [...] *its Origin, Progress, and Present Condition* (London 1845), plate opposite p. 313 (see Harris, Thematic shelving, fig. 1); Ernst Braches, 'The first years of the Fagel Collection in Trinity College Dublin' in S. Roach (ed.), *Across the Narrow Seas: Studies in the History and Bibliography of Britain and the Low Countries, Presented to Anna E.C. Simoni* (London 1991), pp. 189–96, here p. 191.

34 Elrington's notes of Board meetings, TCD MS 4960.

35 The catalogue is now TCD MS 1707.

36 TCD MUN/LIB/11/9/5.

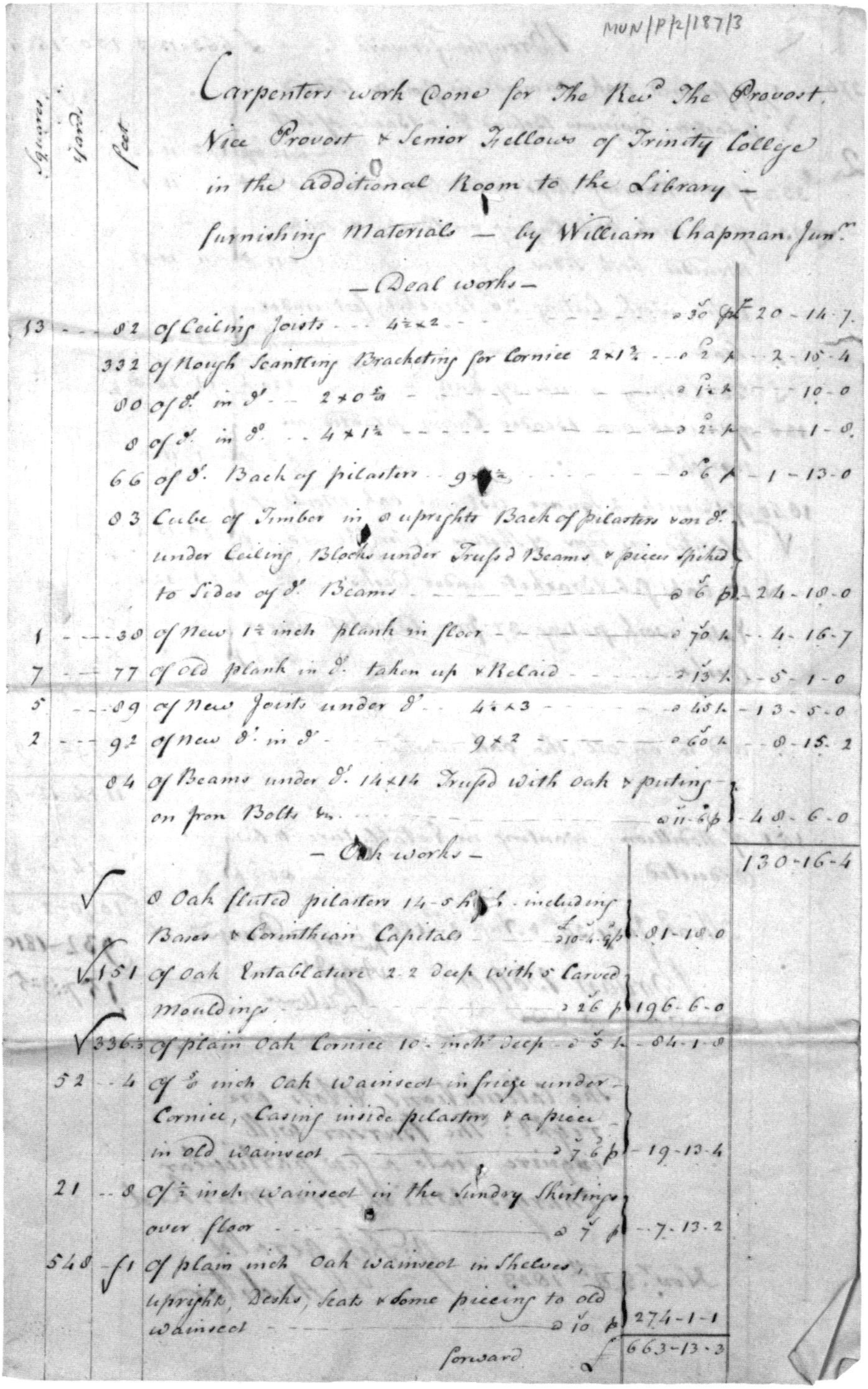
MUN/P/2/187/3

Squares | Yards | Feet

Carpenters work Done for The Revd The Provost, Vice Provost & Senior Fellows of Trinity College in the additional Room to the Library — furnishing Materials — by William Chapman Junr.

— Deal works —

13 — 82 of Ceiling Joists — 4½×2 — 0 30 p — £20 - 14 - 7
332 of Rough Scantling Bracketing for Cornice 2×1½ — 0 2 p — 2 - 15 - 4
80 of do. in do. — 2×0½ — 0 1½ p — 10 - 0
8 of do. in do. — 4×1½ — 0 2½ p — 1 - 8
66 of do. Back of pilasters — 9×[illegible] — 0 6 p — 1 - 13 - 0
83 Cube of Timber in uprights Back of pilasters von do. under Ceiling, Blocks under Trussed Beams & pieces spiked to Sides of do. Beams — 0 6 p — 24 - 18 - 0
1 — 38 of New 1½ inch plank in floor — 0 70 p — 4 - 16 - 7
7 — 77 of old plank in do. taken up & Relaid — 0 13 p — 5 - 1 - 0
5 — 89 of New Joists under do. — 4½×3 — 0 45 p — 13 - 5 - 0
2 — 92 of New do. in do. — 9×2 — 0 60 p — 8 - 15 - 2
84 of Beams under do. 14×14 Trussed with Oak & puting on Iron Bolts &c. — 0 11 6 p — 48 - 6 - 0
130 - 16 - 4

— Oak works —

8 Oak fluted pilasters 14 - 5 high including Bases & Corinthian Capitals — £10 - 4 - 6 p — 81 - 18 - 0
151 of Oak Entablature 2. 2 deep with 5 Carved Mouldings — 2 26 p — 196 - 6 - 0
336½ of plain Oak Cornice 10 inch deep — 0 5 p — 84 - 1 - 8
52 — 4 of ⅞ inch Oak Wainscot in frieze under Cornice, Casing inside pilasters & a piece in old Wainscot — 0 7 6 p — 19 - 13 - 4
21 — 8 of ½ inch Wainscot in the Sundry Skirtings over floor — 0 7 p — 7 - 13 - 2
548 — 1 of plain inch Oak Wainscot in Shelves, uprights, Desks, Seats & some piecing to old Wainscot — 0 10 p — 274 - 1 - 1
forward £663 - 13 - 3

Fig 2: Part of William Chapman's bill for the shelving for the Fagel Collection. (TCD MUN/P/2/187/3)

At an early date the Board decided that duplicates would not be kept with the collection but would be placed in the Lending Library. From 1804 to 1808 books were regularly being sent to a range of binders and throughout the first half of 1808 Michael Logan was employed to letter and number about 8000 of the books.[37] Logan was also commissioned to transcribe from a rough copy 'into one fair volume all the classes of the Fagel Library in alphabetical order', to prepare a catalogue in numerical order, 'marking off the above so as to distinguish their place', and to prepare a local catalogue.[38]

Though work was still under way during much of the first decade of the nineteenth century, it is clear that the newly acquired collection became a matter of increasing pride to the College and was shown to visitors at every opportunity. In 1806 the antiquary and book collector Sir Richard Colt Hoare wrote of the recent acquisition of the library in his *Journal of a Tour in Ireland*,[39] and, the year before, Sir John Carr noted in his book *The Stranger in Ireland*: 'At the further end [of the Long Room] is another room, which is not yet opened, in which is the celebrated library of baron Fagel from Holland: the books are not yet arranged, some of them are most beautifully illuminated'.[40]

Finally, on 1 March 1809 all was ready and the Board ordered that the Fagel Library should be opened. Graves, the Librarian, was paid £200 for his work. That, together with what had been paid to Elrington and Barrett, to the students who had worked on sorting the collection, and to the binders, brought the total cost of the acquisition closer to £10,000 than to the £8000 that had been paid to Fagel. But, as anyone who has seen some of the riches in the collection will attest, this was still a small sum, given the value of what is there.

Before the acquisition of the Fagel Collection, books on theology and biblical exegesis, many in Latin, had predominated in the College Library. But the Fagel was essentially a secular collection – the working library of an eighteenth-century Dutch political family – in which history, politics and geography (including maps) were significant, and so its acquisition fundamentally altered the character of Trinity's Library. Kinane has calculated that the subject coverage was as follows:[41]

37 TCD MUN/LIB/11/9/16.

38 TCD MUN/LIB/11/9/21; MUN/LIB/11/10/3.

39 Sir Richard Colt Hoare, *Journal of a Tour in Ireland in 1806* (London 1807), p. 8.

40 Sir John Carr, *The Stranger in Ireland; or, A tour in the Southern and Western Parts of that Country in the Year 1805* (London 1806), p. 54.

41 Kinane, 'The Fagel Collection', p. 164.

	%
History/topography	37.6
Theology	18.1
Politics/law	6.4
Geography/cosmography/travels	6.3
Classics	6.2
Literature	5.9
Philosophy (including natural philosophy and mathematics)	2.6
Natural history	2.6
Visual arts	2.5
Medicine	0.7
Military	0.6
Agriculture/horticulture	0.5
Economics	0.4
Miscellaneous	9.6

The history section is dominated, naturally, by works on the Netherlands, and then by books on its allies and enemies, chiefly France, Great Britain and Germany. Kinane remarks that 'the breadth of the Fagels' collecting habits is something more often associated with a royal or national library than with a family collection' and Jean-Paul Pittion's assessment of the collection in relation to French culture is that it was 'a monument to the *ancien régime*', showing both its strengths and the cracks that led to its downfall.[42]

The bulk of the collection consists of seventeenth- and eighteenth-century books. Some of these are in large multi-volume sets that are represented in the sale catalogue by just one entry. There is, for example, the *Mercure historique et politique* in 192 volumes, the *Europesche Mercurius* in sixty-five, as well as the *Hollantse Mercurius*, of which the collection holds a full set, forty-one numbers covering the years 1650 to 1690 (see fig. 3). Just one number in the sale catalogue was estimated by Paterson to contain upwards of 10,000 pamphlets on the history and politics of every state in Europe, though recent scholarship suggests that the figure is in fact closer to 4500 (see p. xxi). The section on natural history contains perhaps the most visually spectacular books, including John Johnstone's *Historia naturalis* (Frankfurt am Main 1650), the *Harmonia macrocosmica* of Andreas Cellarius (Amsterdam 1661), Maria Sibylla Merian's *Metamorphosis insectorum Surinamensium* (Amsterdam 1719) and Pierre Cramer's *Papillons exotiques* (Amsterdam 1779–82) (see plates 15–17 and 3).

42 J-P. Pittion, 'The Fagel Collection', *Hermathena*, 121 (1976), 108–16, here 115.

Fig 3: *Hollantse Mercurius, vervaetende het gepasseerde in Europa, voornamelijk den Enghels ende Nederlantsen oorloch, voor gevallen in't geheele iaer 1653*, Haerlem: Pieter Casteleyn, 1654. This, the fourth in a series of forty-one annual reviews of European affairs (published 1651–91), is dominated by hostilities between England and the Netherlands. The woodcut frontispiece that precedes the title-page has at the top a representation of Oliver Cromwell dissolving Parliament. (Fag. H.7.1)

The collection contains few incunabula or sixteenth-century publications and very few manuscripts. The main exceptions to this are the so-called Agostini Plutarch, the manuscript which has become known as the Fagel Missal and the seventeenth-century record of Simon van der Stel's journey in the Cape Colony (see plates 32, 18, 19).

The Agostini Plutarch is a magnificent example of the work of the celebrated Venetian printer Nicolaus Jenson. It is a two-volume edition of Plutarch's *Lives*, printed on vellum and dated 2 January 1478. The Fagel copy was decorated for a wealthy Venetian family, the Agostini. The frontispiece to each volume is magnificently painted in gold and brilliant colours and almost every section is decorated with a painted initial.[43]

The Fagel Missal (TCD MS 81) is one of the largest and most elaborately decorated works from the convent of St Agnes in Delft. It dates from around 1460. As well as the standard Missal text it contains twenty-six illuminated initials and two full-page miniatures, one showing the Crucifixion and the other the two patrons of the convent, St Augustine and St Agnes.

In 1681 some Namaqua tribesmen had brought specimens of copper ore to the Dutch East India Company's headquarters at the Cape of Good Hope, and in 1685 Simon van der Stel, commander at the Cape, was dispatched with an expedition to try to identify the location of the copper mountains. The only surviving manuscript of the journal kept by van der Stel during the expedition, which includes seventy-two coloured drawings of animals and plants, was placed in the Colonial Archives of the Dutch East India Company.[44] It was removed from the archives at the end of the seventeenth century, but how it came into the possession of the Fagel family is not known. It is now TCD MS 984.

The Fagel maps have been described by John Andrews, one of Ireland's greatest map experts, in the following terms:

> In breadth of territorial coverage and cartographic subject-matter the Fagel Collection can only be described as dazzling: there can have been few map libraries quite so cosmopolitan in the England of 1802 and surely none in Ireland [...] Its subjects embrace virtually the whole world as known to contemporary Europeans, and its imprints cover almost all the major map-publishing centres of the period.[45]

43 Lilian Armstrong, 'The Agostini Plutarch: An illuminated Venetian incunable' in Fox, *Treasures of the Library*, pp. 86–96.

44 *Simon van der Stel's Journey to Namaqualand in 1685*, with a revised introduction by Gilbert Waterhouse (Cape Town 1979).

45 J.H. Andrews, 'Maps and atlases' in Fox, *Treasures of the Library*, pp. 170–83, here p. 177.

They consist of 2880 sheets of loose maps, plans, charts and views and over one hundred volumes of atlases.[46]

The Fagel Collection is one of the glories of Trinity College Library, but because it is essentially a continental collection housed in an Irish library it is less well known than it deserves to be. It is to be hoped that this volume and the symposium that gave rise to it will help to draw the attention of scholars to it and encourage the sort of research that will undoubtedly unearth more gems.[47]

46 T.K. Abbott, *Catalogue of the Manuscripts in the Library of Trinity College, Dublin; to which is Added a List of the Fagel Collection of Maps in the same Library* (Dublin 1900), lists 1631 maps, but some of these consist of multiple sheets and recent scholarship has put the number of individual map sheets in the Fagel collection at 2880.

47 I must acknowledge the research of Leendert Brummel, Director of the Koninklijke Bibliotheek, the Royal Library of the Netherlands, who laboured extensively on the Fagel archives in the Algemeen Rijksarchief in the 1950s and whose published work supplied much of the information about the movements of the Fagel Collection and its history while it was still in the Netherlands; I also owe a debt to my late colleague Vincent Kinane, formerly of the Early Printed Books Department in Trinity, whose chapter in *Treasures of the Library* was the source of much of my information about the contents of the collection (see notes 33 and 41).

Plate 1: Johann Wolfgang von Goethe, *Das römische Carneval*, Berlin, gedruckt bey Johann Friedrich Unger, Weimar und Gotha, In Commission bey Carl Wilhelm Ettinger, 1789 (plate 4): Pulcinello as a cuckold. The horns of this carnival costume could be drawn in and out; the figure of the magician hints at the Roman zeal for lotteries. (Fag. GG.4.13)

Plate 2: St Petersburg album of architectural drawings (plate 4): façade of the Monastery of St George, a design that was not in fact realized. (Fag. GG.I.18)

10.

Plate 3: Pieter Cramer, *Uitlandsche kapellen. Papillons exotiques*, Amsterdam: S.J. Balde, and Utrecht: Barthelemy Wild, 1779 (plate 25). The species are identified as: *Pompeus* (A), *Maja* (B/C) and *Galanthis* (D/E). (Fag. GG.4.1)

Plate 4: Abraham Munting, *Naauwkeurige beschryving der aardgewassen*, Leyden: Pieter van der Aa, and Utrecht: François Halma, 1696 (plate following fol. 535/6): *cyclamen bipenninum*. The various trees, herbs and flowers are placed in landscapes, bucolic or urban settings, or, as here, maritime scenes. (Fag. GG.3.1)

Plate 5: The garden pavilion of Noordeinde 140, ceiling, detail. (Wikimedia Commons, 's-Gravenhage 20380109, Rijksdienst voor het Cultureel Erfgoed)

Plate 6: Johan Barents (?), title-page, 'Fagel Tulip Album' (c. 1637–41), 307 x 195 mm, watercolour and gouache. (TCD MS 1706/1)

Plate 7: Johan Barents, *De Paus van Roomen*, 'Fagel Tulip Album' (c. 1637–41), 307 x 195 mm, watercolour and gouache. (TCD MS 1706/1, fol. 66)

Plate 8: Attributed to Michiel Jansz van Miereveld, *Portrait of Gijsbert van Beresteyn* (1614), oil on panel. (Museum Mayer van den Bergh, Antwerp, RKD-Nederlands Instituut voor Kunstgeschiedenis, IB-nr. 38227)

Plate 9: Johan Barents (?), *Viceroy*, 'Fagel Tulip Album' (c. 1637–41), 307 x 195 mm, watercolour and gouache. (TCD MS 1706/1, fol. 6)

Plate 10: Johan Barents (?), *Semper Augustus*, 'Fagel Tulip Album' (c. 1637–41), 307 x 195 mm, watercolour and gouache. (TCD MS 1706/1, fol. 3)

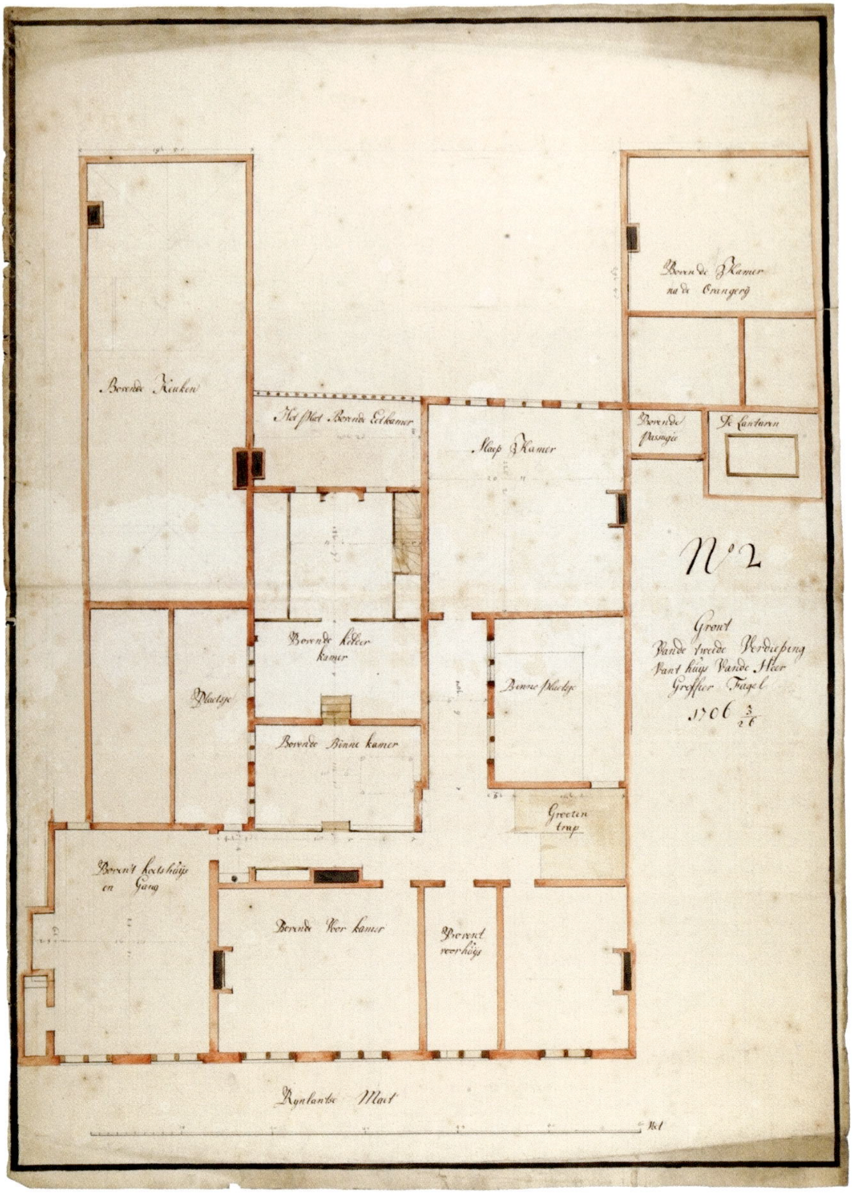

Plate 11: Proposed plan for the first floor of the Fagel House, The Hague (26 March, 1706), 53 x 73 cm. (Fagel Portfolio 14:063/3; Abbott 920)

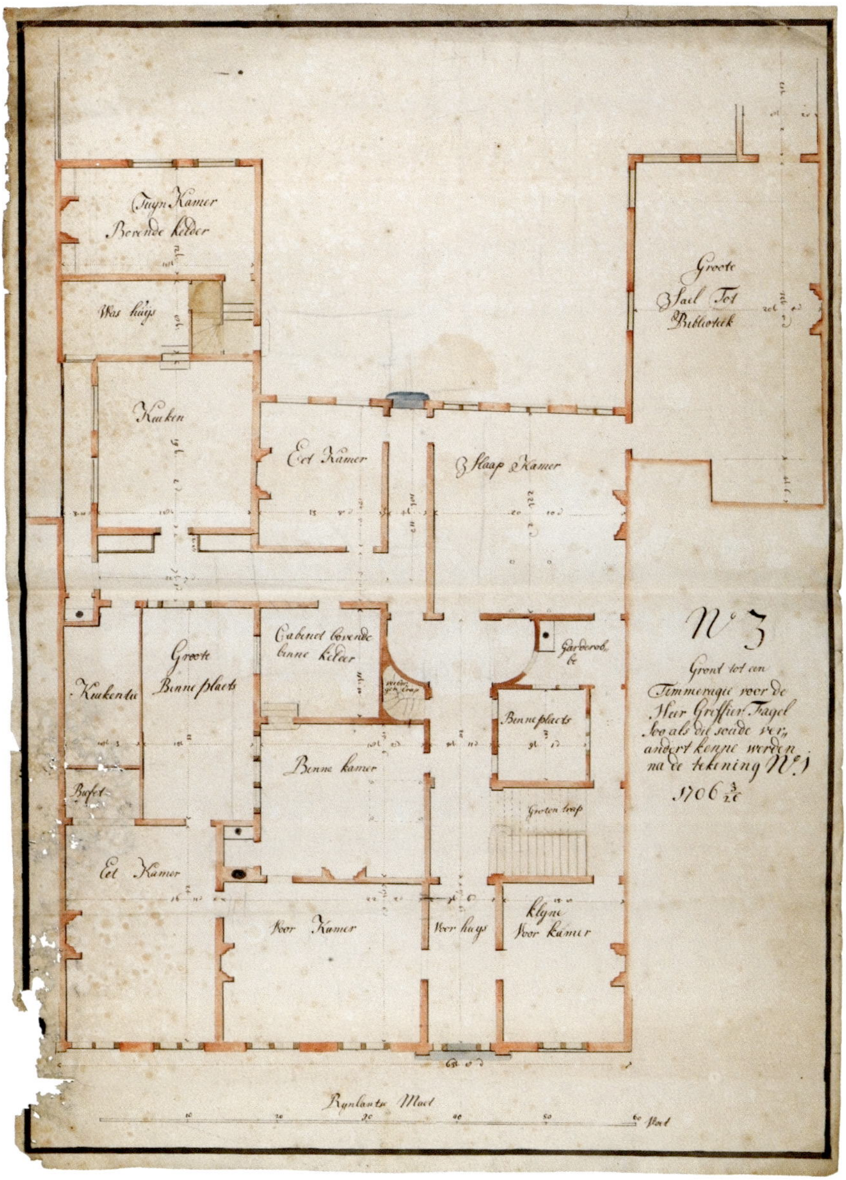

Plate 12: Proposed plan for the ground floor of the Fagel House, The Hague (26 March, 1706), 53 x 73 cm. (Fagel Portfolio 14:063/2; Abbott 920)

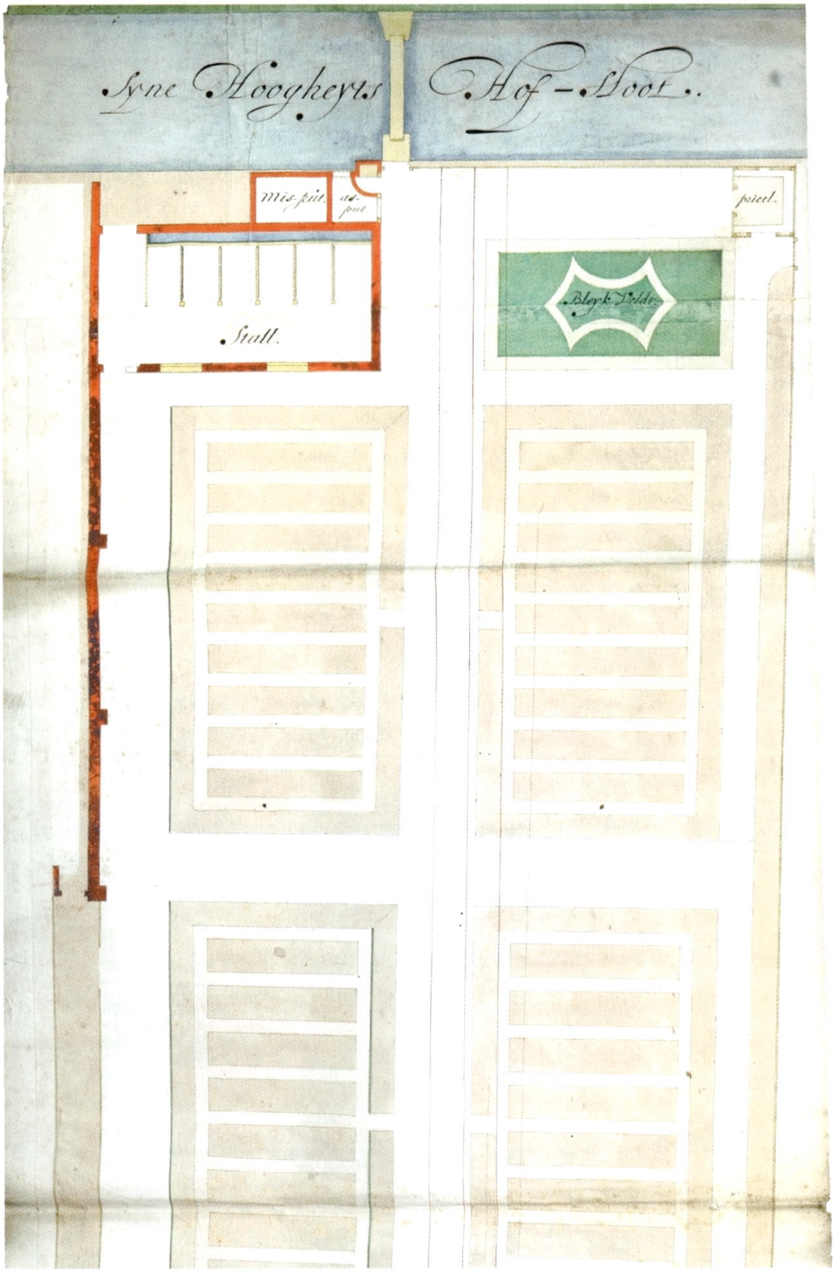

Plate 13: Plan of the ground floor and garden of the Fagel House, The Hague (c. 1706), 53 x 160 cm. (Fagel Portfolio 14:063/1; Abbott 920)

Eet-Saal
Koock Keucken
Binne Keucken
Kelder Kamer
Binne Kamer
Kelder
Coets-Huijs
Salet
Voor-Huijs
Voor-Camer

Plate 14: *Portrait of François Fagel the Elder* (?)
(Detail of plate 13)

Thematic shelving in the Old Library: The evidence of the Fagel Collection

Jason Harris
UNIVERSITY COLLEGE CORK

THE ACQUISITION – partly adventitious and partly planned – of enormous numbers of books over the centuries has created formidable problems for the staff managing the collections of the library in Trinity College Dublin. How they have chosen to classify, locate and catalogue this material reflects a compromise between exigency and intellectual factors. Pressure of circumstance has manifested itself in a recurring tendency towards haphazard shelving of new purchases and frequent relocation of existing collections, a procedure that has unfortunately helped to obscure evidence of earlier plans or patterns of shelving. Nevertheless, several sources are at hand to guide the researcher as to earlier arrangements of the collections. Two of the most useful are a copy of the auction catalogue of the Fagel Collection that was used as a checklist in the early nineteenth century, and the old handwritten local catalogues held in the Early Printed Books reading room.[1] In addition, one may supplement these with information from other sources that provide more limited evidence of various periods in the library's history, such as early manuscript catalogues of the collections.[2] Examination of these sources is valuable both as a contribution

1 Samuel Paterson, *Bibliotheca Fageliana. A Catalogue of the Valuable and Extensive Library of the Greffier Fagel, of the Hague* (London 1802). Local catalogues of the Long Room and of the Fagel Collection are kept on the open shelves in the Early Printed Books reading room. Details of the shelving process are given by Vincent Kinane, 'The Fagel Collection' in Peter Fox (ed.), *The Treasures of the Library, Trinity College Dublin* (Dublin 1986), pp. 158–69.

2 See Jane Maxwell, 'A guide to the manuscript sources in TCD for the history of the library' in Vincent Kinane and Anne Walsh (eds), *Essays on the History of Trinity College Library, Dublin* (Dublin 2000), pp. 91–103.

to the history of the library as a whole and as a study of the intellectual criteria that informed the decisions of successive librarians as to how to manage and best display the collections. In what follows, I will examine this evidence in order to throw light on the extent to which subject classification was a factor in the shelving of books both in the Fagel Collection specifically and in the Old Library as a whole (see fig. 1).[3]

The auction catalogue of the Fagel Collection

There are two copies of the Fagel auction catalogue that Trinity librarians used during the shelving and organization of the collection. The first is Fag.N.12.61a, which is a copy of the first part of the catalogue that appears to have been used as a checklist when the books were unpacked in Dublin.[4] The second is Fag. N.12.61, which contains marginal notes of class marks as assigned in the early nineteenth century. Braches dates the annotation of this copy to some time after 1836, yet indicates that it was based upon an earlier register.[5] By 1836 some re-shelving had already taken place, a process repeated several times later in the century. Earlier evidence of class marks is available in the form of the local catalogue of the Fagel Collection as well as a copy of Barrett's catalogue that was completed in 1826 and annotated with shelf-marks.[6] These provide the most direct evidence of the earliest shelving; in the small number of instances where they differ from the annotated auction catalogue, they indicate for the most part deviation in shelf position, not class mark. However, because one is arranged by author and the other is essentially a concordance of class mark and auction lot number, the auction catalogue itself is by far the most useful tool for assessing the intentions of the librarians when they unpacked the Fagel books.

Paterson's auction catalogue divided the 9844 lots into sections arranged broadly by subject, with further subdivisions within these sections. In some sections these subdivisions are very detailed. For example, under the heading of 'History' one finds a section on the Low Countries that is subdivided into

3 Some brief but helpful remarks on the subject, and on the desirability of further research, may be found in Ernst Braches, 'The first years of the Fagel Collection in Trinity College, Dublin' in Susan Roach (ed.), *Across the Narrow Seas: Studies in the History and Bibliography of Britain and the Low Countries* (London 1991), pp. 189–96.

4 Handwritten references to the storage cases are found on pp. 135, 153, 170 and 176.

5 Ernst Braches, 'Rapport Fagel-Bibliotheek', unpublished typescript held in the Early Printed Books reading room, Trinity College Dublin, p. 9.

6 The local catalogue is held in the Early Printed Books reading room. The copy of Barrett's catalogue is held by the Manuscripts department of the library: MUN/LIB/1.22.

Fig 1: W.B.S. Taylor, *The History of the University of Dublin*, London 1845 (facing p. 313): the Fagel Collection *in situ* in the first half of the nineteenth century, by F. Williams. (Gall. BB.13.1)

a section on general history, chronicles of Belgium and Batavia, the Belgian war, regional and urban histories and genealogies of both the southern and the northern Low Countries – all of which covers roughly one thousand lots.[7] By this means the contents of the collection are classified according to broad subject area. One might imagine that any librarian wishing to shelve the material by subject would have taken the convenient route of following

7 *Bibliotheca Fageliana*, lots 6795–7713.

the subject classification employed in the auction catalogue, but this is not in fact the approach taken. A selection from the section on 'Grammars and lexica of various languages' may illustrate the point. The following are lots 52 to 80, though I have abbreviated the entries to author, title, and shelf mark and have omitted the 'Fag.' prefix to the latter:

52. Albert Schultens, *Vindiciæ originum Hebræarum*: D.6.27
53. *idem*, *Institutiones ad fundamenta linguæ Hebrææ*: C.3.14
54. *idem*, *Origines Hebrææ*: D.8.2–3
55. *idem*, *Vetus et regia via Hebraizandi*: D.10.42
56. *idem*, *Excursus tres de lingua primæva*: D.7.14–16
57. Hendrik Albert Schultens, *Specimen proverbiorum Meidanii*: D.8.1, no. 3
58. Gerardus Outhovius, *Linguæ Græcæ rudimenta*: G.14.85
59. Philippus Munckerus, *Pandæsia grammatica, et introductio in grammaticam Græcam*: C.8.66
60. Bernardus de Montfaucon, *Palæographia Græca*: F.4.6
61. Gregorius Corinthius, *De dialectis*: G.6.25
62. Johannes Rodolfus Westenius, *Pro Græca et genuina linguæ Græcæ pronunciatione*: G.10.1
63. Theophilus Christophorus Harles, *Introductio in historiam linguæ Græcæ*: C.4.59
64. Henricus Hoogeveen, *Doctrina particularum linguæ Græcæ*: C.3.47–8
65. Gulielmus Otho Reizius, *Belga Græcissans*: G.4.5
66. Henricus Stephanus, *Thesaurus Græcæ linguæ*: F.3.12–16
67. Benjamin Hedericus, *Græcum lexicon manuale*: C.4.13
68. Humphredus Hodius, *De Græcis illustribus linguæ Græcæ instauratoribus*: G.4.25
69. Christophorus Fridericus Boernerus, *De doctis hominibus Græcis litterarum Græcarum in Italia instauratoribus*: F.8.49
70. Thomas Linacre, *De emendata structura Latini sermonis libri sex*: C.7.51
71. Gerardus Vossius, *Latina grammatica*: C.8.72
72. [Pierre Chompré], *Traduction des modèles de latinité*: C.8.33–6
73. Johannes Fridericus Reitzius, *De ambiguis, mediis et contrariis*: G.4.10
74. *Gradus ad Parnassum*: no shelf-mark
75. Fridericus Matthæus Grapaldus, *Onomasticon*: C.11.43
76. Robertus Stephanus, *Thesaurus linguæ Latinæ*: F.3.8–11
77. Johannes Gesner, *Linguæ et eruditionis Romanæ thesaurus*: F.4.13–14
78. Henricus Spelmann, *Glossarium archaiologicum*: E.4.20
79. Carolus Dufresne, *Glossarium ad scriptores mediæ et infimæ latinitatis*: F.4.15–24
80. [Plexiacus], *Lexicon philosophicum, sive index latinorum verborum*: C.4.60

This sample suggests that the Fagel books were not shelved in accordance with their classification in the auction catalogue (except, perhaps, as a short-term solution while the appropriate subject classification was determined).[8] Yet the shelf mark attached to each book only contains information about the location assigned to it, not its content. The initial letter refers to the case in which the books are stored, and proceeds from *A* to *Z* (later in the century, extra shelving was added with doubled letters, e.g. *AA*). The first number refers to the shelf. The lower shelves have lower numbers and probably tended to contain larger-format books, such as folios and large quartos, though expediency and space conservation may have caused local deviations from the pattern. The second number refers to the order in which the books were placed on the shelf. One could surmise that lower numbers were shelved first, left to right, but it is perhaps more likely that much shuffling of books took place prior to the final arrangement and numbering of the volumes. It is worth noting that the shelf marks for the Fagel Collection operate identically to those in the Long Room, though the latter contain two alphabetical and only one numerical element. This purely locative system is typical of the era and contrasts with modern approaches such as the Dewey decimal system and the Library of Congress system, both of which are, to a greater or lesser degree, subject-descriptive.[9] However, if the Fagel books were shelved thematically by subject then the shelf marks could effectively have been treated by users as subject designations.

It is clear that lots 52 to 80, although grouped thematically in the auction catalogue, were shelved separately. Nevertheless, they were not scattered randomly throughout the entire library, but were mostly housed in cases *C*, *D*, *F* and *G*. A few of these items ended up side by side, though they were not so in the auction catalogue. For example, Harles's introduction to the history of Greek (lot number 63), an octavo from 1778, was shelved beside Plexiacus's work on Ciceronian philosophical vocabulary (lot number 80), which was printed in quarto.[10] Since the difference in format is not an infallible guide to size it would not necessarily be more efficient to shelve all books in the same format together

8 See Braches, 'The first years of the Fagel Collection', p. 191.

9 See, for example, Sargent Bush, Jr and Carl J. Rasmussen, *The Library of Emanuel College, Cambridge, 1584–1637* (Cambridge 1986), p. 9. For a wider account of libraries in the period see N.R. Ker, 'Oxford college libraries in the sixteenth century', *Bodleian Library Record*, 6 (1957–61), 459–515; and Philip Gaskell, *Trinity College Library: The First 150 Years* (Cambridge 1980), pp. 3–10 and 92–106. According to Gaskell, books in Trinity College Cambridge were at first shelved in order of accession rather than by subject (p. 93).

10 Theophilus Christophorus Harles, *Introductio in historiam linguæ Græcæ* (Altenburg 1778); Plexiacus [Henri du Sauzet], *Lexicon philosophicum, sive index latinorum verborum descriptionumque ad philosophos et dialecticos maxime pertinentium* (Hague 1716).

and hence also the difference in format of these two items does not rule out size as a factor in where they were placed.[11] Further evidence that the librarians' decisions as to shelving were the product of some deliberation can be found in the distribution of the works of Albert Schultens. His basic textbook of Hebrew (lot 53) was placed in case *C*, separated from his other more discursive studies of Hebrew and the other ancient languages, which were shelved in various parts of case *D*.[12] Moreover, the linguistic, encyclopedic and palaeographical tools found among these lots, such as the Latin and Greek dictionaries of Robert and Henri Estienne (lots 76 and 66), or Du Cange's dictionary of post-classical Latin (lot 79), appear to have been placed in case *F*.[13] One might, however, reasonably object that since the books in the sample are necessarily linked by content, isolated analysis of their distribution throughout the library is liable to create the optical illusion of subject clusters where in fact there were none. This small sample is thus suggestive, but not in itself a reliable indication of the existence of thematic shelving.

An alternative explanation for the dispersal of these lots must also be considered. The physical arrangement of books suggested by the auction catalogue would not necessarily have been preserved when the collection was shipped to Dublin. It is quite possible, therefore, that these lots were separated in transit and that their arrangement on the shelves in Dublin largely reflects the order in which they were unpacked.[14] Yet this runs against the evidence of the catalogue used to unpack the books, where a note on page 135 reads 'these are in first 36 cases'.[15] If this were so, however, one would expect that the holdings in any section of the library that is large enough to provide a statistically significant sample should more or less match the proportions of books by subject in the collection as a whole. Local variations should be expected, but if

11 The number of books in the library muniments reveal that librarians in the nineteenth century were concerned that space was wasted by shelving different formats together, a concern which indicates that the practice had not been uncommon: MUN/LIB/19.

12 Albertus Schultens, *Vindiciæ originum Hebræarum* (Leiden 1737); *idem*, *Institutiones ad fundamenta linguæ Hebrææ* (Leiden 1737); *idem*, *Origines Hebrææ* (Franeker 1724; Leiden 1738); *idem*, *Vetus et regia via Hebraizandi* (Leiden 1738); *idem*, *Excursus tres de lingua primæva*, (Leiden 1739).

13 Henricus Stephanus, *Thesaurus Græcæ linguæ* (Paris 1573); Robertus Stephanus, *Thesaurus linguæ latinæ* (London 1734–5); and Du Cange, *Glossarium ad scriptores mediæ et infimæ latinitatis* (Paris 1733–6).

14 A detailed account of the packing and shipping of the books is provided in the diary of Thomas Elrington, who was sent to London to supervise proceedings: MUN/LIB/12 (see above, pp. 81–84).

15 See Fag. N.12.61a, p. 135. The hypothesis that the books were disordered during shipping also runs counter to the plausible suggestions offered by Braches, 'The first years of the Fagel Collection', p. 191.

an overwhelming preponderance of books from one or other subject area occurs frequently, then, in the absence of other determining criteria, the existence of thematic shelving is probable.

On the basis of his assessment of the auction catalogue, Vincent Kinane offered the following estimate of the proportion of books in each subject area:[16]

	%
History/topography	37.6
Theology	18.1
Politics/law	6.4
Geography/cosmography/travels	6.3
Classics	6.2
Literature	5.9
Philosophy (including natural philosophy and mathematics)	2.6
Natural history	2.6
Visual arts	2.5
Medicine	0.7
Military	0.6
Agriculture/horticulture	0.5
Economics	0.4
Miscellaneous	9.6

The content of selected sections of the library may be examined with these proportions in mind. The first sample I wish to discuss is case *G*, in which, as we have seen, several items from lots 52 to 80 were shelved. The content of the case cannot be fully reconstructed on the basis of the auction catalogue, but can be supplemented from information given in the local catalogue.[17] Further, the copy of Barrett's catalogue that was made in the 1820s and annotated with shelf marks can be used to double-check the evidence of the auction catalogue, though it is clear that relocations took place early on, so that one must be careful not to overestimate the reliability of the evidence.[18] Nevertheless, the lots assigned to case *G* in the auction catalogue reveal a heavy preponderance of material pertaining to one or other aspect of the study of the Classics, broadly conceived. This does not mean merely those books listed under 'Classics' in Kinane's statistics, but rather reflects a combination of material from several

16 Kinane, 'The Fagel Collection', pp. 158–69, here p. 164.

17 The local catalogue records the presence of substantial infill after the arrival of books under copyright legislation and it is a matter of speculation as to the extent to which this required relocation of books shelved previously. For some observations in this regard see Braches, 'The first years of the Fagel Collection', pp. 192–3.

18 MUN/LIB/1.22.

other categories too, most notably 'literature'. The subject categories of the past do not coincide precisely with those of today.

The most reliable designation to use for the material in case *G* is *litteræ humaniores*, the term employed in the auction catalogue that Kinane renders 'literature'. The phrase *litteræ humaniores* encompassed those areas of the arts and humanities that pertain to *belles-lettres*, stylistics and philology. Thus, case *G* houses books as seemingly diverse as editions of the works of Cicero, a treatise on ambiguous language by Johann Reitz, a posthumous edition of Johann Burkhardt Mencke's literary writings, an edition of the correspondence of Leibniz, and the writings of Abelard and Heloise.[19] What unites these is a concern with language and style, whether explicitly treated in the books or merely in so far as the author's style was admired. Thus, anything that was read for its literary or stylistic value could be included in this section, as, for example, Richard Stanihurst's account of Irish history, which was more highly regarded for its Ciceronian Latin than for its value as a historical study (see fig. 2).[20] Accordingly, books classified in numerous different ways in the auction catalogue found their way into case *G*.

One might object that it is possible to include almost anything under such an expansive category or that the looseness of *litteræ humaniores* as a subject category creates the illusion of coherence in what is in fact a miscellaneous gathering of books. Yet the almost total absence from case *G* of books on mathematics, logic, or the natural sciences, and the fact that the majority of the books have an unambiguously literary character or linguistic focus, supports the contention that there is a thematic core to what is housed in the case. The combination of 'literature' and 'Classics' in Kinane's list amounts to a mere 12.1 per cent. Even assuming a substantial level of infiltration from other categories, it is certain that the proportion of books in case *G* that falls within the subject area outlined above greatly exceeds the proportion in the collection as a whole.

To corroborate these findings, it is instructive to consider a sample of starkly contrasting character, such as case *N*. Although the subject category that best describes the content of this case has no precise equivalent in the modern day, it is immediately evident that the books have what we would regard as a scientific subject matter. The early-modern category that best describes them is

19 Johann Reitz, *De ambiguis, mediis et contrariis* (Utrecht 1736); Johann Burkhardt Mencke, *Dissertationes literariæ* (Leipzig 1734); Johann Daniel Gruber (ed.), *Commercii epistolici Leibnitiani prodromus* (Hannover 1745); and *Abelardi et Heloisæ opera* (Paris 1616).

20 Richard Stanihurst, *De rebus in Hibernia gestis* (Antwerp 1584).

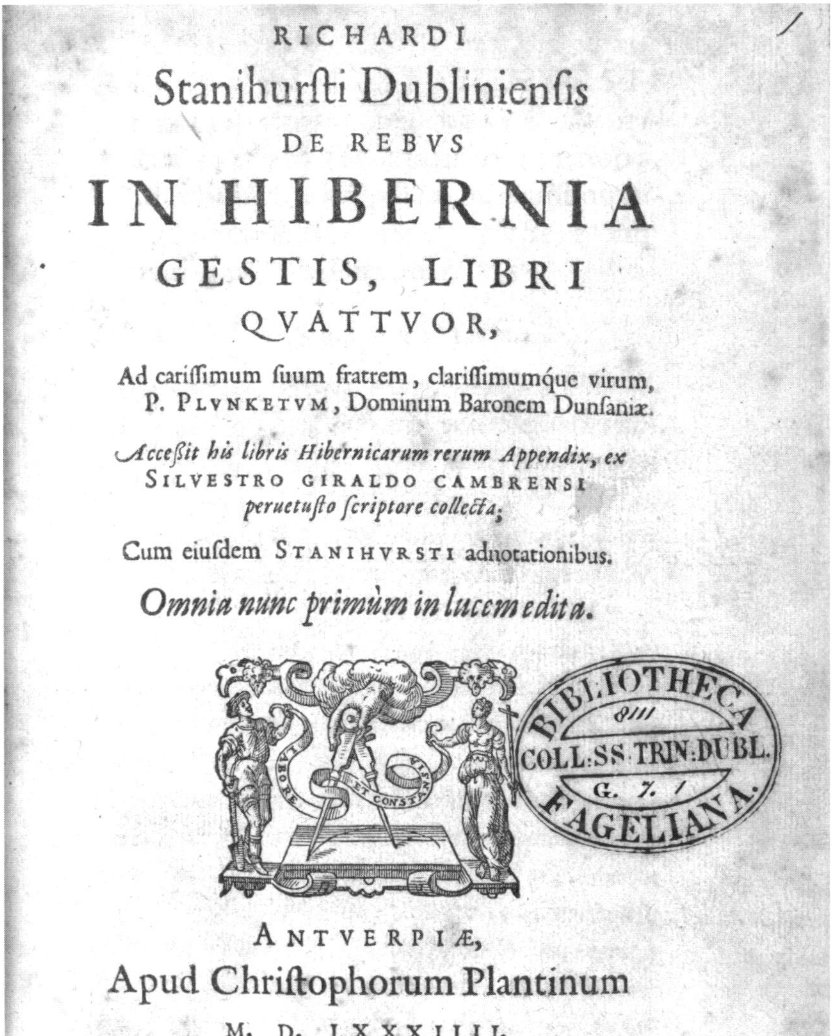

RICHARDI
Stanihurſti Dublinienſis
DE REBVS
IN HIBERNIA
GESTIS, LIBRI
QVATTVOR,

Ad cariſſimum ſuum fratrem, clariſſimumq́ue virum,
P. PLVNKETVM, Dominum Baronem Dunſaniæ.

Acceßit his libris Hibernicarum rerum Appendix, ex
SILVESTRO GIRALDO CAMBRENSI
peruetuſto ſcriptore collecta;

Cum eiuſdem STANIHVRSTI adnotationibus.

Omnia nunc primùm in lucem edita.

ANTVERPIÆ,
Apud Chriſtophorum Plantinum
M. D. LXXXIIII.

Fig 2: Richardi Stanihursti Dubliniensis, *De rebus in Hibernia gestis*, Antwerp: Christophorus Plantinus, 1584. (Fag. G.7.1)

'natural philosophy', but one can be still more specific. The books discuss the mathematical and physical sciences, largely from the perspective of the 'new science' of the seventeenth and eighteenth centuries. This means that scholastic science is largely absent, yet so are medicine and the natural history of the animal world. Geography is missing too, though mathematical and esoteric cosmographies are present. Thus one finds here the works of Athanasius Kircher, Robert Boyle, John Locke, Gottfried Leibniz, Isaac Newton and Antoon van Leeuwenhoek (see fig. 3), accompanied exclusively by other writers who responded to or developed their work, or who pursued cognate studies.

Fig 3: Antoni van Leeuwenhoek, *Ontledigingen en ontdekkingen van levende dierens*, vol. 1, Leyden: Cornelis Boutenstyn, 1686 (frontispiece preceding title-page). The inscription on the monument proclaims the discovery of invisible things in the natural world. (Fag. N.7.38)

The proportion of these books in case *N* is as close to one hundred per cent as one could expect, given the vicissitudes that have affected the shelving of the collection. Bearing in mind that Kinane's statistics suggest that books of this kind amount to less than 10 per cent of the collection as a whole, there can be no question but that the collocation of these volumes was not accidental but intentional. A significant gathering of cognate books, including some by the same authors, can be found in case *D*; there, however, the shelves reveal a greater preponderance of philosophy and natural theology, so that one can surmise that apparent similarities with case *N* arise from the overlap between these fields and that of natural philosophy. This confluence reflects very well the intellectual world of the Royal Society as well as the personal interests of authors such as Locke, Boyle and Newton. Nevertheless, the areas of overlap between cases *D* and *N* are not sufficiently extensive to cause ambiguity about the difference in thematic focus between the two areas. Further, the wider context of what is omitted helps to underscore the coherence of what is included. For instance, although natural theology is found in case *D*, the majority of controversial theology is found in the cases with shelf marks towards the end of the alphabet. A detailed study of the placement of the extensive theological holdings in the Fagel Collection is beyond the scope of this article, but in general it appears that their disposition on the shelves supports the evidence that thematic arrangement was one of the considerations that most influenced the librarians.

The imperfect nature of the evidence for the original shelving of the Fagel Collection does not negate the value of the extensive and detailed picture that can be reconstructed. Nevertheless, everywhere one looks in the collection one sees that thematic concerns were not always of paramount importance to the library staff. From the outset, space must have been a central factor, as indeed was time. Accordingly, nowhere in the collection can one find holdings perfectly arranged by subject. Rather, it is appropriate to speak of a prevalent tendency towards thematic shelving, vitiated by circumstance. Bearing in mind these caveats, it is possible to offer the following tentative results from the test cases that I have examined to date:

Bookcase	Materials
A–B	Geography, travel, astronomy, cosmology and navigation
C	Lexica and pedagogical works
D	Philosophy and natural theology
E–G	Classics and litteræ humaniores
H	Political tracts
I	Numismatics
M–N	Natural philosophy (mathematical and physical sciences)
O–P	Law and politics
Q–U	Regional histories and topographies
W–Z	Church history and theology[21]

21 These results may be compared with the observations of Braches, 'The first years of the Fagel Collection', p. 192.

Although this selection does not cover the entire collection – and indeed the depth of my scrutiny has not been the same in each case – nevertheless the sample is sufficiently large to establish with some degree of certainty both the extent and the structural coherence of the thematic shelving that was envisaged for the Fagel Collection.

Local catalogues of the Long Room

It may with reason be surmised that the approach taken to the shelving of the Fagel Collection was not altogether fortuitous, but rather based upon an already established *modus operandi* within the library in Trinity College. Unfortunately, there is no subject catalogue that captures the original plan of the collections. Yet the very fact that subject catalogues were not felt to be necessary during the first centuries of the library's existence might suggest that librarians had an alternative means of locating books by topic, such as shelving similar items in proximity to one another where possible. A survey of the shelves confirms that there is some basis for this conjecture, with two very large caveats – the arrangement of books by provenance and the infill of later acquisitions. Both of these factors were further qualified by the increasing pressure to use space efficiently as the library filled up. Some description of the physical housing of the collections is therefore requisite.[22]

The Long Room consists of a central aisle, some 64 metres in length, on either side of which the books are displayed in double-sided bookcases, each labelled alphabetically, which together form bays. There are twenty bays on either side, each formed out of two cases, each containing between twelve and eighteen shelves of varying distribution to accommodate different book sizes. For ease of access and structural stability, the large folios are situated on the bottom shelves, quartos in the middle, and folios and smaller formats on the highest shelves. The two sides of the library have parallel class marks, thus case *A* is opposite case *AA*, *B* is opposite *BB*, and so forth. Each shelf is labelled alphabetically, with 'a' at the bottom and 'j' omitted, ascending to a minimum of 'm' and a maximum of 's' at the top – the number of shelves varies according to the heights of the books in the case. On the other side of the same case, the shelves are labelled with doubled letters, aa, bb, and so forth. Thus, at one end of the library the first case commences with shelf-

22 For what follows, see Anne Crookshank, 'The Long Room' in Fox (ed.), *The Treasures of the Library*, pp. 16–28.

mark A.a.1 on one side and A.aa.1 on the other, while the parallel case across the aisle commences with shelf-marks AA.a.1 on one side and AA.aa.1 on the other. Although the shelf numbers originally only went up to 'w' and 'ww', in later years, owing to shortage of space, small double-sided cases three or four shelves high were placed in the middle of each bay, which served to extend the shelf numbers up towards the end of the alphabet.

The overall physical arrangement of the cases and shelves is important because it determines that the lowest shelf numbers in each class will contain large folio volumes, often atlases or hefty reference works. Higher shelf numbers will contain progressively smaller-format books, and the highest shelf numbers in each class will contain late acquisitions that are placed in the smaller cases in the middle of each bay. Larger formats were more expensive and better suited to particular types of book, generally more monumental in scope, while the smaller formats were often used for pamphlets, cheap editions, and so forth. Hence the subject matter and type of the books in each case often varies according to these physical determinants, even where there is a broad uniformity of subject within the case. In addition, one entire side of the library, that with double-lettered bookcases, is filled with collections acquired from private benefactions; on the other side, the college's own purchases are stored. Accordingly, provenance has been an organizing principle in the Long Room that therefore set limits within which thematic shelving could operate.

This process of discerning patterns in the arrangement of books in the Long Room can be aided greatly by consultation of the local catalogues held in the Early Printed Books reading room. Rarely consulted by anyone other than library staff, these catalogues document the holdings of the library shelf by shelf. Thus one can check the contents of each bay at a glance. The entries are often only the name of an author, but these can readily be checked against the printed catalogues under that name. Some of these volumes have been moved from the location they had when the local catalogues were compiled, but normally a record has been inserted to indicate this. The process of infill is evident from the local catalogues where changes in handwriting signal clearly the passage of time. What is of the greatest value in the study of these catalogues is that the links that were perceived by the librarians between what we would now regard as disparate areas of scholarship can clearly be seen.

A fine example that supports the analysis of the Fagel Collection offered earlier may be found in case *L*, which houses natural philosophical material not dissimilar to that found in case *N* of the Fagel Collection. Kircher, Locke, Newton, and so forth, are found side by side, accompanied by Gassendi, Malebranche, and even examples of scientific writings by scholastic authors. The thematic coherence of the material is incontestable, yet the detail offered by the local catalogues reveals that the physical arrangement of books on each shelf within these themed areas often appears arbitrary and in fact may have been driven by circumstances such as book size and date of acquisition.

Further sampling of the structure of the college collections using the local catalogues confirms the impression that thematic shelving was originally in operation, only to be modified later through pressure of space. The following is an imprecise conspectus of the thematic disposition of cases in the first half of the collections:

A–G	Theology
H–I	Law
K	Medicine
L	Natural philosophy
M	Geography
N	History etc.

Work still needs to be done on the physical arrangement of the named collections in the Long Room, which have been affected by infill and relocation in much the same way as the Fagel Collection. Nevertheless, some brief remarks about the contents of the two largest collections, those of James Ussher and Claudius Gilbert, may lend support to the evidence presented thus far from the Fagel Collection. The Ussher Collection, acquired by the university in 1658 and allocated to the college in 1661, for the most part occupies cases *AA* to *EE*.[23] The character of the collection is overwhelmingly theological, but admits of thematic subdivision. Notably case *EE* contains philological and scientific matter, the clustering of which suggests that further research might unearth more detailed thematic arrangements within the Ussher bookcases. The collection of Claudius Gilbert (donated in 1743) is more diverse in character. It occupies the shelves from case *II* to *TT* and, partly, *UU*. Subject-specific clusters of material can be seen in the following locations:

23 On the acquisition of the collection see T.C. Barnard, 'The purchase of Archbishop Ussher's library in 1657', *Long Room*, 4 (1971), 9–14.

II.i	Classics
II.k–n	Geography and history
KK–MM	Theology
NN	Law
OO	Natural philosophy, botany and medicine
PP	Geography and chronology; history from *m* upwards
QQ–SS	History
TT	Classics

These findings are very tentative but offer some indication that the personal collections in the Long Room were, like the Fagel Collection, shelved with an eye to thematic coherence. In addition, substantial infill in case *FF*, situated between the Ussher and Palliser collections, and in case *HH*, between the Palliser and Gilbert collections, suggests that the initial housing of these collections left sufficient space for gaps to be left between them. These empty (or partially filled) cases seem to have been used in later centuries for new accessions, particularly after Trinity became a copyright library in 1801.[24] Given the dramatic rise in scientific output during the nineteenth century and the growing presence of science on the curriculum, it is not surprising to see these cases filled with localized gatherings of scientific material. Nevertheless, such clusters are merely adventitious and provide a salutary warning that the current disposition on the shelves is late of origin and that circumstance can lend coherence to chance.

Finally, further evidence of the deployment of thematic shelving in the Old Library may be found in the manuscript catalogues of the earliest collections. In TCD MS 1, for example, a seventeenth-century catalogue of the library collections, clear patterns can be discerned in the assigning of class marks to each volume. The catalogue is arranged alphabetically by author. The following data are derived from detailed analysis of the material listed under the letter *A*, and have been checked against more widespread but less thorough sampling of material from the remainder of the catalogue as well as against detailed thematic scrutiny of the shelving of natural philosophical and medical material:

24 Peter Fox, '"They glory much in their library"' in *idem* (ed.), *The Treasures of the Library*, pp. 1–15; and Vincent Kinane, 'Legal deposit, 1801–1922' in Kinane and Walsh (eds), *Essays*, pp. 120–37.

h.1	Grammar and logic
h.2	Philosophy and rhetoric
h.3	Astrology
h.4	Cosmology
h.5	Natural philosophy
h.6	Medicine
h.8	History
h.10	Law

Theology is omitted from this classification system because theological books were catalogued separately with the class-mark *t* instead of *h*. The evidence of this catalogue, set beside that of the local catalogues for the Long Room, serves to reaffirm the conclusion reached through analysis of the Fagel auction catalogue: notwithstanding the impact of pragmatic criteria such as the size of volumes, the date of their acquisition and the need to display them according to provenance, thematic shelving was the standard practice of Trinity's librarians throughout the first two centuries of the library's history. By contrast, in subsequent years, as shortage of free space became an increasingly pressing problem, the librarians were compelled to shelve new accessions wherever they could, without much concern about congruence with surrounding volumes.

Conclusion

The lack of subject catalogues produced during the first two centuries of the library in Trinity College is not an indication that the librarians disregarded thematic links between books in the collections. On the contrary, a subject catalogue might have seemed redundant for collections that were already arranged on the shelves by content. Until the collections grew unmanageably large, the physical arrangement of the books would have sufficed as a thematic 'search engine'. The sudden influx of new material caused by the acquisition of the Ussher Collection must have put this system under some pressure, but it was probably only towards the end of the eighteenth century that it began to break down in earnest as the size of the holdings grew in leaps and bounds with the procurement of the Gilbert, Palliser and Fagel collections, and the assignment of copyright status. The piecemeal accession of new materials in no way undermined the viability of the system of thematic shelving; by contrast, the sudden inundation of a large personal collection presented as significant a logistical problem as it did an intellectual opportunity.

How the college's librarians dealt with this challenge can best be seen in the case of the last great accession of a private library, the Fagel Collection, thanks to the survival of the auction catalogue that was used to record class marks while the books were unpacked and shelved. It is especially fortunate that this record survives because it illustrates the contrast between two subject classifications of the same material. This draws attention to a conscious plan of thematic shelving that was formulated around the time of the acquisition of the collection, whereas for all the other collections we must rely upon the murky evidence of the end product, after the books have been shelved, re-shelved, and intermingled with other materials. What is more, we can see from the Fagel auction catalogue that considerable thought was put into creating a thematic arrangement of the books that suited the library users better than the classifications offered by the auctioneers. Rearranging the collection in this way was a time-consuming and therefore expensive process, particularly because it required broad familiarity with the contents of each book. This factor must be considered when evaluating the delays caused by the building work undertaken to house the collection.[25]

To some extent, the librarians' arrangement of the books into broadly defined subject areas offers a useful measure both of their understanding of early-modern disciplinary boundaries and of their knowledge and view of the material in the Fagel Collection. As we have seen, the arrangement of books in each section of the Old Library followed a slightly different plan. The subject areas in each section are broadly commensurate, but their physical location in relation to one another varies. No doubt this reflects the influence of chance circumstances in addition to the peculiarities of each collection. Yet, once the formative role of thematic shelving in the Old Library is acknowledged, it may be possible to study these topological variations with an eye to the intellectual frameworks that, at least in part, lie behind them. On the other hand, lack of space and the desire to privilege provenance rather than subject often intervened to rule out the implementation of a predefined schema. Indeed, whatever arrangement of books was chosen, the reasons for the decision were always grounded in practicalities of access and storage. As we have seen, one consequence of this is that the librarians have frequently had to rearrange parts of the existing collections in order to house later accessions. The books in the Long Room are not, therefore, organized systematically by subject in

25 On the time taken shelving the books see Kinane, 'The Fagel Collection', pp. 162–4.

the manner of a modern library following the Dewey decimal or Library of Congress system; but their physical arrangement offers, nevertheless, a ragged palimpsest that may yet disclose further traces of the intellectual history of the college.

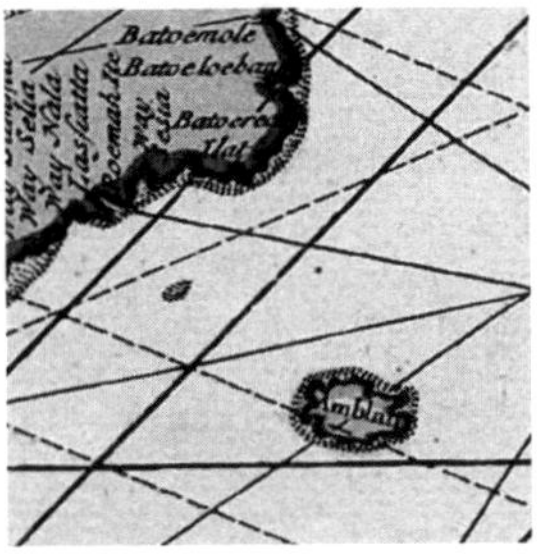
Batoemole
Way Sela
Way Nala
Tlat

Developing the Fagel Map Collection

David Brown
TRINITY COLLEGE DUBLIN

THE FAGEL Map Collection in Trinity College Dublin is one of the finest in the world, and unsurpassed in terms of quality and standard of preservation. Very large collections of early modern maps include the George III Topographical Collection in the British Library, the Royal Collection in the Bibliothèque Nationale de France, the National Library of the Netherlands and the Royal Library of Denmark. The Frederik den Femtes Atlas in Copenhagen is similar in arrangement to the Fagel Atlas, approximately 3500 maps bound into portfolios, although it is comprised mainly of plates from published atlases as opposed to the unbound, limited circulation and early state copies in the Fagel Collection. This latter is the largest surviving discrete collection to have been assembled as the material was published, as opposed to retrospectively. As a working library it provides a valuable insight into how the geographical understanding of the world developed among the ruling elite of the Dutch Golden Age. The Fagel Map Collection comprises:

> 600 volumes of contemporary accounts of travels, books on geography and other geographical material, including 4500 engravings of maps.
>
> 142 bound atlases comprising approximately 8200 double folio maps.
>
> The Fagel Atlas: 2880 single map sheets contained in 25 portfolio boxes.

The portfolios comprising the Fagel Atlas are arranged by geographical region, and a catalogue of these maps was published as the 'Catalogue of the Fagel Collection of Maps, Plans, Etc.' as an appendix to the catalogue of manuscripts in Trinity College Library prepared by T.K. Abbott in 1900.[1] The maps are unbound and the term 'Atlas' follows the convention of the Femtes Atlas, to indicate that the collection has been assembled by the Fagels and not subsequently by the Library. Catalogue descriptions are based on information given on the printed maps, but many items in this catalogue are either undated or have very brief descriptions. The single sheets are housed in new library boxes and examples of the original library portfolios have been preserved.

The material ranges in date from 1490 to 1798, with the greater volume published in the eighteenth century, and relates to all parts of the world, but with a particular emphasis on Europe and areas outside Europe with Dutch colonial or trading interests. The content includes all levels of cartographic material, from celestial charts to detailed plans of buildings and fortifications, in addition to volumes on geographical theory and methodology. Highlights of the collection include:

The complete coloured set of Blaeu's *Atlas Major.*

The complete set of atlases published by Jacob van Meurs.

Atlases, many coloured, by Frederik de Witt, Jans Jansson, Jean Baptiste d'Anville, Johann Baptist Homann, Nicolas Sanson, Alexis Hubert Jaillot, Pieter van der Aa, Giacomo Cantelli and Vincenzo Coronelli.

A large collection of first-hand accounts of voyages of exploration, including those of Henry Hudson, Abel Tasman, James Cook and William Bligh.

Several hundred battle plans relating to all the major conflicts in Europe from 1650 to 1800, approximately thirty of which are in manuscript.

In excess of 1200 detailed city maps, including John Ogilby's twenty-sheet map of London (1676) and Pierre Bullet's twelve-sheet map of Paris (1676), the majority in colour.

The celestial atlases of Andreas Cellari and Johan Gabriel Doppelmayr.

Sea atlases by Jacob Colom and Johannes van Keulen, and the *Neptune Français.*

1 T.K. Abbott, *Catalogue of the Manuscripts in the Library of Trinity College, Dublin* (Dublin and London 1900), pp. 438–529.The collection has recently been discussed by J.R. Bartlett, 'Fagel's maps: The eighteenth-century world' in W.E. Vaughan (ed.), *The Old Library Trinity College Dublin 1712–2012* (Dublin 2013), pp. 133–48.

Although the collection was acquired for the Trinity College Library in 1802, much of it – for example, the atlases and their contents – has never been catalogued and is unknown to the outside world. Some maps, like the Nicolaes Witsen map of Asia on six sheets, are the only surviving examples. The cataloguing of the atlases is particularly important as many were assembled on an ad hoc basis – atlases of the same name do not necessarily contain the same maps but reflect the individual requirements and budgets of each customer. Thus Jacob Colom's *World Sea Atlas* of 1668 contains eighteen charts in the standard version, fifty-six in the Fagel edition.[2] The special nature of this collection, in terms of both its scope and its condition, makes it an invaluable resource of primary material for research across a number of disciplines. A project to digitize the cartographic material has already been completed, resulting in an image bank of pre-1800 maps.

The Fagel Archive, held in the National Archive of the Netherlands, comprises the papers of Gaspar Fagel (Greffier 1670–72), Hendrik Fagel the Eldest (Greffier 1672–90), François Fagel the Elder (Greffier 1690–1744), Hendrik Fagel the Elder (Greffier 1744–90) and Hendrik Fagel the Younger (Greffier 1790–95). The papers relate to their work for the States General and include both private and administrative material. The interaction of the Fagel Archive and the Fagel Library is an obvious candidate for further study, providing insights into how the composition of the library and the knowledge that it contains contributed to the formation of policy and statecraft at the highest governmental levels in the Dutch republic.

The collection can also be used as a tool for comparative research. Comparing the Fagel Map Collection with contemporary collections held elsewhere allows for the comparison of the level of geographical knowledge available to different régimes. The Topographical Collection assembled by George III (reigned 1760–1820), now in the British Library and currently the subject of a major digitization project ('The King's Topographical Collection'), comprises approximately 50,000 maps, plans and views, both printed and hand-drawn, relating to all parts of the world but particularly Great Britain and the British Empire. The material ranges in date from about 1540 to 1824. The collection was donated to the nation by George IV in 1828, shortly after the Fagel Collection came to Trinity College Dublin.

2 Jacob Colom, *De Groote Zee Atlas ofte Water-Werelt* (Amsterdam 1668). Library shelf mark: Fag. Z.1.18.

The George III collection differs from the Fagel Collection in that it was mainly assembled through purchase and acquisition by a single collector whereas the Fagel Collection was a working library built up over time. Although the collections were assembled using a different methodology, comparisons of the eighteenth-century material are valid and allow the researcher to determine the comparative level of knowledge concerning different parts of the world held by two of the Great Powers. A remarkable deficiency in the Fagel Map Collection is the lack of material relating to the British Isles, an area in which it could be assumed the Dutch would have a keen interest. Replete with maps and atlases of all corners of the globe, it does not include a copy of William Petty's *Hiberniæ delineatio*, first published in 1687 and the only detailed atlas of Ireland then available. We can only presume that William III would have found it most useful.

There is no duplication in the collection; most items appear to have been acquired only if they represented advancement in the knowledge of an area or concerned a recent event or discovery. The Fagel family were evidently most particular in only acquiring material of the highest quality. Many items in the Fagel Atlas are private printings, in that they were not made available to the public at large, and are very scarce.

This internationally important collection of early printed maps is now being developed as a publicly available digital resource through the Fagel Project, a collaborative research initiative undertaken by the departments of History and Computer Science at Trinity College Dublin and supervised by Professor Mícheál Ó Siochrú. The project is supported by a philanthropic donation arranged through the Trinity Foundation and receives direct technical support from Google. Using technology developed for the recently completed Down Survey project at Trinity College, the Fagel maps will be geo-referenced and overlaid onto Google's web-based map interface, the Google Maps API.[3] A virtual seventeenth-century globe is a real possibility, with links to other content in the collection or content related to the Fagels held in other institutions.

The key tasks of the project include combining the geographical sections from the existing 1802 auction listing and the 1903 Abbott catalogue into a consolidated database, which will then be updated into a modern catalogue useful to scholars. The new catalogue will be created in a portable version of MARCXML to facilitate its incorporation into the Trinity College Library's main catalogue and to provide an interface with online resources held at other institutions.

3 The Down Survey website is available at http://downsurvey.tcd.ie.

The project will use the image bank of 10,000 high-resolution digital images of the Fagel maps, created by Leslie Brown and donated to the College. In addition to allowing the user to view a digital version of each map in the collection, these images will be used to create a number of pilot visualizations underlining the potential of the collection to transform the way in which history can be interpreted through cartographical material. These tasks include the development of three-dimensional visualizations of streetscapes and battle plans. The aim of this module of the project is to enable the user to experience an early-modern city or military engagement using realistic three-dimensional renderings generated from the early-modern engravings.

A feature of the site will be a route-planning function that will allow the user to get directions and an estimate of travel time between two points in Europe during the seventeenth and eighteenth centuries. Using the large number of post road maps in the collection the route planner will make adjustments for the quality of the road along a given route and for the time of year, which had a great impact on the length of a journey. The aim of this module, apart from providing useful historical information, is to make this part of the material accessible to a wide audience. Following the completion of the pilot map project, it is intended to use the material and website as the basis for a major funding application with additional partners in order to further develop the potential of the Fagel Library.

Examples of maps from the Fagel Map Collection

To curate a small representative sample of maps from so rich a collection as that assembled by the Fagels requires a high degree of subjectivity. The following are essentially personal favourites, but include some of the more important and rare maps in order to indicate the scope of the collection.

Each entry contains the information that is to be found on the map in question, followed by details of its production, and finally the Fagel shelf mark and the relevant number in Abbott's catalogue.

1. *Tabula Selenographica in qua Lunarium Macularum exacta Descriptio secundum Nomenclaturam Præstantissimorum Astronomorum tam Hevelii quam Riccioli* [...] *exhibetur* à Joh. Gabr. Doppelmajero Math. P. P. Opera Joh. Bapt. Homanni, Norinbergæ (see plate 21).

Johan Gabriel Doppelmayr, Lunar chart, engraved by Johann Baptist Homann (Nürnberg 1718), 58 x 46 cm
Fagel Portfolio 1:028 (Abbott 0028)

Two coloured and contrasting maps of the moon, one by Johannes Hevelius, the other by Giovanni Battista Riccioli, both originally published in the mid seventeenth century. Although the topography of the moon obviously does not change much, this work charts how the nomenclature of the moon's features was subject to vigorous debate. Hevelius' system, favoured in Protestant countries, assigned the names of terrestrial countries and features to lunar ones. Riccioli's system was favoured in Catholic countries at first, not becoming the standard until the middle of the eighteenth century, and invoked the names of famous astronomers used alongside more evocative names. Parts of the moon that appeared darker were called 'seas', such as the Sea of Tranquillity, lighter parts were termed 'land', for example the Land of Fertility or the Land of Health.

Doppelmayr (1677–1750) was a prolific writer on astronomy, mathematics and instrumentation whose most enduring work, his *Atlas Cœlestis*, included this lunar map along with star charts, the planetary systems of Tycho Brahe, Nicolas Copernicus and Riccioli, and Edmund Halley's cometary theory. Although the atlas was not published until 1742, most of the charts contained within it were produced between 1709 and 1720. The charts were collected by the Fagels as they were produced, as evidenced by the fact that they were never bound, and complement the magnificently illustrated *Atlas Cœlestis* or *Harmonia Macrocosmica* by Cellarius found elsewhere in the collection (see plate 16).[4]

2. *Planisphærium Terrestre cum utroque Cœlesti Hemisphærio, sive diversa orbis Terraquei pro variatis divisionis conspectus, variarumque positionum et observationum circumstantiis multis in locis correcta variisque huc facientibus cosmographicis illustrationibus pluriumque Naturæ Phænomenorum explicationibus, ex præclaris Auctoribus excerptis, aucta et ornata repræsentatio*: Opera et studio A. F. Zürneri. Ex officina Petri Schenkii (see plate 22).

   Adam Friedrich Zürner, World Map (Amsterdam: Gerhard Valk and Petrus Schenk, 1708), 58 x 51 cm
   Fagel Portfolio 1:001 (Abbott 0001)

4 Andreas Cellarius, *Harmonia Macrocosmica* (Amsterdam 1661), Fag. A.2.36.

A magnificently coloured double hemisphere world map updated to c. 1700. California is shown as an island with an indistinct *Fretum Anian* and *Terra Esonis* above it. Australia is now known to be separate from New Guinea, and Nova Britannia is shown as a separate island off the coast of New Guinea with the annotation that it was discovered by William Dampier in 1700. Several navigators' routes are shown, including those of Ferdinand Magellan, Dampier and Tasman. There are two insets of celestial maps arranged between the two hemispheres. Zürner (1679–1742) is better known as a land surveyor and the developer of the post road system in Saxony during the 1720s.

3. *Nieuwe Lantkaarte van het Noorder en Ooster deel van Asia en Europe strekkende van Nova Zemla tot China aldus getekent, beschreven, in kaart gebragt en uytgegeven sedert een Nauwkeurig ondersoek van meer als twintig Jaaren.* Door Nicolaes Witsen, Consul Amst. 1687 (see plate 20).

   Nicolaes Witsen, Map of Northern and Central Asia, a private printing (Amsterdam 1687), over six sheets, 210 x 180 cm
   Fagel Portfolio 1:054 (Abbott 0054)

This six-sheet map of Asia printed by Nicolaes Witsen (1641–1717) was the first map available to Europeans showing overland trade routes in central Asia, including the overland Silk Road from Beijing (Peking) in China to Astrakhan on the shores of the Caspian Sea. Witsen had been employed by Peter the Great to survey the Tsar's new Asian empire. Although he had this map engraved and printed in Amsterdam, it was not intended to be sold and this six-sheet impression is exceptionally rare. In 1692 he published a compendium, *Noord en Oost Tartarye*, describing Siberia and the surrounding areas.

The map caused a sensation when it first appeared in a smaller four-sheet format as it allowed European eyes to see another 'New World'. Witsen was careful to show the territories of each ruler, representations of different styles of building and the established caravan routes. Along the routes he named were the great *caravanserais* of the East–West Silk Road and he indicated pictorially the relative size of each settlement and marked the territory in which it was to be found.

The eastern side of the map shows the Great Wall of China in considerable detail, and Witsen is careful to indicate those gates in the wall open to foreign travellers wishing to go on to Peking and those closed to foreigners, but outside which they were permitted to conduct trade. The western side of the map shows the Silk Road converging on Astrakhan, the great Caspian seaport that also provided access to the Volga river system. The Black Sea and Constantinople lay to the west, European Russia was accessible via the Volga to the north, while Persian goods, including transhipments from India, could enter via the Caspian ports to the south.

Our European understanding of the Silk Road is often based on Marco Polo, leading us to see it as no more than an east–west highway from Peking to Venice. The Witsen map shows clearly that it was one of many important trade routes linking the peoples of Central Asia in a complex and interrelated society.

4. *De Landvoogdy van Amboina met de elf onderhoorige Eylanden* (see plate 23)

François Valentyn, Map of Seram and the outlying islands (Dordrecht: Joannes van Braam, Amsterdam: Gerard onder de Linden, 1724), 75 x 31 cm
Fagel Portfolio 19:022 (Abbott 1278)

A composite in two parts from the original, first published in Valentyn's *Oud en nieuw Oost-Indien*, this special printing includes an inset map featuring an enlargement of the Western peninsula of Seram and the island of Hoeamohel. By means of an engraved legend the map associates a number of locations with the history of the discovery and original cultivation of nutmeg and clove trees, which provided spices of immense value to the East India Company, for example:

A is het grote notenmuschaten bosch verdistrueert in November 1667
B mede een notenbosch by niboru met het voorsz. 3300 bomen alle verdistrueert
C Anno 1668 in may syn hier omtrent Massili by de 600 grote nagelbomen gevonden die nog in wesen zyn
D in Iuly 1668 gevonden omtrent 300 nagelbomen groot en klyn
by E en F syn ook eenige in do. maand gevonden dog wyd verspreyt alhier is t land overal styl en niet wel te beklimmen [...]

A The large nutmeg bush destroyed in November 1667
B With a nut bush near Niboru with the above mentioned 3300 trees all destroyed
C Here, around Massili, in May of the year 1668 some 600 large clove trees were found, which still exist
D In July 1668 some 300 large and small clove trees found
At E and F in the same month some more were found, but widely scattered – all around here the land is steep and not easy to climb

François Valentyn (1666–1727), a native of Dordrecht who spent much of his working life in the East Indies, first as a theologian and later as a geographer, devoted the latter part of his life to the production of *Oud en nieuw Oost-Indien*, which can also be found in the Fagel Library.[5] For almost two centuries this work was the standard reference text in Dutch for south east Asia, containing topographical maps and sea charts, town plans and descriptions of people and places.

5. *Platte Grondt van de Stad Miaco,*[6] *Zetel van den Geestelyken Erf-Keyzer van Japan*, na een Origineele Japansche Kaart van vyf en een halve voet lang, en vier voet breedt, onder den Ridder Hans Sloane berustende, in 't klein gebracht door J.G. Scheuchser [*sic*] (see plate 24)

   Johannes Gaspar Scheuchzer, Plan of the Imperial city of Kyoto ('s Gravenhage: Pierre Gosse and Jean Neaulme, c.1692), 42 x 27 cm
   Fagel Portfolio 19:053 (Abbott 1309)

A German national, Engelbert Kaempfer (1661–1716) took up a post as a doctor at the Dutch trading post at Nagasaki in 1690. Seventeenth-century Japan was almost completely closed to the outside world, save for the small Dutch colony comprising about two dozen merchants and their families on the outskirts of Nagasaki – the only Europeans permitted to live in the country, and then only at its westernmost extremity. This plan of the imperial city of Kyoto shows the Emperor's palace at the centre of a coloured town plan.

Kaempfer learned the language and travelled widely with a Japanese chaperone, collecting material on Japanese culture, society and geography for a book unpublished during his lifetime. After his death the manuscripts were acquired by Sir Hans Sloane, the wealthy London merchant and philanthropist after whom Sloane Square is named, who had the work translated into English and published as *The History of Japan* (London 1727). The subsequent French translation of this book is in the Fagel Collection.[7]

There are six coloured Kaempfer maps relating to Japan in the Fagel Atlas that are similar to the maps published in the *History of Japan*, but they are older, slightly larger and appear to have been a special, oversize edition of the

5 F. Valentyn, *Oud en nieuw Oost-Indien*, 8 vols, folio (Dordrecht and Amsterdam 1724–26), Fag. A.4.15–22.

6 The Dutch knew Kyoto as Miaco/Miako.

7 Engelbert Kaempfer, *Histoire naturelle, civile, et ecclésiastique de l'Empire du Japon*, 2 vols (La Haye 1729), Fag. U.6.19-20.

maps engraved as an undertaking separate from the publication of the general volume. Kaempfer's *History* was ultimately translated into Japanese, completing the journey of a work that had been originally intended to inform Europeans about Japan.

6. *Insulæ Canariæ, olim Fortunatæ Dictæ*, Amstelodami apud G. Valk et P. Schenk (see plate 25)

   Joan Blaeu, The Canary Islands (Amsterdam: Gerhard Valk and Petrus Schenk, 1662), 51 x 38 cm
   Fagel Portfolio 20:040 (Abbott 1366)

The Canary Islands were a major hub for commerce and shipping throughout the early modern period. Mount Teide on Tenerife is the highest point of all the islands in the Atlantic and was vital for navigation.

El Hierro, the westernmost island of the Canaries, was in common use as the prime meridian until the general adoption of the Greenwich meridian during the nineteenth century. The use of El Hierro to mark 0 degrees of latitude dates back to Ptolemaic geography, when the island was considered to be the westernmost point in the known world.

Following a decree by Louis XIII in 1632, the majority of engravers of early printed maps, including Blaeu and D'Anville, adopted the island as their standard meridian. The island was considered to be 20 degrees west of Paris, a calculation that caused some distortion of the rest of the world as it came to be mapped in more detail at the latter end of the Age of Exploration. Blaeu (1596–1673) only published this map as part of his *Atlas Major*.[8] As this example shows no evidence of having been originally bound it can be assumed that it was presented by Blaeu to the Fagels prior to their acquisition of the complete atlas.

7. *Plan de l'Isle de Gorée*, Gravé par F. Bailleul l'Ainé (see plate 26)

   Jacobus van der Schley, The Island of Gorée (Amsterdam 1772), 36 x 20 cm
   Fagel Portfolio 20:038 (Abbott 1364)

The island of Gorée lies off the coast of Sénégal, opposite Dakar, and was the largest slave trading centre on the African coast. It was first settled by the

8 Joannis Blaeu, *Geographia Blaviana* (Amsterdam 1662), Fag. Z.1.3, Plate 39.

Portuguese in 1444 and captured by the Dutch in 1588, who named it after the Dutch island of Goeree. The island fell into British hands in 1664 and then came under French control in 1667. Until 1960, when it became part of the newly independent Sénégal, the French ruled the island, with the exceptions of the periods 1758–63, when it was captured by the British during the Seven Years War, and 1779–83, when it was occupied by the British again.

This map thus dates from a time when the island was highly contested and shows fortifications and gun-battery placements in addition to the usual navigational aids of compass and soundings. It also details some of the infrastructure of the slave trade and can be viewed with a detailed map of the Slave Coast, also in the collection. The nature of the slave trade was of some concern to the Fagels, as evidenced by numerous volumes within the library containing arguments for and against emancipation.[9]

8. *Plan van het Geweese Fort Nassau en daar bij gestaan hebbende Stad Nieuw Amsterdam in de Colonie de Berbice* […], F. De Veije, P. Aelmans, 1764 (see plate 27)

   F.S. de Veije and P. Aelmans, Plan of the former Fort Nassau and the nearby town of New Amsterdam in the colony of Surinam (manuscript, 1764), 107 x 57 cm
   Fagel Portfolio 21:046 (Abbott 1423)

This manuscript plan of the Dutch Berbice colony, now in the Republic of Guyana, was drawn in 1764 in the aftermath of the Great Slave Uprising, February 1763 to February 1764. After an initial skirmish in late February 1763 and an offer of free passage from the colony, Dutch and English settlers were attacked by 600 African slaves and the plantations in the hinterland of New Amsterdam were abandoned by the colonists. They had hoped for help from Captain James Cook who was nearby on a separate trading mission, but Cook's only contribution was to load all of the valuables from the town onto his vessel and sail away. Disease and desertion prevented the local colonial

9 James Ramsay, *An Essay on the Treatment and Conversion of African Slaves in the British Sugar Colonies* (London 1784), Fag. B.5.5. no. 1, Fag. B.5.6. no. 1; [James Tobin] *Cursory Remarks upon the Reverend Mr. Ramsay's Essay on the Treatment* […] (London 1785), Fag. B.5.5. no. 2, Fag. B.5.6. no.2; *idem*, *A Short Rejoinder to the Rev. Mr. Ramsay's Reply* […] (London 1787), Fag. B.5.6. no. 3; Willem Bosman, *Nauwkeurige beschryving van de Guinese goud-tand- en slave-kust, met fyne kopere plaaten* (Utrecht 1704), Fag. B.6.48, Fag. H.11.12; William Snelgrave, *A New Account of Some Parts of Guinea, and the Slave Trade* (London 1734), Fag. B.8.28; *Copies of Several Acts for the Regulation of Slaves, Passed in the West India Islands* ([London] 1789), Fag. P.3.1.

administrator, Wolfert Simon van Hoggenheim, from putting down the rebellion and the colony remained under the control of the slave population until help arrived from the Netherlands in November, paid for by the directors of the Society of Berbice. The Slave Revolt is a key national symbol and central to the historiography of Guyana, which became a republic on 23 February 1970, the anniversary of the revolt. This plan shows the colony as the company wished to have it reconstructed in the aftermath of the revolt, with a strengthened fort and secured lodgings for slaves who were kept within the town's precincts (the *Neegerÿ*). The colony was abandoned in 1785 and a new settlement established downstream at Fort Sint Andries on the confluence of the Berbice and Canje rivers. This fort was subsequently renamed Fort Amsterdam but is otherwise unrelated to the settlement depicted on this manuscript.

The Fagels took a great interest in the development of the colony, publishing Anthony Blom, *Verhandeling van den Landbouw, in de colonie Suriname* (Amsterdam 1787).[10]

9. *Tabula Islandiæ* (see plate 28)

 Iceland, from Joan Blaeu, *Atlas Major* (Amsterdam 1662), 11 vols, vol. 1, plate 8, 51 x 38 cm
 Shelfmark: Fag. Z.1.22

This map was first published by Blaeu's father, Willem Janszoon Blaeu in 1645. The map is based on the work of Juris Carolus (c. 1566–c. 1636), a Dutch traveller who probably drew this version in the 1620s. The *Atlas Major* marks the beginning of the major acquisitions of the Fagel cartographical collection, contemporaneous with Johannes Jansson's four-volume atlas of town plans, *Theatrum urbium Italiæ, Galliæ, Germaniæque superioris et inferioris* (Amsterdam c. 1662, Fag. A.2.32-35) and Cellari's *Macrocosmica* (see plate 16), also engraved and coloured by Jannson. The major Dutch cartographical works of the late sixteenth century, those by Mercator, Ortelius and de Jode, are not present in the Fagel collection although it includes most of the major

10 Fag. H.10.8. For further reading on the Slave Rebellion see Marjoleine Kars, '"Cleansing the land": Dutch-Amerindian cooperation in the suppression of the 1763 Slave Rebellion in Berbice' in Wayne E. Lee (ed.), *Empires and Indigenes: Intercultural Alliance, Imperial Expansion, and Warfare in the Early Modern World*, Warfare and Culture Series 2 (New York 2011), pp. 251–76; J.J. Beyerman, 'De Nederlandsche kolonie Berbice in 1771', *Nieuwe West-Indische Gids*, 15 (1934), 313–7.

Dutch works *post* Blaeu. It is possible that the collection follows the fortunes of the Fagel family, a coloured atlas being then, as now, an expensive item.

10. *A Map of the British Empire in America with the French, Spanish, and Hollandish Settlements adjacent thereto* by Henry Popple. Printed at Amsterdam for I. Cóvens and C. Mortier (see plate 29).

    Henry Popple, Map of North America (Amsterdam: Johannes Cóvens and Cornelis Mortier, 1733), 59 x 50 cm
    Fagel Portfolio 22:008 (Abbott 1434)

Map showing the eastern part of North America, Central America and the northern part of South America. Cartographic elements include lines of latitude and longitude, sea banks, topographical details and a compass rose. The decorative cartouche includes a native American with an alligator, monkeys, maize and a scene of a harbour with goods being loaded onto ships. Four insets of Niagara Falls, Mexico City, Quebec City and New York City are at the top. At right are eighteen small insets of named harbours. Decorative elements include a scene of naval warfare, and the map is framed with a scale of latitude and longitude.

This map is state 1 of the key map for the twenty-sheet map of North America produced by Popple (d. 1734), which is also present in the Fagel Collection as a bound atlas. The plates can be arranged into a huge 240 x 230 cm wall map. It was the first map to show all thirteen British colonies in North America. The information in the map was based on Popple's work at the Board of Trade and Plantations in London, where he had access to estate maps created by landowners, although he appears to have relied heavily on de L'Isle's work for the region west of the Alleghenies.[11] The map and atlas were very popular and widely distributed, not least by the Board of Trade, which instructed that each of its offices should have one.

11 Guillaume de L'Isle, *Atlas* (Paris ?1718), Fag. L.1.14. This volume lacks a title page; a similar one in the Bibliothèque Nationale de France is catalogued as 1718.

LABORE ET CONSTANSIA

The place of Neo-Latin in the Fagel Collection

Jason Harris
UNIVERSITY COLLEGE CORK

THE FAGEL Collection has justly been characterized as a 'working library' and 'at least in part a reference library where the various *Greffiers* amassed the reference works they needed – sources mostly printed, sometimes manuscript, which were the tools of their office'.[1] Such judgements point towards the overwhelming preponderance of pamphlets, histories, collections of correspondence and geographical publications in the library. The present study is intended to supplement that account by focusing upon the number and character of Latin imprints in the collection, paying particular attention to those purchased in the latter half of the eighteenth century and to accounts of the education and reading of François Fagel the Younger. Jean-Paul Pittion has noted that the collection preserves a record of 'a major change already taking place in the eighteenth century: the emergence of English as the successful rival of French in the literary field', but to what extent does it map the decline of Latin?[2]

Latin

By the time the Fagel Collection was sold in 1802 the use of Latin as a language of communication among scholars and diplomats or as a language of preference among literary writers had long passed its zenith. Although Italy retained a high

1 Vincent Kinane, 'The Fagel Collection' in Peter Fox (ed.), *The Treasures of the Library, Trinity College Dublin* (Dublin 1986), pp. 158–69, here p. 165; Jean-Paul Pittion, 'The Fagel Collection', *Hermathena*, 121 (1976), 108–16, here 109.

2 Pittion, 'The Fagel Collection', 112.

proportion of printed books in Latin (roughly 50 per cent at the beginning of the eighteenth century), in the areas in which the Fagels bought most of their books the statistics speak overwhelmingly of the decline of Latin.[3] In Germany too, Latin was the language of roughly 50 per cent of imprints at the start of the eighteenth century but declined to less than 15 per cent by the end. In the Netherlands, Dutch imprints outnumbered Latin two to one in the first half of the century and six to one in the second half. In England already a century earlier Latin printing held only about 10 per cent of the market, and in France it was half that again.[4] Such figures may be misleading in that they do not take account of the size of print runs or the distinction between pamphlets and broadsheets on the one hand and multi-volume tomes on the other. Nevertheless, evidence of the print trade can be supported by the widespread, albeit uneven, decline in the religious, administrative and spoken use of Latin throughout Europe, as well as the broad-based attack upon the prestige of Latin as an elite language in an age of increasing democratization in the educational sphere.[5] While the Fagels were amassing their book collection, an enormous shift was taking place in the linguistic balance of Europe, in which development Latin was the main loser.

Reading through the auction catalogue of the Fagel Collection, one gains a rather different impression of the linguistic contours of the Fagels' world.[6] Latin holds a prominent position alongside French, English and Dutch, perhaps surpassing all of them. To some extent this may be an optical illusion, since an individual lot number may refer to many separate items, such as number 7593, which was estimated to contain 'upwards of 10,000 tracts'. Recent work on the pamphlet collection suggests a figure closer to 4500, of a total of some 6000, but a very large proportion of these would have been in Dutch, since they pertained to the history, politics and laws of the Dutch Republic (see p. xxi). Nevertheless, the presence of Latin in the Fagel library far exceeds its presence in the wider world of printing, particularly when one bears

3 Françoise Waquet, *Latin: or, The Empire of the Sign from the Sixteenth to the Twentieth Centuries*, trans. John Howe (London 2001), p. 82. As to where the Fagels bought their books, see Pittion, 'The Fagel Collection', 110, and Kinane, 'The Fagel Collection', p. 164.

4 For Germany, France and England, see Waquet, *Latin*, pp. 81–2; for the Netherlands, see Theo Hermans, 'Dutch tradition' in Mona Baker (ed.), *Routledge Encyclopedia of Translation Studies* (London 1998), p. 397.

5 The best overall account is Waquet, *Latin*. For a concise account see Nicholas Ostler, *Ad Infinitum: A Biography of Latin* (New York 2007), pp. 292–301.

6 Samuel Paterson, *Bibliotheca Fageliana. A Catalogue of the Valuable and Extensive Library of the Greffier Fagel, of the Hague* [...] (London 1802).

in mind that the great majority of the books in the collection were printed post 1650, and more particularly in the eighteenth century. A survey of the auction catalogue suggests that a conservative estimate would provide a figure of around 30 per cent for books printed primarily in Latin.[7] When one adds to this the large number of historical books containing lengthy extracts in Latin (which in some cases amount to more than half of the entire text) and the many other items in which Latin figures prominently as the language of aphorism, citation, commentary or reference, its presence in the collection looms larger still.

That this is so is owing to several factors. The upward social trajectory of the Fagels during the course of the seventeenth and eighteenth centuries is reflected in their acquisition and display of cultural capital to enhance and render conspicuous their increasingly elevated social standing. In addition, although French and English operated widely as the languages of diplomacy in this period, the well-educated diplomat was expected to be familiar with the Classics as a shared framework of reference, wit and allusion. Although many gentlemen who lacked classical learning relied rather on equestrian, military or natural philosophical interests to adorn their conversations, it is by no means surprising that a family that amassed a large library should have encompassed the Classics within it. Finally, the size and character of their library reflects intellectual encyclopedism – not merely indiscriminate purchasing of ephemera, but the desire to represent the universe of learning through preservation of all that was worth knowing. This prioritization of works of erudition, though not rigorously or exclusively pursued, naturally tended to give Latin greater prominence than it had in the wider public sphere.

François Fagel the Younger (1740–73)

The acquisition and display of cultural capital, both through book collecting and polite conversation, can be demonstrated in relation to several members of the Fagel family, but particular detail is available regarding the education of François the Younger. In 1768 David Ruhnkenius, who had recently succeeded Frans Hemsterhuis as professor of Greek in the University of Leiden, dedicated to François an edition of the grammarian Rutilius Lupus, in the preface to which he recounted having taught him Greek:

7 I have discounted books with Latin titles but vernacular text, books mostly in Greek but with the scholarly apparatus in Latin, and translations of Latin texts where the presence of the source language is not specifically indicated.

Veneras ad nos supra ætatem Latine doctus, Latinorum inprimis poetarum flagrantiore studio, quam quod expleri et satiari legendo posset. Verum cum patri tuo, cujus sapientiam in maximis reipublicæ caussis spectatam tanta exornat ingenuarum artium scientia, quantam vix credibile sit in vita tam occupata comparari potuisse; cum igitur patri tuo credidisses, vim et venustatem Virgilii, non nisi cognito Homero, Ciceronis, non nisi Demosthene, penitus percipi posse: nihil antiquius habuisti, quam ut Græcas literas conjungeres cum Latinis.[8]

You had come to us learned above your age in Latin, possessed in particular of a more burning love of the Latin poets than could by reading be sated or satisfied. But since you trusted your father, whose evident wisdom amid the greatest affairs of the state was furnished by such knowledge of the liberal arts as can scarcely be believed to be attainable in the midst of such a busy life – since, I say, you trusted your father who said that one could not fully grasp the force and beauty of Virgil if one did not know Homer, nor of Cicero if one did not know Demosthenes, you thought nothing more desirable than to conjoin Greek learning to your Latin.

This passage offers us a useful portrait of the linguistic accomplishments of both François and his father Hendrik the Elder (1706–90). On the one hand, the picture is conventional. It is a humanist commonplace that one requires knowledge of Greek literature to fully appreciate Latin, and in particular the pairings of Virgil and Homer, Cicero and Demosthenes, are often cited. On the other hand, Ruhnkenius's comments derive from the specific context of having taught François Greek and he continues to offer concrete details that lend verisimilitude to the account:

Itaque una legebamus ingeniorum principem, Homerum, eique, ut Atticam etiam elegantiam et suavitatem gustaremus, Xenophontem adjungebamus. Qua lectione confirmati non dubitamus ad grandem, et Homero in dispari genere similem poetam, Sophoclem, et dulcem subtilemque de scæna philosophum, Euripidem accedere. Tum vero, qualis in te materia et indoles esset, intelligere coepi. Nihil dicam de docilitate, qua intra biennium consecutus es hoc, ut, qua facilitate Cornelium et Racinium, eadem Sophoclem et Euripidem legeres. Majorem admirationem mihi

8 David Ruhnkenius, *P. Rutilii Lupi de figuris sententiarum et elocutionis libri duo* (Leiden 1768), p. iv. For details on Ruhnkenius see the biographies written by his former student Daniel Wyttenbach, *Vita Ruhnkenii* (Leiden 1799) and Friedrich Theodor Rink, *Tiberius Hemsterhuys und David Ruhnken: Biographischer Abriss ihres Lebens* (Königsberg 1801). Brief notes may also be found in Helgus Nikitinski (ed.), *David Ruhnkenius: Elogium Tiberii Hemsterhusii*, Bibliotheca Teubneriana (Munich 2006).

> *movebat vis judicandi, quæ in locis dubiis et obscuris cernebatur, inprimisque acerrimus pulcri et veri sensus, quo, sæpe magistrum præcurrens, ante latentes veneres deprehendebas, quam ipse earum demonstrandarum locum habuissem.*[9]
>
> And so together we read Homer, the prince of wits, and to him we added Xenophon so that we might taste Attic elegance and sweetness too. Emboldened by this reading, we were not afraid to approach Sophocles, that grand poet who is similar to Homer but in a different genre, and Euripides, the sweet and subtle philosopher of the stage. Then in truth I began to understand what kind of substance and character you possessed. I will say nothing of your readiness to learn, by means of which within two years you attained to this, that you could read Sophocles and Euripides with the same ease that you read Corneille and Racine. I was moved to greater admiration by the force of your judgement, which was evident when faced with doubtful or obscure passages, and especially by your extremely acute sense of beauty and truth, with which, running ahead of your teacher, you uncovered hidden charms before I had the chance to show them to you.

Setting aside the eulogistic commonplaces in this passage, one can see that Fagel is being described not merely as a gentleman who possesses a casual acquaintance with Greek as well as Latin literature, but rather as someone with considerable scholarly faculties. His discernment in dealing with philological problems is singled out for praise, as is his aesthetic judgement. These were key characteristics of a textual critic, not the accomplishments of an *homme d'affaires*. Nevertheless, Ruhnkenius proceeds to describe how, after completing his education in Greek, François embarked upon a Grand Tour in which he visited the more highly cultured parts of Europe (*cultiores Europæ partes*), but he closes with a final commonplace of humanist education to the effect that François was as much concerned about visiting libraries and meeting the learned as about dallying in the courts of princes: *Nec tamen frequentior eras in aulis, quam in bibliothecis, aut magis purpuratos, quam doctrina et ingenio claros, appetebas.*[10] (And you were not more often in courts than in libraries, nor did you prefer to meet princes than those renowned for learning and intellect.)

From this account we may derive a clue as to the provenance of some of the volumes in the Fagel library. Yet, before assessing the nature of the Latin collections it is worth examining the evidence offered by another close

9 Ruhnkenius, P. Rutilius Lupus, pp. iv–v.

10 *Ibid.*, p. vi.

friend of François Fagel, the renowned Greek scholar Frans Hemsterhuis, who was also a very good friend of Ruhnkenius.[11] Hemsterhuis dedicated his *Lettre sur l'homme et ses rapports* to François the year before the latter's death.[12] This treatise is an attempt to refute materialist and idealist philosophies that tend towards scepticism and to propose a sound basis for moral and epistemological reasoning. It was followed, after François's death, by the *Description philosophique du caractère de feu M.F. Fagel*, a short eulogy that presents an idealized portrait of the man, but includes some specific details as to his education and literary taste:

> *Pour ce qui regarde ses connoissances, il possédoit presque toutes les langues modernes, et en parloit plusieurs avec facilité. Pour les langues grecque et latine, il les sçavoit d'autant plus en grand maître, qu'il avoit une connoissance profonde du gouvernement, du caractere et des moeurs des anciens. Parmi les auteurs grecs, ceux dont il aimoit le plus la lecture étoient Homere, Théocrite, Aristophane et Xénophon. Entre les auteurs latins, c'étoit Horace, Pétrone et Tacite. Aristophane et Tacite ont eu peu de lecteurs comme lui.*[13]
>
> As regards intellectual attainments, he knew almost all the modern languages and spoke several of them with ease. As regards the Greek and Latin languages, he had a particularly great mastery of them because he had a profound knowledge of the government, character and customs of the ancients. Among Greek authors he most liked to read Homer, Theocritus, Aristophanes and Xenophon; among Latin authors it was Horace, Petronius and Tacitus. Aristophanes and Tacitus have had few readers like him.

Once again, in the midst of idealizations the reader is offered personal details. Like Ruhnkenius, Hemsterhuis suggests that François balanced Latin and Greek evenly; but he also provides a list of favourite authors, and then alludes to the specific quality of François's ability to read Aristophanes and Tacitus. It might be noted that these are authors who present acute philological problems, so that it may be that one is meant to infer from his taste something about his linguistic prowess. In addition, Hemsterhuis

11 On Hemsterhuis see H. Moenkemeyer, *François Hemsterhuis* (Boston 1975) and the older, more detailed biography by Leendert Brummel, *Frans Hemsterhuis: Een philosofenleven* (Haarlem 1925).

12 Frans Hemsterhuis, *Lettre sur l'homme et ses rapports* (Paris 1772).

13 Frans Hemsterhuis, 'Description philosophique du caractère de feu M. F. Fagel', *Journal encyclopédique ou universel*, 8: 2 (December, 1773), 329.

offers numerous remarks about the advantages that accrue from François's learning, not to mention his character as a whole: *Avec ses amis, ses discours étoient énergiques, profonds et instructifs par son immense lecture.*[14] (Among his friends, his conversation was energetic, profound and instructive because of his immense reading.)

Yet all his erudition, Hemsterhuis tells us, is not merely an end in itself, but serves a larger purpose: to comprehend man. One ought to be wary of accepting at face value this effort to make of Fagel an exemplar of Hemsterhuis's own philosophical enterprise; nevertheless, one can readily perceive why he dedicated to his friend his *Lettre sur l'homme et ses rapports*, which treats of this very subject. Accordingly, he sums up his friend's learning as follows:

> *Mais il rapporta tout à sa science favorite, qui étoit analogue à son état: c'étoit celle de l'origine, des moeurs, du caractère, des loix, des rapports, des facultés et des ressources des nations, qui a pour base la connoissance parfaite de l'homme et des hommes.*[15]
>
> But he brings everything back to his favourite area of knowledge, which had relevance to his own condition: this was the origin, customs, character, laws, interconnections, faculties and resources of nations, which has as its foundation the perfect knowledge of man and men.

One cannot, of course, simply assume that the educational philosophy of Hemsterhuis was shared by Fagel, to whom he dedicates it and by whom he exemplifies it, but it is not hard to imagine that the Latin elements of the Fagel Collection stem from this kind of cultural outlook. François Fagel does not appear to have been one of the major collectors in the family (perhaps because he died young) and not all of his relatives seem to have moved in elevated academic circles, but Ruhnkenius and Hemsterhuis both suggest that he derived his view of culture from his family, and their library attests to an impressive intellectual patrimony that can readily be viewed as encompassing all knowledge under the guidance of the contemporary notion that 'the proper study of mankind is man'.[16]

14 *Ibid.*, 330.

15 *Ibid.*, 329–30.

16 Pope, *An Essay on Man* (London 1733), 2: 2.

A learned family

The comments of both Hemsterhuis and Ruhnkenius point towards the fact that François Fagel was adept at philological analysis of the texts he read. Further evidence for his having an interest in such matters may be deduced from the fact that Ruhnkenius chose to dedicate to him an edition of Rutilius Lupus, a relatively obscure ancient grammarian, accompanied by extensive commentary, and editions of a couple of other short philological works of antiquity.[17] While philological training was necessarily a component of any serious classical education in the early-modern period, one might wonder at its pertinence in the library of a family of politicians. Yet François was not the only family member to have an interest in this subject, nor, given his early death, can much of the shape of the library collection be attributed to him. The kind of education that François acquired relied of necessity upon the support of a parent favourably disposed towards funding it, and the testimony of Ruhnkenius quoted above specifically attributes François's study of Greek to the influence of his father Hendrik Fagel the Elder. The library collection itself is manifestly the product of a family culture that was passed on from generation to generation, at least since the lifetime of the brothers Hendrik the Eldest (1617–90) and Gaspar (1634–88) who first brought the family to national and international prominence.

We may surmise something of the intellectual pedigree of Gaspar Fagel through the sale of some of his books, which is recorded in an auction catalogue printed in London early in 1690.[18] The catalogue also contains books from the libraries of Stephen Le Moyne and an unidentified 'learned person', without clear indication of provenance for individual items, so that it is not possible to be certain about which books belonged to Fagel. We are told in the preface written by the bookseller John Ballard that the anonymous learned person owned many 'excellent editions of the best Roman and Greek Authors, of the Editions of Aldus, Stephen, Elzevir, etc' and that several of Le Moyne's books are heavily annotated – the few that are noted in the catalogue are in the section on history and philology. Unfortunately, no remarks are made as to the character of Fagel's books,

17 See note 8.

18 *Bibliotheca instructissima, sive Catalogus librorum in omnigena literatura, præsertim vero antiqua Romana et Græca maxime insignium* (London 1690).

except that 'there are numbers of very choice Books'.[19] Nevertheless, the overall character of the collections is clear. There are 288 items categorized under theology, 294 under history and philology, 21 Delphinus editions of the Classics, 127 items classed as miscellaneous but with a heavy preponderance of Classics, 36 items classed as miscellaneous theology but actually mostly editions of pagan classical authors, and finally 176 items classed under medicine but including some studies of natural philosophy. There is a notable absence of books on law and comparatively little on contemporary history, politics or geography. Roughly 90 per cent of the items are in Latin or Greek. The great majority of books were printed in the 1670s and 1680s, though this is less the case for folios in all sections, and markedly less so for history and philology. The overwhelming majority of books devoted to the Classics were printed in Amsterdam, Leiden and Paris. The consistent character of the combined collection is striking and there is no reason to suppose that Fagel contributed an unrepresentative portion of it – indeed, had he done so one would expect it to have been adverted to in the preface.

What do we learn from this catalogue? Firstly, the sale of Gaspar Fagel's books upon his death suggests that he did not contribute much to the compilation of the Fagel Collection as we know it. Secondly, the intellectual character of the auctioned material is similar in many respects to that of the Fagel Collection. The most striking differences are the relative lack of vernacular material and of contemporary political matter. It may have been that these were sold at earlier auctions in the Netherlands, but it is also possible that ephemeral and foreign vernacular material was not regarded as being so well suited to the English market. Nevertheless, one may tentatively surmise from this catalogue that Gaspar Fagel received an intellectual formation through study of the Classics similar to that of his great-great-nephew François the Younger, yet the linguistic worlds that they inhabited were starkly different. A fall in the proportion of Latin and Greek books from roughly 90 to 30 per cent in the course of the century that separates the two auction catalogues underscores the fact that François's classical erudition was somewhat more *recherché* by contemporary standards than that of his distinguished ancestor.

19 *Ibid.*, preface 'To the Reader' (unpaginated).

Neo-Latin works in the Fagel Collection

The Neo-Latin holdings of the Fagel Collection may, for the sake of analysis, be divided into three classes: literary Latin, classical scholarship, and functional or professional Latin. I will say little here about the third class, which contains works written by theologians, doctors, lawyers and other scholars, with the principal aim of international scholarly communication rather than literary or linguistic felicity. Such are the works of writers who sought to express themselves in clear, grammatical and idiomatic Latin, perhaps with simple eloquence, but who did not aspire to impress greatly with their style. The distinction between these writers and those in the first category is a matter of judgement. For example, Richard Stanihurst's study of Irish history, *De rebus in Hibernia gestis*, is very clearly an exercise in writing Ciceronian Latin to the highest standard, whereas James Ware's study of Irish antiquities eschews rhetoric in favour of simple, lucid expression; the former was greatly admired for its style, the latter for its content.[20] Yet there are certain genres of Neo-Latin writing that by their very nature place in the foreground concerns with style; these include oratory, epistolography and poetry. All three genres are represented by separate sections in the sales catalogue.

Within the section on epistolography (lot numbers 2807 to 2920) can be found many Renaissance classics of the genre. The letters of Salutati, Bruni, Erasmus, Lipsius and Scaliger are all represented in collected editions, some with scholarly annotations.[21] These writers were used as models of style, but also consulted for the observations on classical texts with which they are bejewelled. The letter collections of several purist Ciceronians, such as Pietro Bembo and Christophorus Longolius, are included alongside those of such as Marc-Antoine Muret and Erycius Puteanus, who, in company with Lipsius, represent the development of a contrasting style characterized by esoteric vocabulary, abrupt expression and elliptical wit.[22] Those whose letters were read perhaps more for their erudition than for the form they took include William Camden, Hubert Languet and Hugo Grotius, although none of these three is lacking in eloquence, and early-modern notebooks (commonplace

20 Richard Stanihurst, *De rebus in Hibernia gestis* (Antwerp 1585); James Ware, *De Hibernia et antiquitatibus ejus disquisitiones*, 2nd edn (London 1658). See Harris, Thematic shelving, fig. 2.

21 *Bibliotheca Fageliana*, lots 2901–2 (Salutati), 2823 (Bruni), 2841 (Erasmus – see also 2717), 2862–4 (Lipsius) and 2904 (Scaliger).

22 *Ibid.*, lots 2818 (Bembo), 2865 (Longolius), 2882–5 (Muretus), and 2895–8 (Puteanus).

books) reveal the voracious appetite of readers for the well-turned phrase on any subject and from every available source.[23]

The preoccupation of readers with stylistic refinement can be observed at the opening of the epistolography section in the Fagel auction catalogue, where can be found a selection of guides to letter writing. It is not surprising to see here the two standard works on the topic, Erasmus's *De conscribendis epistolis* (lot number 2809) and Lipsius's *Epistolica institutio* (lot number 2810).[24] Erasmus's treatise decisively marked the break away from formalism in letter-writing, advocating a varied and spontaneous style appropriate to the subject matter; Lipsius emphasized to a still greater degree the conversational tone to be employed in letters, enlivened by vivid and fresh expression. Perhaps inevitably, prescriptive models were derived from both authors because of their use in educational contexts and despite their shared emphasis on variety and spontaneity of expression.[25]

The Fagels' collection of Neo-Latin treatises on epistolography is, however, not particularly extensive. Oporinus's Basel 1549 edition of the fifteenth-century Italian author Aurelio Lippo Brandolini's *De ratione scribendi* contains the important works of Erasmus, Juan Luis Vives and Conrad Celtes, but not the widely popular textbook of Georgius Macropedius, which was added to later editions, but is nowhere contained in the Fagel library.[26] Also present in the collection is the 1541 Basel printing of Vitruvius Roscius's *De commoda ac perfecta elocutione* and *De conficiendis epistolis isagogicon*, printed along with the inevitable Erasmus as well as Marinus Becichemus's *Epistolarum scribendarum ratio* and Georgius Valla's *De orthographia*, but the much more popular work of Christopher Hegendorf is not.[27] The sizeable Ciceronian manual of Andreas Diether, the *Thesaurus epistolarum contexendarum, formandæque linguæ ad imitationem Ciceronianæ dictionis locupletissimus*, contrasts with the slighter but more eclectic compendium of Simon Verepaeus, the *De epistolis latine*

23 *Ibid.*, lots 2829 (Camden), 2858–60 (Languet) and 2848 (Grotius). On commonplace books generally see Ann Moss, *Printed Commonplace-Books and the Structuring of Renaissance Thought* (Oxford 1996).

24 Desiderius Erasmus, *De conscribendis epistolis* (Amsterdam 1680); Justus Lipsius, *Epistolica institutio* (Frankfurt 1592).

25 See, in this regard, Judith Rice Henderson, 'Humanism and the Humanities: Erasmus's *Opus de conscribendis epistolis* in sixteenth-century schools' in Carol Poster and Linda C. Mitchell (eds), *Letter-Writing Manuals and Instruction from Antiquity to the Present* (Columbia 2007), pp. 141–77.

26 *Bibliotheca Fageliana*, lot 2807. Macropedius was added to the next Basel edition, having originally been published as Georgius Macropedius, *Epistolica* (Antwerp 1543).

27 *Ibid.*, lot 2812. Christoph Hegendorf, *Methodus epistolas conscribendi* (Hagenau 1526).

conscribendis.[28] It is striking that these are all sixteenth-century imprints, several from prestige publishers such as Oporinus and Plantin. While it is true that they were still current in the seventeenth and eighteenth centuries, it seems likely that this small and sporadic selection reflects more of an interest in book-collecting than in the precepts of letter-writing.

The oratory section in the catalogue is much less substantial and of rather different character. It consists mostly of eighteenth-century anthologies, particularly, though not exclusively, of Dutch orators. In part this may be a matter of cataloguing. For example, the influential orations of Muretus and Scaliger are listed under epistolography because they were printed along with the authors' collected correspondence. Similarly, the hugely important *Prolusiones academicæ* of Famianus Strada, which are oratorical in format, were listed among the works of philologists because of the nature of the matters treated in the orations.[29] In like manner, the orations and epistles of Angelo Poliziano were both included in the edition of his *Opera omnia* that is listed under the section in the catalogue for philological works.[30] Notwithstanding exceptions like these, the paucity of volumes devoted exclusively or even principally to Latin oratory is, no doubt, a reflection both of the interests of the Fagel family and of the fact that Latin oratory had little place in the political life of northern Europe in this period. This is in marked contrast to Latin letter-writing, for the epistolary holdings of the Fagel Collection might provide models for imitation, a stylistic repertoire, and a stock of anecdote with which to pepper polite conversation.

Among explicitly literary holdings one must include the short section of jokes and satires as well as the rather longer section devoted to modern Latin poets. The former contains a dozen items without coherence or any approximation to comprehensiveness. Elsewhere are found the *Facetiæ* of Poggio, Thomas More's ludic *Utopia*, and Erasmus's *Laus stultitiæ*, though Sebastian Brant's *Stultifera navis* takes pride of place here at the head of the list.[31] Neo-Latin poetry fares rather better, amounting to 58 lots, including several of the national anthologies so popular in the seventeenth century.[32] Some of the most celebrated writers are represented by complete collections of their verse: Girolamo Fracastoro, Jacopo Sannazaro, Janus Secundus, both Scaligers, George Buchanan, John

28 *Ibid.*, lots 2808 and 2811.

29 *Ibid.*, lot 2788.

30 *Ibid.*, lots 2775–6 (see plate 33).

31 While this work is part of lot 2998 in Paterson's catalogue, it was not assigned a shelfmark and is not in the collection today.

32 *Ibid.*, lots 2976–80.

Owen, Daniel Heinsius, Caspar Barlaeus and numerous others. If one were to supplement this list with those writers whose collected works are listed elsewhere in the catalogue, the resulting list would look rather more impressive, including the works of such eminent figures as Angelo Poliziano and Andrea Navagero.[33] Nevertheless, the list is not long enough to indicate sustained or far-reaching interest in the Latin poetic corpus of the early-modern period. Only in the vast anthologies edited by Janus Gruterus can one find the Latin verse of celebrated writers such as Baptista Mantuanus, Marco Girolamo Vida, Giovanni Pontano, Conrad Celtes, Ulrich von Hutten, Eobanus Hessus, Joannes Stigelius, Jean du Bellay, Janus Lernutius and Janus Dousa.[34] The poetry of Marullus, Balde, and Sarbievius, to mention only a few of the most eminent, is markedly absent. On the other hand, during the latter half of the eighteenth century purchase of Neo-Latin verse seems to have increased, notable acquisitions including the poetic works of the classical scholars Jan van Broekhuizen and Pieter Burman.[35]

Although the Neo-Latin literary holdings just discussed attest to the Fagels' rather fitful interest in contemporary Latin literature, particularly in comparison with their extensive collection of classical authors, their engagement with Neo-Latin linguistic and textual scholarship appears to have been more enduring. Their collection of critical editions of the works of ancient authors is filled with gems of Renaissance philological erudition that would reward sustained study in a manner beyond the scope of this short survey. The culture of Latin scholarship is also, however, represented in the 120 lots devoted to the works of those whom the auction catalogue describes as '*Philologi, Critici, Polygraphi*' (philologists, textual scholars, wide-ranging writers) – a description that conveys the difficulty of categorizing works that engage in multifarious ways with linguistic concerns that were at the heart of much early-modern scholarship. Perhaps the best designation for this section in modern scholarly terms would be 'cultural history'. Here one finds the works of Famianus Strada and Angelo Poliziano, both mentioned above, on philology, stylistics and textual interpretation.[36] Yet, also included in this section are the letters of Abelard and Heloise, the speculative historic-linguistic studies of Johannes Goropius Becanus, Guillaume Budé's treatise on dealing with the vicissitudes of

33 *Ibid.*, lot 2765 (Navagero).

34 Janus Gruterus, *Delitiæ CC. Italorum poetarum* (Frankfurt 1608); *idem*, *Delitiæ poetarum Gallorum* (Frankfurt 1609); *idem*, *Delitiæ poetarum Germanorum* (Frankfurt 1612); *idem*, *Delitiæ C. poetarum Belgicorum* (Frankfurt 1614).

35 *Bibliotheca Fageliana*, lots 2946 (Broekhuizen) and 2949 (Burman).

36 *Ibid.*, lot 2788 (Strada).

fortune, and Paolo Cortesio's series of literary biographies that encompasses the rise of Renaissance humanism itself.[37] The section is filled with the *adversaria* (notes), *opuscula* (short studies) and *opera omnia* (collected works) of the leading Latin writers of the age. While much of the material is erudite and often abstruse, in the early-modern republic of letters such things were depicted as entertainments for the well-cultivated mind. To some extent this reflects the topos of false modesty whereby scholars claimed (with increasing frequency towards the end of the early-modern period) that the product of their careful studies was in fact a thing of nothing, or the kind of thing a gentleman does in his spare time. While in many cases this was a fair description of their working schedule, the rhetoric belies the egos and agenda embedded in their labours. The title of Philipp Camerarius's tendentious Lutheran commentaries on current affairs and recent history, *Operæ horarum succisivarum, sive meditationes historicæ* ('Works of Leisure, or, Reflections on the Past'), captures well the tone of such disclaimers.[38] Yet amid biographies of ancient and modern writers or witty observations on contemporary *mores*, this section contains an impressive array of serious scholarly works by Poggio, Poliziano, Cardano, Erasmus, Lipsius, Scaliger, Vossius and numerous others. Whether or in what depth they were studied by the Fagels is impossible to tell, yet they represent a valuable repository of some of the best Neo-Latin literary and linguistic scholarship.

Deliciæ eruditorum

Among these works is found the multi-volume *magnum opus* of the Italian scholar Giovanni Lami, the *Deliciæ eruditorum*.[39] A vast miscellany of historical fragments and antiquarian notes, these tomes reflect much of the intellectual character of the Fagels' Neo-Latin collection. The notion that entertainment could be derived from meticulous philological scholarship of a scattered and arcane nature, and that such study could prompt reflections upon the present and provide jewels of anecdote with which to adorn polite conversation and elevate political considerations, lies, it seems to me, behind the enormous investment of several generations of the Fagel family in the purchase of Neo-Latin literature and scholarly works. The rhetoric of the early-modern period

37 *Ibid.*, lots 2686 (Abelard and Heloise), 2696 (Goropius Becanus), 2704 (Budé) and 2714 (Cortesius).

38 *Ibid.*, lot 2707.

39 *Ibid.*, lot 2747.

presented gentlemanly discourse and private reading as a mere diversion of polite society, but in fact it was woven into the fabric of such serious business as politics, diplomacy and religious polemic. How large a part it played in these affairs, and whether its contribution was diminishing in the same way that the production of Neo-Latin books was declining, is moot. The Fagels certainly devoted substantial resources to the acquisition of classical texts, works which aid in their interpretation, and books by those who sought to emulate them. Their intention was to purchase cultural capital as much as to amass a collection of books.

The Neo-Latin holdings of the Fagel Collection are wide-ranging but by no means comprehensive. This was not a scholar's library, but the delight of learned gentlemen. The purchase of serious philological works reflects the kind of education procured for François Fagel and the estimate of him offered by Ruhnkenius and Hemsterhuis. Cultural attainment was the child of classical learning, which in turn was the child of philological scholarship. Yet the engagement of most politically active learned gentlemen in such abstruse matters was necessarily fitful, circumstantial and no doubt often accidental. The Fagel Collection reflects a pattern of engagement along these lines, but it is exceptional for the depth and continuity of effort that was devoted to maintaining and developing its holdings. The Fagels appear to have reflected in many ways the cultural values and aspirations of their peers, but in this respect at least they outclassed the majority of them.

Italian literature and Humanist scholarship in the Fagel Collection

Clare E.L. Guest
TRINITY COLLEGE DUBLIN

THIS ARTICLE covers just one area of the Fagel Collection – that of holdings in Italian literature, focussing on Italian Humanist editions of classical poetry and Italian Renaissance poetry and poetics. This is a very simple outline and it must be emphasized that this area of the Fagel Collection is not one that permits us to build up speculations about intellectual or cultural motives for acquisition. Following the Italian collections themselves, this article will necessarily take the form of *disjecta membra*. To make it clear which of the books discussed are in the Fagel Collection, those volumes have their titles in bold text.

In terms of Trinity College Library holdings, Fagel can be compared with the other eighteenth-century collections that have rich resources in this area, namely those of Gilbert and Quin – collections that have quite distinct characteristics. The Quin Library is a small but highly select collection of rare copies of early continental printings in fine bindings, mainly in the area of classical and Italian literature, collected in the last decades of the eighteenth century by Henry George Quin (1760–1805).[1] The Vice-Provost and Regius

1 On Quin's library, see Veronica Morrow, 'Bibliotheca Quiniana' in Peter Fox (ed.), *Treasures of the Library, Trinity College Dublin* (Dublin 1986), pp.184–96; *idem*, 'Biblioteca Quiniana: A description of the books and bindings in the Quin Collection in the Library of Trinity College Dublin' (Unpublished Master's thesis, University College London 1970). Quin was the son of a successful Dublin doctor, Henry Quin, who took his doctorate in Padua; he was appointed King's Professor of the Practice of Physic at Trinity College and was repeatedly President of the King's and Queen's College of Physicians in Ireland. On his life and art collecting, see T. Percy C. Kirkpatrick, *Henry Quin, M.D., President and Fellow of the King and Queen's College of Physicians in Ireland: and King's Professor of the Practice of Physic (1718–1791)* (Dublin 1919); John Fleetwood, *History of Medicine in Ireland* (Dublin 1951), pp. 48; 135–6.

Professor of Divinity Claudius Gilbert (1669/70–1743) amassed a large library of 13,000 works in philosophy, theology and Humanist studies.[2]

In terms of the Fagel Collection, this area gives some idea of the interest in classical literature, in Humanistic scholarship and in canonical modern literature, as represented by the more famous Neo-Latin poets and vernacular classics such as Petrarch or Tasso. While the eighteenth century is often seen as a period of cultural decadence and stagnation in Italy, earlier Italian literature maintained an international status, as evinced by the numerous and often lavish editions of poets such as Tasso that appear in the period. There is a considerable body of eighteenth-century Italian scholarship on Renaissance literature, exemplified by the monumental *Storia della letteratura italiana* (Modena 1772–82) of Girolamo Tiraboschi (1731–94). The eighteenth century is also the period when we start to see a changing attitude to the Italian literary canon from abroad, most notably in the re-evaluation of Dante, whose growing international fame was assisted by the aesthetics developed in Burke's *Philosophical Enquiry into the Origin of our Ideas of the Sublime and the Beautiful* (London 1757).[3] Amongst attempts to present Italian literature to the English-speaking public is the three-volume history by the Irish peer Lord Charlemont, *An Essay towards a History of Italian Poetry* [...] *from Dante to Metastasio* (composed between c. 1785 and 1799), an enterprise that has been described as 'establishing the Italian canon for the English-speaking world as Dr Johnson and Thomas Wharton had done recently for English literature, with their respective *Lives of the Poets*

2 On Gilbert, see Robert Armstrong, 'Claudius Gilbert and his books' in W.E. Vaughan (ed), *The Old Library, Trinity College Dublin, 1712–2012* (Dublin 2013), pp. 112–21. I am grateful to Robert Armstrong for having generously allowed me to read a manuscript of his article.

3 Giuseppe Baretti's *Dissertation upon the Italian Poetry* (London 1753), written in response to Voltaire and French seventeenth-century critics such as Boileau, helped establish Dante's reputation. On the growing French eighteenth-century interest in *Inferno* and episodes such as Count Ugolino (*Inferno* 33), see Michael Pitwood, *Dante and the French Romantics* (Geneva 1985), pp. 35–40. In England the Count Ugolino episode is translated by the painter Jonathan Richardson in 1717; he also noted Milton's debt to Dante in *Explanatory Notes and Remarks on Milton's* Paradise Lost (London 1734). Reynolds' painting of Count Ugolino dates to 1773 and was linked to his reverence in old age for the anti-classical genius of Michelangelo. Pre-Romantic and Romantic images of Dante include inventions inspired by Dante (e.g. Fuseli) and illustrations, like those of Flaxman (1793, reissued 1807) and the watercolours that Blake carried out for John Linnell (1824–27). Gray's enthusiasm for Dante included the use of *Purgatorio* 7,5 as the inspiration for the opening lines of the 'Elegy Written in a Country Churchyard'; Joseph Wharton also praised him in *Essay on the Genius and Writings of Pope* (London 1756). The first complete, albeit loose translation of Dante was by the Irish vicar Henry Boyd in 1802, following the success of his Dublin 1785 translation of *Inferno*. The turning point of Dante's fortunes in England comes in 1810 with Cary's Dante translation, praised highly by Coleridge, and the subsequent wide and deep use of Dante by Byron and Shelley. For discussion of Dante's English reception in the eighteenth century, see Werner Paul Friedrich, *Dante's Fame Abroad 1350–1850: The Influence of Dante Alighieri on the Poets and Scholars of Spain, France, England, Germany, Switzerland and the United States* (Rome 1950), pp. 181ff.

(1779–81) and *History of English Literature* (1774–81)'.[4] If the role of Italy as a source of cultural inspiration in eighteenth-century Ireland were to be more thoroughly examined, Charlemont's *History* might be considered in relation to other manifestations of engagement with Italian high culture, such as the rare editions pursued by Quin.

The Italian Humanist holdings in the Fagel Collection

By contrast with Gilbert and Quin, the Fagels' holdings in this area appear quite sparse, especially when compared with their extensive collections of French and English literature.[5] This said, I should emphasize that I have not included the reprinting of Italian Humanist material in large, multi-volume antiquarian encyclopaedias, like Graevius' ***Thesaurus antiquitatum Romanarum*** (Leiden 1694–9) or ***Thesaurus antiquitatum et historiarum Italiæ*** (Leiden 1704–23), or the republication of minor critical or textual apparatus to classical texts by Italian Renaissance Humanists. It should also be reiterated that I am not treating areas of history (including church history), topography and political writings, where literature in Italian is more abundant. Later Italian literature is slightly better served, with four editions of the works of the eighteenth-century Venetian dramatist Goldoni. The Fagel Collection also includes a copy of the ***Rime*** (London 1717) of Paolo Rolli (1687–1765), who worked on the first Italian translation of *Paradise Lost* in the 1720s. As we shall see, this is not the only case of Anglo-Italian collaboration in the books of the collection. This narrow

4 George Talbot, *Lord Charlemont's History of Italian Poetry from Dante to Metastasio: A Critical Edition from the Autograph Manuscript*, 3 vols (Lampeter 2000), vol. 1, p. xxxiv. Talbot's is the only published edition of the work; a selection of Charlemont's translations of Petrarch's sonnets from the *Essay* appeared in a limited edition of twenty copies twenty-three years after his death in 1799 (*Select Sonnets of Petrarch*, Dublin 1822). The manuscript is held in the Royal Irish Academy, MS 12 R 2–4, its full title being 'An essay towards the history of Italian poetry, attempted in translated specimens of the noted classical poets from Dante to Metastasio'. The dating of the manuscript comes from Charlemont's allusion to a paper delivered to the Royal Irish Academy and printed in the Academy's *Transactions* in 1787; see Talbot, *Lord Charlemont*, vol. 1, p. xxxiii. In the year of his death, Charlemont was urged by the Italianist J.C. Walker to publish the work (Talbot, *Lord Charlemont*, vol. 1, p. xxii).

5 The section entitled 'Libri Italiani; Poesie e Mescolanze' covers just two pages of the sales catalogue, *Bibliotheca Fageliana. A Catalogue of the Valuable and Extensive Library of the Greffier Fagel, of the Hague* [...], digested by Sam[uel] Paterson (London 1802), pp. 136–7, nos. 3010–63. These pages do not cover Latin works, which appear in the preceding sections of the catalogue, 'Philologi, Critici, ac Polygraphi', 'Epistolæ clarorum Virorum' and 'Orationes clarorum Virorum', pp. 121–32. Researches on Fagel Collection material require one to check the sales catalogue against the Trinity College 1872 printed catalogue, which on occasion gives a Fagel shelf mark to material not in the collection, such as material published after its entry into TCD.

range of material limits what one can say and the inferences that can be made concerning the selection of material. Thus this article can only comment on where the Italian books in the Fagel Collection lie (or do not lie) and how they compare to the interests apparent in the richer Italian Humanist and Renaissance acquisitions of Gilbert and Quin.

The presence of Italian Humanists in the Fagel Collection does not lie so much in poetry or philology as in epistles, orations and histories. Discussion of the holdings in history (including translations or versions of ancient historians) and historiography must remain beyond the scope of this essay, as do occasional historical writings, such as funeral orations or political addresses. Thus the 'three crowns' of Italian poetry (Dante, Petrarch, Boccaccio) are covered by a mere six volumes, while the Humanists now studied for their literary interests are represented by their letters. Amongst these are the Florentine Chancellor, historian, translator and exemplary figure of 'civic Humanism' Leonardo Bruni, 1370–1444 (***Epistolæ***, Florence 1741; ***Epistolæ***, Hamburg 1724; ***Epistolæ***, Basel 1535; ***Historiarum Florentinarum libri XII***, Strasbourg 1610), or the Venetian linguist, editor, poet and proponent of Tuscan purism, Pietro Bembo, 1470–1547 (***Epistolæ***, Nuremberg 1703; ***Lettere***, Venice 1562; ***Rerum Venetarum historiæ libri XII***, Paris 1551). Other Humanist notables represented by their letters or orations include the Florentine poet and philologist Angelo Poliziano, 1454–94 (***Epistolæ***, Lyon 1528), the Neo-Latin poet Giannantonio Campano (1429–77), who formed part of the Roman academy of Pomponio Leto, 1428–97 (***Epistolæ ac poemata***, Leipzig 1707), the great jurist Andrea Alciati, 1492–1550 (***Epistolæ***, Leiden 1695 and 1708; ***Rerum patriæ seu historiæ Mediolanensis libri IV***, Milan 1625) and Giovanni Antonio Flaminio, 1464–1536 (***Epistolæ familiares***, Bologna 1744) – father of the better-known Neo-Latin poet Marcantonio Flaminio (1497/8–1550). The interest in epistolary literature continues into the works of eighteenth-century historians of earlier Italian literature, such as the ***Lettere*** (Venice 1752) of the Venetian bibliographer Apostolo Zeno (1669–1750) and his annotations to Giusto Fontanini's ***Biblioteca dell'eloquenza italiana*** (Venice 1753) and the ***Anecdota quæ ex Ambrosianæ bibliothecæ codicibus*** [...] (vols 1/2 Milan 1697, vols 3/4 Padua 1713) of the historian Ludovico Antonio Muratori (1672–1750), also represented by his ***Rerum italicarum scriptores ab anno æræ christianæ 500 ad annum 1500*** (Milan 1723–51) and his antiquarian works ***Antiquitates italicæ medii ævi*** (Milan 1738–42) and ***Novus thesaurus veterum inscriptionum***

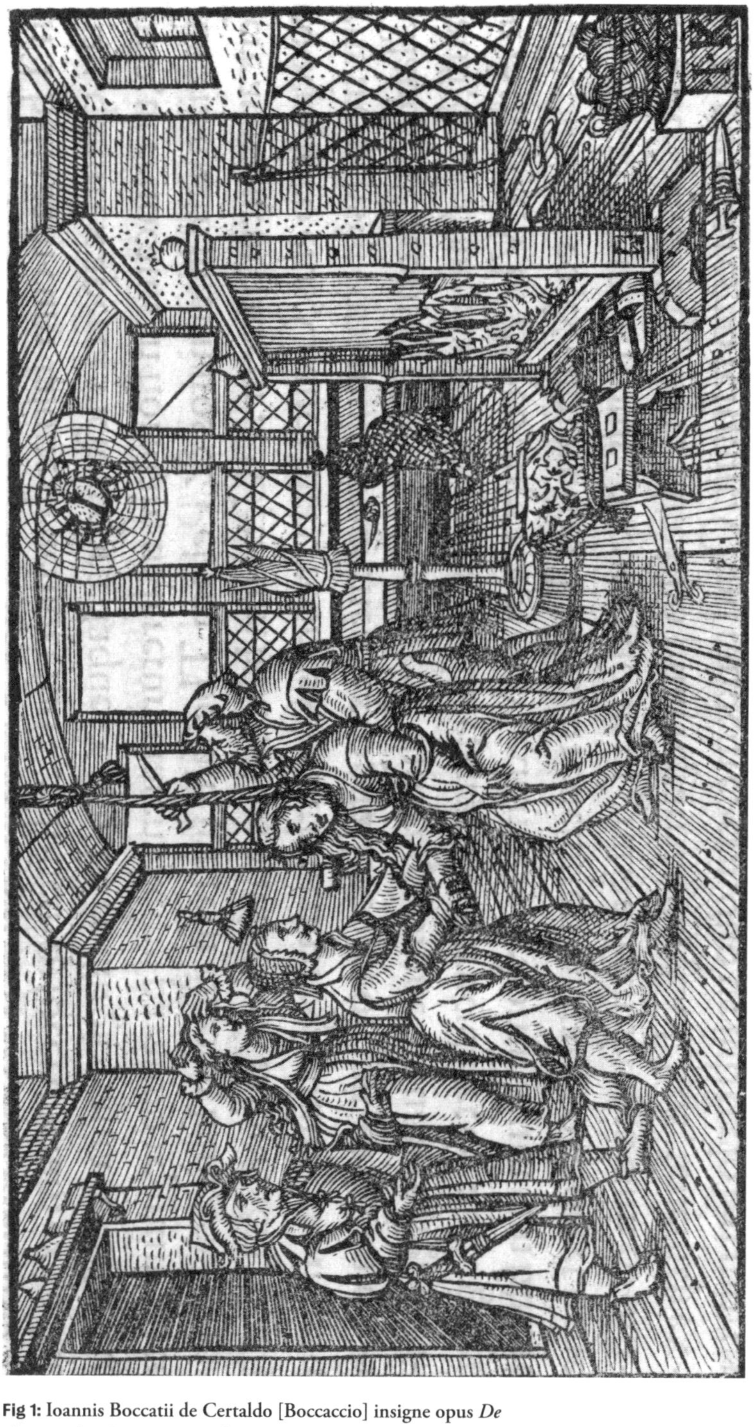

Fig 1: Ioannis Boccatii de Certaldo [Boccaccio] insigne opus *De claris mulieribus*, Bernæ Helveticæ: Mathias Apiarius, 1539 (fol. 12v): the woodcut that is attached to the chapter *De Arachne Colophonia muliere*. The same image, with the spider's web erased, is used on fol. 33r to illustrate the chapter *De Leæna meritrice*. (Fag. w.4.18)

(Milan 1739–40). Alongside histories and bibliographies of Italian literature is the famous vernacular lexicon, the ***Vocabulario degli Accademici della Crusca*** (Venice 1623).

This interest in biographical or anecdotal information concerning *viri illustres* is also evident in other choices of Humanist and Renaissance authors, such as Boccaccio's ***De casibus*** (Augsburg 1544) and ***De claris mulieribus*** (Bern 1539, Italian translation of Venice 1558) (see fig. 1), the ***De hominibus doctis*** (Florence 1734) of the fifteenth-century Humanist Paolo Cortesio (1465–1510) and in historical writings. The latter include the ***Vitæ summorum pontificum ad Sixtum IV*** (Nuremberg 1481) of the Vatican librarian Bartolomeo Platina (1421–81), the ***Commentarii*** (Frankfurt 1614) of Pius II, Aeneas Sylvius Piccolomini (1405–64), the ***Opera*** (Basel 1578) and ***Vitæ duodecim vicecomitum Mediolani principum*** (Paris 1549) of Paolo Giovio (1483–1552), and the ***Discorsi historici universali*** (Genoa 1582) of the Medici Humanist Cosimo Bartoli (1503–72). Other historians represented include Carlo Sigonio, 1524–84 (***Opera***, Milan 1732–7), the historian of Florence Scipione Ammirato, 1531–1601 (***Opere***, Florence 1637–42), and Paolo Sarpi (1552–1623), critical historian of the Council of Trent (***Opere***, Venice 1687), while the Italian author who features most prominently is Machiavelli.[6] Contemporary Italian political thought is represented by Cesare Beccaria (1738–94) and his seminal work in penology, ***Dei delitti*** (Paris 1780); earlier Italian political philosophy appears in the ***De institutione reipublicæ*** (Paris 1534) and ***De regno et regis institutione*** (Prato 1531) of Francesco Patrizi of Siena (1413–94), the ***Opuscula moralia et politica*** (Paris 1645) of Agostino Nifo (c. 1473–1538/1545), the ***De rei publicæ dignitate*** (Cremona 1556) of Marco Girolamo Vida (1485?–1566), and the ***Arcana politica*** (Leiden 1635) of Girolamo Cardano (1501–76).

This list of titles shows the Fagels selecting historical or political writings, rather than the most celebrated works of the authors in question. Nifo, for example, was most famed as a philosopher, especially for his writings on the immortality of the soul (*De immortalitate animæ*, Venice 1518), which refuted Pietro Pomponazzi's argument that the rational soul fails to survive the death of the material individual, while Vida's name is best remembered for his pedagogic treatise on poetics, which promoted adherence to Virgil as principal

6 The prominence of Machiavelli may have reflected his high standing as a model of Italian prose in Voltaire's *Essay on the Epick poetry of the European Nations* (composed in English 1727, rewritten French version 1733). The Fagel Collection contains a 29-volume edition of Voltaire's *Œuvres* (Amsterdam 1764).

literary model (*De arte poetica*, Rome 1527). Cardano is remembered chiefly as a doctor, mathematician (for his work on algebra) and natural philosopher who incurred ecclesiastical disapproval for casting Christ's natal horoscope. Similarly, while there are works by the literary theorist Giulio Cesare Scaligero (J.C. Scaliger, 1484–1558), his influential *Poetices libri septem* (Lyon 1561) does not appear – instead there are copies of his poem ***Epidorpides*** (Geneva 1573), two editions of his letters (Leiden 1600, Hanau 1603), his ***Adversus Erasmum*** (Toulouse 1623) and a miscellany entitled ***Electa Scaligerea: hoc est ejus sententiæ, præcepta etc.*** (Hanau 1634).

If we can form any interpretations on the basis of this short list, it does seem that the interest in Italian Humanism in the Fagel Collection is historical rather than literary. The Italian Humanists feature in the collections as political thinkers, historians or as notable men whose lives and correspondence were worthy of study for their detail or exemplarity. The major Italian holdings, however, appear in the areas of antiquarianism and history. The ample collections in these areas occupy more than half the Fagel catalogue (lots 4631–9634, including travel books) and are indicated by the sale cataloguer Paterson as the particular attraction of the library: 'Various antiquities – many very choice'. There is a representative selection of Italian sixteenth-century antiquarian scholarship on numismatics and topography, often in early editions, such as: the Roman antiquarian Fulvio Orsini (1529–1600): ***Illustrium imagines*** (Antwerp 1609), ***Imagines et elogia virorum illustrium*** (Rome 1570) and ***Familiæ Romanæ quæ reperiuntur in antiquis numismatibus*** (Rome 1577); Antonio Agustín (1516–86): ***Dialogo sopra le medaglie*** (Rome 1698); Agustín and Orsini: ***De Romanorum gentibus et familiis*** (Lyon 1592); Onofrio Panvinio (1529–68): ***Republicæ Romanæ commentariorum libri tres*** (Frankfurt 1597); Sebastiano Erizzo (1525–85): ***Sopra le medaglie de gli antichi*** (Venice 1559); Jacopo Strada (1507–88): ***Imagines imperatorum*** (Lyon 1553 and Regensburg 1557); Enea Vico (1523–67): ***Augustarum imagines*** (Venice 1558); Jacopo Lauro (1550–1605): ***Antiquæ urbis splendor*** (Rome 1612); and Girolamo Mercuriale (1530–1606): ***De arte gymnastica*** (Venice 1573), a groundbreaking study of ancient sports. Orsini's fine textual scholarship is also represented by the ***In omnia opera Ciceronis notæ*** (Antwerp 1581); Erizzo's ***Discorso dei governi civili*** appears with Bartolomeo Cavalcanti's ***Trattati overo discorsi sopra gli ottimi reggimenti delle republiche antiche e moderne*** (Venice 1571), in keeping with the Fagels' interest in political theory. Further publications by Panvinio include his work on Veronese antiquities, ***Antiquatum Veronensium libri octo*** (Padua 1648), his ***Effigies pontificum maximorum numero XXVIII*** (Strasbourg 1573) and ***Chronicon ecclesiasticum*** (Louvain 1573). The last two are early productions of the Christian archaeology that becomes a major antiquarian theme with the works of Baronius and Possevino in the late sixteenth century.

These authors include the noted antiquarians of sixteenth-century Italy, mostly associated with the papal Farnese family in Rome (Agustín, Orsini, Panvinio, Strada). French and Flemish antiquarians who studied Roman remains, such as Étienne Du Perac (1520–1607), Jean-Jacques Boissard (1528–1602) and Stephanus Vinander Pighius (1520–1604) are also represented. The ample antiquarian section contains much post-sixteenth-century material, such as the works of Bellori, Bartoli and Montfaucon and leads into a substantial historical literature, topographical and political, on Rome and on the other major Italian states – the Kingdoms of Naples–Sicily and of Piedmont–Sardinia, the Duchies of Tuscany and Milan and the Venetian and Genovese republics.

In keeping with the antiquarian interests, the sections on visual arts contain a fine selection of the major art treatises composed in sixteenth-century Italy: Giorgio Vasari (1511–74): ***Vite*** (Rome 1759–60); Pomponio Gaurico (1482–1530): ***De sculptura*** (Antwerp 1609); two editions of Leonardo's writings on painting (Paris 1651 and 1716); Ludovico Dolce (1508/10–68): ***Aretino*** (Florence 1735); Benvenuto Cellini (1500–71): ***Vita*** (Cologne 1740); Ascanio Condivi (1525–74): ***Vita di Michelangelo*** (Florence 1746); Andrea Palladio (1508–80): ***I quattro libri dell'architettura*** in French translation (The Hague 1726); the art treatises of Gian Paolo Lomazzo (1538–92): ***Trattato dell'arte della pittura*** (Milan 1584), ***Idea del tempio della pittura*** (Milan 1590), ***Della forma delle muse*** (Milan 1591); and Giovanni Battista Armenini (1530–1609): ***De' veri precetti della pittura*** (Ravenna 1587). The works of Lomazzo and Armenini are first editions.

The art literature extends into the seventeenth and early eighteenth century, with the ***Notizie de' professori*** (Florence 1702) of Filippo Baldinucci (1624–97) and a generous selection of the writings of Gian Pietro Bellori (1613–96): those concerning the art of his day – ***Vite*** (Rome 1672), ***Ritratti di alcuni celebri pittori del secolo XVII*** (Rome 1731) – his description of Raphael's works in the Vatican (Rome 1695) and numerous antiquarian studies. These include ***Fragmenta vestigii veteris Romæ ex lapidibus Farnesianis*** (Rome

1673); ***Veterum illustrium philosophorum, poetarum, rhetorum, et oratorum, imagines ex vetustis nummis, gemmis et alijsque antiquis monumentis desumptæ*** (Rome 1685); ***Veteres arcus Augustorum triumphis insignes ex reliquiis quæ Romæ adhuc supersunt*** (Rome 1690); and ***Adnotationes in XII priorum Cæsarum numismata ab Ænea Vico edita*** (Rome 1730). Bellori's works with the artist and engraver Pietro Santi Bartoli (1635–1700) are also represented: ***Admiranda Romanarum antiquatum ac veteris sculpturæ vestigia*** (Rome 1693), ***Columna Antoniana*** (Rome *s.a.*) and the vernacular version ***La Colonna Triana*** (Rome *s.a.*); ***Picturæ antiquæ cryptarum Romanarum et sepulcri Nasonum*** (Rome 1738) and ***Le pitture antiche del sepolcro de Nasonii nella Via Flaminia*** (Rome 1680). The most precious of Bartoli's works in the Fagel Collection is the ***Recueil de peintures antiques*** (Paris 1757), one of only thirty copies printed, and with hand-coloured illustrations showing frescoes from ancient tombs (see plate 31). The antiquarian writings of Athanasius Kircher (1601/02–80), the polymath Jesuit of the Collegium Romanum, and a major figure in seventeenth-century Roman artistic and intellectual life, are likewise well represented: ***Obeliscus Pamphilius*** (Rome 1650), ***Obelisci Ægyptiaci*** (Rome 1653), plus three works on his museum: ***Romani Collegii Societatis Jesu museum*** (Amsterdam 1678), ***Musei Kirkeriani*** [*sic*] ***in Romano Societatis Jesu Collegio ærea notis illustrata*** (Rome 1763–5) and ***Musæum Kircherianum*** (Rome 1709). The collection contains further works by the prolific Kircher, on Egyptology, technology, universal music, combinatory logic, volcanology, Sinology, Biblical chronology and geology, which lie beyond the scope of this article. Particularly notable is the lavishly illustrated edition of Kircher's geological work ***Mundus subterraneus***, bound by Albert Magnus (Amsterdam 1678 – see plate 30).[7] This area of the library also includes the two most successful works of Renaissance iconography, Alciati's ***Emblemata CCXI*** (Frankfurt 1567) and the ***Iconologia*** (Paris 1644) of Cesare Ripa (c. 1560–c. 1622). Thus while the Fagel Collection contains a fair selection of sixteenth-century artistic literature, it becomes much richer as we pass into the seventeenth- and eighteenth-century reprintings. This Baroque artistic literature concerns both ancient and High Renaissance art, especially the work of Raphael; amongst Bartoli's works in the collection is his publication on the Sala di Costantino in the Vatican, decorated by Raphael's atelier, notably by his pupil Giulio Romano (1492/99–1546): ***Monocromata, in***

7 See Kinane, 'The Fagel Collection' in Fox, *Treasures of the Library*, pp. 158–69, here p. 168.

Constantiana Vaticani aula, ab artifice summo Julio Pippio Romano (Rome, *s.a.*). Bartoli's engravings of Giulio Romano's Sala di Costantino decorations also appear in ***Imagines Constantini pietatem designantes; a P.S. Bartolo insculptæ*** (Rome, *s.a.*).

Thus the Italian material lies principally in history, topography, antiquarianism and literature on fine art, less in philological scholarship and barely at all in mathematics, philosophy and theology – although there is a copy of the ***Opera*** (Basel 1557; also vol. 2 of the Basel 1573 edition) of Giovanni Pico della Mirandola (1463–94), and of his letters in the edition of Christopher Cellarius (Zeitz 1682). At first glance we do indeed see the eclipse of Italy's cultural achievement, with its significance restricted to the past and in particular to material culture or remains. Thus we can say that there was not a policy of collecting early editions of the Italian Humanists, in a period when such collection was interesting to other bibliophiles, as we can see in the libraries of Gilbert and Quin. One notable exception is the glorious illuminated edition of Plutarch's ***Vitæ*** (Nicolas Jenson, Venice 1478), justly described by Paterson as 'a most beautiful and matchless copy' (see plate 32).[8]

The Fagel collections in classical philology date generally from the mid sixteenth century, thus neglecting previous scholarship. Vincent Kinane remarked: 'The coverage in the Classics section is comprehensive, encompassing the seventeenth-century Leiden editions of the Elzevirs through to the eighteenth-century Glasgow editions of the Foulis press.'[9] The collection is 'comprehensive' only if one overlooks the foundational work of the fifteenth- and sixteenth-century philologists. The holdings in classical literature consist, as Kinane observed, mainly of seventeenth- and eighteenth-century editions, with the work of the French and Dutch philologists such as Henricus Stephanus who take over classical scholarship from the Italians from the mid sixteenth century. Where Italian material does appear, it is in the variorum editions of the seventeenth and earlier eighteenth century, compiled by Dutch editors such as Dousa, Heinsius and Burmann, who include fifteenth-century Italian scholarship by figures associated with the early stages of Humanist textual scholarship, such as Domizio Calderini (1446–78), Antonio Mancinelli (1452–1505) and Girolamo Avanzi (c. 1460–post 1534),

8 On the Plutarch, see Lilian Armstrong, 'The Agostini Plutarch: An illuminated Venetian incunable' in Fox, *Treasures of the Library*, pp. 86–96.

9 Kinane, 'The Fagel Collection', p. 165.

who prepared the first Aldine editions of Catullus and Lucretius.[10] Of earlier editions of ancient poets and theorists commented by Italian Humanists, I have found to date just four works – a 1555 Basel reprint of the 1548 Latin ***Paraphrasis*** by Francesco Robortello (1516–67) on Horace's *Ars poetica* and his ***Explicationes*** of Aristotle's *Poetics* (the first full-length modern commentary) and three editions from the press of the Parisian editor Badius Ascensius of Horace, ***Opera*** (1529), bound with a commented edition of Persius' ***Satyræ*** (1523), and finally Virgil, ***Opera*** (1529) printed by Ambrose Girault.[11]

Excepting the area of material remains, the Fagel Collection seems to reflect the established early modern world rather than the genesis of that world with Italian Humanism – possibly reflecting the concerns of a family active in public life. It seems safe to say that there is no evidence of a bibliophilic pursuit of early Humanist texts as examples of book or printing history (e.g. incunable, early Greek printing, *editio princeps* established by a famous scholar). The character of the collection becomes defined by comparison with the acquisitions of the bibliophile Quin or a scholar like Gilbert, both of whom pursued early editions of classical literature assiduously. Gilbert's large collection of incunables and Quin's pursuit of valuable books, both in terms of text and binding, show them acquiring early Italian printings as rare books but also with an interest in creating something like a history of scholarship. Gilbert amassed a large collection of early editions of the major figures of the classical canon and shows interest in early commentary, as he buys commentaries without accompanying texts, such as the 1583 edition of the commentary on Pindar by Francesco Porto (1511–81). This suggests an interest in the development of literary criticism, as well as acquisition of early editions.

10 Calderini's printed works include commentaries on Martial (often reprinted), plus polemics over the readings of rival commentators Perotti and Merula, on Ovid's *Ibis* and *Letter of Sappho*, on Juvenal, on Statius' *Silvæ*, on pseudo-Quintilian's *Declamationes maiores*, Ptolemy's *Cosmographia*, the *Appendix Virgiliana*, plus a partial commentary on Pausanias. Despite the longevity of Calderini's works, he was heavily criticized by the Pliny scholar Hermolao Barbaro, by Antonius Codrus Urcaeus, and repeatedly by Poliziano. Avanzi was a Veronese Humanist who edited texts for Aldus Manutius. Antonio Mancinelli commented on Juvenal and on the *Rhetorica ad Herennium*, and produced an epitome and other critical or introductory works to Lorenzo Valla's *Elegantiæ linguæ latinæ*, plus a series of works on grammar and rhetoric; his commentaries on Virgil and Horace were frequently reprinted, as were his grammatical writings.

11 The Horace edition contains ancient glosses by Pseudo-Acro and Porphyrio, Renaissance commentaries by Antonio Mancinelli and Badius and annotations corrected by Matteo Bonfini and Aldus Manutius. The Virgil contains the ancient commentaries of Servius, Donatus and Probus, plus those of Mancinelli, corrections by Pierio Valeriano (author of the *Hieroglyphica*), an exposition by Badius and remarks by Cristoforo Landino and Filippo Beroaldo.It also contains lively illustrations, reprinted from the 1502 Strasbourg edition of Sebastian Brant.

Quin's collections are most noted for their bindings, luxurious production or celebrity provenance, but he also pursued editions for their scholarly standing, such as the rare and prized Aldine Virgil (Venice 1514), with the text corrected by Andrea Navagero, or the 1473 Parma commentary published by Portilia on Petrarch's *Triumphs* of which there are only fifty copies extant today.[12]

In the Fagel Collection we do not see a comparable pursuit of early editions or publishers – there is nothing to suggest an interest in famous early printers, such as Aldus or Giunta, as late editions and reprintings of international editions of Italian authors are purchased, such as a Basel 1581 reprint of Henricus Petrus' two-volume edition of Petrarch's ***Opera*** (Basel 1554) or a Florence 1578 reprint of Dante's ***Commedia*** with the commentaries of Landino (1480) and Alessandro Vellutello (1544). Amongst these later editions is the single book notable for its binding in this area of the Fagel Collection.

This is the two-volume octavo ***Opera*** of Poliziano, printed in 1546 in Lyon by the German printer Sebastian Gryphius, who established a successful business there, printed Erasmus and Dolet, and was friends with Alciati and the French Humanists Aneau and Scève.[13] It is one of two Poliziano *Opera* in the Fagel Collection, the other being an elegant edition printed in Basel in 1553 by Nicolaus Episcopius (Bischoff) junior, the nephew of the printer Froben's son-in-law and collaborator. The Gryphius two-volume octavo *Opera* has a rare stamped panel binding showing the theological virtues (see plate 33). The stamp shows a female figure in classical dress with arms crossed, gazing at the heavens where a cross appears amongst the clouds in the upper left corner. She stands on a square pedestal named *Fides*; behind her are *Charitas* and *Spes*. The words *Meritum Christi* appear beside the cross. To the left of the figure are stamped the words from Psalm 70 *In te domine speravi: non confundar in ęternum, in iustitia tua libera me et eripe me*. In the border of the image lines from Psalm 90 are stamped, with each word separated from

12 The 1514 Aldine version is also noted because in the dedication to Pietro Bembo Aldus mentions the library of Bernardo Bembo (father of Pietro) as an inspiration for the octavo format. The anonymous Portilia commentary, with a misleading distich that ascribes it to Francesco Filelfo, is based on transmitted manuscript glosses on Petrarch's *Triumphs*, corrected and expanded. The Portilia commentary was the first printed commentary on Petrarch's poetry to appear, predating the commentaries of Filelfo on the *Canzoniere* (Bologna 1476) and Bernardo Ilicino's commentary on the *Triumphs* (Bologna 1475).

13 The front pages of both volumes show traces of varied provenance. In the upper right margin *me possidet Anno 1700* appears following an erased name; thus the book entered the Fagel library after that date.

the next by an asterisk: *Quoniam in/ me speravit liberabo/ eum, proteg/ am eum quoque*. The monogram that appears in the bottom left corner is that of Jacob Bathen, the Louvain bookbinder, bookseller and publisher. These so-called 'Spes' panels were used by Bathen and the binder I.P., possibly Jacob Pandelaert.[14] They were introduced in the 1520s and reach their peak between c. 1530 and 1550; they appear with and without the virtue *Charitas*, a variant that has been regarded as a reflection of confessional differences.[15] Thus it has been surmised that the bindings without *Charitas* were produced for a Protestant market, as an attempt to promote Lutheranism in Louvain, or – more cautiously – as simply catering to a market. The panels without *Charitas* cease to appear after 1542, possibly in response to censorship.

The two mid sixteenth century editions of Poliziano suggest some interest in Neo-Latin Renaissance literature in the Fagel holdings, even if one edition may have been purchased for the binding.[16] This interest is also suggested by eighteenth-century editions of some of the most highly regarded Neo-Latin poets: the Neapolitan Jacopo Sannazaro, 1458–1530 (***Opera***, Amsterdam 1728), who created the marine eclogue and wrote *Arcadia*, the prototype of the vernacular pastoral; Andrea Navagero or Naugerius, 1483–1529 (***Opera omnia***, Padua 1718), a scholar, poet and diplomat in the circle of Flaminio, Castiglione and Raphael, remembered as a master of Latin pastoral lyrics he termed *lusus*; and Girolamo Fracastoro, 1478–1553 (***Poemata omnia***, Padua 1718), natural philosopher and physician, best known for his study of infection and the first

14 It has been argued that the Bathen panel is based on that designed by I.P. For discussion of this and the other Spes panels, see Staffan Fogelmark, *Flemish and Related Panel-Stamped Bindings* (New York 1990), pp. 135–7 and 157–69; Mirjam Foot, *The Decorated Bindings in Marsh's Library, Dublin* (Aldershot 2004), pp. 114–5. Fogelmark devotes considerable attention to the I.P. panel, taking it as the example in his discussion of flaws and reproducing it as the image on the title page of the work. He discusses other stamped panel bindings in the collection of Trinity College Library and reproduces an identical I.B. (Jacob Bathen) binding in the Chester Beatty Library, Binding no. 392 (Fogelmark, Pl. xlii, R. 109).

15 Prosper Verheyden, 'La reliure en Brabant' in *Le livre, l'estampe, l'édition en Brabant du XVe au XVIe siècle. Mémorial de l'exposition d'art ancien à Bruxelles* (Gembloux 1935), p. 177, cited in Fogelmark, *Bindings*, pp. 157–9; Nathalie Coilly, 'Une plaque "Spes" à la Bibliothèque de l'Arsenal: l'acte de foi du relieur luthérien Jacob Bathen', *Bulletin du bibliophile* (2000), 416–8. Fogelmark, *op. cit.*, p. 159, also notes that the I.P. Spes panel was sometimes combined with the binder's panel showing Lucretia, an exemplar of virtuous pagan despair. See also E.P. Goldschmidt, *Gothic and Renaissance Bookbindings, Exemplified and Illustrated from the Author's Collection* (London 1928); H.M. Nixon, *Twelve Books from the Library of J. Hely Hutchinson* (Oxford 1953); Jane Greenfield, 'Notable bindings, pt. 13', *Yale University Library Gazette*, 70 (1995–6), 170–73.

16 The Fagel Collection also contains the 1608 Frankfurt anthology ***Delitiæ CC italorum poetarum***. This is part of a series with companion volumes for France, the Low Countries and Germany, so it cannot be taken to show particular interest in Italian writers.

detailed account of the pathology and treatment of syphilis.[17] The last two poets are linked by Fracastoro's celebrated dialogue on poetics, entitled *Naugerius*, in praise of Navagero, who appears as the principal speaker of the dialogue.

The works of Fracastoro and Navagero in the Fagel Collection are in the editions of the scholarly Paduan press of Giuseppe Comino, set up in 1717 by the Paduan philosopher and literature professor Giannantonio Volpi (1686–1766) and his bibliophile brother Gaetano.[18] The quality of scholarship and textual editing means that the Volpi–Cominiana press is regarded as one of the most prestigious publishing ventures in eighteenth-century Italy. The editions of Fracastoro and Navagero are valuable philological works, which contain an anthology of poems dedicated to the respective authors – the Fracastoro edition reconstructs the Veronese poetic milieu of Fracastoro's day, the Navagero edition includes material relating to Navagero's textual scholarship, poems and letters addressed to him and translations of his Latin poetry, plus Fracastoro's *Naugerius*.[19] The Fagel Collection also has another work edited by Volpi, a 1710 edition of **Catullus** – another Veronese poet – possibly a reflection of the extensive study of Veronese history, culture and manuscripts carried out in the early decades of the eighteenth century by the Arcadian academician Scipione Maffei (1675–1755). Maffei's ***Verona illustrata*** indeed appears in the collection in two copies of the edition Verona 1732 and one of Verona 1771. The Volpi–Cominiana Petrarch *Rime* (Padua 1732), in the Quin Collection, shows similarly high standards of scholarship, with careful collation of manuscript sources and early editions plus slightly more anecdotal material, such as the epitaphs composed on the supposed 'tomb of Laura'. Quin did not purchase this book just because it was printed on turquoise paper – he was a collector of good editions, as other parts of his library show.

When we turn from Italian Neo-Latin to Italian vernacular poetry we find the Fagel Collection is indeed thin: two editions of Tasso's ***Gerusalemme liberata*** (Paris 1644 and Venice 1745) (see fig. 2), more notable for lavish

17 The disease took its name from Fracastoro's Neo-Latin poem *Syphilis*, 1530, the mythological third book of which described the shepherd Syphilis, afflicted with venereal disease for blasphemy to the sun god; the poem was praised lavishly by contemporaries as a masterpiece of Neo-Latin prosody.

18 The Volpi–Cominiana press produced more than 200 works from 1717 to 1756. The editions were eagerly sought after the press was sold in 1758. Gaetano Volpi provided a chronological and alphabetical catalogue of the press in *La libreria de Volpi: e la stamperia Cominiana; illustrate con utili e curiose annotazioni* (Padua 1756). For an overview of the Volpi–Cominiana press see the entry of Lorenzo Baldacchini in *Dizionario biografico degli italiani*, vol. 27 (Rome 1982), *s.v.* Comino, Giuseppe.

19 The Navagero edition was the first on which Comino collaborated with the Volpi brothers.

Plate 15: John Johnstone, *Historia naturalis*, two vols, Frankfurt am Main: Heredum Math. Meriani, 1650–3: title-page preceding the last two sections in vol. 2, *De insectis. De serpentibus et draconibus.* (Fag. M.4.52)

PLANISPHÆRIVM
Sive
ORBIVM MVNDI
PTOLEMA=
NODI=
SEV CAPRICORNVS
TICA AQVARIVS
ECLIP PISCES
ARIES
TAVRVS
GEMINI
VIA
IOVIS
ORBITA
SEPT
CIRCVLVS
PLA NE
MVNDVS SVBLVNARIS QVATVOR ELE
ITER MER
VENERIS
CVRRICVLVM
ORBE
SATVRNI

Plate 16: Andreas Cellarius, *Harmonia macrocosmica, seu Atlas universalis*, Amsterdam: Joannes Janssonius, 1661 (plate 1): Planisphærium Ptolemaicum. (Fag. A.2.36)

Plate 17: Maria Sybilla Meriaen [German form: Maria Sibylla Merian], *Over de voortteeling en wonderbaerlÿke veranderingen der Surinaemsche insecten*; second title-page: *Metamorphosis insectorum Surinamensium*, Amsterdam: Joannes Oosterwÿk, 1719 (plate 23): an atlas moth resting on a species of banana (*musa serapionis*). In some plates, as here, Merian's standard representation of the life cycle of a butterfly or moth along with a botanical specimen is supplemented by a reptile. (Fag. GG.2.10)

Plate 18: The 'Fagel Missal' (fol. 10v): St Augustine and St Agnes. (TCD MS 81)

Plate 19: 'Dagh Register gehouden op de voiagie gedaen naer der Amacqua [*sic*] Land onder 't beleÿdt van den E. Heer Sÿmon van der Stel. Commander van Caap de Goede Hoop' [first entry: 25 August 1685] (fol. 63r): Meerkat, described on 64r as 'sweet and friendly'. (TCD MS 984)

Plate 20: Nicolaes Witsen, *Nieuwe Lantkaarte van het Noorder en Ooster deel van Asia en Europe*, Amsterdam 1687 (detail showing the Seven Brothers rock formation located in the Urals, the so-called *Cingulum orbis* – girdle of the world – the Riphean mountains and the river Barantsa). (Fagel Portfolio 1:054)

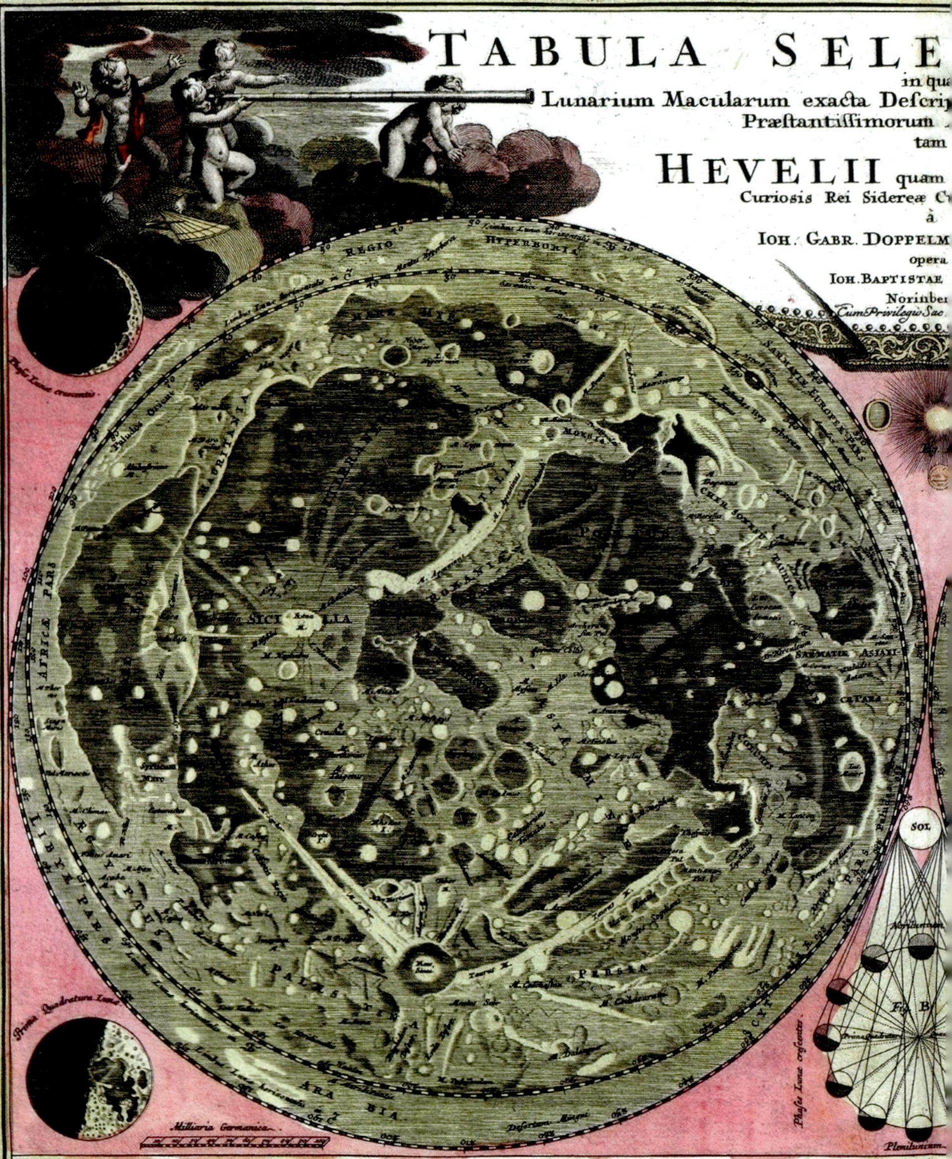

Nullum inter corpora cælestia, ex quo tempore Veteres sacræ Uraniæ addicti omne moverunt lapidem, ut Siderum naturæ et affectiones quam maxime forent in aprico positæ, cunctorum vicit magis admirationem, et multiformi ambage (si cum Plinio loqui liceat) torsit contemplantium ingenia, proximum quippe ignorari sidus indignantium, quam ipsa Luna, varietate macularum imprimis miranda; sed nec mirari nos subeat, cum mediis tunc destituti, quibus nunc Lunam accuratius inspicere et contemplari nobis hodie datum, oculis scilicet armatis; hinc etiam deficiente hoc Tuborum opticorum apparatu diversas de Lunæ substantia è maculis nudo oculo visis fovere opiniones non potuere non Antiqui illi rei sidereæ Cultores; alii enim cum Cleardo et Argesinace maculas Lunares nostri Oceani imaginem in Luna tanquam in speculo conspicuam esse, alii hasce è certis corporibus, quæ Solem inter et Lunam jaceant originem ducere existimarunt; alii Lunam vitream, non quidem exacte pellucidam, sed ex parte opacam; alii partim igneam, partim opacam putarunt; et quæ sunt multæ aliæ de corporis Lunaris substantia sententiæ.

At multo feliciori successu omnium primus celeberrimus ille Florentinorum Mathematicus Galilæus de Galilæis anno superioris seculi decimo, quo utilissimum Tuborum opticorum inventum luci publicæ traditum, id negotium tentavit, quod dein Scheinerus et alii satis superq; dedere probatum, imò plures hodie Tubis prædictis ad majorem perfectionem nunc perductis, rem acu, quod ajunt, multo felicius tangere videntur, si pro indubio asserunt, quod Luna innumeris scateat montibus, qui nostros altitudine, habito respectu globi Lunaris ad nostrum, sexagies ferè minoris, superent; porro quod eædem profunditates, quæ prægrandibus semper in ambitu suo exteriori, plerumque circulari, mœnium instar, cinguntur eminentiis, innumeras fere et multò plures, sed non tantas et tam profundas, quam nostra exhibeat Terra, si huius cavitates suis destituerentur maribus; denique quod partes multæ in Luna obscuræ, quæ sub primo conspectu non apparent profundæ, ideoq; pro materia liquida, maribus scilicet multorum forsan judicio censendæ, adhibita accuratiori inspectione, teste Viro celeberrimo D.no de la Hire, nihilominus profundæ nec tamen liquidæ deprehendantur; ut hinc haud pauci cum acutissimo Galilæo Lunam pro corpore, materiam à Terra diversam habente existimare possent, in qua etiam fortasse substantiæ et res creatæ existant, quæ operationes edant ab imaginatione nostra sicut remotas, ita et prorsus alienas; quippe quæ nullam cum nostris similitudinem habeant, et proin omnino sint à nostra cogitatione discrepantes.

*Quamvis autem Luna profunditatibus et eminentiis quamplurimis sit referta, sæpissime tamen contingit, superficiem Lunæ in certis à Sole distantiis adeò immutatam videri, ut magnus ille montium et profunditatum numerus, qui nuper admodum distinctissime observari poterat, non amplius tunc sub conspectum cadat; ratio huius mutationis ex ipsa figura superiori **A** intermedia facile patescit, quod scilicet profunditates inter novilunia et quadraturas, Luna crescente à dextris maxime, decrescente autem hac à sinistris potissimum altissimorum circumjacentium montium obtegantur umbris; et quidem quod insuper tales pro vario Solis ad Lunam positu perpetuò immutentur (quæ proinde etiam novæ maculæ denominari solent) semi-*

Plate 21: Johan Gabriel Doppelmayr, *Tabula selenographica in qua lunarium macularum exacta descriptio*, Nürnberg 1718. (Fagel Portfolio 1:028)

Ex Officina Petri Schenkii in Platea vulgo
Planisphærium Terrestre cum utroque Coelesti Hemisphærio, sive diversa orbis Terraquei,
pro variatis divisionis, conspectus, variarumque positionum et observationum circumstantiis, multis in locis correcta, variisque huc facientibus
Cosmographicis illustrationibus, pluriumque Naturæ Phaenomenorum explicationibus, ex praeclaris Auctoribus excerptis,
aucta et ornata repraesentatio:
Opera et studio A. F. Zürneri, Reg: Maj: Pol: et El: Sax: Provinciarum finiumq, Comissarii et Geographi ut et Reg: Soc: Sc: B. M.
America Septentrionalis
America Meridionalis
Mare Pacificum
Mar del Zur
Tropicus Cancri
Tropicus Capricorni
Circulus Arcticus
Circulus Antarcticus
Zona Frigida Septentrionalis
Zona Frigida Australis
Mare Magellanicum
Nova Zeelandia
Regiones Australis necdum cognitæ
Venti Variabiles
Benevole Spectator in illustrandis præcipuis
Hemisphærium Australe

Plate 22: Adam Friedrich Zürner, *Planisphærium Terrestre*, Amsterdam: Gerhard Valk and Petrus Schenk, 1708. (Fagel Portfolio 1:001)

Plate 23: François Valentyn, *De Landvoogdy van Amboina*, Dordrecht: Joannes van Braam, and Amsterdam: Gerard onder de Linden, 1724 (detail). (Fagel Portfolio 19:022)

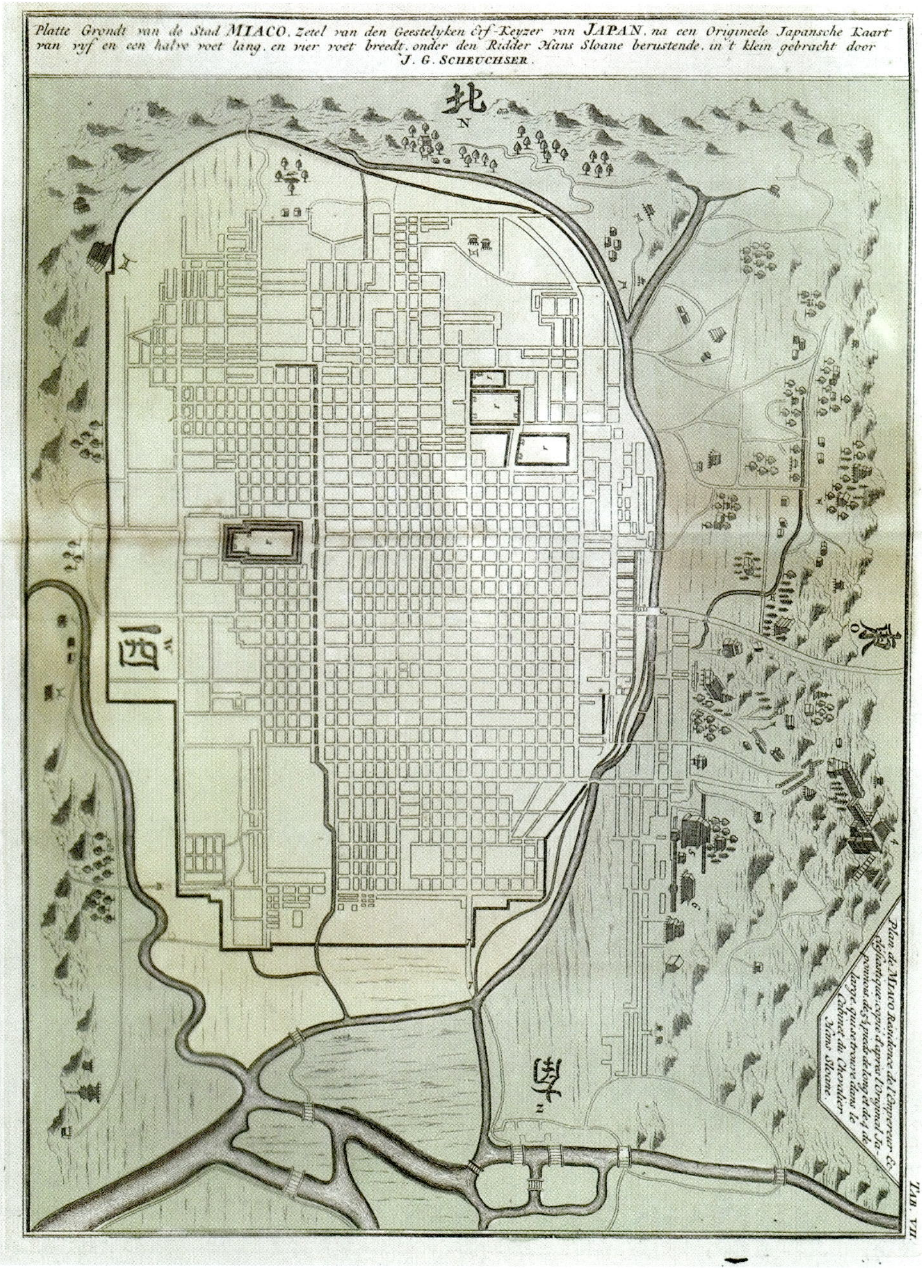

Plate 24: Johannes Gaspar Scheuchzer, *Platte Grondt von de Stad Miaco*, 's Gravenhage: Pierre Gosse and Jean Neaulme, c. 1692. (Fagel Portfolio 19:053)

Plate 25: Joan Blaeu, *Insulæ Canariæ*, Amsterdam: Gerhard Valk and Petrus Schenk, 1662. (Fagel Portfolio 20:040)

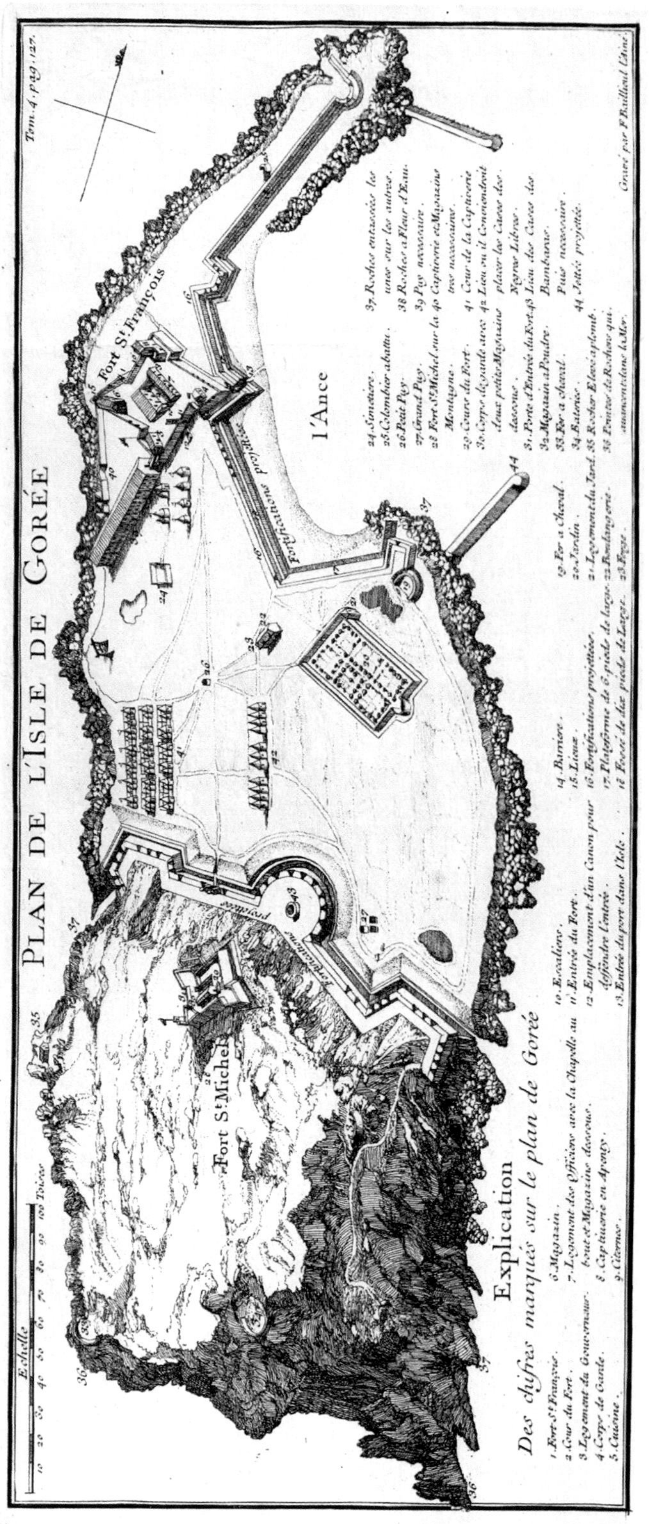

Plate 26: Jacobus van der Schley, *Plan de l'Isle de Gorée*, Amsterdam 1772. (Fagel Portfolio 20:038)

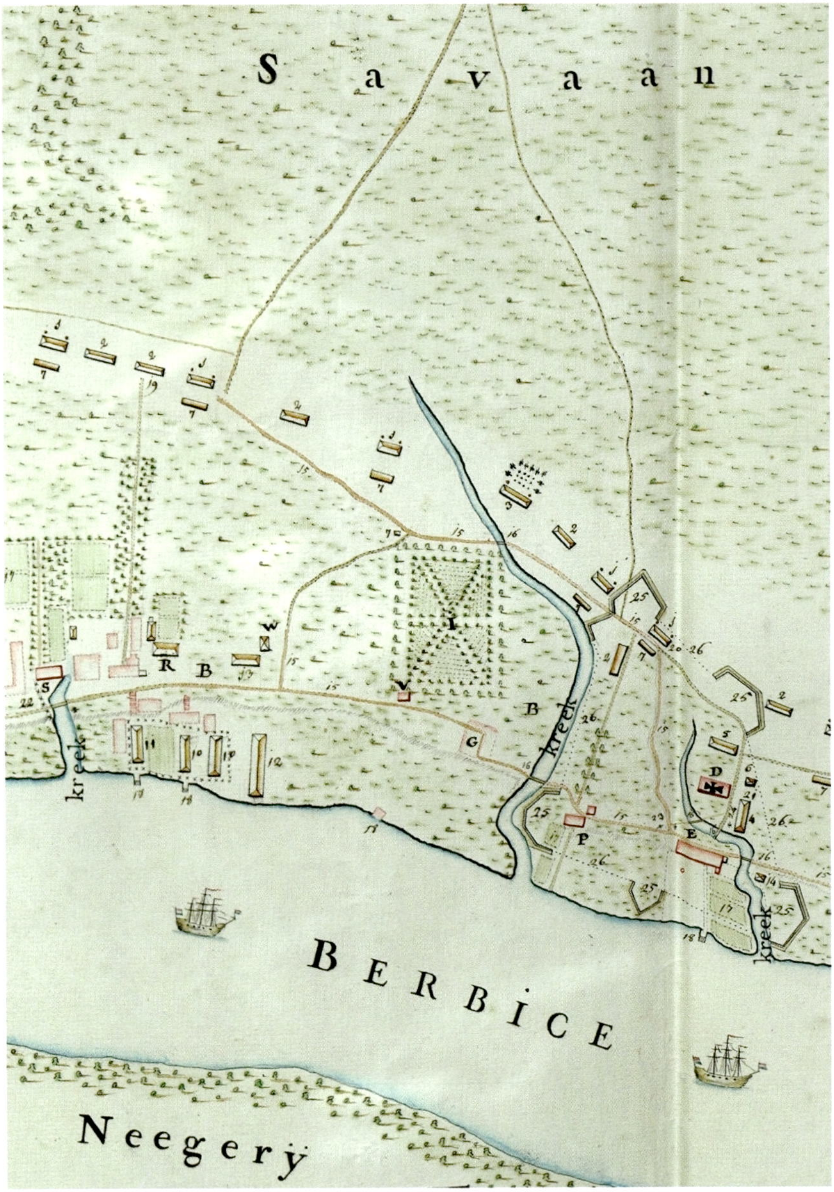

Plate 27: F.S. de Veije and P. Aelmans, 'Plan van het Geweese Fort Nassau' (Colonie de Berbice), manuscript, 1764 (detail). (Fagel Portfolio 21:046)

presentation than textual apparatus, the reprints of Dante's ***Commedia*** and Petrarch's ***Opera*** mentioned above, plus a further eighteenth-century Paduan edition of Petrarch – a 1750 reprint of the 1635 ***Petrarchus redivivus*** of Bishop Giacomo Tomasini (1595–1655). *Petrarchus redivivus* contains serious scholarship on the manuscripts, printing history and reception of Petrarch, including ample detail on his poetic coronation or laureation in Rome in 1341 (he prints the text of the diploma or *privilegium* that Petrarch received at his laureation ceremony). Tomasini also includes four early studies of Petrarch – three fifteenth-century biographies by Leonardo Bruni, Pier Paolo Vergerio the elder and Gianozzo Manetti, and the sixteenth-century biography of Ludovico Beccarelli. The book also explores Petrarch through a series of 'antiquities' – the so-called Laura tomb, with its verses of dubious authenticity, the reconstruction of Petrarch's villa in Arqua, said to be decorated with scenes of triumphs, *symbola* or emblematic figures, sculpted names of various nations, a museum or 'museoleum' with a bust of Aristotle and a bedroom with a sculpture of Cleopatra. The range of objects described – the triumphs, emblems, inscriptions, the choice of statues and the play on *museolum* as place of the Muses and monument – all suggests a much earlier antiquarianism, of the kind that we might associate with Renaissance *studioli* or topical decorative schemes, like those of the *Musæum* of Paolo Giovio on the shores of Lake Como. The oddity of this antiquarian part of the book culminates with description and illustration of Petrarch's mummified cat, which was enthroned above the door of his *museolum*. Following this is a section entitled *Mythologia iconum eodem spectantium* – a series of six emblematic images with explanations and glosses, reminiscent of a Baroque emblem book and showing the longevity of Petrarch's association with emblematics.[20]

Of the three great Tuscan authors, it is not Petrarch or Dante but Boccaccio who is most represented. Here the Fagel Collection is consistent with other library collections and the large number of early editions of Boccaccio.[21] Sixteenth-century Boccaccio editions in Trinity Library show the range of interest that Boccaccio aroused, or the uses to which he was put during the

20 Petrarch is praised as the father of post-medieval emblems or devices in sixteenth-century treatises on devices, such as Luca Contile, *Ragionamento di Luca Contile sopra la proprietà delle imprese* (Pavia 1574), 11v.

21 Trinity Library has fifteen early editions of Boccaccio's poetic works, including the manual of poetic mythography *Genealogia deorum gentilium* – and sixteenth-century works on the *Decameron* such as Vincenzo Borghini's *Annotazioni e discorsi sopra alcuni luoghi del Decameron* (Florence 1574) and Lionardo Salviati's *Avvertimenti della lingua sopra'l Decamerone*, Books I–III (Venice 1584) – but excluding his historical works such as *De casibus*. Three of the fifteen are in the Quin Library. The collection is however small compared to the holdings of the John Rylands Library, which possesses ninety-six fifteenth- and sixteenth-century editions of Boccaccio; Bacchi della Lega counted 192 early editions.

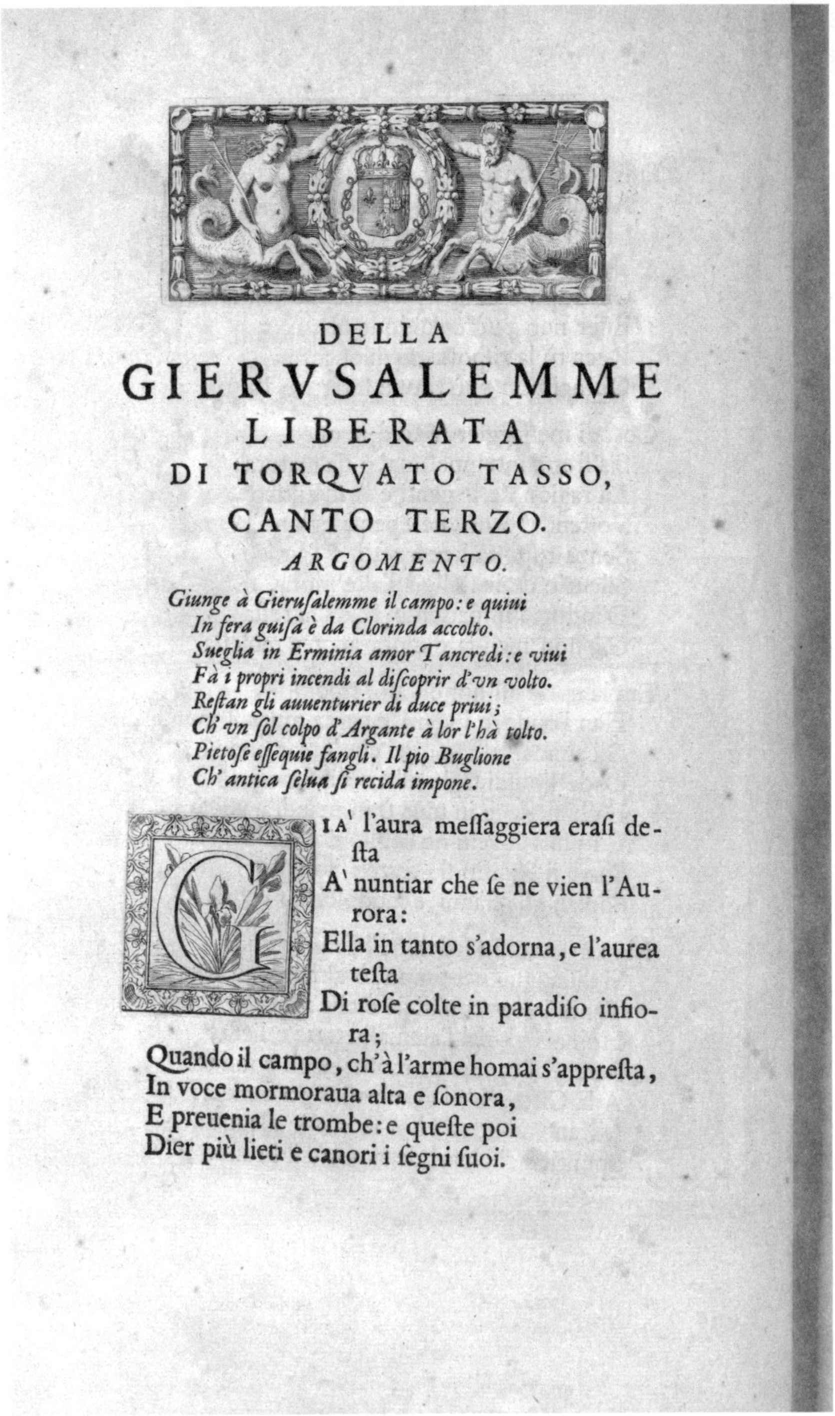

DELLA

GIERVSALEMME

LIBERATA

DI TORQVATO TASSO,

CANTO TERZO.

ARGOMENTO.

Giunge à Gieruſalemme il campo: e quiui
In fera guiſa è da Clorinda accolto.
Sueglia in Erminia amor Tancredi: e viui
Fà i propri incendi al diſcoprir d'vn volto.
Reſtan gli auuenturier di duce priui;
Ch'vn ſol colpo d'Argante à lor l'hà tolto.
Pietoſe eſſequie fangli. Il pio Buglione
Ch'antica ſelua ſi recida impone.

GIA' l'aura meſſaggiera eraſi deſta
A' nuntiar che ſe ne vien l'Aurora:
Ella in tanto s'adorna, e l'aurea teſta
Di roſe colte in paradiſo infiora;
Quando il campo, ch'à l'arme homai s'appreſta,
In voce mormoraua alta e ſonora,
E preuenia le trombe: e queſte poi
Dier più lieti e canori i ſegni ſuoi.

Fig 2: Torquato Tasso, *Il Goffredo overo La Gierusalemme liberata*, Paris: Stamperia Reale, 1644 (p. 50 and plate 3): the beginning of Canto 3, with mention of Erminia and Tancredi. (Fag. D.I.34)

Saluta il campo la città sacrata
Colmo di riuerenza, è pien d'ardire
Delle squadre primiere incontro armata
S'oppon Clorinda à l'impeto, e al ferire
L'antica fiamma Erminia innamorata
Nel giouanetto cor torna à sentire
Morte, e tomba riceue il gran Dudone
E fà tagliar la selua il pio Buglione:
III

Renaissance – they also show a variety of provenance, signalling wide interest in acquisition. Part of this interest was linguistic, in establishing the forms of Tuscan, as propounded by Bembo, but the *Decameron* also provides the material for such works as *Le Lettere di M. Francesco Sansovino sopra le diece giornate del Decamerone* (Venice 1543) of the Venetian *poligrafo* Francesco Sansovino (1521–86), which takes Boccaccio's text as a point of departure for a miscellany of moral and satiric essays, which return repeatedly to questions of religious reform.

The Fagel Boccaccio editions include a copy of the dream poem ***Amorosa visione*** (Venice 1531), making it the earliest printing of Italian vernacular literature in the Fagel Collection, an Amsterdam 1674 ***Decameron*** and a Basel 1532 copy of his ***Genealogia deorum gentilium***, which may have been collected as the first modern manual of mythography.[22] (Another Renaissance mythographic manual, the *Historia de deis gentium* of Lilio Gregorio Giraldi or Lelius Gyraldus (1479–1552), appears in Fagel as part of Giraldi's ***Opera***, Leiden 1696.) The Amsterdam 1674 *Decameron* is a false imprint; it was probably printed in Geneva.[23] This edition declares on the title page that it reprints the Giunta press 1527 Florentine edition, which was an object of considerable historic interest – it was reprinted by Elzevier in 1665, for example. This same 1527 Giuntine edition appears in a 1761 Lucca reprinting of the *Decameron* in Trinity's collections, which discusses Giunta's dependence on a 1384 manuscript written by the scribe Francesco Manelli and gives considerable detail on Manelli.[24] Quin was also interested in the Giuntine Boccaccio and pursued it assiduously, discarding a counterfeit edition sold to him and searching out an original copy (Quin 14).

These seventeenth- and eighteenth-century Boccaccio editions bring us finally to the question of whether the sparse holdings of Italian literature in Fagel share any features with other Trinity holdings in the same area and whether they can reveal similar patterns in seventeenth- and eighteenth-century collection of Italian Renaissance books and literature. The answer is a cautious 'yes', although the assumption that the acquisition of Fagel expanded greatly the literary holdings in Trinity College Library is in need of revision. This may be true for other national literatures, but in Italian the two most valuable endowments came – as I have stressed – with Gilbert for Humanist scholarship and Quin for vernacular literature.

22 The 1532 edition of the *Genealogia deorum gentilium* re-uses the figures that appear in incunable editions, such as the Venice 1497 edition (TCD EE.a.28).

23 See the British Library Short Title Catalogue entry for details.

24 The 1761 Lucca *Decameron* (TCD R.pp.40) was valued for its text.

Fagel in the context of eighteenth-century tastes and criticism

We glanced above at the flowering of literary history in eighteenth-century scholarship, represented in the Fagel Collection by the Volpi–Cominiana editions. We see this scholarly production in Trinity's other collections in such works as the 1714 Naples edition of the commentary by Castelvetro (1505–71) on Bembo's *Prose della volgar lingua* – the annotations of one of the most lucid of Renaissance critics on one of the most influential works on vernacular style.[25] Also notable are the six-volume Florence 1724 edition of Tasso, which includes the critical debates on *Gerusalemme liberata*, the Venice 1730 edition of Ariosto plus sixteenth-century commentaries, and the Florence 1747 *Gesta Landini* of Angelo Maria Bandini (1726–1803), librarian of the Laurentian Library.[26] This last work was the fragment of a projected twelve-volume literary history of Florence from the thirteenth to fifteenth centuries that predates the anglophone interest in the Florentine Renaissance with William Roscoe's *Life of Lorenzo de' Medici* (London 1796). Trinity possesses two early editions of Tiraboschi's *Storia della letteratura italiana* (Modena 1772–6; Florence 1805–13, the former being the first edition), and a selected edition, *Storia della poesia italiana* (London 1803). There was also considerable acquisition of Italian literature from other sources, whether endowment or purchase; in the case of Italian Renaissance literature purchase can certainly be traced in the 1840s, when the scholarly editions by the Typographic Society of Milan, published in the Napoleonic period, were acquired.

Sixteenth-century writers whom we find published in eighteenth-century editions, such as Sperone Speroni, Lodovico Castelvetro or the academicians who debated the relative merits of Ariosto and Tasso, often fell into neglect and did not appear in modern editions until the work of scholars such as Bernard Weinberg in the 1960s, with his two-volume *History of Literary Criticism in the Italian Renaissance* (Chicago 1961) and three-volume *Trattati di retorica e poetica*

25 Muratori also produced a *Vita e opere di L. Castelvetro* (Milan 1727).

26 The Venice 1730 Ariosto reprinted the considerable bulk of sixteenth-century commentary by *poligrafi* such as Ludovico Dolce, Tommaso Porcacchi, Orazio Toscanella, Simon Fornari, Girolamo Ruscelli and the literary theorist Giambattista Pigna. The Florence 1724 Tasso is still more extensive, running to six volumes including variants, rhyme schemes, Tasso's dialogues, letters and academic controversies (two volumes). The full title of Bandini's two-volume *Gesta Landini* is *Specimen literaturæ Florentinæ sæc. XV in quo dum Christophori Landini gesta enarrantur virorum ea ætate doctissimorum in literariam remp. merita, status Gymnasii Florentini a Landino instaurati et Acta Academiæ Platonicæ a Magno Cosma excitatæ recensentur et illustrantur* (Florence 1747–51). Bandini also produced a series of *Lives* of notable Tuscan Humanists, researches on the Giuntine press, on Florentine Platonism and on the unedited works of Poliziano, as well as codicological studies of the Laurentian Library manuscripts.

del cinquecento (Bari 1970–2). In certain cases, editions like those of Volpi still remain a valuable scholarly source. What we find in the Fagel Collection, as in those of Gilbert and Quin, is a pre-nineteenth-century view of Renaissance literature – one in which Neo-Latin and vernacular still have equivalent standing, and in which we do not find the rejection of sixteenth-century Italian literature or theory (especially that of the mid to late century) as the pedantic or aestheticized product of a decadent political order.

These early reprintings are free from the prejudices that led many nineteenth- and twentieth-century historians to privilege certain Italian centres – notably Florence – at the expense of other cities. The preoccupation with Florence – evident from Roscoe in the late eighteenth century to the civic humanism of Hans Baron in the post-war period[27] – has also fostered chronological imbalances in anglophone scholarship, with attention focused on the centres that flourished in the fifteenth century to the detriment of states that rose in eminence in the late Renaissance, for example Turin. On a similar and important theme, the eighteenth-century reprintings of sixteenth-century texts are unhampered by the concept of mannerism as a reaction to, development or decline of a posited 'classical' or high Renaissance phase – a concept that has so often served to distort judgement and shape preconceptions concerning later sixteenth-century culture.[28] Such confusions increase as concepts that function ambiguously as stylistic terms or historical labels – such as 'mannerism' – are passed between the arts, so that a term used to describe differences in artists of successive generations becomes adopted in literature to signify stylistic choices.

27 The German Jewish scholar Hans Baron, who fled Nazi Germany in 1933, introduced the term 'civic Humanism' to describe the life of republican citizenship, which he saw exemplified in the reflections and activities of Leonardo Bruni and his circle.

28 'Mannerism' as a term in literary criticism was used by Ernst Robert Curtius in *Europäische Literatur und lateinisches Mittelalter* (Bern 1948) and by Gustav Hocke in *Manierismus in der Literatur* (Hamburg 1959) to denote tendencies that arise in tension with or reaction to periods of classicism. In studies of visual art, the term provoked sustained disagreement as to whether it signalled a deformation of classicism, analogous to expressionism (see Max Dvořak, 'On El Greco and mannerism' in *idem*, *The History of Art as the History of Ideas*, trans. John Hardy [London 1984], pp. 97–108; Walter Friedländer, 'Die Entstehung des antiklassischen Stiles in der italienischen Malerei um 1530', *Repertorium für Kunstwissenschaft*, 46 [1925], 49–86); a sign of spiritual crisis, as argued by Arnold Hauser in *Der Manierismus: Die Krise der Renaissance und der Ursprung der modernen Kunst* (Munich 1964) and *Der Ursprung der modernen Kunst und Literatur: Die Entwicklung des Manierismus seit der Krise der Renaissance* (Munich 1973); or a stylistic tendency (John Shearman, *Mannerism* [Harmondsworth 1967]). For a summary of the art historical debates, see Elizabeth Cropper's introduction to the second edition of Craig Hugh Smyth, *Mannerism and Maniera* (Vienna 1992). *Maniera* appears as a derogatory term from the seventeenth century for post-Raphael art of the sixteenth century in writers such as Gian Pietro Bellori in *L'Idea del pittore, dello scultore e dell'architetto scelta dalle bellezze naturali superiore alla Natura*, given as a discourse at the Accademia di San Luca, Rome in 1664 and used as a preface to *Vite de' pittori, scultori e architetti moderni* (Rome 1672).

There is also the question of the eighteenth-century interest in minor or counter-genres of Renaissance literature, such as erotic-satiric literature and burlesque. The limited Italian literature section in the Fagel Collection includes a 1584 reprint of the ***Ragionamento*** of Pietro Aretino (1492–1556), a series of dialogues between a nun and a prostitute. The edition advertises its place of publication as 'Bengodi', the fictitious city in *Decameron* (story 3, day 8), and the 'printer' as Barbagrigia (Greybeard), a pseudonym used by the Roman printer Antonio Blado.[29] These 'Bengodi'–'Barbagrigia' editions were in fact published by the English printer John Wolfe in London; they were also reprinted in a number of early seventeenth-century Amsterdam editions.[30]

The Aretino is printed with a work of burlesque commentary on the *Figiad* (*Ficheide*) of the poet Francesco Maria Molza (1489–1544) composed by the Humanist Annibal Caro (1507–66). Caro's ***Commento di Ser Agresto da Ficaruolo sopra la prima ficata del Padre Siceo*** (Rome 1539) is a *capriccio* that vaunts the fantastic and absurd character of its invention and amplification. The *Commento* opens by relating the entry of the burlesque poet Francesco Berni (1497/8–1535) into the garden of the Muses, a parody Parnassus that is soon revealed to be the *hortus* of Priapus where the luscious growth of vegetables extolled and consumed by the poets parallels the fecundity of burlesque invention and lends itself to parody encomia and obscene *double entendres*. This kind of parody cornucopia text is best known through Rabelais, who visited Rome in the years when Molza, Caro and Berni were collaborating there.[31] Such burlesque writing is also full of invented and

29 The first edition (Rome 1539) refers to the printer as 'Barbagrigia da Bengodi' and gives the place of publication as 'Baldacco' – Baghdad or Babylon, also with reference to a quarter and inn of Florence, noted for prostitution.

30 For discussion of Wolfe's edition of Aretino's *Ragionamento*, see Michael Wyatt, *The Italian Encounter with Tudor England: A Cultural Politics of Translation* (Cambridge 2005), p. 191; Soko Tomita, *A Bibliographical Catalogue of Italian Books Printed in England, 1558–1603* (Farnham 2009), p. 17; Sonia Massel, 'John Wolfe and the impact of exemplary go-betweens on early modern print culture' in Andreas Höfele and Werner von Koppenfels (eds), *Renaissance Go-Betweens: Cultural Exchange in Early Modern Europe* (Berlin 2005), pp. 104–18. Castelvetro carried out editorial work on Wolfe's Italian editions. For printings of the 'Bengodi' Aretino in early-seventeenth-century Amsterdam, see British Library online catalogue. Antonio Blado was the first printer of Aretino's *Ragionamento*; he also printed such serious scholarly works as the 1542 Greek edition of Eustathius' Homeric commentaries or *Parekbolai*.

31 Caro moved to Rome in 1529, in 1535 entering the Accademia dei Vignaiuoli, better known from that year as the Accademia dei Virtuosi or Accademia della Virtù, whose projects included Claudio Tolomei's scheme for an encyclopaedic edition of Vitruvius that would include a comprehensive survey of the material remains of Roman antiquity in their entirety and Tolomei's attempts to apply Latin-style quantitative metre in Tuscan poetry (*Versi et regole de la nuova poesia toscana*, Rome 1539). At the Accademia, Caro's associates included Francesco Berni, Francesco Maria Molza and Tolomei. Rabelais was in Rome in 1534 and 1535–6, in the entourage of Cardinal Jean du Bellay and as agent for Geoffroy d'Estissac.

nonsense words that mean approximately caprice, fancy, whimsy, madness etc. and celebrate fantasy and mental disorder as creative forces of the *copia* or abundant style sought after by Humanist learning and promulgated in such celebrated texts as Erasmus' *De copia*. Burlesque poetry envisages variety as escalating, ungovernable transformation that simultaneously multiplies difference and undermines categories of distinction.

This burlesque literature often takes as its 'founder' the fifteenth-century Tuscan poet Burchiello (1404–49) and as its master the early-sixteenth-century Tuscan writer Francesco Berni. The writers who produced such literature, amongst them Annibal Caro, Francesco Maria Molza, Lodovico Dolce, Benedetto Varchi, Angelo Firenzuola and Giovanni della Casa, are often remembered in their 'serious' work for highly polished verse or study of classical models (Molza, Caro), treatises on elegant deportment (della Casa's *Il Galateo*, Venice 1584), feminine beauty (Firenzuola's *Dialogo delle bellezze delle donne*, c. 1542, publ. Venice 1552), painting (Dolce's *L'Aretino*, Venice 1557) and metaphysical essays on Michelangelo's sculpture (Varchi's *Lezzioni*, Florence 1549). Berni's most substantial achievement was his recasting or *rifacimento* of Matteo Boiardo's epic romance *Orlando innamorato* (left unfinished c. 1486) in a more polished style. As with Alberti in the fifteenth century, we find satire and subversive fantasy as the other side of concerns with classicism, elegance and elevated aesthetic reflection.[32] These burlesque poems derive from satiric conventions of address and they also parody the vogue for the epigram, a poem inscribed on or dedicated to an object. Typical parodic subjects are verses in praise of vegetables, gelatine, eels, urinals and other such subjects. There is a carnival mixture of high and low subjects, so that a poem in praise of Aristotle will be followed by a poem in praise of syphilis or boiled eggs. Such juxtapositions could also be seen as a burlesque of the judicious 'proportioning' of contrasting things to create *copia* or *varietas*.

The *Commento* survives in another exemplar in Trinity Library, this being a rare first edition that shares its armorial binding with two other works by Caro.[33] The other editions of Renaissance burlesque verse are of varied

32 Alberti produced the disturbing fantastic and satiric literature contained in *Momus* at the same time (1440s) as he was composing the rationalist treatise on architecture as civic art, *De re ædificatoria* (according to Paolo Portoghesi c. 1443–52).

33 The spine of the binding of the Rome 1539 *Commento* (TCD R.i.7) has a repeated, gold-tooled, armorial motif of a hanged animal that appears on the spines of the Aldus 1574–5 edition of Caro's *Lettere familiari* (TCD R.i.5–6) and Caro's *Rime* (R.i.3), also printed by Aldus, 1569.

provenance, although Quin does stand out for a superb vellum-printed and illustrated Paris 1790 edition of the *Priapea* of Niccolò Franco (1515–70), Aretino's former secretary, who was executed for his satires of members of the papal court. The *Priapea* was printed with another noted production of obscene verse, *Il Vendemmiatore* (Naples c. 1532–34) by the Neapolitan poet Luigi Tansillo (1510–68), which was censored for indecency by Paul IV in 1559.[34] The Paris 1790 title page continues the tradition of the fictitious imprint, advertising itself as *à Pe-King, regnante Kien-long*. Quin's edition of Berni's poems (Venice 1542), published alongside burlesque verse of Molza, della Casa, Varchi, Dolce, Bino, Mauro and Firenzuola is a small, heavily annotated, well-used copy, unusual for a fastidious bibliophile who rejected a precious Grolier binding because the book had several stained pages.[35] The burlesque works of Berni and his followers are reprinted in a Naples 1721 edition, *Il primo libro delle opere burlesche di M. Francesco Berni, di M. Gio. Della Casa, del Varchi, del Mauro, del Bino, del Molza, del Dolce, e del Firenzuola*. This volume also has a false imprint, as it gives 'London' as its publication place. These editions, coming from such varied libraries and states, suggest that burlesque writing, now seen as a minor and specialized area of Renaissance literature, had considerable popularity with eighteenth-century collectors.

We can form a better picture of how the thin Fagel Italian collections fit into the context of international interest in Italian literature in the eighteenth century by reference to critics who sought to promote it abroad, such as Giuseppe Baretti (1719–89), based in London from 1751. His *Remarks on the Italian Language and Writers. In a Letter from M. Joseph Baretti to an English Gentleman at Turin, Written in the Year 1751* (London 1753), discusses Bembo and Speroni – authors who receive scholarly eighteenth-century editions: Bembo, *Prose della volgar lingua* (Naples 1714); Speroni, *Opera* (Venice 1740). Baretti's ***Account of the Manners and Customs of Italy*** (London 1768, published in Dublin 1769) was dedicated to Lord Charlemont: he acted as an agent for

34 *La Priapea*, printed with *Il Vendemmiatore* of Luigi Tansillo, Paris 1790 (TCD Quin 117); *Il Vendemmiatore* also appeared in an edition of 1786 which gives the place of publication as Caserta. The opulence of Quin's edition shows the demand for high-quality productions of erotic literature; the date and place of publication suggest the breakdown of censorship in a revolutionary period. In his *New Observations on Italy and its Inhabitants* (London 1764), vol. 1, p. 19, Pierre Jean Grosley described the custom of vintagers who shouted obscenities at passersby and noted that Tansillo's poem 'known all over Italy [...] heaped together all the scurrilities and obscenities of these vintagers. This is not unlike the new kind of poetry which [...] has got footing in France of late years, by the name of the *style Poissard*, Billingsgate style'.

35 See Morrow, 'Bibliotheca Quiniana', p. 188, on Quin's returning an *exemplar Grolierii* to the bookseller Payne.

Charlemont, buying rare Italian books for him.[36] Charlemont used – and challenged – Baretti's views, such as his anti-Arcadian bias, in his *Essay towards the History of Italian Poetry*. Charlemont also used Crescimbeni's *Istoria della volgar poesia* (Rome 1698), Muratori's *Della perfetta poesia italiana* corrected with the annotations of Anton Maria Salvini (Venice 1748), Francesco Saverio Quadrio's *Della storia e della ragione d'ogni poesia* (Bologna 1739–52), Giusto Fontanini's *Biblioteca della eloquenza italiana* with the annotations of Apostolo Zeno (Venice 1753), and the 1757–8 Zatta edition of Dante, which carried the sixteenth-century annotations of Vellutello.[37]

If we turn to Charlemont's comments on Renaissance literature, we see that he echoes themes touched on in my treatment of Fagel and other contemporary Italian collections in Trinity.[38] Again we find the Veronese Scipione Maffei, who appears as an opponent of Baretti in the latter's endorsement of anti-Arcadian poetry and his interest in the burlesque tradition represented by Francesco Berni.[39] We also find extensive engagement with Castelvetro, and with the notorious polemic waged against him by Annibal Caro, whom we have seen as author of the burlesque *Commento*.[40] Caro's translation of the *Aeneid* is endorsed by Charlemont against Dryden's condemnation.[41] Charlemont's interest in 'low' genres is also attested by the considerable attention he gives to

36 Charlemont's library contained over 8000 volumes when it was sold in London by Sotheby's in 1865, despite the fire that partly destroyed the collection prior to sale. It included a first edition of the *Dittamondo* (commenced c. 1345) of Fazio degli Uberti (1301?–67?), an encyclopaedic poem in *terza rima* based on Dante. It also contained one of five vellum-printed editions of 1532 of Ariosto's *Orlando Furioso*, with an autograph dedication to Veronica Gambara. On this edition, see Conor Fahy, *'L'esemplare già 'Charlemont' dell'Orlando furioso del 1532'*, *Lettere italiane*, 14 (1962), 441–50; *idem*, 'More on the 1532 edition of Ludovico Ariosto's *Orlando Furioso*', *Studies in Bibliography*, 41 (1988), 225–33. On Charlemont's library and his relations with Baretti, see Talbot, *Lord Charlemont*, vol. 1, pp. xxv–xliv; Charlemont and Baretti first met in 1748 in Turin, during Charlemont's Grand Tour, and Charlemont invited Baretti to take up the newly created chair in Italian and Spanish at Trinity College Dublin (1776).

37 See Talbot, *Lord Charlemont*, vol. 1, pp. xliv–v.

38 The question of whether there were any links between Charlemont and Quin remains beyond the scope of this essay.

39 See Talbot, *Lord Charlemont*, vol. 2, p. 146, for Charlemont's discussion of Berni's 1542 parody rewriting of Boiardo's epic *Orlando innamorato*; p. 201 on Maffei's republication of Trissino (Verona 1729); p. 238 on Berni as opponent of Aretino but 'far his Superiour in poetical Talent'.

40 Charlemont refers to Castelvetro repeatedly: see Talbot, *Lord Charlemont*, vol. 2, pp. 18, 28, 34, 37, 45, 46, 48, 49, 68, 74; in condemnation of Castelvetro at pp. 77, 78, 81; as 'Petrarch's great commentator' at p. 90; in disagreement with him at pp. 93, 107; at p. 110 noting the criticisms of Vellutello and Castelvetro; at p. 310 in reference to the Caro–Castelvetro controversy. At vol. 2, p. 239 Charlemont calls Aretino's *Ragionamento*, published in the Fagel 1583 edition with Caro's *Commento*, 'shameless', referring to 'his prostituted Muse, reeking from the Steams of the Brothel'.

41 See Talbot, *Lord Charlemont*, vol. 2, pp. 306–7 on Dryden's bad opinion of Caro's translation of the *Aeneid*, which suggests to Charlemont that Dryden never read it.

Tansillo's lascivious *Il Vendemmiatore*, purchased as we have seen by Quin in a lavish 1790 illustrated edition.[42] We also see in Charlemont the use of sixteenth-century critics, such as Pigna, Lilio Giraldi and Giraldi Cinthio, the histories of Varchi and Giovio, commentators such as Vellutello and *poligrafi* such as Rucellai, prolific, wide-ranging writers attached to the productive Venetian presses in the mid sixteenth century. Charlemont provides a late manifestation of the old Ariosto–Tasso debate that compared the various merits of the two poets to landscapes and gardens (in Charlemont's case), palaces or decorated rooms.[43]

In these ways, Charlemont shows a sense of continuity with the sixteenth century, rather than treating it as a period whose literary ideals are distant and separated from the present by a gulf in taste and *mentalité*, as it would become in the more nostalgic treatments of the nineteenth century – or in Burckhardt's vision of the Renaissance as the great age of cultural design in *Die Kultur der Renaissance in Italien* (Basel 1860). The strong narrative of individualism and the 'designing' of the state in readings of the Renaissance influenced by Burckhardt has difficulty in providing a meaningful account of the host of academicians, editors, commentators, imitators and *poligrafi* whose labours propagated Renaissance literature – both in the promulgation of neoclassical models and their constant inversion through satires, burlesques and other low genres.

Where we do see the sense of historical difference emerging is in Charlemont's treatment of Dante, who is described in terms that smack of the Burkean sublime. Thus Charlemont writes that Dante's 'unadorned sublimity' was 'proper to that dusky Period' when he wrote and 'His Ideas are too vast to

42 See Talbot, *Lord Charlemont*, vol. 2, pp. 321–7, who admits that Tansillo's *Vendemmiatore* has obscene allusions but is 'perfectly guarded' in its words, and praises its 'natural Playfulness'; he also notes Tansillo's condemnation of his poem as unchaste and notes Crescimbeni's praise for Tansillo. Charlemont translates the poem and inserts four stanzas into his text, on the pretext of its rarity. He returns to it at pp. 335–40, declaring that it is less harmful than a 'French or frenchified novel' and quotes the canzone in which Tansillo repents of having published *Il Vendemmiatore*. Charlemont mentions Niccolò Franco in vol. 2, pp. 238–9, as Aretino's enemy, using skills learnt from his former master (Aretino).

43 For Charlemont's discussion of Ariosto and Tasso, see Talbot, *Lord Charlemont*, vol. 2, pp. 360–5. Ariosto is compared to a great river, running through varied countryside, Tasso to a stream that has been trained to water gardens embellished by art; Tasso is praised for superior judgement. The tradition of comparing the two poets to palaces appears in the academic debates of the later sixteenth century, largely centered on exchanges with the Florentine literary Accademia della Crusca; Galileo made a celebrated contribution to the debate in *Considerazioni al Tasso* (c. 1590) where he stigmatized Tasso's poem as a bizarre, dingy cabinet of curiosities compared with Ariosto's palatial gallery. Charlemont notes the attack on Tasso by Boileau and French critics and attempts to exonerate him from the charge of having allegorized his poem. At pp. 372–3 he praises Tasso's late poem *Le sette giornate del mondo creato*.

admit of comparatively trifling Ornament'.[44] Charlemont took an active role in promoting translation of Dante, through his sponsorship of Henry Boyd's *Inferno* translation (Dublin 1785) and his own renderings in the first volume of his *Essay*.[45] The beautiful–sublime polarity that would help to elevate Dante in the Romantic period could also be seen as contributing to the rupture with the tradition of academic Humanist literary criticism with which Charlemont still appears to feel continuity, as well as signalling rejection of French classicism, as shown in Baretti's criticisms of Voltaire.[46] It was that Humanist literary tradition, as promoted by figures such as Bembo, which had in its day rejected Dante as a model in terms such as those of Giraldi Cinthio, who described Dante as a scythe that cuts flowers and weeds without distinction in contrast to Petrarch as a judicious gatherer of the most fragrant and beautiful flowers – a passage quoted by Charlemont.[47]

Lord Charlemont's essay, like Baretti's *The Italian Library* (London 1757), with its defence of Italian life and culture, attempts to appraise a literary tradition in a way that goes beyond the grand tourists' combination of artistic raptures and bigoted cultural condescension, as exhibited by William Beckford's travel writings, for example.[48] It suggests a cultural context for the informed collections of Quin, which show some knowledge of the editorial and critical history of Italian literature. The Fagel holdings in this area, however limited, display conformity with the tendencies shown by other acquisitions – in the longevity of the philological scholarship of the fifteenth-century Italian Humanists, as it was reprinted well into the eighteenth century; in the serious contemporary scholarly interest in the *letterati* of the sixteenth century and the editing of their work; and in the enthusiasm for the counter-genre fantasies and burlesques of the Humanists.

44 Talbot, *Lord Charlemont*, vol. 1, pp. 2–3.

45 Charlemont's sponsorship of Boyd ended badly as Boyd produced too free a translation for Charlemont's taste and dedicated his work to Charlemont's rival, Frederick Hervey, the Earl-Bishop of Derry. See Talbot, *Lord Charlemont*, vol. 1, p. xx.

46 Baretti's *Dissertation on the Italian Poetry, in which are Interspersed some Remarks on M. Voltaire's Essay on the Epic Poets* (London 1753) challenges the numerous inaccuracies of Voltaire's *Essay on Epick Poetry of the European Nations.* Paolo Rolli also objected to Voltaire's disdain for Italian literature and Dante in *Remarks on M. Voltaire's Essay on Epick Poetry of the European Nations* (London 1736).

47 Talbot, *Lord Charlemont*, vol. 2, p. 6.

48 See William Beckford, *The Grand Tour of William Beckford*, ed. Elizabeth Mavor (Harmondsworth 1986).

Dutch interest in Irish affairs in the seventeenth and eighteenth centuries, as evidenced by the Fagel Collection

Timothy R. Jackson
TRINITY COLLEGE DUBLIN

THE AIM of the pages that follow is modest: to establish whether the Fagel Collection contains sufficient material to be of interest to somebody working in Irish studies.

There have been occasions in history when Ireland was a focus of international interest. In the early nineteenth century Daniel O'Connell was a political figure of European stature, and the Irish famine of the 1840s was an event that impinged on the consciousness of the world – but these belong already to a time when the fruits of the Fagels' book collecting were safely stored in Dublin. In the seventeenth and eighteenth centuries, while the collection was being amassed, Ireland was largely peripheral to the interest, and interests, of most continental Europeans. But at least for a Protestant Dutch family, one with a century and a quarter of service at the highest level, principally as greffier to the States General (see Thomassen, fig. 2), the significance of the Rebellion of 1641 and the Williamite War of 1689–91 in Ireland will have been clear. And writers like Swift and Goldsmith, Ussher and Berkeley were known far beyond the boundaries of Ireland. How much of this is reflected in the holdings of books and maps that the Fagel family had accumulated by the time that Trinity College was able to purchase them in 1802?

Of course, not to have a book on a topic does not mean that one has no interest in it – and it is even more true that to have bought a book is not necessarily to have read it. However, the presence of a given book or pamphlet in the collection may mean that the Fagels knew that it had an importance within a given framework, that it contributed to a picture of a given author, period, area or issue. In conjunction with other purchases it may thus fit into a meaningful and systematic pattern of book-buying in relation to, say, Ireland.

Method

I have sought to identify publications in the collection that would have informed the Fagels about Ireland, recounting its history or describing its topography, disseminating the writings or documenting the activities of those who came from and/or lived and worked in Ireland. The tools for even such a limited undertaking are far from adequate – and one of the purposes of the symposium that this volume partly documents was to point this out. My first step was to go lot by lot through the catalogue prepared by Samuel Paterson for the intended auction of the collection in 1802, looking for authors and topics of Irish interest.[1] The issue as to who is to be identified as Irish is complex: Paterson catalogued all English-language creative writing under the rubric 'English Poetry and Miscellanies', but his lot no. 3342, 'Select English plays', an eight-volume collection with the title *Divers Plays*, includes two playwrights with a claim to be recognized as Irish. I will draw attention below to persons whose nationality is not clear cut.

A potentially greater problem for the attempt to identify material of Irish interest is that in many lots a smaller or larger number of publications is bundled together, often with only a sketchy description of their content in the auction catalogue. The most striking example is lot 7593, containing 243 volumes, each with up to thirty or more pamphlets bound in together. Fortunately the Library possesses the 'Inventaris van Politique en andere Tractaaten' (TCD MS 3726), which François Fagel the Elder (1659–1746) compiled c. 1739, a volume-by-volume short-title list of the many thousands of pamphlets that these volumes contain. My second step was thus to work systematically through this manuscript, again noting all titles of Irish interest. The volumes of pamphlets that are contained in three further, much smaller, lots (7594, 7595, 7596) had to be checked individually.

The other major source of information was the printed catalogue of the TCD library, published between 1864 and 1887, and generally referred

1 *Bibliotheca Fageliana. A Catalogue of the Valuable and Extensive Library of the Greffier Fagel of the Hague: Comprehending a Choice Collection of Books, in Various Languages* [...], Digested by Sam[uel] Paterson ([London:] Barker and Son [1802]). See frontispiece.

to as the '1872 catalogue'. Any consultation of this in recent years has been greatly facilitated by the new online version, available at https://www.cs.tcd.ie/1872catalogue/index.php.

Since I was primarily looking for names that were familiar to me and for titles that unambiguously pointed to Ireland I will doubtless have passed over relevant publications, unaware of their Irish connection. I believe, however, that even my less-than-exhaustive list of the material fulfils the limited intentions outlined above.[2] And such is the wealth of the holdings that one could carry out a similar exercise in relation to Sweden or Turkey or a given Dutch town. To do the same for one of the larger political and social powers in Europe, however, perhaps Great Britain or France, Spain or Italy, would be a major undertaking.

Of the aspects of Irish experience reflected in the Fagels' purchasing of books it is religious affairs, in their political and historical contexts, that are most extensively represented. I will briefly consider other areas of interest and then deal with religious matters at greater length. The survey will conclude with an account of such Dublin imprints as are to be found in the collection.

History and topography of Ireland; the Irish abroad

Among the seventeen titles in the section of Paterson's catalogue that covers 'History and Antiquities of Ireland' a substantial number of the early general histories of the country are present: Peter Lombard (1632),[3] James Ware (1658), Roderic O'Flaherty (1685), Richard Cox (1689–90), Geoffrey Keating (1726), Ferdinando Warner (1763) and Thomas Leland (1773). Two such works are Low Countries publications: Richard Stanihurst's *De rebvs in Hibernia gestis* (Antwerp: Plantijn, 1584) (see Harris, Thematic shelving, fig. 2) and the anthology ascribed to Johannes de Laet, *Respublica, sive status regni Scotiæ et Hiberniæ* (Leiden: Elsevier, 1630), the second half of which draws mainly on William Camden for information about Ireland.[4] A further, small number of book-length publications, by Warner, John Davies and Edmund Borlase,

2 A small number of works of Irish interest listed by Paterson are, for one reason or another, not to be found in the collection today.

3 Where not otherwise indicated, publication dates refer to the copy in the collection, not necessarily to the first edition of the work in question. Fuller bibliographical details are to be found in the list that begins on p. 213 below.

4 The collection also contains editions of works by Camden himself that touch upon Ireland: *Anglica, Normannica, Hibernica, Cambrica, a veteribus scripta* […] (1603); *Annales rerum Anglicarum, et Hibernicarum, regnante Elizabetha* (1625); and *Britannia: or, A Chorographical Description of Great Britain and Ireland* […] (translation of 1772).

concentrate on English attempts to control Ireland, two of them in the specific context of the rebellion of 1641; these will be considered below. There are in addition two volumes of memoirs from the first half of the eighteenth century, one by the first Duke of Ormond (1610–88) from 1737 and the other by the first Marquess of Clanricarde (1604–58) from 1744.

The second Duke of Ormond (1665–1745), grandson of the foregoing, became involved in controversy in the course of the War of the Spanish Succession, the result of being sent as commander-in-chief to Flanders in 1712 with ambiguous instructions: ostensibly he was to prosecute the war, while secretly he was ordered to avoid contact with the enemy for fear of jeopardizing the chances of peace with France. This gave rise to a flurry of pamphlets striving to attach the responsibility for this policy of timidity either to him or to the ministers who had sent him. From an Irish point of view two of the most interesting pamphlets were published anonymously by Jonathan Swift: *The Conduct of the Allies, and of the Late Ministry, in Beginning and Carrying on the Present War* (1711) and *Some Remarks on the Barrier Treaty, between Her Majesty and the States-General* (1712); in dealing with these matters Swift shows an informed knowledge of Low Countries affairs.[5] For the rest, the collection has *The Conduct of His Grace the Duke of Ormonde, in the Campagne of 1712* (1st and 2nd edns 1715), as well as a number of equally anonymous, direct or indirect responses to this: *A Vindication of Her Late Majesty Queen Anne, of Glorious Memory; of His Grace the Duke of Ormonde; and of the Late Ministry* [...] (1715); *An Examination of a Book Intituled,* The Conduct of the Duke of Ormond, anno 1712 [...], by an Officer who Made the Campaign with His Grace (1715); *An Address to the Good People of Great Britain, Occasion'd by the Report from the Committee of Secrecy* (1715); and (with, exceptionally, a named author) Thomas Burnett's *The Necessity of Impeaching the Late Ministry* [...] (2nd and 3rd edns 1715).[6]

The collection is relatively poor in topographical information about Ireland. According to Abbott's *Catalogue* the rich cartographical holdings include only four maps of the country, by Herman Moll, William Petty,

5 In his *Sentiments of a Church-of-England Man* (in vol. 1 of the four-volume edition of *Miscellanies* – see below) Swift reflects on the relationship of religion and politics among the Dutch and the British.

6 There are of course many publications in the collection that have a minor bearing on Irish history. An example would be two pamphlets, which, in slightly different Dutch translations, recount the execution in 1641 of Thomas Wentworth, Earl of Strafford and Lord Lieutenant of Ireland, noting for example that he was accompanied to the scaffold by James Ussher, the Church of Ireland Archbishop of Armagh.

Peter Schenk and Johann Baptist Homann.[7] Paolo Giovio's early description of Ireland (1578) is only a brief section in a more general work: *Regionum et insularum atque locorum descriptiones: videlicet Britanniæ, Scotiæ, Hyberniæ, Orchadum*. Beyond that we find *Survey of the South of Ireland* (1777) by 'John Watkinson', the fictitious persona of an Englishman adopted by Rev. Thomas Campbell, and two accounts of tours through the country from the last quarter of the eighteenth century, by Richard Twiss (1776) and Arthur Young (1780).

From the small sample that the collection offers it seems that the travellers are more dispassionate, or even positive, in their assessment of the Irish than the historians. Though some of Twiss's more critical observations caused annoyance, he begins by remarking on the pleasant voyage from Aberystwyth and the beautiful entrance to Dublin harbour and continues by admitting that his expectation of a populace whose hospitality is dominated by an addiction to drink was mistaken: 'Hospitality and drinking went formerly hand in hand, but since the excesses of the table have been so judiciously abolished, hospitality is not so violently practised as heretofore' (p. 8). Young's account of his tour in Ireland in the late 1770s concentrates on the rural economy of the country, with, for example, detailed tables and analyses of the rotation of crops grown in different parts of the country, yields per acre and prices obtained. He also, however, has space for an enthusiastic description of Powerscourt waterfall and its surrounds, finding them 'romantic' and 'melancholy' (pp. 92–3). Of the two illustrations at the back of the volume an untitled one shows a waterfall similar to that at Powerscourt, while the other depicts an Irish cabin, with weed-grown thatch and neither windows nor chimney, and behind it a group of 'lazy-beds' for growing the potatoes on which the peasantry were already tragically dependent (see fig. 1). And finally there are accounts of travels abroad by Irishmen: John Toland writing on Prussia and Hanover (1705),[8] John Talbot Dillon on Spain (1780) and the fifth Earl of Orrery[9] on Italy (1773); Richard Pococke (1704–65), an Englishman, who from 1725 held a succession of positions in the Church of Ireland, produced in his *Description of the East* (1743–5) an early work of

7 T.K. Abbott, *Catalogue of the Manuscripts in the Library of Trinity College, Dublin. To which is Added a List of the Fagel Collection of Maps in the Same Library* (Dublin and London 1900), p. 498, nos 1040–3.

8 The collection has a copy of the edition of 1714, which includes the ordinances of the Royal Academy, Berlin, and the declaration of the Elector Palatine in favour of his Protestant subjects, as well as a translation into French from 1706.

9 John Boyle (1707–62), who was also the fifth Earl of Cork. Philip Luckombe's *Tour thro' Ireland* (London 1783) was not retained by TCD: perhaps it already possessed the edition of 1780.

Fig 1: Arthur Young, *A Tour in Ireland* [1776–9], London: T. Cadwell/J. Dodsley, 1780 (unnumbered penultimate page): an 'Irish cabbin' [*sic*] (Fag. S.10.57 – previously Fag. A.6.33)

Egyptology, while Robert Clayton, who is discussed in greater detail below, published an annotated translation of a *Journal from Grand Cairo to Mount Sinai* (1753), with remarks on hieroglyphics and heathen mythology.

Philosophy; politics

The philosopher and churchman George Berkeley was born in Kilkenny in 1685 and educated at Kilkenny College and TCD. He spent the early part of his working life as a Fellow of the College and subsequently was Bishop of Cloyne from 1734 until 1752. He died in the following year. The collection contains his three most important works, those in which he advanced his arguments against the existence of matter. Duplicate copies of the *Essay towards a New Theory of Vision* of 1709 are to be found following *Alciphron, or the Minute Philosopher* in two copies of the first edition of the latter (1732), a further two as freestanding editions (1733).[10] The *Treatise Concerning the Principles of Human Knowledge*

10 Where I refer to duplicates I mean publications that appear to have been printed from the same setting of type and to have the same fingerprint. There may, however, be differences in the amount of wear, the application of ink etc., which could suggest different impressions; I have not looked for differences in paper or watermarks.

of 1710 is represented by a relatively late edition (1776); the *Dialogues between Hylas and Philonous* are contained in this volume, as well as being present in the first edition of 1713.[11]

Francis Hutcheson (1694–1746) was a founder of the Scottish Enlightenment who influenced the thinking of such luminaries as Adam Smith and Thomas Jefferson. Born of Presbyterian stock in Drumalig, Co. Down, he studied for the ministry at Glasgow University until 1717, but by 1718 had returned to Ireland, where he set up an academy in Dublin, remaining there until 1730, when he took up the chair in Moral Philosophy in Glasgow. Of the writings from his time in Dublin the collection possesses two editions of both his *Inquiry into the Original of our Ideas of Beauty and Virtue* (1725, 1753) and the *Essay on the Nature and Conduct of the Passions and Affections* (1728, 1742). Of his later works, the *Philosophiæ moralis institutio compendiaria* in an edition with the imprint Rotterdam 1745, the third edition of the *Synopsis metaphysicæ* (1749) and the posthumously published two-volume *System of moral philosophy* (1755) are also present. The list of some 400 subscribers to the publication of this last is distinguished by the inclusion of 'The Hon. Henry Fagel, Principal Secretary to their High Mightinesses the States General of the United Provinces', i.e. Greffier Hendrik Fagel the Elder. Finally, there is the edited correspondence between Hutcheson and Gilbert Burnet (1735) and John Taylor's *Examination of the Scheme of Morality, Advanced by Dr Hutcheson* (1759).

It may seem inappropriate to categorize Edmund Burke (1729–97), born in Dublin and like Berkeley a distinguished graduate of TCD, under the rubric 'Politics'. However, while the Fagels did possess a volume with the title, *The Beauties of the late Right Hon. Edmund Burke*, being an anthology of brief passages culled from his works and arranged alphabetically by subject (from 'Act of grace' to 'Zeal'), they did not have *The Sublime and Beautiful*. But the collection contains copies of the fifth and tenth editions of the *Reflections on the Revolution in France* (and Thomas Paine's answer, *Rights of Man*), as well as records of speeches on army estimates, American taxation and conciliation with the colonies.

Richard Steele (1672–1729) may also conveniently be classified as a political writer, though like so many men of his time he published in more than one field. A more pertinent question might be whether to classify him as

11 The collection also holds John Hervey's *Remarks on the Minute Philosopher* and two copies of Bernard Mandeville's *Letter to Dion* (i.e. Berkeley).

Irish. He was born in Dublin, but by the mid 1680s – he entered Charterhouse school in 1684 – he was living in England, where he spent the rest of his life; Twiss, however, places him on his list of Irish writers (p. 159). The collection contains three of his political works in pamphlet form: *The Crisis* [...] *the Just Causes of the Late Happy Revolution* (1714); duplicate copies of *A Letter to a Member of Parliament Concerning the Bill for Preventing the Growth of Schism* (1714); and *Mr. Steele's Apology for Himself and his Writings; Occasioned by his Expulsion from the House of Commons* (1714) – for allegedly seditious criticism of Queen Anne. These also comprise the last three of the eight titles in the collection, *The Political Writings of Sir Richard Steele* (1715), dedicated to the Earl of Clare. There are two religious works: *The Romish Ecclesiastical History of Late Years* (1714) and *The Christian Hero* (1727), as well as a French translation of the latter.[12] Finally, Steele is represented by two comedies – *The Funeral: or, Grief a-la-mode* (1721) and *The Conscious Lovers* (1723) – and the anthology *Poetical Miscellanies* (1727), dedicated to Congreve.

Science

Robert Boyle (1627–91), son of the first Earl of Cork, is well represented, not just for the importance of his scientific work, but also for his religious commitment. The Fagel holdings include some volumes that reflect both concerns, such as *Some Considerations about the Reconcileableness of Reason and Religion* (1675), the *Discourse of Things above Reason* (1681) and the *Disquisition about the Final Causes of Natural Things* [...] *Some Uncommon Observations about Vitiated Sight* (1688). Unambiguously scientific are the *Experiments and Considerations Touching Colours* (1664) and the *Essay of the Great Effects of Even Languid and Unheeded Motion* (1690), while Boyle's religious faith is expressed in such works as *Some Considerations Touching the Style of the H. Scriptures* (1661), the *Free Enquiry into the Vulgarly Receiv'd Notion of Nature* (1685/6) and *Of the High Veneration Man's Intellect Owes to God* (1711), as well as Richard Boulton's three-volume epitome of his theological works (1715).[13] Finally, a summation of both interests is

12 The dedicatory epistle prefacing Urbano Cerri's *Etat présent de l'Eglise romaine* (1716) ascribed to Steele appears in fact to be the work of Bishop Benjamin Hoadly.

13 In addition, in the section 'Sermons by Eminent English divines' in Paterson's catalogue, twenty-three volumes are glossed as 'at Boyle's lecture', which institution he established by his will; there are also five copies of anthologies of these sermons, including duplicate copies of a French translation.

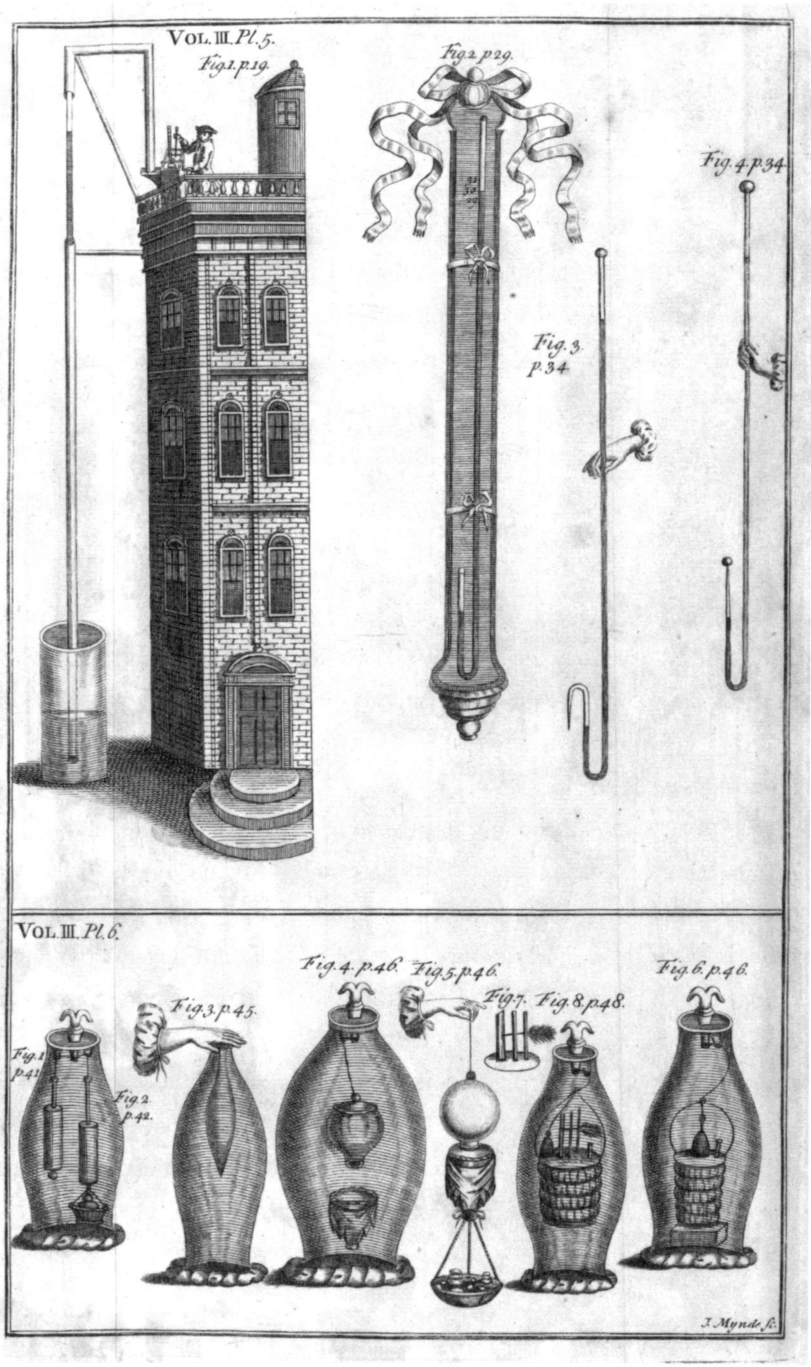

Fig 2: *The Works of the Honourable Robert Boyle. To which is Prefixed The Life of the Author* [by Thomas Birch], 5 vols, London: A. Millar, 1744 (vol. 3, plates 5 and 6): equipment for the conduct of various experiments, e.g. fig. 1 of plate 5, 'About the greatest height, to which water can be raised by attraction or sucking pumps' (cf. pp. 19–22). (Fag. N.1.27)

constituted by the massive *Works of the Honourable Robert Boyle* (1744) – five volumes with some 3200 folio pages ranging in subject from the *Martyrdom of Theodora, and of Didymus* to hundreds of medical remedies (see fig. 2); the list of subscribers ('the encouragers to the Works') includes Rev. Patrick Delany, The Earl of Orrery, Sir Hans Sloane and, not least, 'The Right Honourable Greffier *Fagel* at the *Hague*'.[14]

The same Sir Hans Sloane (1660–1753), best known for his botanical work and for the fact that his library and museum were the basis for the collections of the British Museum, was a native of Killyleagh, Co. Down. He is represented by his *Catalogus plantarum quæ in Jamaica sponte proveniunt* (1696).

Literature and art

Although Jonathan Swift (1667–1745) spent much of his working life in England and was closely involved in English politics, he was born in Dublin, was a graduate of TCD (BA 1686), served for many years as Dean of St Patrick's Cathedral in Dublin and often addressed Irish concerns in his satires. He is represented by eleven lots, more than any other author in Paterson's section 'English Poetry and Miscellanies', suggesting that the Fagels were aware of his importance. However, the following lots are not present in the collection as we have it today: a thirteen-volume London edition of his works from 1760–2, several individual volumes (some of them from other multi-volume editions) and a German translation of Thomas Sheridan's biography of Swift. Of the titles that were retained two are multi-volume collections: *Works* in six volumes (1741–3), published in Dublin by George Faulkner, and four volumes of *Miscellanies* edited by Swift and Pope (1732–3). Something of the range of Swift's œuvre is conveyed by a further number of individual titles or volumes, several of which in their language and imprints show evidence of the reception of Swift on the continent. In addition to *Gulliver's Travels* in three volumes (1726–7)[15] we find Swift's own *Memoirs of the Court of Lilliput* (1727) as well

14 In 1744 François the Elder died and the position as *greffier* passed to one of his sons, Hendrik the Elder. Two of the above-mentioned volumes have (rare) evidence of use by a Dutch reader: inserted at the title-page of *Vitiated Sight* is a bookmark made of a slip of paper torn from another publication on which is printed [...]*erigt daer bi*; on the titlepage of *Things above Reason* the author is named simply as *a Fellow of the Royal Society*, but identified in handwriting in the margin as *R: Boÿle*.

15 The third volume, however, appears not to have belonged originally with the other two: see the bibliography below.

as *Gulliver Decypher'd* (1728?), a humorous work (possibly by his friend John Arbuthnot) supposedly designed to absolve Swift of authorship of the *Travels*. As well as the *Second Tale of a Tub* (1715) we find a French adaptation of the first *Tale of a Tub* by René Macé, *Les trois Justaucorps* (1721) – and French interest is further attested by a translation of *A New Journey to Paris* (1711) with its fictitious author, Sieur Du Baudrier, and *Le grand mistère* (1729), attributed to Swift, but seemingly the work of the Abbé Desfontaines, the first translator of *Gulliver's Travels*. And Swift appears to have been known to the Fagels not just as a creative writer and spirited satirist: as well as the pamphlets relating to the War of the Spanish Succession mentioned above they possessed two others: *The Publick Spirit of the Whigs* (1714), and the *View of the Present State of Affairs in the Kingdom of Ireland* (1730), which begins by treating the problem of absentee landlords and concludes with the famous *Modest Proposal*. Finally, there is a collection of his correspondence (1741), and the fifth Earl of Orrery's *Life and Writings of Dr. Jonathan Swift* (1752).

Other authors with greater or lesser connections to Ireland fare less well. In an eight-volume anthology of *Divers Plays*, William Congreve (1670–1729), who was born at Bardsley, Yorkshire, but studied in TCD (though his BA is not recorded), is represented by *The Old Batchelour* and *The Double-Dealer* (1720), and George Farquhar (1678–1707), born in Derry and another graduate of TCD, by *The Constant Couple*, *The Recruiting Officer* and *The Beaux Stratagem* (1720). There is also a two-volume edition of the works of Congreve (1719).

Thomas Parnell, who was born in Dublin in 1679, graduated from TCD in 1700 and was ordained in the Church of Ireland two years later, at his death in 1718 left behind a substantial body of poetry. Steele's *Poetical Miscellanies* (see above) include four poems by him and the collection also holds his *Poems upon Several Occasions* (1773) edited by Pope and prefixed by Oliver Goldsmith's biography of him.[16] I have not located Goldsmith elsewhere in the collection.

Three works of classical scholarship require mention: Samuel Molyneux (1689–1728, MA TCD 1710), son of the more famous William, figures as the recipient of an *Epître dédicatoire de Mr. Binauld* (1715), containing reflections on Virgil; the fifth Earl of Orrery was the translator of the *Letters of Pliny the Younger* (1751); Richard Pococke published a collection of Greek and Roman inscriptions (1752).

16 **A volume catalogued by Paterson as: 'Parnell's *Hermit*, Pope's *Messiah*, and other Poems' is no longer in the collection. Through the Scriblerus Club Parnell was also an associate of Swift, John Gay and others.**

Finally, the collection contains two works relating to the fine arts that have an Irish connection. James Barry was born in Cork in 1741, spent a number of years in Italy and died in London in 1806. One of the most important of Irish painters, his œuvre included many large-scale canvases, often on mythological or historical topics, sometimes used as allegorical vehicles for his strong commitment to political and religious liberty. The Fagels possessed his study of the *Obstructions to the Acquisition of the Arts in England* (1775). Also in the collection is the fine folio volume of prints, *Tombeaux des Princes, des grands Capitaines et autres hommes illustres qui ont fleuri dans la Grande Bretagne* (n.d.), published by Owen (or: Eugene) Mac Swiney (or: Swiny, Swinny, MacSwinny) (1680–1754), a native of Enniscorthy whose working life was largely spent as a playwright and theatre manager in London (see fig. 3).

Doctrinal controversies

The Fagels were anxious to record religious controversies and conflicts – and also, as we will see below, cooperation. Again and again one comes across books or pamphlets that relate to Pelagianism, predestination/Arminianism or Socinianism. Men with a greater or lesser Irish connection contributed to these theological disputes – be it on the side of freethinking or orthodoxy – in particular to that concerning the deism expounded by such Englishmen as Anthony Collins and Matthew Tindal.

One such was Henry Dodwell, who was born in Dublin in 1641, resigned his fellowship of TCD in 1666, moved to London in 1674 and died near Maidenhead in Berkshire in 1711. He was a so-called 'non-juror', one of the beneficed clergy who refused to take the oath of allegiance to William and Mary, but it seems likely that he interested the Fagels less for his political views than as a religious controversialist. He created a storm with his *Epistolary Discourse, Proving* [...] *that the Soul is a Principle Naturally Mortal* (1706). No fewer than fifty titles in the collection treat the nature of the soul, six of them comprising explicit challenges to Dodwell's arguments – as early as 1706 Edmund Chishull raised the accusation of heresy. It also holds another doctrinal work by Dodwell, his *Eternal Rewards or Punishments* (1708), as well as two works of classical scholarship: *De veteribus cyclis* (1701) and *Chronologia Xenophontea* (1700). Dodwell's son, also Henry, who was born in England around the turn of the century and died in 1784, followed in his father's controversialist footsteps

Fig 3: *Tombeaux des Princes, des grands Capitaines et autres hommes illustres qui ont fleuri dans la Grande Bretagne vers la fin du XVII., et le commencement du XVIII. siecle* [*sic*], *gravés par les plus habiles maitres [sic] de Paris* [...], *dirigé et mis au jour par les soins de Eugene Mac Swiny* [no imprint]: an unnumbered plate following the dedicatory plate to 'Guillelmi III. libertatis Anglicæ vindicis memoriæ immortali'. (Fag. A.I.79)

by espousing the cause of deism, principally in *Christianity not Founded on Argument* (1743). This produced numerous hostile responses, not least from John Leland. Born in 1691 in Lancashire, his family moved not long afterwards to Dublin, where from 1716 he was active as a Presbyterian minister and polemicist, particularly in the anti-deist cause; he died in 1766. The collection contains duplicate copies of his first attack on Dodwell the younger in *Remarks on a Late Pamphlet, Entitled,* Christianity not Founded on Argument (1744) and one copy of the follow-up *Second Letter* (1744); Dodwell in turn, in his *Remarks on the Several Answers to the Pamphlet* (1744), devoted a section to Leland. In his *Divine Authority of the Old and New Testament Asserted* [...] *against* [...] *a Book Entitled,* The Moral Philosopher (1739–40) Leland directed his ire at Thomas Morgan, and further targets were Bolingbroke in *Reflections on the Late Lord Bolingbroke's* Letters on the Study and Use of History (1753), and Tindal in *An Answer to a Late Book Entituled,* Christianity as Old as the Creation (the so-called 'Deist's Bible') (1733). Leland continued his attack on the deists in his *View of the Principal Deistical Writers* (1754–6), while his orthodox views also found expression in works on *The Advantage and Necessity of the Christian Revelation* (1764) and *Forms of Devotion for the Use of Families* (1766), in addition to four volumes of homiletic *Discourses on Various Subjects* (1768–9), such as the nature of God, divine providence, the means of redemption and Christ as an exemplary figure.

Robert Clayton (1695–1758), who was a Fellow of TCD from 1714 (the year of his graduation) and held various Irish bishoprics from 1730, is also to be seen as a controversialist, his thought being dominated by Arian doctrines. In addition to *A Dissertation on Prophecy* [...]; *together with an Explanation of the Revelation of St. John* (1749) the collection holds two works that illustrate his interest in millenarian aspects of the history of religion: *The Chronology of the Hebrew Bible Vindicated* (1747) and the more elaborate three-part study, *A Vindication of the Histories of the Old and New Testament*. Of this, the first part, *In Answer to the Objections of the Late Lord Bolingbroke* (1753) and the second, *The Mosaical History of the Creation and Deluge* (1754), are in the collection, in addition to Catcott's *Remarks on the Second Part of the Lord Bishop of Clogher's* Vindication (1756). What is considered his most significant work, the anonymously published *Essay on Spirit* [...] *With remarks on the Athanasian and Nicene Creeds* (1752), had already exhibited clear Arian tendencies, and when he continued his attack on the doctrine of the Trinity with the publication of the third part of the *Vindication* in 1757 (the Fagels appear not to have possessed it), he provoked a charge of heresy, escaping trial only by dying before the ecclesiastical commission opened.

John Toland, born in Co. Donegal in 1670, held unorthodox, specifically deistical beliefs. At the age of sixteen he rejected the Catholicism in which he had been brought up and in 1690 qualified for an MA from Edinburgh University. Thereafter much of his life was spent in Presbyterian circles in London and travelling on the continent, and he seems to have spent little of the rest of his life in Ireland; he died in 1722. He is represented in the collection in various ways, firstly, by his most important works: *Christianity not Mysterious* (1702), in its insistence that religious truth must be wholly in accord with reason, was found so offensive that (as the title page of the edition of 1702 in the collection notes) it was burned by the hangman in Ireland; in *Amyntor* (1699) he discussed the authenticity of the canonical and apocryphal scriptures and in *Nazarenus* (1718) aspects of ecclesiastical history.[17] The two-volume *Collection* of 1726 includes tracts that discuss classical Rome, Giordano Bruno, the early Church, Druidic worship and Celtic languages – Toland prided himself on his knowledge of Irish – as well as contemporary politics, an interest that is also reflected in his *Oratio philippica ad excitandos contra Galliam Britannos* (1709) and the *Second Part of the State Anatomy* (1717). He also published an edition of James Harrington's *Oceana* (1700).

Secondly, as with Dodwell, we find numerous responses to Toland in the collection, much of it negative. A study of two of his works by Elie Benoist, Johann Lorenz von Mosheim's attack on the *Nazarenus*, and Pierre Des Maizeaux's anthology, with its *Memoirs*, provide evidence of the reception of Toland's ideas on the continent, as does the fact that Benoist's work was published in Delft. As for Britain and Ireland, he attracted the ire of Jonathan Swift, who referred to him as 'the great Oracle of the Anti-Christians' and one of his publications as 'trumpery'.[18] Among the combative responses to *Amyntor* came one from Peter Browne; of uncertain birthdate, he became Provost of TCD in 1699, bishop of Cork and Ross in 1710 and died in 1735. When still a fellow he appears to have been encouraged by the college to challenge Toland through his *Answer to a Book Entituled,* Christianity not Mysterious (1703). Browne's

17 In the edition in the collection *Nazarenus* is followed by an account of Toland's life and writings attributed to Edmund Curll.

18 *An Argument against Abolishing Christianity*, pp. 125 and 113 respectively, in vol. 1 of the four-volume edition of the *Miscellanies*.

Things Divine and Supernatural (1733) was criticized by George Berkeley, who had been his pupil, while his *Discourse of Drinking Healths* (1716), which one might expect to be merely moral and social in intention, in fact illustrates the political tensions of the day: his disapproval of the practice led to his being suspected of Jacobite leanings, since such toasts were often drunk in honour of the memory of William III.

Charles Leslie (1650–1722) became an MA of TCD in 1673 and Chancellor of Connor in 1686, but as a non-juror he was deprived of his office. In a campaign of pamphlet warfare he attacked William III, various Whig clergy, Quakers, Deists and Jews. In addition to both his *Short and Easie Method with the Deists* (1715 – it also contains arguments against Judaism) and *The Truth of Christianity Demonstrated* [...] *A Vindication of the Short Method with the Deists* (1711) – the latter pamphlet being a response to criticism of the former – the collection holds duplicate copies of *The Good Old Cause* (1710), his oblique reply to an attack upon him by Bishop Gilbert Burnet, and *The Finishing Stroke* (1711), a response to the constitutional views of Benjamin Hoadly and William Higden.

Other religious writings

Of the remaining writers on religious matters James Ussher (or Usher) (1581–1656) was one of the first students of Trinity College Dublin, graduated in 1598, became a fellow of the college in 1600, Bishop of Meath in 1621 and finally Archbishop of Armagh in 1625. He was also one of the first scholars of distinction to emerge from TCD. Toland, in his *Relation of an Irish Manuscript of the Four Gospels* (p. 2 – see *Nazarenus*), refers to him as 'the incomparable Archbishop Usher (the glory of Ireland)' and Campbell in his *Survey of the South of Ireland* (p. 10) as 'without comparison the most learned man it [Trinity College] ever produced'. In William Bates' *Vitæ* Ussher is the last of thirty worthies, among them such British and continental figures of distinction as Wainflete and Bodley, Savonarola, Erasmus and Scaliger.[19] The collection holds a range of his work, including the most important: the *Annales Veteris et Novi Testamenti* of 1650–4, albeit in a relatively late edition (1686), but interestingly with a Bremen imprint. It was in this study (see p. 1 of this edition) that he first published his assertion that the events described

19 *Vitæ selectorum aliquot virorum qui doctrina, dignitate, aut pietate inclaruere* (Londini: apud Georgium Wells, 1704) – cf. pp. 734–49 of the edition in the collection.

in the first chapter of Genesis took place in 4004 BC – the product of an approach to the historicity of the Bible that was groundbreaking in its day. Other titles attest equally to the geographical and chronological range of his studies of Church history: *Dissertatio de Macedonum et Asianorum anno solari* (in the same Bremen volume); *Historia dogmatica controversiæ inter Orthodoxos & Pontificios* (1690); *Britannicarum ecclesiarum antiquitates* (1687); *De christianarum ecclesiarum successione & statu* (1658); *De episcoporum, et metropolitanorum origine* (1687); and *De Asia proconsulari* (1687). Another work concerns the relationship of the divine and the secular: *The Power Communicated by God to the Prince and the Obedience Required of the Subject* (1661) (see fig. 4). A later generation credited him with prophesying *i.a.* the events of 1641 (see below).

William King (1650–1729) was born a Presbyterian, but converted to Anglicanism while studying at TCD, where he obtained his BA in 1671. He was bishop of Derry 1691–1703 and Archbishop of Dublin 1703–29. The Fagels possessed his two major works: *De origine mali* (1702) and the sermon *Divine Predestination and Fore-Knowledge* (1728). The first gave rise to Edmund Law's *Essay on the Origin of Evil* (1731), comprising a translation into English and a commentary designed to defend King from the objections that had been published by scholars such as Bayle and Leibnitz.[20]

The subscription list for Hutcheson's *Moral Philosophy* mentioned above also contains the entry, 'Rev. Archibald M'Lean, Minister of the English church, The Hague'. Better known under the form 'Maclaine', he was born in Monaghan in 1722, the son of a Presbyterian minister. He himself studied for the ministry under Hutcheson and from 1747 was for some fifty years co-pastor of the Episcopal Church at The Hague, where his house was situated opposite the palace of the Prince of Orange and he had close connections with the royal family. He died in Bath in 1804.[21] The collection holds his translations of Mosheim's *Historia ecclesiastica antiqua et recentior* into English (1765, along with his *Supplement* of 1768) and into French (1776),[22] and his

20 The second led to the anonymous pamphlet, supportive of his ideas on predestination, *A Vindication of the Divine Attributes. In some Remarks on his Grace the Archbishop of Dublin's Sermon Intituled,* Divine Predestination [...] (London: A. Baldwin, 1710).

21 See p. 245. Maclaine's younger brother James, the so-called 'gentleman highwayman', was hanged in 1750.

22 Both are dedicated to William V as Stadtholder of the United Provinces. In the section on the fifth century in volume I of the English translation a number of passages – mainly concerning doctrinal controversies, but also the conversion of the Irish – are marked with a pencilled X in the margin.

Fig 4: James [Ussher], late Lord Archbishop of Armagh, *The Power Communicated by God to the Prince and the Obedience Required of the Subject*, London: Anne Seile, 1661: portrait and title-page. The difference in dimensions suggests that the former has been pasted in separately. (Fag. x.9.2)

THE POWER

Communicated by GOD to

THE PRINCE,

AND

THE OBEDIENCE

Required of

THE SUBJECT.

Briefly laid down, and Confirmed out of

The { *Holy* Scriptures, / *Testimony of* the Primitive Church. / *Dictates of* right Reason, *and* / *Opinion of the Wisest among the* Heathen *Writers.* }

By the most Reverend Father in God, JAMES, *late* Lord Archbishop of *ARMAGH*, *and* Primate of all Ireland.

Faithfully Published out of the *Original Copy*, written with his own hand, by the Reverend Father in God, *Robert Lord Bishop of Lincoln*, with his Lordships Preface thereunto.

Prov. 24. 21. *My Son, fear thou the Lord and the King, and meddle not with them that are given to change.*

LONDON:

Printed for *Anne Seile*, over against St. *Dunstans* Church in *Fleetstreet*, 1661.

letters to Soame Jenyns on the latter's *View of the Internal Evidence of the Christian Religion* (second edition, 1778).[23]

A number of other clergymen also appear in the collection, albeit less prominently. The Englishman Jeremy Taylor (1613–67), who was Bishop of Down and Connor from 1661 until his death, is represented by his life of Christ, *The Great Exemplar,* in a very handsome Dutch translation (1700): in folio format, it contains a number of full-page engravings (see fig. 5). Charles Hickman (1648–1713), also English, was bishop of Derry 1703–13 and contributes a volume of *Fourteen Sermons* (1706). Patrick Delany (1685–1768), a close friend of Swift and Thomas Sheridan, was fellow and tutor of TCD, and the holder of various appointments in the Church of Ireland; of his works the collection holds *Revelation Examined with Candour* (1732–3), his *Historical Account of the Life and Reign of David King of Israel* (1740) and a volume of *Fifteen Sermons upon Social Duties* (1744). Of the writings of James Duchal (1697–1761), a Presbyterian minister of liberal views, we find the *Short Explanation of the End and Design of the Lord's Supper* (1766) and duplicate copies of his sermons on the *Truth and Divine Authority of the Christian Religion* (1753). Finally the Fagels possessed the *Sermons of Mr Yorick* (1765–6) by Laurence Sterne (1713–68), as well as the ironic funeral discourse that marked his death, *Alas! Poor Yorick!* (1761) by the pseudonymous Christopher Flagellan.[24]

Religio-political cooperation and conflict

The pattern of the Fagels' purchasing suggests a strong interest, not only in doctrinal controversies generally, as we have seen above, but specifically in the aftermath of the Protestant Reformation, not least in the violent confrontations that characterized the two centuries that followed it. In the collection, the Irish dimension to these events is reflected in book form in publications such as John Davies' *Why Ireland was Neuer Entirely Subdued* (1747), Ferdinando Warner's

23 Paterson also listed the first edition (London 1777), but it was not catalogued by the college. The second translation into French of Lady Mary Wortley Montagu's *Letters* (1763), which is not in the collection, has been attributed to a collaborative effort by 'MacLaine, Tavel and Fagel'; MacLaine is presumably Archibald, while Fagel will have been Hendrik the Elder or possibly François the Younger. (See Rachele Raus, 'Lady Mary Wortley Montagu's *Letters* in France' in Alison E. Martin and Susan Pickford [eds], *Travel Narratives in Translation, 1750–1830* [New York and London 2012], pp. 157–80, here pp. 159, 176.)

24 Sterne would tend to be thought of as an English novelist, though he was born in Clonmel in Co. Tipperary and his family had a number of Irish connections; however, by 1723 or 1724 they had left Ireland. His *Sentimental Journey* is in Paterson's catalogue, but not in the collection today.

Fig 5: Jeremias Taylor, bisschop van Down en Conner [*sic*] in Yrland: *Historie van 't leven en de doot van onsen saligmaker Jesus Christus*, t'Utrecht: Wilhelm Broedelet, 1700 (part 3, plate facing p. 112): the Crucifixion of Christ, by Jan Luyken. (Fag. z.2.3)

History of the Civil-War in Ireland (1767) and Edmund Borlase's *History of the Irish Rebellion* (1743). Davies (1569–1626) was solicitor-general and then attorney-general for Ireland, where he advocated severe measures of repression. Borlase (c. 1620–82), historian and physician, sat on various committees of the Irish parliament between February 1641 and April 1644, that is, at the time of the rebellion; the first edition of his *History* (1680), in referring on the title page to the 'execrable' rebellion indicates clearly that his sympathies, too, did not lie with the opponents of English rule in Ireland. Warner (1703–68), a Church of England clergyman and historian, hoped on the other hand that his *History* would lead to greater tolerance in Ireland.

However, it is in pamphlets – of which the collection holds many thousands – that the fatal nexus of politics and religion most frequently found expression in these centuries. The experience of Protestant groupings across Europe provides the theme for an identifiable portion of the pamphlet holdings, e.g. those that record the vicissitudes of the Huguenots, Waldensians and Hussites. The degree of solidarity and shared purpose engendered by these difficulties is exemplified by one of a number of pamphlets relating to the position of the Huguenots in La Rochelle in the years 1626–8: *Brief van de belegerde binnen Rochelle, aende predicanten, onderlinghen ende diaconen vande ghereformeerde kercken vande Geunieerde Provintien* (1626). Similarly, connections between Waldensians and the Dutch Reformed Church are evidenced by the *Brief van de leeraren der euangelysche kercken in de valleyen van Piedmont aan de leeraren der euangelyscher kercken in Nederland* (1663). A more clearly political dimension to such contacts is suggested by *Een verclaringhe der oorsaken beweghende de coninghinne van Enghelandt, hulpe te gheuen tot bescherminghe des benauden ende verdructen volckes der Nederlanden* (1585) (see Harskamp, fig. 2) – and such contacts retained their importance within the Cromwellian republic: cf. *Vier voornaemste redenen waerom de protestanten vande republijck van Engelandt noodtsaeckelijck van noode hebben een religieuse correspondentie met de uytheemsche protestantse kercken* (1654). Indeed there are extensive holdings designed to inform a Dutch audience about the development of the Reformed Church in Britain and Ireland and the political challenges it faced; and the idea that hardship need not be borne alone is also central to some of the pamphlets relating directly to Ireland. Nor were spiritual developments ignored: cf. a pamphlet like *De gereformeerde Engelsche liturgie* (1645), outlining the liturgy for use in the Anglican churches of England, Scotland and Ireland.

From the mid sixteenth century on it was a primary policy of those in power in England to establish and maintain Protestant control of the kingdoms of England, Scotland and Ireland. Of the numerous pamphlets that reflect this policy one example would be the group relating to the Solemn League and Covenant, which committed the Scots and English to work towards the civil and religious union of England, Scotland and Ireland, based on Presbyterian principles. It was approved by the Church of Scotland on 17 August and by the Westminster Assembly (summoned by the Long Parliament) on 25 September 1643. I have not located a copy of the English text of the Covenant in the collection, though it is to be found elsewhere in the TCD Library, e.g. in a printing of 1643: *A Solemn League and Covenant for Reformation and Defence of Religion, the Honour and Happinesse of the King, and the Peace and Safety of England, Scotland and Ireland.* However, the text was in the possession of the Fagels in a number of Dutch-language versions, in some instances accompanied by other material. The following account does not constitute a publishing history of the Dutch pamphlets that transmitted the Covenant to a Dutch public, but is a rough chronology of those held in the collection.

A pamphlet entitled *De vierde Schotsche-post*, which appeared before the end of 1643, contains a translation of *het verbondt selfs, ofte den nieuwen eedt/ de welcke* [...] *soude ghedaen ende genomen werden.* The same translation appears in 1649, but with a slightly altered layout and a different title: *Convenant* [*sic*] *ofte verbont, tusschen de drie koninck-rijcken, te weeten; Engelandt, Schotlandt, ende Yrlandt*, and to this are appended two further short documents (the first of which is also in the *Schotsche-post*).

Another translation is also found in two printings, firstly as *Het verbont/ of naerder vnie van de drie koninckrijcken, Engelant Schotlandt en Yerlandt.* The title page of this pamphlet, which goes on to list other documents, lacks details of publication – they may have been trimmed off in the binding process – but the surrounding material in the volume appeared in 1643. The second printing appears alongside other, but different documents in *Declaratie van beyde huysen des parlements* (1645), and here the *Verbondt ofte unie* is in last position. The differences between the two largely involve orthography and minor aspects of format, the wording of the text of the Covenant being virtually identical.

A third translation in the collection is represented by a pamphlet published in 1645 in London as *Een solemnele ligue ende verbont van weghen de reformatie / ende de bescherminge van religie* [...]. This, too, appeared in another printing, in 1660, with a more elaborate title: *Solemnel covenant ofte heyligh verbondt gemaeckt ende besworen door de Heeren ende Gemeenten van de drie koninckrijcken van Engelandt, Schotlandt ende Yerlandt.* Apart from the wording of the title pages there are differences in layout, morphology and orthography between the two printings; the first also has a preface, *Aen de christelijken leser*, found in no other version in the collection, but neither contains the supplementary documents mentioned above.

Fourthly, in 1649 a further translation had been published (by Abraham Andriessz): *Covenant, ofte verbondt tot reformatie ende defensie van de religie, eere ende welstant van den koning, den vrede* [...]. This item is interesting in that it has, in ink, what appear to be suggested improvements to the translation and, in pencil, suggested corrections of typographical errors. Some of this information has been lost in the process of cutting the pamphlet down for binding. In the same year this translation also appeared under a different imprint (Jan van Hilten) and with variations in orthography and layout; and a third copy of this translation is a duplicate of this second printing.

Finally, there is a pamphlet with, as its only content, a Latin translation of the text of the Covenant: *Pactum et foedus sanctum pro religione reformandâ* [...]. It is interesting that this appeared as early as 1643, but in the absence of accompanying material or even a place of publication I cannot say in whose interest it might have been produced.

Of the English-language original we thus have no fewer than five translations – four of them in two printings – with a total of ten copies in the collection: this would seem to indicate a lively interest in this religio-political policy of consolidation on the part of the Dutch reading public and, by extension, the Fagel family.

If Ireland might be said to figure in this group of pamphlets as a minor aspect of a wider interest in the islands of Britain and Ireland as a whole, it is central to a number of pamphlets that reflect the external threats to the policy of Protestant English control of Ireland, the internal efforts to implement it and Catholic Irish resistance to it. Thus there are two copies of *Sekere verclaringhen wt Yrlandt / aengaende het verlies ende benautheden der Spaenscher Armado toegheuallen op de west custen van Yrlandt* [...] (1588), which details the ships that were lost and where they foundered, how many men were drowned and how many saved, with the names of those who were of social or military importance (see fig. 6); another pamphlet, *Nieuwe tijdinghe* [...], based on a letter from

Nota.

Daer moghen wel fauten zijn int schrijuē vande Spaensche namen uit Engels/door dien sy ghescreuen zijn by middele van interpretatie / maer daer is geen faute van het ghetal der persoonen die doot oft leuendich zijn/Ghedaen den 26. September 1588.

Voor het verlies vande voorsz. 17. schepen voor Yrlant zijnder noch vergaen in Julij eñ in Augusti 15. andere groote schepen in het geuecht tusschen de Engelsche eñ Spaensche vlooten inde smalle Zee van Engelant/daer niet een Engels schip ofte man van qualiteyt/vergaen ofte ghenomen is.

T'ghetal der schepen ende menschen die ghebleuen zijn.

	schepen	menschen
Galeyen	4	1622
Niet verde van Edeston by Pleymuyē	1	000
⁑ { Datmael wert mede ghenomen het schip van Don Pedro de Valdes.	1	422
Datmael verbrant eē Bisschaper	1	289
Voor Calis wert ghespolieert die principaelste Galiasse van Napels / daer in Don Hugo de Moncado doot bleef.	1	686
Inden slach sonck een groot Bisschaeper	1	000
* { Dat Galioen S. Philippo.	1	532
Het Galioen S. Matheus.	1	397
Een groote Bosschaper ghestrant by oosteynde	1	000
Den dach nae het ghevecht soncken twee Veneetsianen	2	843
Een grooten Bosschaper ghedwonghen aen strant by Habel neuf door twee vande Coninginnen schepen.	1	000

Somma 15. schepen 4791. menschen.

⁑ Dese twee bleuen aen Engelandt.

*Dese twee zijn in ghedwongen tot Vlissinghen/ zijnde seer gequetst. Ende in sint Mat. was Don Diego Piemontelle.

In Tireconel in Langgefoyl een schip / wt dit selue schip ende anderen diet ontquamen 1100. menschen.

In Connaught	In Slig hauen	3	1500
	In Tireauley	1	400
	In Cleer Eylandt	1	300
	In Finglas	1	400
	In Offerti	1	200
	In Irrise	2	*000
	In de Baye Garliawe	1	70
In Munster	In die Shena	2	600
	In Treale	1	24
	In Dingele	1	500
	In Desmont	1	300
	In de Shinnau	1	⁑ 000

Somma total 17. schepen 5394. menschen.

* Dese menschē ontquamen in een ander schip.

⁑ Dit schip verbrandt/eñ de menschen worden ghebercht in een andr schip.

Somma in beyde verliesen 32. schepen / 10185. menschen/benessens vele schepen daer niet af ghehoort wordt/die vermoedet worden verloren te zijn/ waer van geuangen soo in Engelant als Zeelant ten minsten 1000. benessens een groote menichte hier niet gerekent / die doot ghebleuen zijn int ghevecht/eñ van honger gestoruen alst blijckt.

FINIS.

Fig 6: *Sekere verclaringhen wt Yrlandt / aengaende het verlies ende benautheden der Spaenscher armado toegheuallen op de west custen van Yrlandt*, Eerst, ghedruckt in Londen by Ridtsaert Filde. Daer nae tot Amstelredam by Cornelis Claesz, 1588 (p. Biv verso): a table giving the numbers of ships and men of the Spanish Armada lost on or off the Irish coast. (Fag. H.3.8, no. 20)

Milorde Grey / gouuernuer [*sic*] *van Yrlandt*, gives similar information, but more briefly and less systematically. A pamphlet of 1624 contains the *Proclamatie vant bannissement der iesuwyten ende paepsche priesters uyt Yrlandt*, while a House of Commons Committee *Report* of 1734 on the seizure of papers belonging to 'one Mcc. [*sic*] Carthy, alias Rabah, a reputed titular Popish bishop' indicates that concern over Catholic ecclesiastical organization was still very much alive a century later. Support for the policy of Protestant hegemony on the part of loyal Irish institutions is expressed in a pamphlet like the *Besluyt ende verklaringe van 't parlement in Yrlandt* (1640), a declaration of fidelity to King Charles as he prepares to confront the rebellious Scots – *de slimste ende boseste van dese sijne Onderdanen* – and an assurance that the four *subsidien* already granted can be supplemented if necessary.[25] Another coercive measure was the imposition of forfeitures of land. *The Case of the Forfeitures in Ireland Fairly Stated* (1700) and *Jus regium* (1701) are attempts to justify the practice, while the *Short View of both Reports* (1701) is a response to the parliamentary reports of 1699 and 1701 on the subject.

Religio-political conflict: the rising of 1641

That such measures produced reactions is not surprising. The most spectacular act of Irish Catholic resistance in the seventeenth century was the rebellion or rising of 1641. The library of Trinity College possesses a massive collection of contemporary or near-contemporary manuscript depositions arising out of this event.[26] Their formal purpose was to register claims for compensation for property that had been lost, but inevitably they contain details of the massacres and other horrific atrocities allegedly perpetrated by Catholics on Protestants during the rising. Beyond the assumption that these accounts are greatly exaggerated, their degree of accuracy is still a matter of controversy. However, to the extent that the allegations were believed at the time, the rebellion constituted a kind of test case: the reformist project in one European country could be presented as facing an existential threat, with implications for other countries. A number of Dutch-language pamphlets arising from this conflict are also to be found in the

25 This item consists of a single sheet, originally of a size roughly comparable to A4 and printed on one side only: one wonders why such a document, in what is effectively poster format, should have been produced in the Netherlands.

26 These depositions, which are not part of the Fagel Collection, have been the subject of a large-scale collaborative research project: cf. http://1641.tcd.ie.

collection, most, it would seem, again the result of translation. An example would be *Yrelandtsche traenen*: [...] *een lijste, vande noyt gehoorde wreetheden/ ende barbarische verraderyen der bloet-dorstighe jesuwijten* (1642). Inspired by *The Teares of Ireland* by James Cranford (?1592–1657), this is a relatively long (sixty-four pages), systematic and detailed account of the alleged atrocities of 1641, with each of twenty-four participants being treated in turn. That the translation appeared in the same year as the original may suggest not just an urgent interest shared by the British and the Dutch public, but also a close relationship between the respective printers.[27] The rising is also the subject of another complete pamphlet – *Nieuwe ende goede tijdinge uyt Yrlant* (1644) – in which the opposition of Lord Inchiquin and others to a ceasefire with the *bloet-dorstige Yrische rebellen* is expressed, and claims of outrages carried out by monks, priests and Jesuits in the province of Munster are recorded.

Other pamphlets contain only brief references to the events of the rising, which their titles do not necessarily lead the reader to expect. Thus from the title *Den Enghelschen paus* ('the English pope' – probably 1643) one might not anticipate the allusions to massacres by Irish rebels that are found e.g. on pp. 35–6. And it is only far down on the title page of the *Ootmoedige requeste, van de raetheeren* [...] *van Londen* (1642) that one finds that *Daer by gevoecht zijn de copien van twee bysondere missiven uyt Yerlandt*, which describe the allegedly barbaric and inhuman acts of violence inflicted on Protestants there. Of these brief missives – they were read to the Westminster parliament on 24 December 1641 and together take up two pages – the first, signed by Thomas Partington and dated 17 December 1641, describes alleged atrocities, particularly in Munster; the second, neither signed nor dated, portrays one incident, involving the murder of a woman and her newborn child.

Similarly, it is only at the end of the title page of *Regis Caroli casus* (1649) that we find mention of *de Rebellie in Yerlandt*, and the long title of the first number of *De Schotsche post* (1643) ends with a reference to the *comploot van de Yrijsche/ Engelsche/ ende Schotsche papisten* and the arrest of the Earl of Antrim, *een vande voornamste paepsche rebellen in Yrlandt*, as the text describes

27 That such links were possible in later years is indicated by the career of William Smith, a native of Belfast, who by the early 1720s was based in Amsterdam and operating as 'continental book buyer for J[ohn] Smith & [William] Bruce'. His marriage to Agatha Cornelia Wetstein (cf. *Ex officina Wetsteniana* on the title-page of Toland's *Oratio philippica*) gave rise to the imprint 'R. & J. Wetstein and W. Smith'. See pp. 219 and 208, and M. Pollard: *A Dictionary of the Members of the Dublin Book Trade 1550–1800 Based on the Records of the Guild of St. Luke the Evangelist Dublin* (London 2000), p. 539.

him (p. A3r). The opening pages of *Den Brittannischen donderslach* (1643) place the rising of 1641 in an apocalyptic context of wars and rumours of wars: *t' Vyer van Godts toorn is aenghesteecken* [...] *Men hoort niet dan van* Oorloghen, *ende* gheruchten van Oorloge [...] *Het Koninckrijcke van* Ierlandt *treurt, de Arme Protestanten werden aldaer vermoort* [...]. A Dutch origin for this pamphlet may be indicated by the way in which it expresses solidarity with other countries in referring, five years before the end of Thirty Years War, to *De miserien van Duytslandt, de ellenden die onse nabueren in* Engelandt *ende* Jerlandt *sijn overghekomen* (p. A3r).

The two missives that I have just discussed express the wish that the help that has been promised will be sent speedily. A more elaborate attempt on the Irish side to appeal to Dutch solidarity is represented by the pamphlet *Yrlands bloedende request aen de gereformeerde kercken der vereenigde Nederlandsche Provintien* [...] (1643) (see fig. 7). This claims that the *Papisten*, advised by the Jesuits *en andere gespanjoliseerde Geestelicheyt* ('and other Hispanicized clergy'), are conspiring to exterminate all Protestants in Ireland in the rebellion that began with the attack on the city and castle of Dublin in October 1641. The grossly exaggerated figure of 154,000 dead in the first four months of the rebellion is quoted and those who have suffered are likened to the victims of the Roman emperors, to the Waldensians, Hussites and Bohemians, Protestants under Charles IX in France, under Mary in England, and under the Duke of Alba in the Netherlands. On the basis of shared faith, religion and baptism they seek the help of their *Eerwaerde en geliefde Vrienden* in the Netherlands.

The complex publishing history of this pamphlet and the presence of five copies in the collection seem to suggest a high degree of interest. So does the fact that one copy has much underlining of the text and two lines of manuscript comment, though this did not necessarily come from the pen of one of the Fagels: there is evidence that they purchased many pamphlets second hand. All five copies were published in 1643, but they represent three different printings (including two pairs of duplicates), and up to three different publishers may also be involved: the only pair of duplicates to name one, Isaac Reyers in Dordrecht, differs in format and linguistic morphology from the other pair, and the singleton is different again (see fig. 7). There is also a significant difference in content: one of the pairs of duplicates and the singleton contain an additional section: *Requeste van de gecommitteerde des parlements in Engelant/ aen-gaende den bedroefden toe-stant van vele duysenden arme protestanten in*

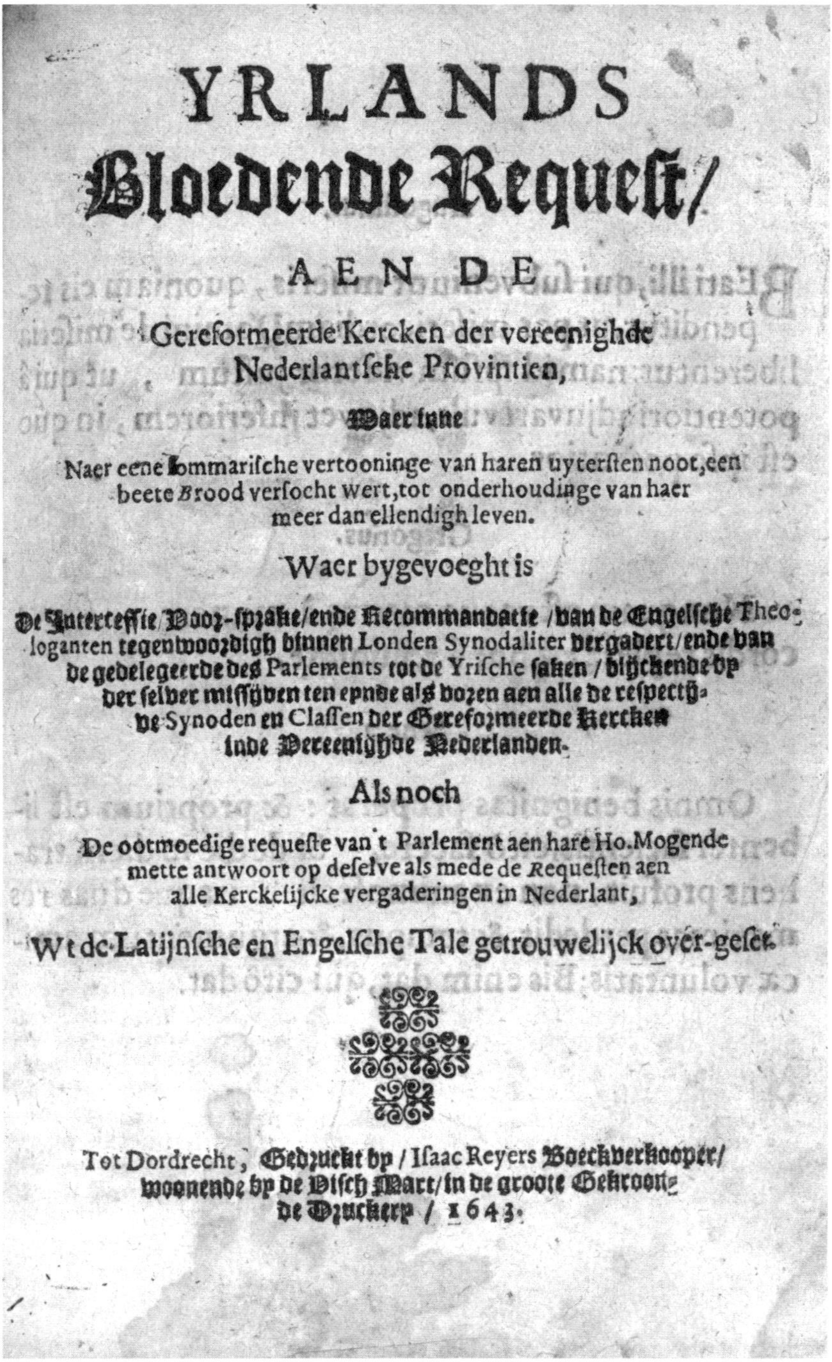

YRLANDS
Bloedende Request/
AEN DE
Gereformeerde Kercken der vereenighde
Nederlantsche Provintien,
Waer inne
Naer eene sommarische vertooninge van haren uytersten noot, een beete Brood versocht wert, tot onderhoudinge van haer meer dan ellendigh leven.
Waer bygevoeght is
De Intercessie/Voor-spraecke/ende Recommandatie /van de Engelsche Theologanten tegenwoordigh binnen Londen Synodaliter vergadert/ende van de gedelegeerde des Parlements tot de Yrische saken / blijckende by der selver missyven ten eynde als voren aen alle de respectyve Synoden en Classen der Gereformeerde Kercken inde Vereenighde Nederlanden.
Als noch
De ootmoedige requeste van't Parlement aen hare Ho. Mogende mette antwoort op deselve als mede de Requesten aen alle Kerckelijcke vergaderingen in Nederlant,
Wt de Latijnsche en Engelsche Tale getrouwelijck over-geset.
Tot Dordrecht, Gedruckt by / Isaac Reyers Boeckverkooper/ woonende by de Visch Mart/ in de groote Gekroonde Druckerye / 1643.

Fig 7: *Yrlands Bloedende Request / aen de Gereformeerde Kercken der vereenighde Nederlantsche Provintien* [...], Wt de Latijnsche en Engelsche Tale getrouwelijck over-geset, Dordrecht: Isaac Reyers, 1643. (Fag. H.1.50, no. 16)

het koninghrijcke van Yrlant. Finally, this same section is also present in the collection as a separate publication in two duplicate copies.

That the sense of solidarity among the Reformist churches of Europe extended to material support in such circumstances as the rising of 1641 is evidenced by a further pamphlet in the collection: the *Sent-brief van de Nationale Synode van Schotlant, aen de Nederlantsche kercken,* thanking them for their s*poedighe Collecte in de Kercken voor de broederen van Yerlant*, their *vertroosten van de Yersche Kercken* (p. A2v). We may assume that pamphlets like the *Bloedende request* will have helped to stimulate such generosity.

As an aside one should mention that a later generation would claim that in a sermon preached in 1601 the 'excellent' James Ussher had foreseen the 'Rebellion in Ireland Forty years before it came to pass'.[28] This pamphlet soon found its way to a Dutch public as *Vreemde en aanmerkelijke voorzeggingen van de heylige, geleerde en uitstekende Jacobus Usher*. The collection has one copy of each of three editions of the translation (1678, 1686 and 1688).

The Fagels' interest in prophecy, astrology and other forms of prognostication is also seen in another curio: *Verhael van de seer beklaechlicke afbrandinge der stadt Corke*, concerning the burning of Cork in 1622; the battle between large numbers of starlings over the city a year previously, in which thousands of birds were reported to have died, was seen as a portent of the later disaster, which in turn was interpreted as an exemplum encouraging repentance.

Religio-political conflict: the Williamite period

The persistent fear of a repetition of the events of 1641 led the British authorities and public to accept Titus Oates' claim of an imminent 'popish plot' in 1678. Two pamphlets in the collection – *Waerachtig verhael, van het schrickelijck verraet, en samensweering van de paepsche partye* (1679 – two duplicate copies) and *Engelants verraed ontdeckt* (1679 – three duplicate copies) – outline the allegations, including the Irish dimension: the supposed involvement of persons such as *Vader Suinam een Yersche Jesuit tot Madrid* and the plan for the conquest of Ireland with the assassination of the Duke of Ormond as the signal for a general uprising and massacre of Protestants as in 1641 – *als voor desen* – (pp. 9 and 50 respectively).

28 *Strange and Remarkable Prophesies* [*sic*] *and Predictions, of the Holy, Learned, and Excellent James Usher* (1678).

Unsurprisingly there is a considerable amount of material in the collection dealing with the Williamite period. One group of pamphlets is of particular interest in that it presents a member of the family, Pensionaris of Holland Gaspar Fagel (1634–88), as a participant in an issue that related to Ireland: the Penal Laws and the Sacramental Test by which anybody wishing to hold public office in Great Britain or Ireland was required to take Holy Communion according to the rite of the Anglican Church. In November 1687 he wrote a letter to James Stewart (1635–1713), from 1692 Lord Advocate of Scotland, who had been instructed by King James to ascertain the views of the Prince and Princess of Orange on these matters. In the letter, which appeared as *Een brief, geschreeven door den heer pensionaris Fagel* early in 1688, he writes of *de publyke en vastgestelde religie van* Engeland, *Schotland, en Yerland* and notes the high proportion of Roman Catholics in Ireland (pp. 3 and 5 respectively). By the end of the year he had caused a flurry of publications containing translations of and comments on the letter by other writers in Dutch, English and French, five of which are in the collection. The anonymous *Reflectien op den heer Fagels brief* and *Considération sur la lettre de Mr. Fagel* probably came first. Then there is the *Réponse à la lettre supposée écrite par Monsieur Fagel*, authorship of which is assigned to Stewart in the TCD printed catalogue, though the text itself says that it was written by *une personne qui estime & qui honnore beaucoup M. Stewart.* This in turn produced *Réflexions sur un écrit, intitulé Réponse à la lettre supposée écrite par Monsieur Fagel.* Finally, Fagel himself takes up his pen again in the *Missive* [...] *Aen den heere marquis d'Albyville*, who was the Extraordinaris Envoyé of King James to the States General of the Netherlands. The pamphlet attributed to Stewart suggests that, even though Fagel is a Calvinist, his position on these issues is that only those restrictive measures should be abolished whose removal will not threaten Anglican supremacy.

A series of pamphlets relates to the context of William III's war in Ireland. The *Declaratien van syn hoogheyt Wilhem Henrik* (1688), of which the collection holds three copies, state that his decision to cross over to England with an armed force is partly motivated by the knowledge that the government of Ireland is in the hands of Papists; Protestants there live under such fear of arbitrary power that many have emigrated; and, not least, they are still mindful of the events of 1641 (*die wreede en bloedige moort*, p. 8). Similar sentiments are found in the *Apologie voor de protestanten van Ierland* (1689), with its claims that Catholics increasingly hold positions of power, are stockpiling weapons and plan a rebellion like 1641, while *Koning William of koning Louis* (n.d.) places memories of 1641 and allegations of current anti-Protestant discrimination in the context of a wider argument that sees James II as Louis XIV's stalking horse and asserts the importance of the security of Holland for *de Universeele Protestantse Kerk* (pp. 7–8). The *Antwoord op de declaratie van de gewesen koning Jacobus* (1689) relates to the time when James was still in possession of Dublin, while the *Verhaal van een gevecht, voorgevallen tusschen de Franschen en Yeren* (n.d.) claims that there have been instances of hostility between Irish administrators serving James, such as Major General Justinus Maccarty [*sic*], Governor of Cork, and French officials attempting to take over their positions. The *Pertinent dagh-relaes* (1689) concludes (pp. 18–19) with a declaration of the Protestant nobility of Munster that they wish to place themselves under the command of Lord Inchiquin and Henry Boyle. Lastly, the *Voornaame tydinge uyt Ierland* (1689) is in effect recruiting propaganda: given the possibilities of employment and the low cost of land and living, the war in Ireland currently offers the best opportunities for service (*de voorteeligste dienst*, p. 3) in Europe.

Other publications inform the reader about the war itself, in particular the siege of Derry (or Londonderry) that lasted from 16 September 1688 until 1 August 1689. It is another event of pivotal significance in Irish Protestant construction of the past. At sixty-three pages the *Waarachtig en pertinent dag-verhaal* (1689) of George Walker is by some distance the longest account. Walker, who in different pamphlets and contexts is given the titles Rev., Dr and Col., was born between 1643 and 1648 and was the governor of Derry. He gives a brief description of the city, an account of the siege and its eventual relief, as well as the wording of various documents and letters, lists of enemy officers killed or captured, and the prices of such foods as a cat, a dog's head, a handful of seaweed etc. The *Historisch verhaal van het gepasseerde in Engelant, Schotland en Yerlant* (1689) has a much narrower focus, reporting on the events of May and June 1689, including successful operations against those besieging Derry, as well as rumours of dissent between the Irish and French forces and an estimate that the city could hold out for a further seven weeks; it concludes (pp. 26–9) with a *Iournael*, a concise, but detailed, daily account of the defensive and offensive measures taken by those under siege between 3 and 26 May 1689, written by an officer defending Derry; he also reports on a sermon preached by Walker, in which he encouraged the troops with the thought that the safety of three kingdoms depended on their bravery. Of the three reports, dated June 1689 and printed recto and verso on the single sheet comprising *De drie laatste post-tydinge uyt London*, two bring news of the siege of Derry: one records an assault on the city by the forces of King James on 29 May, the efforts to bring men and munitions from Britain to reinforce the defence, and speculation as to how long the siege might last; the other notes that in a sally forth from the city the defenders killed 1800 of the besiegers. The *Waarachtig verhaal van de tegenwoordigen toestand van Ierland* (1689) contains, *i.a.*, information on the strength of James's forces, a list of the Irish nobility and a letter from the hand of Col. Walker. The *Pertinent verhael van 't* [...] *ontsetten en verlaten van Londonderry* (n.d.) describes the aftermath of the siege. Little more than a year later Walker would be among those who died in the decisive engagement of William's war in Ireland, the Battle of the Boyne; his last words are recorded in *Waarachtig verhaal van de laatste reden, van den eerwaardigen Dr. George Walker* (n.d.). Another combatant at the Boyne, Godert de Ginkel, is the subject of the bilingual pamphlet, *The Character of the Lord Baron Ginckle / De ware verbeeltenis van sijn excellentie den baron van Ginckel* (1691), which celebrates his character and his contribution to William's campaign.

The *Memorie van 't geene gepasseert is in 't leger van konink William* (1690) is a two-page account by an engineer, as the title page tells us, from his disembarkation at Carrickfergus on 17 June, via the Battle of the Boyne (in which, he says, Schomberg was killed no more than ten paces away from him) to the hearty welcome received by William's troops as they entered Dublin: the formulation, *De Gereformeerde ontfangen ons met groote blyschap*, might suggest a Dutch author. The *Tweede oprecht en waere journael uyt Yerlandt* (n.d.) consists of four brief eyewitness reports dated 16–19 July 1690, i.e. following the Battle of the Boyne on 1 July (old style). They too describe William's entry into Dublin on Sunday 6 July and the warm welcome that his troops received, including the quotation, with its Hiberno-English flavour, *God blesh youw all, brave Gentlemen*, as well as noting the capture of prisoners and the desertion of some of James's troops to William's side; the munitions and provisions that were found in the city's magazine; and – not least – the advantages of the city and its setting, and the respectability of its inhabitants: *wel soo groot als Rotterdam* [...] *een schoone Baey* [...] *een gesonde lucht* [...] *fatsoenlijcke Luyden*. The comparison with Rotterdam seems again to indicate a Dutch author. In the *Brief van Tyrconnel* (1690) the author refers to the achievement of General de Lauzun and himself in fortifying Galway and Limerick, the latter being the object of an unsuccessful siege by William's forces in August of that year.

Three pamphlets give a retrospective view of the war. William's brief *Aenspraeck, aen beyde de huysen des parlements* (1690?) begins by mentioning his endeavours in the year in question (presumably 1690) to ensure that Ireland would no longer be a burden on England. The *Gereformeerde Mercurius* of 25 July 1690 (old style) includes reflections on William's successes in Ireland and the role of his personal qualities in his victories, especially at the Boyne. At ninety-six pages *Yerlant verlost en hersteld* (1690) is the most substantial and detailed pamphlet that I have considered. After a very short account of Ireland and its people it moves to the events of 1689–90: the siege of Derry, William's arrival in Ireland, the Battle of the Boyne, the surrender of Dublin, James's flight to France and the rejoicing in Paris at the mistaken report of William's death in late July 1690, William's departure from Ireland, a list of dead and wounded on William's side. It is also unusual in having copious illustrations, for the most part depictions of surrendered towns, but also including a panoramic view of the Battle of the Boyne (see fig. 8).

The Dublin book trade

Nearly all the English-language publications in the collection have London imprints, with a scattering from Oxford and Cambridge, Edinburgh and Glasgow. As regards genuine Dublin publications, I have located no more than the fourteen that are listed in the final section of the Bibliography (including five relating to Ireland that were reprinted elsewhere from Dublin editions and three that have no Irish dimension apart from the fact of publication itself). This means that most of the books by Irish authors in the collection are not in Irish editions.

However, even this small number of publications contains information about the Dublin book trade, its printers and publishers and their places of business. For example, the full imprint of Leland's 'answer' to Tindal's *Christianity as Old as the Creation* runs:

> *DUBLIN*: Printed by S[tephen] Powell, For Abraham Bradley, at the *Two Bibles* in *Dame's-street*, opposite to *Sycamore-Alley*, Bookseller. M.DCC. XXXIII.

Ten other publications name publisher-booksellers. Swift's correspondence is presented as 'Printed by and for' George Faulkner, as are the six volumes

Fig 8: *Yerlant verlost en hersteld, door den onvermoeide victorieuzen William de III$^{de.}$ koning van Groot-Britannien. Waar in kortelijk verhandelt werd zijn maijesteits heyrtogt na Yerland*, Amsterdam: Jan ten Hoorn, 1690 (facing p. 52): panoramic view of the Battle of the Boyne. William III and the Duke of Schomberg (who was to die in the battle) are identified by the numbers 1 and 2. (Fag. 11.1.26, no. 13)

in the edition of his works, four of which add 'in *Essex-Street*' and two 'opposite to the Bridge'; Clayton's *Vindication* Part II is simply 'Printed by' Faulkner 'in Essex-street'. In two further cases we also have printer, publisher and the latter's place of business. The *Works* of Josephus are:

> Printed by R[ichard]Reilly: For George Ewing Bookseller, at the *Angel* and *Bible* in *Dame's-street*

and Clanricarde's Memoirs are:

> Printed by S[tephen]Powell, For C[harles] Connor, at *Pope's Head* on the *Blind-Key*, near *Essex-Gate*

Hutcheson's works on *Beauty and Virtue* and the *Passions and Affections* were printed in London for 'Wil. and John Smith on the *Blind Key* in *Dublin*' and '*John Smith* and *William Bruce*, Booksellers in *Dublin*' respectively. The 'Advertisement' to the *Reflexions* of Duncan Forbes (1685–1747), a Scottish lawyer with an interest in theological matters, tells us that through the good offices of a number of his friends they were published after his death by George and Alexander Ewing and Robert Main in Dublin; the title page refers to them as 'Booksellers in *Dame-street*'. The account of Englishman Charles Thompson's travels in Europe was published by Peter Wilson 'at *Gay's* Head [*sic*] in *Dame-street*'. Finally, Borlase's *History of the Irish Rebellion* (see fig. 9) appeared under the imprint:

> *DUBLIN:* Printed by and for Oli[ver] Nelson, at *Milton's Head* in *Skinner-Row*; and for Charles Connor, at *Pope's Head*, near *Essex-Gate*. M DCC XLIII.

These publisher-booksellers have to advertise their wares: the edition of Josephus has at the back of volumes 1 and 4 respectively 'A CATALOGUE of BOOKS lately printed for and sold by George Ewing, Bookseller at the *Angel* and *Bible* in *Dame-street*' and 'A CATALOGUE of BOOKS, lately imported from *England* and *Holland* [...]'. Similarly, at the back of Forbes' *Reflexions* we find 'The following BOOKS, printed in *Scotland*, sold by Robert Main, Bookseller in *Dame-street*, opposite *Fownes's street*', while Faulkner's edition of Swift's correspondence concludes with a list of 'BOOKS lately published and sold by the Printer hereof'. At the end of Thompson's *Travels* is a catalogue of books 'To be sold by Peter Wilson' at his Dame Street address.

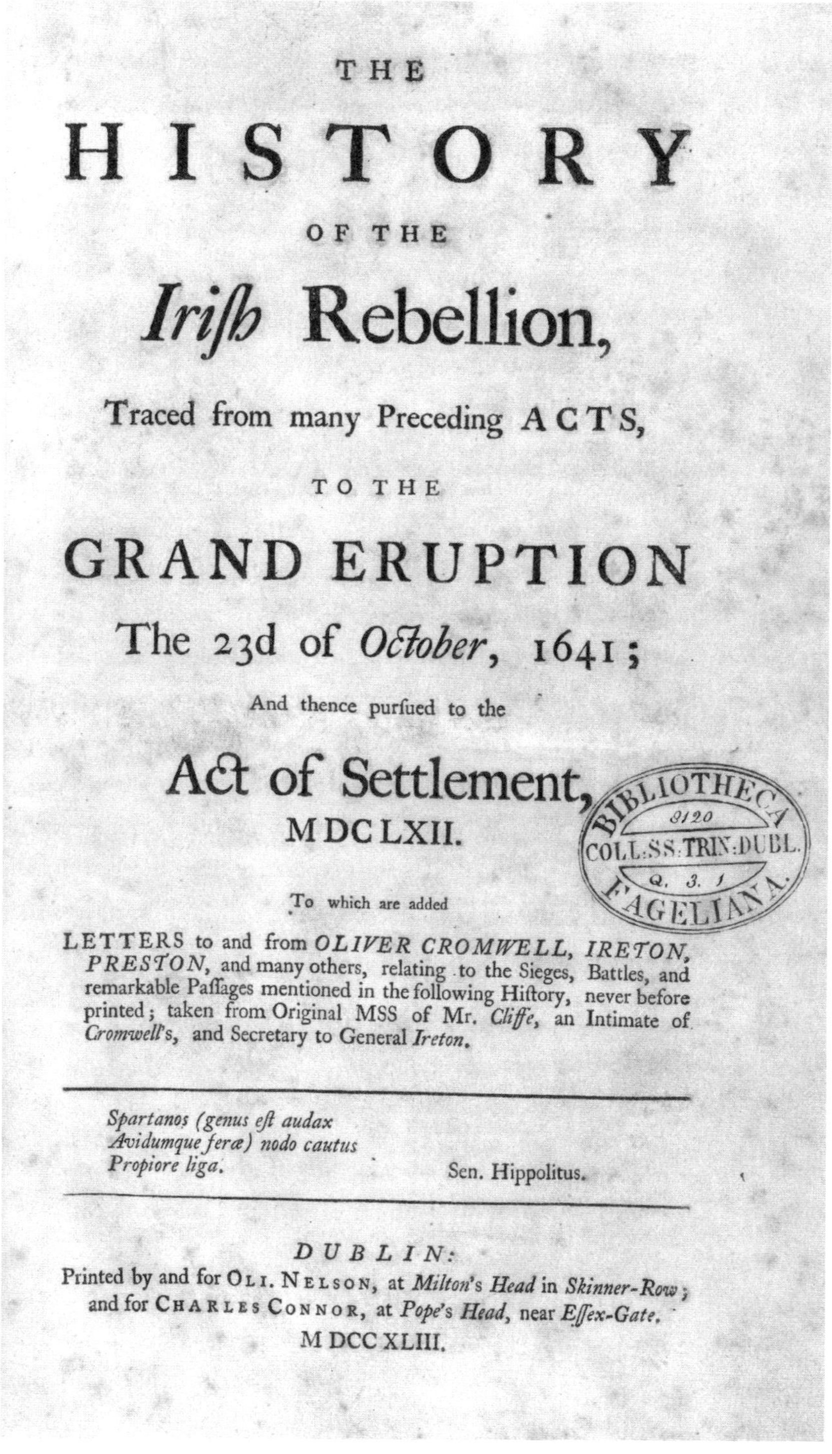

THE

HISTORY

OF THE

Irish Rebellion,

Traced from many Preceding ACTS,

TO THE

GRAND ERUPTION

The 23d of *October*, 1641;

And thence pursued to the

Act of Settlement,

MDCLXII.

To which are added

LETTERS to and from *OLIVER CROMWELL*, *IRETON*, *PRESTON*, and many others, relating to the Sieges, Battles, and remarkable Passages mentioned in the following History, never before printed; taken from Original MSS of Mr. *Cliffe*, an Intimate of *Cromwell's*, and Secretary to General *Ireton*.

Spartanos (genus est audax
Avidumque feræ) nodo cautus
Propiore liga.
Sen. Hippolitus.

DUBLIN:
Printed by and for OLI. NELSON, at *Milton's Head* in *Skinner-Row*;
and for CHARLES CONNOR, at *Pope's Head*, near *Essex-Gate*.
M DCC XLIII.

Fig 9: Edmund Borlase, *The History of the Irish Rebellion*, Dublin: Oliver Nelson and Charles Connor, 1743. (Fag. Q.3.1)

If the books coming onto the market indicate the interests of the reading public, subscription lists do so even more clearly. I noted above that, in addition to Greffier Fagel (probably François the Elder), a number of Irish personages are among the subscribers to the five-volume edition of the works of Robert Boyle; similarly, Hendrik Fagel the Elder stands alongside six Irish bishops, seven fellows of TCD and at least twenty other Irish names in the list of those subscribing to Hutcheson's *Moral Philosophy*; those supporting the publication of Borlase's work include Luke Gardiner; Lady Howth; the Earl of Kildare; the Reverend Charles Meredyth, Dean of Ardfert; Joseph Nicholls, Store-keeper of Duncannon; and Mr. Cornelius Wynne, Bookseller [Capel Street, Dublin]. Still more informative is Thompson's book of travels: even a cursory examination of the subscription list appended to the last volume identifies some thirty subscribers as Irish or having a residence in Ireland, among them such persons as the Bishop of Cork and the Bishop of Clogher, Lady Drogheda and Mrs Mary Montgomery of Stephen's Green (Dublin) – and there may well be many more. Fourteen are explicitly associated with Trinity College Dublin; and fourteen booksellers are named, of whom eleven are trading in the city, including Powell, Faulkner, Ewing and Connor. Arthur Young, in the pages that precede his account of his Irish tour (not published in Dublin), presents the process of publication by subscription as complex and risky: again, the names of the subscribers are listed, the Irish separately from the British, but more striking is his criticism of Dublin booksellers, of whom he alleges that they are so greedy that they demand as much as three shillings to deliver a copy of his book.

Conclusions

Returning to the question that I posed at the outset, the answer is that when the Fagel Collection found its new home in Trinity College it contained much material that relates to Ireland – and two centuries later some of it, as Jaap Harskamp and Andrew Pettegree have established (see p. xxi), is known to be unique. I have listed over 200 titles, but I have no doubt that a more thorough search would identify more, particularly relating to religious topics: I have, for example, not examined lots 1601–1764 in Paterson's catalogue, 'Sermons by eminent English divines'; nor have I in general listed, say, the many responses from non-Irish theologians to the contributions of Irish writers to religious controversies. Although the holdings might allow us to draw some conclusions about the reception of the works of Swift and Burke, Berkeley and Toland in the Netherlands, the more significant material lies in the largely anonymous pamphlets. However, not until there is a catalogue that records every pamphlet and broadsheet will we know exactly what is there to be studied: nothing had led me to expect the single-sheet *De drie laatste post-tydinge uyt London*.[29]

Another, more complex, question has remained implicit above: whether in the quantity and nature of this Irish material there is evidence that the Fagel family collected it because they were aware of Ireland as a political, historical, cultural and social entity, distinct from England or Britain. As regards the collection as a whole, systematic purchase by the Fagels is indicated not just by the sheer volume of the holdings in certain areas (e.g. religious controversies), but also by the evidence of second-hand acquisition: for example, on a paste-down inside the front cover of Dodwell's book on the mortality of the soul the name 'Rich Dashwood' is written. That is to say, the massive holdings of pamphlets are not simply the result of standing orders with certain publishers, but were augmented by other means. Whether, however, one should have expected more than 200 titles or fewer I cannot judge. Nor can I say whether these titles are present as the result of a targeted interest in Ireland on the part of the Fagels, the more so since there is no evidence of systematic use. Persons mentioned cryptically in *Gulliver Decypher'd* are identified in manuscript in the margins, and elsewhere we find very occasional underlining, marginal notes and doodles, but I am not in a position to say from whose hand these derive. Only in the case of Gaspar and the Sacramental Test is there evidence of an active interest in an issue that was relevant to Ireland.

My intention in this article was limited to giving a descriptive account of the material that I have been able to locate in the collection. Somebody with the requisite expertise – and access to the Fagel Archive – would be able to cast more light on the principles according to which the Fagels selected books for purchase and the pattern of their use. In addition, however, to such an attempt to clarify the genesis and original function of the collection, an analysis of its content would add to our knowledge of at least three aspects of early modern European history.

29 See p. xxv, note 12, and p. xxxii.

Firstly, one could examine more closely the function of Dutch pamphlets relating to 1641 or 1689–90, be they original Dutch productions or versions of English-language originals. These publications can be seen as part of a Europe-wide enterprise: the establishment and maintenance of the Reformist project, the construction and preservation of Protestant identity in the face of hostile forces. This has implications for the self-image of Dutch Protestantism in its relation to that project and to the Irish (and British) Protestantism with which it is allying itself.

Secondly, one side effect of the Reformation and the Enlightenment was a ferment of theological ideas, some more, some less orthodox. That a substantial number of the theological works of Irish origin in the collection were written by Protestants and Fellows of Trinity College is not surprising: apart from the Fagels' interest in the Protestant churches, Trinity was an Anglican institution and the only university in the country. How distinctive was its contribution to European theological thought?

Thirdly, I had not anticipated just how many pamphlets had been rendered into Dutch from other languages, particularly from English, in the seventeenth century. The first page of *Heer Fagels brief* concerning the Penal Laws notes that there are English and Latin copies of Gaspar's letter to Stewart, but that the English one is to be considered the original (*voor een soort van origineel te houden is*). Moreover, Dutch interest in British and Irish affairs was such that an English-language pamphlet might appear within a short space of time in multiple translations and multiple printings. Title pages frequently refer to a given pamphlet as a translation and in many cases the original can be identified. On the one hand there is scope here for an examination of translation technique. Apart from questions of the accuracy or fluency of a given translation might it be possible, not to put names on anonymous translators, but perhaps on the basis of vocabulary or stylistic choices to group a number of translations together as the work of a single practitioner? Moreover, the existence of multiple renderings of the same original allows for comparative studies of technique. On the other hand, if one reads Jaap Harskamp's comments below on the connections between the printers of London and Middelburg (see p. 246) and bears in mind the sheer volume of translations, it would encourage a closer investigation of what was a veritable translation industry in the Netherlands in the seventeenth century.

Bibliography

Titles are listed in the order in which they appear above. Where the name of an author is placed in square brackets it indicates that it does not appear on the relevant title page.

I have not followed all the idiosyncrasies of type that are found on the original title pages, but have in general retained contemporary abbreviations and spellings. The use of upper/lower case in Dutch titles is based on the Short Title Catalogue Netherlands.

History and topography of Ireland; the Irish abroad

Peter Lombard, *De regno Hiberniæ sanctorvm insvla commentarivs* [...], Lovan.: Apud Viduam Stephani Martini, 1632

Jacobi Waræi *De Hibernia & antiquitatibus ejus, disquisitiones*, editio secunda [...]. *Rerum hibernicarum regnante Henrico VII, Annales* ([both, with separate pagination] Londini: Jo. Crook, 1658)

Roderic O Flaherty, *Ogygia: seu, Rerum hibernicarum chronologia* (Lond.: Ben. Tooke, 1685)

Richard Cox, *Hibernia anglicana: or, the History of Ireland from the Conquest Thereof by the English, to this Present Time* [...], 2 vols (London: vol. 1: printed by H. Clark, for Joseph Watts, 1689; vol. 2: printed by Edward Jones, for Joseph Watts, Matthew Gillyflower, Charles Harper, Samuel Crouch, 1690)

Jeoffry Keating, *The General History of Ireland* [...], trans. Dermo'd [*sic*] O Connor, 2nd edn (Westminster: B. Creake, 1726)

Ferdinando Warner, *The History of Ireland* (vol. 1, London: J. and R. Tonson, 1763 [no more published])

Thomas Leland, *The History of Ireland from the Invasion of Henry II* [...], 3 vols (London: J. Nourse, T. Longman, G. Robinson and J. Johnson, 1773)

Richardi Stanihursti Dubliniensis *De rebvs in Hibernia gestis, Libri quattvor* [...] (Antverpiæ: apud Christophorum Plantinum, 1584)

[Johannes de Laet] *Respublica, sive status regni Scotiæ et Hiberniæ diversorum autorum* (Lugd. Bat.: Ex officina Elzeuiriana, [1630])

[Although the title page has 1627 it is in fact the 2nd edn of 1630 – see colophon.]

Mémoires de la vie de Mylord Duc d'Ormond [...], 2 vols (La Haye: Aux dépens de la Compagnie, 1737)

Memoirs of the Right Honourable the Marquis of Clanricarde [...] (Dublin: C[harles] Connor, 1744)

[Jonathan Swift] *The Conduct of the Allies, and of the Late Ministry, in Beginning and Carrying on the Present War*, 3rd edn (London: John Morphew, 1711)

[Jonathan Swift] *Some Remarks on the Barrier Treaty; Between Her Majesty and the States-General* [...] (London: John Morphew, 1712)

The Conduct of His Grace the Duke of Ormonde, in the Campagne of 1712, 1st and 2nd edns (London: John Morphew, 1715)

A Vindication of Her Late Majesty Queen Anne, of Glorious Memory; of His Grace the Duke of Ormonde; and of the Late Ministry; from the Horrid Reflections Cast upon them in a Late Pamphlet, Intitled, The Conduct of His Grace the Duke of Ormonde in the Campaign of 1712, 2nd edn (London: R. Burleigh, 1715)

An Examination of a Book Intituled, The Conduct of the Duke of Ormond, anno 1712 [...], *by an Officer who Made the Campaign with His Grace* (London: J. More, 1715)

An Address to the Good People of Great Britain, Occasion'd by the Report from the Committee of Secrecy (London: J. Roberts, 1715)

Thomas Burnett, *The Necessity of Impeaching the Late Ministry.* [...], 2nd and 3rd edns (London: J. Roberts, 1715)

De twee laedtste oratien ghedaen ende de wereldt naer-ghelaten door den edel-gebooren heer Thomas Wenthworth [*sic*] [...] *vice-roy van Yerlandt* [...] (Leyden: Willem Christiaens, 1641)

Swaenen-gesangh / gehoort aen den Teems, ofte De twee laeṭste aen-spraken van Thomas Wentworth [...] (Dordrecht: Hendrick van Esch, 1641)

A New Map of Ireland Divided into its Provinces, Counties and Baronies [...] by Herman Moll (London: H. Moll [...], I. Bowles, P. Overton [...], T. Bowles [...] and I. King, [?1740])

Hiberniæ Regnum [...] *noviter delineatum per Guilielmum Petty et in lucem editum per Nicolaum Visscher* (Amst. Bat.: Nunc apud Pet. Schenk Junior, [?1750])

Novissima et accuratissima Regni et Insulæ Hiberniæ delineatio [...] per Petrus [*sic*] Schenk (Amstelodami [c. 1705])

Hiberniæ Regnum [...] *ex prototypo Guil. Petty-Vischeriano deductum et exhibitum à Ioh. Bapt. Homanno* (Noribergæ [?1740])

Pauli Iovii Novocomensis Episcopi Nucerini *Regionum et insularum atque locorum descriptiones: videlicet Britanniæ, Scotiæ, Hyberniæ, Orchadum* [...] (Basileæ 1578, pp. 29–33, in P.I.N., *Opera qvotqvot extant omnia*, vol. 1, Basileæ: P. Pernæ, 1578)

[Thomas Campbell] *A Philosophical Survey of the South of Ireland, in a Series of Letters to John Watkinson* (London: W. Strahan and T. Cadell, 1777)

[Richard Twiss] *A Tour in Ireland in 1775* (London: J. Robson, J. Walter, G. Robinson, G. Kearsly, 1776)

Arthur Young, *A Tour in Ireland; with General Observations on the Present State of that Kingdom: Made in the Years 1776, 1777, and 1778, and Brought down to the End of 1779* (London: T. Cadell and J. Dodsley, 1780)

[John] Toland, *An Account of the Courts of Prussia and Hannover: Sent to a Minister of State in Holland* [...] (London: J. Roberts, J. Harrison, A. Dodd and J. Graves, 1714)

J. T[oland], *Relation des cours de Prusse et de Hanovre, avec les caractéres* [*sic*] *des principales personnes qui les composent* [...], traduite de l'anglois de J. T. (La Haye: Thomas Johnson, 1706)

John Talbot Dillon, *Travels through Spain, with a View to Illustrate the Natural History and Physical Geography of that Kingdom* [...] (London: G. Robinson, 1780)

John Earl of Corke and Orrery, *Letters from Italy, in the Years 1754 and 1755* [...] (London: B. White, 1773)

Richard Pococke, *A Description of the East, and Some Other Countries*, 2 vols in 3 (London: Printed for the Author by W. Bowyer, 1743–5)

Robert [Clayton], Lord Bishop of Clogher, *A Journal from Grand Cairo to Mount Sinai, and back again. Translated from a Manuscript, Written by the Prefetto of Egypt* [...], *to which are Added Remarks on the Origin of Hieroglyphics, and the Mythology of the Ancient Heathens*, 2nd edn (London: William Bowyer, 1753)

Philosophy; politics

[George Berkeley] *Alciphron: or, The Minute Philosopher. In Seven Dialogues. Containing an Apology for the Christian Religion, against those who are Called Free-thinkers*, 2 vols (London: J. Tonson, 1732)

[In this ed. *Alciphron* is followed, with consecutive pagination (starting p. 211), by:]

[George Berkeley] *An Essay towards a New Theory of Vision*. First Published in the Year 1709 (London: n.pub., 1732)

[George Berkeley] *The Author of* Alciphron, or, The Minute Philosopher, *The Theory of Vision, or Visual Language, Shewing the Immediate Presence and Providence of a Deity* [...] (London: J. Tonson, 1733) [two duplicate copies]

Dr. Berkley, since Bishop of Cloyne, *A Treatise Concerning the Principles of Human Knowledge* [...] To which are Added, his *Dialogues between Hylas and Philonous* [...] (London: J. Dodsley and J. Wilkie, 1776)

George Berkeley, *Three Dialogues between Hylas and Philonous* [...] London: Henry Clements, 1713

[Francis Hutcheson] *An Inquiry into the Original of our Ideas of Beauty and Virtue* [...] (London: Printed by J. Darby [...], for Wil. and John Smith on the Blind Key in Dublin; and sold by W. and J. Innys [...], J. Osborn and T. Longman [...], and S. Chandler [London], 1725; also, 5th edn, London: R. Ware, J. and P. Knapton, T. and T. Longman, C. Hitch and L. Hawes, J. Hodges, J. and J. Rivington, and J. Ward, 1753)

[Francis Hutcheson] *An Essay on the Nature and Conduct of the Passions and Affections* [...] (London: Printed by J. Darby and T. Browne, for John Smith and William Bruce, Booksellers in Dublin; and sold by J. Osborn and T. Longman, and S. Chandler [London], 1728; also, 3rd edn, London: A. Ward, J. and P. Knapton, T. Longman, S. Birt, C. Hitch, L. Gilliver, T. Astley, S. Austen, and J. Rivington, 1742)

Franciscus Hutcheson, *Philosophiæ moralis institutio compendiaria. Ethices & jurisprudentiæ naturalis elementa continens* (Rotterodami: Franciscus Bradshaw, 1745)

[Franciscus Hutcheson] *Synopsis metaphysicæ, ontologiam et pneumatologiam complectens*, 3rd edn (Glasgow: Robertus et Andreas Foulis, 1749)

Francis Hutcheson, *A System of Moral Philosophy*, in Three Books [with a Preface by William Leechman], 2 vols (Glasgow: R. and A. Foulis, 1755)

Letters between the Late Mr. Gilbert Burnet, and Mr. Hutchinson [*sic*], *Concerning the True Foundation of Virtue or Moral Goodness* (London: W. Wilkins, 1735)

John Taylor, *An Examination of the Scheme of Morality, Advanced by Dr Hutcheson* (London: J. Waugh and W. Fenner, 1759)

The Beauties of the Late Right Hon. Edmund Burke [...]. To which is Prefixed, *A Sketch of the Life, with some Original Anecdotes of Mr Burke*, 2 vols (London: printed by J.W. Myers, 1798)

Edmund Burke, *Reflections on the Revolution in France* [...], 5th edn and 10th edn (London: J. Dodsley, 1790 and 1791 respectively)

Substance of the Speech of the Right Honourable Edmund Burke, in the Debate on the Army Estimates, in the House of Commons, on Tuesday, the 9th Day of February, 1790. Comprehending a Discussion of the Present Situation of Affairs in France, 4th edn (London: J. Debrett, 1790)

Speech of Edmund Burke, Esq., on American Taxation, April 19, 1774, 3rd edn (London: J. Dodsley, 1775)

Speech of Edmund Burke, Esq. on Moving his Resolutions for Conciliation with the Colonies, March 22, 1775, 2nd edn (London: J. Dodsley, 1775)

Richard Steele, *The Crisis: or, A Discourse Representing, from the most Authentick Records, the Just Causes of the Late Happy Revolution* [...]. *With some Seasonable Remarks on the Danger of a Popish Successor* [...] (London: Ferd. Burleigh, 1714)

Richard Steele, *A Letter to a Member of Parliament Concerning the Bill for Preventing the Growth of Schism*, 2nd edn (London: Ferd. Burleigh, 1714) [two duplicate copies]

Mr. Steele's Apology for Himself and his Writings; Occasioned by his Expulsion from the House of Commons (London: R. Burleigh, 1714)

The Political Writings of Sir Richard Steele (London: printed for J.T. and sold by Owen Lloyd and J. Brown, 1715)

Richard Steele, *The Romish Ecclesiastical History of Late Years* (London: J. Roberts, 1714)

[Richard Steele] *The Christian Hero: An Argument Proving that no Principles but those of Religion are Sufficient to Make a Great Man*, 8th edn (London: T. Johnson, 1727)

> [This work, separately paginated, is bound together with the *Poetical Miscellanies*.]

R. Steele, *Le heros* [*sic*] *chrétien*. Traduit de l'Anglois par A. de Beaumarchais [...] (La Haye: Henry Scheurleer, 1729)

Mr. Steele, *The Funeral: or, Grief a-la-mode*. A Comedy (London: T. Johnson, 1721)

Sir Richard Steele, *The Conscious Lovers*. A Comedy (London: T. Johnson, 1723)

> [These are the first two plays in an anthology of five, by different authors, each with its own title page and pagination.]

Poetical Miscellanies, Consisting of Original Poems and Translations. By the Best Hands. Published by Sir Richard Steele, 2nd edn (London: J. Tonson, 1727)

Science

[Robert Boyle] T.E., a Layman, *Some Considerations about the Reconcileableness of Reason and Religion*. To which is Annex'd by the Publisher, *A Discourse of Mr. Boyle, about the Possibility of the Resurrection* (London: H. Herringman, 1675)

[Robert Boyle] *A Discourse of Things above Reason. Inquiring whether a Philosopher Should Admit there are any such* [...] (London: Jonathan Robinson, 1681)

Robert Boyle, *A Disquisition about the Final Causes of Natural Things* [...] *Some Uncommon Observations about Vitiated Sight* (London: John Taylor, 1688)

Robert Boyle, *Experiments and Considerations Touching Colours* [...] (London: Henry Herringman, 1664)

Robert Boyle, *An Essay of the Great Effects of Even Languid and Unheeded Motion.* Whereunto is Annexed *An Experimental Discourse of some Little Observed Causes of the Insalubrity and Salubrity of the Air and its Effects* (London: Sam. Smith, 1690)

Robert Boyle, *Some Considerations Touching the Style of the H. Scriptures* [...] (London: Henry Herringman, 1661)

R[obert] B[oyle], *A Free Enquiry into the Vulgarly Receiv'd Notion of Nature; Made in an Essay, Address'd to a Friend* (London: John Taylor, 1685/6)

R[obert] B[oyle], *Of the High Veneration Man's Intellect Owes to God, Peculiarly for His Wisdom and Power* (London: printed for Richard Davis [...] and sold by Tho. Shelmerdine, 1711)

The Theological Works of the Honourable Robert Boyle, Esq; Epitomiz'd by Richard Boulton, 3 vols (London: W. Tatlor, 1715)

The Works of the Honourable Robert Boyle. To which is Prefixed *The Life of the Author* [by Thomas Birch], 5 vols (London: A. Millar, 1744)

Hans Sloane, *Catalogus plantarum quæ in Jamaica sponte proveniunt* [...] (London: D. Brown, 1696)

Literature and art

The Works of J[onathan] S[wift] D.D. D.S. P.D. [...], 6 vols (Dublin: George Faulkner, vol. 1: 1742; 2: 1744; 3, 4: 1743; 5, 6: 1741)

> [The Publisher's Preface to vol. 1 and the Advertisement to vol. 2 are dated 1734, the Publisher's Preface to vol. 5, 1738.]

[Jonathan Swift (with Alexander Pope)] *Miscellanies*, 4 vols (London: vol. 1: Benjamin Motte, 1733; 2: 2nd edn, Benjamin Motte, 1733; 3: Benjamin Motte and Lawton Gilliver, 1732; 4: Benjamin Motte, 1733)

[Jonathan Swift] *Travels into Several Remote Nations of the World, by Lemuel Gulliver*, 3 vols (London: Benjamin Motte, vols 1, 2: 1726; 3: 1727)

> [Although the three volumes have the same binding and are catalogued by Paterson as one lot (3387), vol. 3 seems to be separate. In addition to being dated a year later than 1 and 2, it does not in fact give Motte as the publisher. Nowhere does it say how many volumes comprise the set, but the title page of vol. 1 refers to '4 parts' and p. iii lists the contents, concluding, as does vol. 2, with the Houyhnhms as part 4. Vol. 3 has Part 1: *A Second Voyage to Brobdingnag* etc., and Part 2: *A Voyage to Sevarambia* etc.]

[Jonathan Swift] *Memoirs of the Court of Lilliput. Written by Captain Gulliver* [...], published by Lucas Bennet [...], 2nd edn (London: J. Roberts, 1727)

[?John Arbuthnot] *Gulliver Decypher'd: or Remarks on a Late Book, Intitled,* Travels into Several Remote Nations of the World. By Capt. Lemuel Gulliver. *Vindicating the Reverend Dean on whom it is Maliciously Father'd. With some Probable Conjectures Concerning the Real Author* (London: J. Roberts, n.d. [1728?])

[Jonathan Swift] *A Second Tale of a Tub: or, The History of Robert Powel the Puppet-Show-Man* [...] (London: J. Roberts, 1715)

[René Macé] *Les trois Justaucorps*, conte bleu, tiré de l'Anglois du Révérend Mr. Jonathan Swif [*sic*] (Dublin: n.pub., 1721), in: *Recueil de pièces sérieuses, comiques, et burlesques* (n.p., n.pub., 1721), pp. 1–79

[Jonathan Swift] Sieur du Baudrier, *Relation du voyage que fit Monsieur P—r* [viz. Prior], [...], Traduit de l'Anglois (Londres: Jean Morphew, 1711)

[Pierre-François Guyot Desfontaines] *Le grand mistère, ou l'art de méditer sur la garderobe, renouvellé et devoilé, par l'ingénieux Docteur Swift* (La Haye: Jean van Duren, 1729)

> [The volume also includes the *Pensées hazardées sur les études* by George Louis Le Sage; Swift's work occupies pp. 5–40.]

[Jonathan Swift] *The Publick Spirit of the Whigs, Set forth in their Generous Encouragement, of the Author of* The Crisis [...], 4th edn (London: John Morphew, 1714)

Dr. Sw–ft, *A View of the Present State of Affairs in the Kingdom of Ireland; in Three Discourses*. 1. *A List of the Absentees of Ireland, and the Yearly Value of their Estates and Incomes Spent Abroad* [...] 2. *The Present State of Ireland Consider'd* [...] 3. *A Modest Proposal for Preventing the Children of Poor People from Being a Burthen to their Parents or the Country* [...] (Printed at Dublin: Reprinted at London: Weaver Bickerton, 1730)

Letters to and from Dr. J. Swift, D.S.P.D. from the Year 1714, to 1738. [...] (Dublin: George Faulkner, 1741)

John Earl of Orrery, *Remarks on the Life and Writings of Dr. Jonathan Swift* [...], 4th edn (London: A. Millar, 1752)

Divers Plays, 8 vols (London: The Company [of Booksellers], n.d.)

> [Individual plays have their own title page, often with publisher and date. Within this collection we find:]

In vol. 3: William Congreve, *The Old Batchelour* (London: T. Johnson, 1720)

William Congreve, *The Double-Dealer* (London: The Company of Booksellers, n.d.)

In vol. 8: George Farquhar, *The Constant Couple* (London: The Company [of Booksellers], n.d.)

George Farquhar, *The Recruiting Officer* (London: T. Johnson, 1720)

George Farquhar, *The Beaux Stratagem* (London: T. Johnson, 1720)

The Works of Mr. William Congreve, 2 vols (London: Jacob Tonson, 1719)

Poems upon Several Occasions Written by Dr. Thomas Parnell, Late Archdeacon of Clogher and Published by Mr. Pope [...], To which is Prefixed, The Life of Dr. Parnell, Written by Dr. Goldsmith (London: T. Davies, J. Dodsley, R. Baldwin, 1773)

Epître dédicatoire de Mr. Binauld à Mr. Molyneux (London: Pierre du Noyer, 1715)

John Earl of Orrery, *The Letters of Pliny the Younger, with Observations on each Letter; and an Essay on Pliny's Life*, [...], 2 vols (London: Paul Vaillant, 1751)

Richard Pococke, *Inscriptionum antiquarum græc[arum] et latin[arum] liber* [...] (n.p., n.pub., 1752)

James Barry, *An Inquiry into the Real and Imaginary Obstructions to the Acquisition of the Arts in England* (London: T. Becket, 1775)

Tombeaux des Princes, des grands Capitaines et autres hommes illustres qui ont fleuri dans la Grande Bretagne vers la fin du XVII. et le commencement du XVIII. siecle [*sic*], *gravés par les plus habiles maitres* [*sic*] *de Paris* [...], *dirigé et mis au jour par les soins de Eugene Mac Swiny* [no imprint]

Doctrinal controversies

Henry Dodwell, *An Epistolary Discourse, Proving* [...] *that the Soul is a Principle Naturally Mortal; but Immortalized Actually by the Pleasure of God* [...] (London: R. Smith, 1706)

Henry Dodwell, *The Scripture Account of the Eternal Rewards or Punishments of all that Hear of the Gospel* [...] (London: George Straughan, 1708)

Henricus Dodwellus, *De veteribus Græcorum Romanorumque cyclis* [...] *dissertationes decem* [...] (Oxonii: E Theatro Sheldoniano. Prostant apud Benj. Tooke ad Medii Templi Portam in Vico Fleetstreet dicto, 1701)

Henricus Dodwellus, *Chronologia Xenophontea* (Oxoniæ: E Theatro Sheldoniano, 1700)

[Henry Dodwell Jr.] *Christianity not Founded on Argument; and the True Principle of Gospel-Evidence Assigned* [...], 2nd edn (London: T. Cooper, 1743)

John Leland, *Remarks on a Late Pamphlet, Entitled,* Christianity not Founded on Argument [...] (London: printed for R. Hett [...] and sold by J. Stagg, 1744) [two duplicate copies]

John Leland, *A Second Letter, Containing Remarks on a Late Pamphlet, Entitled,* Christianity not Founded on Argument (London: printed for R. Hett [...] and sold by J. Stagg, 1744)

[Henry Dodwell Jr.] *Remarks on the Several Answers to the Pamphlet, intitled* Christianity not Founded on Argument [...] (London: M. Cooper, 1744)

John Leland, *The Divine Authority of the Old and New Testament Asserted* [...] *against* [...] *a Book Entitled,* The Moral Philosopher (London: Richard Hett, vol. 1: 2nd edn 1739; vol. 2 1740)

[Volume 2 was written in response to Thomas Morgan's criticism of volume 1.]

John Leland, *Reflections on the Late Lord Bolingbroke's* Letters on the Study and Use of History [...], 2nd edn (London: Benj. Dod, 1753)

John Leland, *An Answer to a Late Book Intituled,* Christianity as Old as the Creation, 2 vols (Dublin: Abraham Bradley, 1733)

John Leland, *A View of the Principal Deistical Writers that Have Appeared in England* [...], 3 vols (London: B. Dod, 1754–6)

John Leland, *The Advantage and Necessity of the Christian Revelation, Shewn from the State of Religion in the Antient Heathen World* [...], 2 vols (London: W. Richardson and S. Clark, R. and J. Dodsley, and T. Longman, 1764)

[John] Leland and Others, *Forms of Devotion for the Use of Families* [...] (London: W. Johnston and R. Griffiths, 1766)

John Leland, *Discourses on Various Subjects* [...], 4 vols (London: W. Johnston and J. Dodsley, 1768–9)

Robert [Clayton], Lord Bishop of Clogher, *The Chronology of the Hebrew Bible Vindicated: the Facts Compared with Other Ancient Histories* [...] (London: J. Brindley, 1747)

Robert [Clayton], Lord Bishop of Clogher, *A Dissertation on Prophecy* [...]; *together with an Explanation of the Revelation of St. John* (London: Re-printed (from the Dublin Copy Revis'd) by J. Watts and Sold by him and B. Dod, 1749)

Robert Clayton, *A Vindication of the Histories of the Old and New Testament. In Answer to the Objections of the Late Lord Bolingbroke.* In *Two Letters to a Young Nobleman*, 2nd edn (Dublin: Printed, London: Reprinted for W. Bowyer and Sold by M. Cooper and George Woodfall, 1753)

Robert Clayton, Lord Bishop of Clogher, *A Vindication of the Histories of the Old and New Testament, part II. Wherein the Mosaical History of the Creation and Deluge, is Philosophically Explained* [...] (Dublin: George Faulkner, 1754)

[Another edition with the imprint: Dublin: Printed, London: Reprinted for W. Bowyer, and Sold by R. Baldwin, and M. Cooper, 1754, is bound in with:]

Alexander Catcott, *Remarks on the Second Part of the Lord Bishop of Clogher's* Vindication of the Histories of the Old and New Testament [...] (London: E. Withers, R. Clements (Oxford), and the Booksellers of Bristol, 1756)

[Robert Clayton] *An Essay on Spirit, wherein the Doctrine of the Trinity is Considered in the Light of Nature and Reason* [...] *Together with some Remarks on the Athanasian and Nicene Creeds*, 2nd edn (London: J. Noon, G. Woodfall, and M. Cooper, 1752)

John Toland, *Christianity not Mysterious: or, A Treatise Shewing, that there is Nothing in the Gospel Contrary to Reason* [...]. To which is Added, *An Apology for Mr. Toland, in Relation to the Parliament of Ireland's Ordering this Book to be Burnt* (London: n.pub., 1702)

[John Toland] *Amyntor: or, A Defence of Milton's Life* [...] (London: The Booksellers of London and Westminster, 1699)

[The title-page does not have the author's name, but the dedication is signed J.T.]

Mr. [John] Toland, *Nazarenus: or, Jewish, Gentile, and Mahometan Christianity. Containing the History of the Antient Gospel of Barnabas* [...]. *The Original Plan of Christianity* [...]. *The Relation of an Irish Manuscript of the Four Gospels* [...], 2nd edn (London: J. Brotherton, J. Roberts, and A. Dodd, 1718)

[Bound in with the above:]

[Edmund Curll] *An Historical Account of the Life and Writings of the Late Eminently Famous Mr. John Toland* [...] (London: J. Roberts, W. Mears, J. Brotherton, J. Graves, and W. Chetwood, 1722)

A Collection of Several Pieces of Mr. John Toland [...], *with some Memoirs of his Life and Writings*, [ed. P. Des Maizeaux], 2 vols (London: J. Peele, 1726)

[The *Memoirs* are also the work of Des Maizeaux.]

Joannes Tolandus, *Oratio philippica ad excitandos contra Galliam Britannos* [...] (Amstelædami: Ex officina Wetsteniana, 1709)

Patricola [John Toland], *The Second Part of the State Anatomy, &c.* [...] (London: John Phillips, J. Brotherton, P. Meadows and J. Roberts, 1717)

The Oceana of James Harrington [...], *with an Exact Account of his Life Prefix'd*, by John Toland (London: The Booksellers of London and Westminster, 1700)

Peter Browne, *A Letter in Answer to a Book Entituled*, Christianity not Mysterious [...], 3rd edn (London: Robert Clavel, 1703)

[Peter Browne] *Things Divine and Supernatural Conceived by Analogy with Things Natural and Human* [...] (London: William Innys and Richard Manby, 1733)

A Discourse of Drinking Healths. Wherein the Great Evil of this Prevailing Custom is Shewn [...], by Peter [Browne] Lord Bishop of Cork and Rosse (London: Henry Clements, 1716)

[Charles Leslie] *A Short and Easie Method with the Deists: Wherein the Certainty of the Christian Religion is Demonstrated* [...], *To which is Added a Second Part to the Jews* [...], 5th edn (London: Geo. Strahan, n.d.) Between the two parts a new title page: *A Short and Easie Method with the Jews* [...], 3rd edn (London: Geo. Strahan, 1715), the two being separately paginated.

Charles Leslie, *The Truth of Christianity Demonstrated. With a Dissertation Concerning Private Judgment and Authority. To which is Prefixed a Vindication of the* Short Method with the Deists [...] (London: E. Pool and G. Strahan, 1711)

Miso-Dolos [Charles Leslie], *The Good Old Cause, or, Lying in Truth, Being a Second Defence of the Lord Bishop of Sarum* [...] (London: The Booksellers of London and Westminster, 1710) [two duplicate copies]

[Charles Leslie] *The Finishing Stroke. Being a Vindication of the Patriarchal Scheme of Government* [...] (London: The Booksellers of London and Westminster, 1711)

Other religious writings

Jacobi Usserii Armachani *Annales Veteris et Novi Testamenti.* [...] *Chronologia sacra Veteris Testamenti. Dissertatio de Macedonum et Asianorum anno solari*, editio tertia (Bremæ: Hermannus Brauerus, 1686)

Jacobi Usserii *Historia dogmatica controversiæ inter Orthodoxos & Pontificios de Scripturis et sacris vernaculis* [...] (London: Richard Chiswell, 1690)

Jacobus Usserius, *Britannicarum ecclesiarum antiquitates* [...]. *Gravissimæ quæstionis de christianarum ecclesiarum successione & statu historica explicatio* (London: Benjamin Tooke, 1687)

Jacobus Usserius, *Gravissimæ quæstionis, de christianarum ecclesiarum, in occidentis præsertim partibus, ab apostolorum temporibus, ad nostram usque ætatem, continua successione & statu, historica explicatio*, 2nd ed. (Hanoviæ: Typis Hæredum Aubrianorum, 1658)

Jacobi Usserii *Opuscula duo* [...], *De episcoporum, et metropolitanorum origine. De Asia proconsulari* [...] (London: Samuel Smith, 1687)

James [Ussher], late Lord Archbishop of Armagh, *The Power Communicated by God to the Prince and the Obedience Required of the Subject* [...] (London: Anne Seile, 1661)

De origine mali, Authore Guilielmo King (London: Benjamin Tooke, 1702)

His Grace William [King] Lord Archbishop of Dublin, *Divine Predestination and Fore-Knowledge, Consistent with the Freedom of Man's Will. A Sermon Preach'd at Christ-Church, Dublin, May 15, 1709* [...], 3rd edn (London: printed John Darby and Thomas Browne, 1728)

[Edmund Law] *An Essay on the* Origin of Evil. *By Dr. William King* [...] (London: Printed for W. Thurlbourn Bookseller in Cambridge; and sold by R. Knaplock, J. and N. Knapton, and W. Innis in London, 1731)

John Lawrence Mosheim, *An Ecclesiastical History, Antient and Modern* [...], trans. Archibald Maclaine, 2 vols (London: A. Millar, 1765)

Jean Laurent Mosheim, *Histoire ecclésiastique ancienne et moderne* [...], trad. Archibald Maclaine, 6 vols (Maestricht: Jean-Edmé Dufour & Philippe Roux, 1776)

Archibald Maclaine, *A Supplement to the Quarto Edition of Dr. Mosheim's* Ecclesiastical History [...] (London: A. Millar, 1768)

Archibald Maclaine, *A Series of Letters addressed to Soame Jenyns Esq; on Occasion of his* View of the Internal Evidence of Christianity, 2nd edn (London: Charles Bathurst, 1778)

Lettres de Miladi Marie Wortley Montagüe [...] (Rotterdam: Beman, 1763)

Jeremias Taylor, bisschop van Down en Conner [*sic*] in Yrland: *Historie van 't leven en de doot van onsen saligmaker Jesus Christus* [...] (t'Utrecht: Wilhelm Broedelet, 1700) [translation of the 7th English edition]

Charles Hickman, *Fourteen Sermons Preach'd at St. James's Church in Westminister* [...], 2nd edn (London: William Hawes, 1706)

Patrick Delany, *Revelation Examined with Candour* [...] (London: C. Rivington, vol. 1: 2nd edn 1733; vol. 2: 1st edn 1732)

[Patrick Delany] By the Author of Revelation Examin'd with Candour, *An Historical Account of the Life and Reign of David King of Israel* [...], 3 vols (London: W. Innys and R. Manby, C. Rivington, T. Longman, S. Birt, J. and P. Knapton, T. Astley, S. Austin, C. Hitch, J. Woodward and C. Woodward, T. Woodward and C. Bathurst, J. Hodges, R. Dodsley, H. Chapelle, R. Hett and J. Davidson, and J. Leake, 1740)

[Patrick Delany] The Author of The Life of David, *Fifteen Sermons upon Social Duties* (London: J. Rivington, 1744)

[James Duchal] *A Short Explanation of the End and Design of the Lord's Supper* [...] (London: W. Johnston and R. Griffiths, 1760)

James Duchal, *Presumptive Arguments for the Truth and Divine Authority of the Christian Religion*; in Ten Sermons [...] (London: A. Millar, 1753) [two duplicate copies]

Laurence Sterne, *The Sermons of Mr Yorick*, 4 vols (London: vols 1 and 2, 7th edn: J. Dodsley, 1765; vols 3 and 4 [no mention of edn]: T. Becket and P. A. de Hondt, 1766)

Alas! Poor Yorick! or, A Funeral Discourse, Occasioned by the much Lamented Death of Mr. Yorick, Prebendary of Y- - k and Author of the much Admired Life and Opinions of Tristram Shandy, Preached [...] by Christopher Flagellan [...] (London: W. Nicoll, 1761)

Religious conflict and cooperation

John Davies, *A Discoverie of the True Causes why Ireland was Neuer Entirely Subdued, nor Brought vnder Obedience of the Crowne of England, vntill the Beginning of His Maiesties* [James I] *Happie Raigne*. Printed exactly from the edition in 1612 (London: A. Millar, 1747)

Ferdinando Warner, *The History of the Civil-War in Ireland* (London: J. and R. Tonson, 1767)

[Edmund Borlase] *The History of the Irish Rebellion, Traced from Many Preceding Acts, to the Grand Eruption the 23rd of October, 1641; and thence Pursued to the Act of Settlement, 1662* [...] (Dublin: Oli. Nelson, Charles Connor, 1743)

Brief van de belegerde binnen Rochelle, aende predicanten, onderlinghen ende diaconen vande ghereformeerde kercken vande Geunieerde Provintien van alle talen in Nederlandt (s'Graven-Haghe: n.pub., 1626)

Brief van de leeraren der euangelysche kercken in de valleyen van Piedmont aan de leeraren der euangelyscher kercken in Nederland [...] (t'Utrecht: Henrick Versteegh, 1663)

Een verclaringhe der oorsaken beweghende de coninghinne van Enghelandt, hulpe te gheuen tot bescherminghe des benauden ende verdructen volckes der Nederlanden (Delf: Aelbrecht Hendrickz, 1585)

Vier voornaemste redenen waerom de protestanten vande republijck van Engelandt noodtsaeckelijck van noode hebben een religieuse correspondentie met de uytheemsche protestantse kercken [...] (n.p., n.pub., 1654)

De gereformeerde Engelsche liturgie [...] *aengaende den openbaeren godsdienst door de drie conincrijcken van Engelant, Schotland ende Yrlant* ('sGravenhaghe: Ian Vely, 1645)

De vierde Schotsche-post/ mede-brenghende het verbondt selfs, ofte den nieuwen eedt/ de welcke by alle de ondersaten in beyde de coninckrijcken van Engelant ende Schotlant soude ghedaen ende genomen werden (n.p., n.pub., 1643)

Convenant [*sic*] *ofte verbont, tusschen de drie koninck-rijcken, te weeten; Engelandt, Schotlandt, ende Yrlandt. Mitsgaders: De proclamatien van't coninckrijck Schotlandt / tot aenneminghe van haeren wettighen koningh Charles Stuart, den tweeden van dien name* ('sGraven-Haghe: Ludolph Breeckevelt, 1649)

Het verbont / of naerder vnie van de drie koninckrijcken, Engelant [*sic*] *Schotlandt en Yerlandt* [...] (n.p., n.pub., n.d.)

[It is possible that the imprint was trimmed off prior to binding.]

Declaratie van beyde de Huysen des Parlements van Enghelandt. Aende [...] *Staten Generael der Vereenichde Nederlantsche Provintien.* [...] *Hier is noch by gevoecht het verbondt ofte unie vande drie koninckrijcken Engelandt Schotlandt ende Yrlandt* (n.p, n.pub., 1645)

Een solemnele ligue ende verbont van weghen de reformatie / ende de bescherminge van religie / de eere ende gelucksaligheyt des conincks, ende de vrede ende behoudenisse van de drie coningrijcken van Engelandt, Schotlandt, ende Yrlandt (Londen: Ed. Husband, 1645)

Solemnel covenant ofte heyligh verbondt gemaeckt ende besworen door de Heeren ende Gemeenten van de drie koninckrijcken van Engelandt, Schotlandt ende Yerlandt, om de religie te reformeren ende te stabilieren; om de authoriteyt ende de majesteyt van de koningh te defenderen: ende om de vrede ende het welvaren van de drie koninckrijcken vast te stellen (n.p., n.pub., 1660)

Covenant, ofte verbondt tot reformatie ende defensie van der religie, eere ende welstant van den koning, den vrede ende behoudnisse van de dry koningrijcken, Engelandt, Schotlandt ende Yrlandt. Besloten Anno 1643 (Dordrecht: Abraham Andriessz, 1649)

Covenant, ofte verbondt [...] (Amsterdam: Jan van Hilten, 1649) [two duplicate copies]

Pactum et foedus sanctum pro religione reformandâ & conservandâ, pro authoritate, & Majestate Regis tuenda, pro pace, & salute trium regnorum, Angliæ, Scotiæ, & Hiberniæ stabilienda [...] (n.p., n.pub., 1643)

Sekere verclaringhen wt Yrlandt / aengaende het verlies ende benautheden der Spaenscher Armado toegheuallen op de west custen van Yrlandt [...] (Eerst, ghedruckt in Londen by Ridtsaert Filde. Daer nae tot Amstelredam by Cornelis Claesz, 1588)

[Fag. **H**.1.27, no. 18, is a later printing than Fag. **H**.3.8, no. 20: in the marginal print on p. Aiiir '800' has been corrected to '8000'.]

Nieuwe tijdinghe / ghetrocken wt den brief welcke milorde Grey / gouuernuer [*sic*] *van Yrlandt/ ghesonden heeft aen haere ma*[t]*. in sekere articulen vervat / wat daer aende custe van Yrlandt verloopen is, aengaende de Armade van Spaengien* (Amstelredam: Cornelis Claesz, n.d.)

Oratie van sijne co: ma[t]*. van Groot Britannien ghedaen int parlement den 19*[en]*. februarij stilo Angliæ 1624. Mitsgaders, de proclamatie vant bannissement der iesuwyten ende paepsche priesters uyt Yrlandt* (Middelbvrgh: Ian Pietersz vande Venne, 1624)

A Report from the Committee Appointed to Inspect the Original Papers Seiz'd in the Houses or Lodgings of one Mcc. [*sic*] *Carthy, alias Rabah, a Reputed Titular Popish Bishop; and Joseph Nagle, a Reputed Popish Sollicitor, both of the City of Corke* [...] (Dublin printed; London reprinted for T. Cooper, 1734)

Translaet. Besluyt ende verklaringe van 't parlement in Yrlandt ('sGraven-hage: Ludolph Breekevelt, 1640)

The Case of the Forfeitures in Ireland Fairly Stated, with the Reasons that Induced the Protestants there to Purchase them, 2nd edn (London: n.pub., 1700)

Jus regium: or, the King's Right to Grant Forfeitures, and Other Revenues of the Crown [...] (London: n.pub., 1701)

A Short View of both Reports, in Relation to the Irish Forfeitures. In a Familiar Dialogue between A. and B. [...] (London: n.pub., 1701)

Religio-political conflict: the rising of 1641

Yrelandtsche traenen: waer in levendich is affgebeelt/ ende als in een schilderie verthoont/ een lijste, vande noyt gehoorde wreetheden/ ende barbarische verraderyen der bloet-dorstighe jesuwijten, met de papistische factie aldaer (Colophon: Leyden: Willem Christiaens, 20.12.1642)

Nieuwe ende goede tijdinge uyt Yrlant, mede-brengende eene verklaringe van den lord Jnchequin [*et al.*] [...], *vervattende de redenen von hare tegenwoordige oppositie van den stilstant van wapenen/ met de bloet-dorstige Yrische rebellen* [...]. *Insgelijcks mede de gesamentlijcke ende eendrachtige declaratie van sijne majesteyts protestante onderdanen inde provincie van Munster* [...] *verthoonende de menichvuldige* [...] *schrickelijcke t'samen-rottingen van monnicken, priesteren ende jesuiten, om ons te verraden* [...] (Printed: London: I. Wright, reprinted [n.p.]: A. Jacobsz, 1644)

Den Enghelschen paus [...], *De heymelijcke onderhandelinge/ ende 't verborghen verstandt tusschen het Hoff van Enghelandt, ende 't Hoff van Roomen* [...] (First published London: Robert Bostock)

> [Other information has been trimmed off in the binding process – surrounding pamphlets are dated 1643.]

Ootmoedighe requeste, van de raetheeren [...] *van Londen.* [...] *Daer by gevoecht zijn de copien van twee bysondere missiven uyt Yerlandt, daer in vermelt werden de barbarische ende onmenschelijcke wreetheden, die by de rebelle papisten aldaer, aen de protestanten ghepleecht werden* (Amstelredam: Theunis Jacobsz, 1642)

Jan Cooke, *Regis Caroli casus, Of een appel* [...] *'Tsamen met een bygevoeghde opinie/ nopende* [...] *de rebellie van Yerlandt* (n.p., Pieter Cole, 1649)

De Schotsche post, mede brengende eene declaratie vande heeren van sijne majesteyts secreten raedt in Schotlandt. [...] *Als mede een verradelijck ende verdoemlijck comploot vande Yrijsche/ Enghelsche/ ende Schotsche papisten/ ten deele nu ontdeckt/ door de onverwachte apprehensie van den grave van Antrim* [...] (Uyt de Engelsche copye, eerst tot Edenburch, ende daer na tot Londen gedruckt, getrouwelijck overgeset, 1643)

> [The preface is dated $^{19}/_{9}$. Iuny 1643.]

Den Brittannischen donderslach, ofte Naerder ghesprek/ over het teghenwoordighe Engelsche wesen [...] *Brittanischen blixem* [...] (n.p., n.pub., 1643)

Yrlands bloedende request, aen de gereformeerde kercken der vereenigde Nederlandsche Provintien: waer inne naer eene sommarische verthooninghe van haren uyttersten noodt, een beete broods versocht wert, tot onderhoudinge van haer meer dan ellendigh leven. [...] (n.p., n.pub., 1643) [two duplicate copies]

Yrlands bloedende request [...] (Dordrecht: Isaac Reyers, 1643) [two duplicate copies]

Yrlands bloedende request [...] (n.p., n.pub., 1643)

> [The title pages of these three pamphlets have for the most part the same wording, but different imprints and slight variations in format and punctuation; those of the last two also refer to a final section, which at the appropriate point has its own title page, viz.:]

Requeste van de gecommitteerde des Parlements in Engelant/ aen-gaende den bedroefden toe-stant van vele duysenden arme protestanten in het koninghrijcke van Yrlant

> [This section also appears as a discrete publication: without an imprint and with the same wording as the preceding, but with its own pagination and differences in font and layout; two duplicate copies of this are in the collection.]

Eenen sent-brief van de Nationale Synode van Schotlant, aen de Nederlantsche kercken, inhoudende een hertige dancksegginghe, van de liberale collecte aen die van Yerlant, met noch andere considerable materien (Middelburgh: Zacharias Roman, 1644)

Vreemde en aanmerkelijke voorzeggingen van de heylige, geleerde en uitstekende Jacobus Usher eertijts aartsbisschop van Armagh, en primaat van Yrlandt. [...] *Geschreven door die gene welke het gehoort heeft uit de eige mondt van dese uitstekende man, en nu uitgegeven om ons te vermanen tot bekering en verbetering, 't welk alleen onse ruine en vernieling kan afwenden* (Uit het Engels vertaalt na de copye, gedruckt tot Londen voor R. G., 1678)

Vreemde en aanmerkelijke voorzeggingen [...] (n.p., n.pub., 1686)

Vreemde en aanmerkelyke voorzeggingen [...] ('sGtavenhage [*sic*]: Pieter Hagen, 1688)

Plate 28: Joan Blaeu, *Tabula Islandiæ*, from his *Atlas Major*, Amsterdam 1662 (vol. 1, plate 8). (Fag. z.1.22)

CARTE PARTICULIÉRE DE L'AMÉR
FALL of NIAGARA
MEXICO
LAKE SUPERIOUR
LAKE ERIE
PENNSYLVANIA
LOUISIANA
CAROLINA
GEORGIA
FLORIDA
GULF OF MEXICO
TROPICK of CANCER
BAY of CAMPECHE
HONDURAS
NICARAGUA
COSTA RICA
JAMAICA
NUEVA GRANADA
THE SOUTH SEA
A MAP of the BRITISH EMPIRE in AMERICA with the FRENCH, SPANISH and HOLLANDISH SETTLEMENTS adjacent thereto by Henry Popple
at AMSTERDAM
Printed for I. COVENS and C. MORTIER

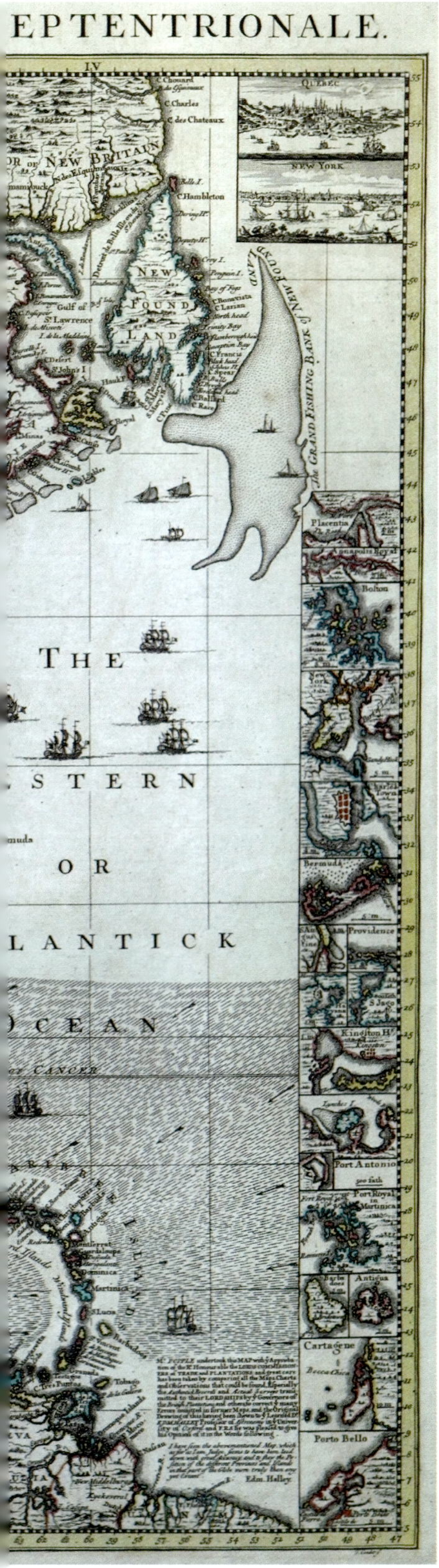

Plate 29: Henry Popple, *North America*, Amsterdam: Johannes Cóvens and Cornelis Mortier, 1733. (Fagel Portfolio 22:008)

Ignis centralis A, undiq; et undiq; per pyragogos canales ex-halationes ſpiritusq; igneos diffundit; ho
qui concavorum antrorum fornicibus illisi, frigore loci condensati in aquas deniq; resoluti fontes r
derivati in metallica corpora coalescunt, aut in novam combustibilis materiæ fœturam ad ignis
vel æstus motum, aquas per subterraneos cuniculos in altisſima montium hydrophylacia ejaculetu
Vides quoq; Subterraneum Orbem, in extima superficie terræ mare camposq; subsequi, et hæc aërem, uti ſchem

Plate 30: Athanasius Kircher, *Mundus subterraneus*, third ed., two vols in one, Amstelodami: apud Joannem Janssonium à Waesberge & Filios, 1678 (p. 186): subterranean water courses. The binding is stamped in gold with the arms of the families of Van Loon and Bas of Amsterdam and the corners of the front cover with the monogram F[rederik] W[illem] V[an] L[oon], who lived 1644–1708. (Fag. GG.2.3)

Plate 31: Pietre-Sante Bartoli, *Recueil de peintures antiques*, Paris: n. pub., 1757 (plate 24): marine idyll (Bacchus and Ariadne on Naxos?). Plates 23–5 are described as 'Peintures découvertes sous le Pontificat d'Alexandre VII, dans un souterrein, au Jardin des Religieux Camaldules de Saint Grégoire sur le Mont-Celio'. (Fag. L.1.50)

THESEI VITA PER LAPVM FLORENTINVM EX PLVTARCO GRAECO IN LATINVM VERSA.

QVEMADMODVM IN ORBIS TERRAE SItu describendo historici solent: ut ad quæ ipsi cognitione aspirare non possunt: extremis tabularũ partibus supprimentes quibusdam adiiciunt locos esse uastos arenosos & cælo terraq; penuriam aquarum: aut limum insuperabilem: aut mõtem stiticum: aut astrictum frigore pontum: ita & nobis in hac uirorum collatione perpetua rerũ historia quantũ probabili oratione assequi potuimus: de his quos supra memorauimus uiris tempora percurrẽtibus uere licuit affirmare. Quæ uero antiquiora ac uetustiora sunt: tragica & monstruosa poetæ & fabulosi rerum scriptores occupant: nec ultra fidem ullam nec certitudinem præse ferunt. Cum igitur Lycurgi legũ latoris & Nume regis res gestas litteris mandauerimus: haud ab re fuerit ad Romulum orationem conuertere: quando historia ipsa ad eius tempora q̄ prope accessimus. Sed mihi diu cogitãti huic uiro (ut inquit Aeschilus) quis conueniret: quem illi opponerem: quis dignus secum in comparatione cõiungi: uisum est tandem faciendum esse: ut a quo celebrata Atheniensium ciuitas amplificata est: eum cum gloriosissimæ atq; inuictissimæ urbis Romæ parente conferrem & compararem. Licet autem nobis reiectis fabulis ad ipsam claram historiæ lucem & ueritatem accedere. Quod sicubi necessitas coget nos ab hac parumper digressos: ad id quod uerisimile sit conferre: a quo fortasse historia abhorreat: nec admittat ullum cũ probabilitate cõmertium: æquis auditoribus opus erit: quiq; benigne & humane initium orationis exaudiant atq; approbent. Videtur igitur Theseus multis de causis Romulo q̄ simillimus extitisse. Ambo.n. cum spurii & obscuri forent: existimati sunt a Diis ĩmortalibus procreati esse. Ambo ẽt belicosi ac manu strenui: hoc quidem omnes scimus: & quanta maxime fieri potuit prudẽtia præstiterunt. ex duabus quoq; clarissimis ciuitatibus Roma & Athenis: alteram hic condidit: alteram ille nouis colonis compleuit. Fœminarum præterea raptus de utroq; feruntur: nec eorum quisq̄ domesticam cladem & crimina suorum effugit: sed ad postremum ambo dicuntur in inuidiam & offensionem ciuium incidisse. Siquid igitur ex his quæ minus tragice dici uidentur ad ueritatem conducit: Thesei quidem paternum genus in erechtheum ac primos indigenas referebatur: maternum uero in Pelopem. Pelops enim non opibus magis & copiis q̄ natorum sobole cæterorum Pelopõnesi regum potentissimus fuit: cũ filias permultas optimatibus in matrimonio locasset: multosq; in rebusp. passim principes dispersisset: e quibus unus Pittheus extitit Thesei maternus auus: qui urbem nõ magnam trœzeniorum incoluit: is qui per id temporis omnibus sapientia & eloquentia plurimum præstare putabatur. Fuit eius sapientiæ ut uidetur talis quædam uis ac forma: qualem complexus Hesiodus cum sua scripta sententiis plurimis refersisset: sapiens imprimis est habitus: atq; eam unam ex Pitthei sententiis fuisse memorant: Esto satis comiti merces promissa laboris. Cuius rei Aristoteles philosophus ẽ auctor. Euripides etiam cum Hippolytum casti Pitthei disciplinam appellet: hanc eandẽ de Pittheo opinionem perspicue attestari uidetur. Aegeo uero cum filiis indigeret: uulgatum illud oraculum Pythiam uatem cecinisse ferũt: quo iussit ne cum muliere coiret: priusq̄ Athenas accederet. quod cum non satis aperte dixisse uideretur: in Trœzenem profectus: de Dei responso cum Pittheo communicauit: quod huiusmodi fuit: Neue

Plate 32: The 'Agostini Plutarch', so named after the Venetian merchant family for which it was produced. Printed on fine vellum in two volumes it has no title-page, but vol. two has the colophon: 'Virorum illustrium uitæ ex Plutarcho græco in latinum uersæ solertique cura emendatæ fœliciter expliciunt: per Nicolaum Ienson Gallicum Venetiis impressæ. M.CCCC.LXXVIII. die. ii. Ianuarii.' The miniaturist is known as the Master of the London Pliny. Each volume has a full-page frontispiece; this one (vol. I, fol. 1r) begins the life of Theseus. (Fag. GG.2.1)

Plate 33: Angeli Politiani, *Opera,* two vols, Lugduni [Lyon]: apud Seb. Gryphium, 1546: front cover of vol. 2. (Fag. G.1.40)

[All three editions have essentially the same content and the title pages have identical wording, except that Hagen's omits the sentence, '*Geschreven* [...] *afwenden.*']

Verhael van de seer beklaechlicke afbrandinge der stadt Corke in 't west-quartier van Irlandt, [...] *gebeurt den laetsten may 1622. Naer de prodigieuse bataille der vogelen genoemt spreeuwen, die welcke over ende ontrent die stadt seer heftichlick vochten den 12. ende 14. may 1621.* [...] ('sGraven-Haghe: Aert Meuris, 1622)

Religio-political conflict: the Williamite period

Waerachtig verhael, van het schrickelijck verraet, en samensweering van de paepsche partye, tegens het leven van sijn geheyligde majesteyt, de regeeringe, en de protestantsche religie [...], *door Titus Oates* [...] (Amsterdam: Weduwe Bruynings and Jan Bouman, 1679) [two duplicate copies]

Engelants verraed ontdeckt, bewesen uyt veel autentijcke brieven en bekentenisse, als van Oates, Bedlow, Prance, Koolman, en andere. [...] Getrouwelijck uyt het Engels vertaelt (n.p., n.pub., 1679) [three duplicate copies]

Een brief, geschreeven door den heer pensionaris Fagel. Aan Mr. James Steward [*sic*] *advocaat, behelzende 't gevoelen der prince en princesse van Orangie, wegens 't affschaffen van de Test en de Penale Wetten* (colophon: t'Amsterdam: By de Weduwe van Steven Swart, 1688)

Reflectien op den heer Fagels brief

[There is no imprint, but the date 12 January 1688 is appended to the text.]

Considération sur la lettre de Mr. Fagel Conseiller Pensionaire d'Holande, en réponce de celle de Mr. J. Steward [*sic*], *Avocat à Londres. Pour l'informer des sentimens de Leurs Altesses Royales* (Cologne: Pierre Marteau, 1688)

[Only the first eight pages are present.]

[James Stewart] *Réponse à la lettre supposée écrite par Monsieur Fagel, Pensionaire de Hollande à Monsieur Jacques Stewart pour expliquer les sentimens de leurs altesses royales, Monseigneur le Prince & Madame la Princesse d'Orange, touchant l'abolition du Test et des loix pénales* (n.p., n.pub., n.d.)

[The date 13 February 1688 is appended to the text.]

Réflexions sur un écrit, intitulé Réponse à la lettre supposée écrite par Monsieur Fagel, Pensionnaire de Hollande, à Monsr. Jaques Stewart: *Ou défense des sentimens de leurs Altesses Royales sur la révocation du Test* (n.p., n.pub., 1688)

[The place and date La Haye and 27 February 1688 are appended to the text.]

Copie van een missive by den heere Fagel, raedt-pensionaris van de edele groot mogende heeren Staten van Hollandt en West-Vrieslandt, geschreven in de Franschetale, op den 9. april 1688. Aen den heere marquis d'Albyville [...]. *Hebbende voor af een aenspaeke* [*sic*] *aen den bescheyden leser, over het subject van de brief by sijn wel-ed: op den vierden november 1687. Aen Dr. Stewart in Engelandt geschreven* (Lleeuwarden [*sic*]: Hero Nauta, 1688)

Declaratien van syn hoogheyt Wilhem Henrik, by der gratie Gods, prince van Orangien, &c. Behelsende de redenen die hem bewegen met de wapenen in het koningrijck van Engelant over te gaen tot bescherming van de protestantse religie, ende tot herstellinge van de wetten en vryheden van Engelant, Schotlant en Yerlant [...] ('s Gravenhage: Arnout Leers, 1688) [three duplicate copies]

Een apologie voor de protestanten van Ierland; bestaande in een kort verhaal van de revolutien in dat koninkrijk, mitsgaders de tegenwoordige staat desselfs (Amsterdam: Aart Dircksz Oossaan, 1689)

Koning William of koning Louis. [...] *Wegens 't gouvernement deeser natien. Geschreeven uyt Cheshire door een edelman die onlangs van Ierland gearriveerd is. Uyt het Engelsch overgeset* [no imprint]

Een antwoord op de declaratie van de gewesen koning Jacobus aan alle sijne gepretendeerde onderdaanen in 't koninkrijk van Engeland, gegeven op 't kasteel te Dublin den 8/18 may 1689. [...] (Amsterdam: Pieter Pijl, 1689)

Een verhaal van een gevecht, voorgevallen tusschen de Franschen en Yeren, op 't weygeren van de Fransche tot gouverneurs aan te neemen van Cork en Waterford in Ierland. Overgeschreeven in een brief van een officier in Ierland aan sijn vriend tot London [no imprint]

Pertinent dagh-relaes wegens het gepasseerde in Engelant van den 5 maert tot den 25 incluys. [...] (Rotterdam: J. Gysen and J. van Reen, 1689)

Voornaame tydinge uyt Ierland. Zijnde motiven van aanmoediginge van de officieren en soldaten die in de tegenwoordige oorlog van Ierland zullen dienen (Amsterdam: Aart Dirksz Oossaan, 1689)

Waarachtig en pertinent dag-verhaal, van de belegering van London-Derry; uytgegeeven door Mr. George Walker rector van Donoghmoore in 't graafschap van Tirone, en laast gouverneur van London-Derry. [...] (Amsterdam: de Weduwe van Steven Swart, 1689)

Historisch verhaal van het gepasseerde in Engelant, Schotlant en Yerlant. Sedert den 28 mey tot den 17 juny 1689. [...] *Nevens een pertinent dagh-iournael van 't gene in de belegering van Londonderry is voorgevallen, geschreven door een officier uyt gemelde stad.* (Rotterdam: J. van Rynen and J. van Gysen, 1689)

[P. 26 is headed by a secondary title for the *Iournael*, dating it to 28 May.]

De drie laatste post-tydinge uyt London (Amsterdam: Laurens Gunter, 1689)

Een waarachtig verhaal van de tegenwoordigen toestand van Ierland. Betreffende de nieuwe vaststelling der regeering, geschied door den geweesen koning Jacobus. [...] *Beneffens de staat van Derry en Enniskilling* [...] *In 't Engelsch geschreeven door een persoon die zeer kommerlyk uyt Dublin is gekomen op den 18 juny 1689 en daar uyt vertaald* (Amsterdam: Aert Dirksz Oossaan, 1689)

Pertinent verhael van 't gene gepasseert is in 't ontsetten en verlaten van Londonderry; met de brieven van den 23 augusti [1689] *uyt Londen* [no imprint]

Waarachtig verhaal van de laatste reden, van den eerwaardigen Dr. George Walker, gouverneur van London-Derry, so als hy deselve sprak tegens Mr. David Maxwel predikant van Donoghaddee, en verscheide messieurs, die by hem waaren toen hy stierf [no imprint]

The Character of the Lord Baron Ginckle, Lieutenant General, and Commander in Chief of their Majesties Forces in Ireland [...] *De ware verbeeltenis van sijn excellentie den baron van Ginckel, luytenant-generael en commandant en chef van hare majesteyten armées in Yrland* ('s Gravenhage: Jan Aelberts, 1691)

Memorie van 't geene gepasseert is in 't leger van konink William, t' zedert zijn komst in Yerland, tot den 6/16 july 1690. [...] *Geschreven door een ingenieur, die alomme by, aan en present is geweest* (Amsterdam: n.pub., 1690)

[The text is signed 'N. N.', presumably indicating anonymity.]

Tweede oprecht en waere journael uyt Yerlandt. [...] ('sGravenhage: Gerrit Rammazeyn, n.d.)

Een brief van Tyrconnel aen den koning van Frankryk uyt Yrlandt. Gedruckt met permissie den 28 augusti 1690 [no imprint as such]

Syne majesteyts allergenadigste aenspraeck, aen beyde de huysen des parlements [no imprint, surrounding pamphlets from 1690]

De Gereformeerde Mercurius, of Den Nieuwen Observator [...], *Vtydag* [*sic*] *July 25 O: St: 1690* (Rotterdam: Barent Bos, 1690)

Yerlant verlost en hersteld, door den onvermoeide victorieuzen William de III$^{de.}$ koning van Groot-Britannien. Waar in kortelijk verhandelt werd zijn maijesteits heyrtogt na Yerland. [...] *Naaukeurig uit de autentyke bewijzen en raporten by een gestelt door en liefhebber der historien.* [...] (Amsterdam: Jan ten Hoorn, 1690)

The Dublin book trade

Details for those works that have an Irish connection can be found in the relevant sections above.

Imprint: Dublin Printer + Publisher-Bookseller

Leland, *An Answer to a Late Book Intituled,* Christianity as Old as the Creation

Letters to and from Dr. J. Swift

Swift, *Works* in 6 vols

Clayton, *A Vindication of the Histories of the Old and New Testament,* part II

The Genuine Works of Flavius Josephus, the Jewish Historian [...], ed. William Whiston, 5 vols (Dublin: George Ewing, 1741)

Clanricarde, *Memoirs*

Duncan Forbes, *Reflexions on the Sources of Incredulity with Regard to Religion* (Dublin: G[eorge] and A[lexander] Ewing and R[obert] Main, 1750)

The Travels of the Late Charles Thompson, Esq; Containing his Observations on France, Italy, Turkey in Europe, the Holy Land, Arabia, Egypt. [...] 4 vols (Dublin: Peter Wilson, 1744)

Borlase, *The History of the Irish Rebellion*

Imprint: originally printed in Dublin

Swift, *A View of the Present State of Affairs in the Kingdom of Ireland*

Clayton, *A Dissertation on Prophecy*

Clayton, *A Vindication of the Histories of the Old and New Testament*, part I

Clayton, *A Vindication of the Histories of the Old and New Testament*, part II – cf. Catcott, *Remarks*

A Report from the Committee Appointed to Inspect the Original Papers [...] *of one Mcc.* [*sic*] *Carthy*

Imprint: London + Dublin Publisher-Bookseller

Hutcheson, *Inquiry into Beauty and Virtue*

Hutcheson, *Essay on the Passions and Affections*

Imprint: false attribution to Dublin

[René Macé] *Les trois Justaucorps* – see Swift

[Claude Barthélemy Morisot] *Carolus I. Britanniarvm Rex, a secvri et calamo Miltonii vindicatus* (Dublini: apud Liberum Correctorem, via Regia, sub signo Soluti fascis, 1652)

[The British Library catalogue suggests Dijon as the actual place of publication.]

Don't worry about Pandora, throw the box wide open: Some thoughts on revealing the riches of the Fagel Collection

William A. Kelly
EDINBURGH NAPIER UNIVERSITY

OTHER PAPERS presented to the symposium confirmed that I was not alone in being unable to claim an acquaintance with the contents of the Fagel Collection beyond the bald facts about it on the website of the library of Trinity College Dublin: the riches of Dutch, French and English publications on politics, religion, economics, the sciences, including natural history and travel. Although I had long been aware of its presence in TCD, it was not until the conference of the Association for Low Countries Studies in Great Britain and Ireland was held there in January 2002 that I learnt about it from the then Keeper of Older Printed Books, Charles Benson – not least that, although it has been there for 200 years, a part of the collection, which is still uncatalogued, is known to contain university dissertations. I was on familiar territory, for I have been closely involved for almost forty years with an enormous collection in Edinburgh, acquired in 1820 by the Advocates Library, where a significant part of the collection, predominantly legal, still remains. The very much larger proportion was transferred to the ownership of the newly established National Library of Scotland in 1925, where a considerable part of the transferred material has still not been entered in the main catalogue. What has this to do with the Fagel Collection? Directly not much, but indirectly a very great deal, as I hope to show. I shall concentrate on the importance of completing the cataloguing of the collection: only when all the contents are known can they best be exploited.

The Edinburgh collection referred to formed part of the personal library of the Nuremberg senator, Georg Septimus Dieterichs, that was put up for sale after his death in 1805. In the 1810s, William Hamilton, member of the Faculty of Advocates (of whose library he was a trustee) and sometime Professor of Philosophy at the University of Edinburgh, learned that a large part of Dieterichs' material still lay unsold and neglected with the Leipzig bookseller Gleditsch. A keen student of German bibliography, he persuaded his fellow trustees to buy it. Once in Edinburgh, the bibliographical and scholarly value of the contemporary imprints by Luther, his associates and his opponents was quickly recognized and the items were catalogued. While these are known to scholars thanks to the relatively recent work of Michael Pegg and the compilers of the National Library's *Short-title Catalogue of Foreign Books Printed up to 1600*, much important information can still be mined from a close inspection of individual items.[1] One of my projects is to send regular descriptions of relevant material in Edinburgh libraries to the head of the Bavarian State Library's sixteenth-century German STC, and already an interesting number of variant or unrecorded titles in the Dieterichs Collection and elsewhere in the National Library's holdings has been revealed. If that can be achieved with material already in the public domain, what unknown treasures might there be in the uncatalogued part of the Fagel Collection? The only way to find out is to catalogue that material and then to collaborate with other librarians and bibliographers in the Netherlands, Flanders and elsewhere, the better to exploit the riches revealed.

If I say that almost all the work on the uncatalogued material in the Dieterichs Collection has been done by me, it is partly because the sheaf catalogues available to the public are so scrappy and partly because, unlike other members of the public, I know how to access the boxes in which the material is stored. It is a recognized fact among those concerned with establishing a national bibliographical record that no one country holds all the necessary materials. A former, long-term member of the National Library of Austria, Helmut Lang, has stated in print that only about 50 per cent of the early bibliographical output of Austria can be found in that library, and those of us

1 Michael A. Pegg, *A Short-title Catalogue of Foreign Books Printed up to 1600: Books Printed or Published outside the British Isles now in the National Library of Scotland and the Library of the Faculty of Advocates, Edinburgh* (Edinburgh 1970); *idem, Bibliotheca Lindesiana and Other Collections of German Sixteenth-century Pamphlets in Libraries of Britain and France,* Bibliotheca bibliographica Aureliana, vol. 66 (Baden-Baden 1977); *idem, A Catalogue of German Reformation Pamphlets (1516–1546) in Libraries of Great Britain and Ireland,* Bibliotheca bibliographica Aureliana, vol. 45 (Baden-Baden 1973).

who have helped in even a small way in a foreign bibliographical project can provide supportive evidence.[2] Jaap Harskamp, formerly of the British Library, has assured me that, when he was cataloguing a collection of Elzevier imprints that lay neglected in the University of London's Senate House, he found a number of editions of monographs not recorded in Willems' bibliography.[3] Fortunately the details of these have been passed to the Royal Library in The Hague, so that even if the STCN project has now officially closed – if indeed a line can ever be drawn under such a project – the bibliographical details and their location are known.

Mention of Willems leads me to one of my longest-standing bibliographical interests: university dissertations. I am grateful to Jos van Heel of the Museum Meermanno-Westreenianum in The Hague for correcting my long-held criticism of Willems' omission of university dissertations from his bibliography by pointing out that it was designed only to describe a collection and was not intended as a complete bibliography of the Elzeviers' activities as printers. It is nevertheless true that this genre used to be considered a kind of bibliographical stepchild, an attitude that still persists in some quarters, as I know from a remark made to me a number of years ago by the director of a large German university library, who lamented the amount of space taken up in his stacks by the thick *Sammelbände* in which large numbers of these individual items had been bound. And I remember the uncomprehending tones in which a senior figure in the National Library of Scotland's Department of Printed Books in the early 1970s told me of a recent visit by two Dutch academics, describing them as academic cannibals for their interest in dissertations as source material for teaching in a particular university faculty. His attitude struck me as somewhat odd at the time and some years later I was able to demonstrate the importance of dissertations as primary evidence for the intellectual history of an individual faculty in my doctoral dissertation on the changing fortunes of the theological faculty of the former University of Helmstedt.[4]

A possible indication that this long-standing attitude is changing is the information given to me by a doctoral candidate at the University of Amsterdam's Department of Book and Manuscript Studies that she would

2 Helmut W. Lang, *Bibliographie der österreichischen (nichtperiodischen) neuen Zeitungen 1492–1705*, Österreichische retrospektive Bibliographie, ser. 2, vol. 1 (Munich 2001), p. 5.

3 Alphonse Willems, *Les Elzevier: Histoire et annales typographiques* (Brussels, Paris, The Hague 1880).

4 W.A. Kelly, *The Theological Faculty at Helmstedt: An Outline of its Intellectual Development, as Mirrored in its Dissertations, together with a Chronological Catalogue*, 2 vols (Strathclyde 1991).

consider her dissertation on the Utrecht university printer, François Halma, incomplete without a catalogue of his entire output, including dissertations. My delight increased when she told me that several dissertations printed by Halma, lying uncatalogued in the Dieterichs Collection and recorded in my project, 'A catalogue of seventeenth century legal imprints from the Dutch language areas of Europe held by selected Edinburgh libraries', cannot be found in any Dutch library.[5] Another Dutch researcher, Barendina Hempenius-van Dijk of Groningen University's Faculty of Law, who visited the National Library in 2008 to pursue her work on legal dissertations defended at Groningen and Franeker, also found in that collection material that she could not find in a Dutch library. If among the uncatalogued, largely German dissertations in the Dieterichs Collection, there are also Dutch ones, who can tell what lies hidden in the uncatalogued part of the Fagel Collection? The only way to find out is to catalogue that part of it.

In my very early days in the National Library of Scotland the aforementioned colleague assured me that the uncatalogued material in the Dieterichs Collection contained mainly legal, theological and general philosophical dissertations. When I asked about possible medical and scientific dissertations, I was told that there were few or none. At that time I knew little about early medical and scientific publishing in the Dutch- and German-language areas, but in the intervening years that has become one of my major bibliographical interests. Examination of the boxes in which the dissertations are stored has revealed that the Dieterichs Collection contains many hundreds of dissertations in these areas from the seventeenth and eighteenth centuries. Indeed entries for these make up a very large part of my projected 'Catalogue of seventeenth- and eighteenth-century medical and scientific imprints from the Dutch- and German-language areas of Europe in Edinburgh libraries'.[6] Obviously one must not rely too much on second-hand information on what is in an uncatalogued part of a collection. If the Dieterichs Collection contains some dissertations printed at Utrecht, Groningen and Franeker that cannot be found in a Dutch library or some of those defended in Helmstedt's Faculty of Law that Werner Kundert could not find in a German or Swiss one, then it is

5 Go to http://www.napier.ac.uk/randkt/rktcentres/scob and then click on one of the publications listed there.

6 Bizarrely, the map that was printed as the endpapers to Douglas Guthrie, *A History of Medicine* (London *et al.* 1945 and 1958), entitled 'Cultural & Medical Centres of Historic Interest', mentions Vienna, which did not rise to prominence until the nineteenth century, but no centre of medical excellence from the German-language area of Europe in earlier centuries.

entirely possible that the Fagel Collection also contains publications of this type that are missing from the bibliographical record.[7]

So far my arguments for the completion of the cataloguing of the Fagel Collection have been based on material that can be said to have a solid scholarly value. However, as Bernard Naylor, former Librarian of the University of London's Institute of Latin American Studies, pointed out at a conference of the former Library Association: high-level scholarship can be conducted using low-level material. Bearing in mind the so-called 'ephemeral' imprints of earlier centuries, it may well be that there is another parallel between the Dieterichs and the Fagel collections. I know that the former also contains numerous ephemeral imprints, which cannot be ignored in the compilation of a national bibliographical record. Many of these concern the day-to-day administration of towns, such as edicts highlighting particular problems, for instance the high risk of fire in wooden houses and attempts to curtail it, or advertisements for theatrical performances, or of universities, such as announcements of an address by an incoming rector or dean of a faculty or worries about the conduct of some members of the student body. It is not at all certain that such materials, which add more light and shade to the sometimes rather staid information already available to us, are to be found in the archive of the individual town or university. It is possible that examples were held in the Fagels' library, but one cannot know until the cataloguing has been completed.

If they are already known to exist in the Fagel Collection, I would be surprised if another important genre whose extensiveness in the Dieterichs Collection cannot yet be ascertained accurately, namely a printed record of those key events in an individual's life – birth, marriage and death – were not there too. Leaving aside the necrophiliac interest of these publications for family historians, they are an important source of increased knowledge of an individual writer's literary output – many important figures contributed occasional verses, which have still not been recorded as fully as they should be. Before the cataloguing of the remaining part of the collection begins, I would suggest that, where appropriate, the description of such an item should include the names of the contributors of congratulatory verses. This was suggested as far back as 1990 by Wolfgang Müller, who refers to such individuals as *beteiligte Personen* (participants) in his monograph, *Die Drucke des 17. Jahrhunderts im deutschen Sprachraum.* It is interesting that Müller's remit – to produce a

7 Werner Kundert, *Katalog der Helmstedter juristischen Disputationen, Programme und Reden, 1574–1810*, Repertorien zur Erforschung der frühen Neuzeit, vol. 8 (Wiesbaden 1984).

template for such a catalogue – has been taken up by those responsible for the chronologically earlier project, *Verzeichnis der im deutschen Sprachbereich erschienenen Drucke des XVI. Jahrhunderts*, known for short as *VD16*.[8]

My regard for the role of serendipity in bibliographical research is borne out by my experience with Jaap Harskamp's *Dissertatio medica inauguralis*.[9] On its appearance I went through all the seventeenth-century items listed by him, to see who had contributed congratulatory verses. After looking at many volumes that contained no contributors or ones whose name meant nothing, I hit gold when I came upon a dissertation defended by a native of Dorpat (now Tartu), Sebastian Wirdig,[10] to which the German poet and mystic, Quirinus Kuhlmann, had contributed a previously unrecorded text. Consisting of four stanzas, each of four lines, it begins with a quotation, *Odi profanum vulgus & arceo* from Horace's *Carmina*, 3.1.1, which chimes with what we know of Kuhlmann's flight from many of his contemporaries because of his early speech impediment and his increasing absorption in mysticism. The rest of the poem is taken up with praise of Wirdig's filial following of his father's profession of physician. The short biographical descriptions appended to the names of contributors to monographs and university dissertations give further clues in identifying writers with a common link.

When some twenty years ago the British Germanist John Flood was beginning work on his bio-bibliography of the poets laureate of the Holy Roman Empire,[11] I was able to provide him with the names of a number of German baroque poets I had located in the Dieterichs Collection. Similarly, I made use of that same collection to alert the North American-based Germanist Gerhard Dünnhaupt to separate monographs by individuals whom he lists in his magisterial *Bibliographisches Handbuch der Barockliteratur* and its much expanded second edition, *Personalbibliographien zu den Drucken des Barock*. One of my largest and most satisfying additions was for the entry on the

8 Wolfgang Müller, *Die Drucke des 17. Jahrhunderts im deutschen Sprachraum: Untersuchungen zu ihrer Verzeichnung in einem VD17*, Beiträge zum Buch- und Bibliothekswesen, vol. 31 (Wiesbaden 1990). *Verzeichnis der im deutschen Sprachbereich erschienenen Drucke des XVI. Jahrhunderts VD16, herausgegeben von der Bayerischen Staatsbibliothek in München in Verbindung mit der Herzog August Bibliothek in Wolfenbüttel*, 25 vols (Stuttgart 1983–2001), now available online at www.vd16.de.

9 Jaap Harskamp, *Dissertatio medica inauguralis* [...]: *Leyden Medical Dissertations in the British Library, 1593–1746. Catalogue of a Sloane-inspired Collection* ([London] 1997).

10 Sebastian Wirdig, *Disputatio medica inauguralis, de pleuritide*, 1674. Listed by Harskamp as no. 648. Kuhlmann's poem appears on leaf A6v.

11 John L. Flood, *Poets Laureate in the Holy Roman Empire: A Bio-bibliographical Handbook* (Berlin 2006).

Lutheran pastor, schoolmaster and Neo-Latin playwright, Johann Sebastian Mitternacht, many of whose *Schulprogramme* – which are difficult to find in German libraries – are present in Edinburgh.[12]

The publication of literary discoveries in specialist scholarly periodicals is one way of bringing a collection to the notice of researchers. Another is to survey a broad class of material in libraries within a particular geographical area. Although I had been aware that there are numerous early Low Countries imprints in Scottish libraries as a result of the close legal, theological and medical links between these countries, it was not until I had begun to gather data for the volume *A Guide to Collections of Books Printed in German-speaking Countries before 1901* that I got a clearer impression of just how numerous such imprints are in both Glasgow and Edinburgh and the rest of the country.[13] It was several years before I was in a position to conduct an in-depth survey of these early Low Countries imprints both as a worthwhile project in its own right and as a way of giving further proof of the validity of the methodology adopted by Bernhard Fabian for the *Handbuch deutscher historischer Buchbestände in Europa*. The result of the survey reveals an impressive variety of subject matter – from astronomy through ballistics, Biblical exegesis and textual criticism, hydraulics, law, theology (both Protestant and Roman Catholic) and urban administration – in holdings that are as important as the early German ones. In spite of the geographical area covered, that survey was relatively easy to conduct and I hope to extend my coverage first to the northern counties of England, i.e. Northumberland, Durham, Yorkshire, Lancashire and Cumbria, and then possibly further south. If such a survey can improve our knowledge of the early Low Countries imprints in parts of Britain, then one covering the holdings in Trinity College (including a fully catalogued Fagel Collection) and other

12 Gerhard Dünnhaupt, *Bibliographisches Handbuch der Barockliteratur: Hundert Personalbibliographien deutscher Autoren des siebzehnten Jahrhunderts*, Hiersemanns bibliographische Handbücher, no. 2, 2 vols (Stuttgart 1980–81); *idem*, *Personalbibliographien zu den Drucken des Barock*, Hiersemanns bibliographische Handbücher, no. 9, 2nd, corrected and extended edn, 6 vols (Stuttgart 1990–93); my discoveries of previously unrecorded texts by Mitternacht are listed in *Personalbibliographien*, vol. 4, pp. 2751–806. See also: W.K., 'Additions to the bibliography of Johann Sebastian Mitternacht', *Daphnis: Zeitschrift für mittlere deutsche Literatur und Kultur der frühen Neuzeit (1400–1750)*, 37/3–4 (2008), 626–44; *idem*, 'Johann Ludwig Praschs früheste gedruckte Dichtung', *Wolfenbütteler Barock-Nachrichten*, 22/1 (June 1995), 35; *idem*,'Drei unbekannte Gedichte Johann Rists', *WBN*, 23/2 (November 1996), 95–106; *idem*, 'Ein unbekanntes Werk Johannes Riemers', *ibid.*, 106; *idem*, 'Ein unbekanntes Gedicht Georg Greflingers', *Daphnis*, 28/1 (1999), 201–2; *idem*, 'Neugefundene Texte des deutschen Barock aus britischen Beständen', *Daphnis*, 29/3–4 (2000), 699–708.

13 Graham Jefcoate, William A. Kelly and Karen Kloth (eds), *A Guide to Collections of Books Printed in German-speaking Countries before 1901 (or in German elsewhere) Held by Libraries in Great Britain and Ireland*, Handbuch deutscher historischer Buchbestände in Europa, vol. 10 (Hildesheim 2000).

libraries in Ireland will have the same beneficial effects. As I wrote in the general introduction to the survey, these benefits are not confined to researchers, but also extend to librarians:

> A much more detailed knowledge is desirable for librarians in both micro- and macro-planning. In the former such information can enable those in immediate charge of departments of early printed collections to offer more accurate advice to the members of their own institution on their Low Countries holdings and will also help them to give more informed advice to their senior management on questions of collection development. In the latter, which has longer term implications for British tertiary education, it can be argued that there is little or nothing to distinguish the information centres of the newer universities which rely on the Internet, e-books and e-journals for the needs of their staff and students, but what does distinguish the older ones not only from the former but also the one from the other are the special collections held by each one.[14]

I was thinking of course of a purely British context but the same principle can apply to Irish institutions in their relations both with one another and with British ones, for we are living in an environment that unites not only economies but so many other aspects of life, including education. If a researcher knows that certain materials are easily available in Dublin, it may be much cheaper and quicker for him or her to go there rather than to the Netherlands or Flanders, however great the intellectual and aesthetic pleasure to be derived from a journey to the latter.

In conclusion I say again to those responsible for the Fagel Collection what I said in the first part of this article's title: put out of your mind the old story of Pandora and the consequences of her action and throw the box wide open. In encouraging the completion of the cataloguing of the Fagel Collection I would hope that restrictions of time and a pragmatic attitude to the task would protect the staff involved from unreasonable expectations as to what a catalogue can achieve. Specialists charged with drawing up a set of cataloguing rules for such a project can spend many hours discussing the placement of a comma or a full stop. That is bad enough when one is dealing with modern imprints, but when one is working with early printed books it can lead to the delusion – as illustrated by the thinking behind the first edition of the Library of Congress Cataloging Distribution Service's *Bibliographic description of rare books* and its

14 William A. Kelly, 'Survey of Pre-1801 Low Countries imprints in Scottish research libraries', part 1, *Gutenberg-Jahrbuch*, 82 (2007), 278–337; part 2, ibid., 83 (2008), 165–232, here 279.

various updates – that a catalogue entry can be accepted by a bibliographer as a trustworthy record.[15] I remember the astonished, uncomprehending look on the face of a former colleague as he left a meeting, at which much time had been expended on trying to fashion a form of words to describe what words on the title page were contained within brackets and how they were disposed there. The truth of course is that no bibliographer worth his or her salt would subscribe to the idea that the personal autopsy of such an item is unnecessary.

15 *Bibliographic Description of Rare Books: Rules Formulated under AACR2 and ISBD (A) for the Descriptive Cataloging of Rare Books and Other Special Printed Materials* (Washington 1981). In the second edition of 1991 (p. v) it is stated that the use of 'bibliographic description' in the title of the 1981 edition was too suggestive of a traditional descriptive bibliography. That phrase was dropped in favour of 'descriptive cataloging' to show that the rules are designed for library cataloguers rather than for bibliographers. However that earlier, admirable determination seems to have been forgotten in the catalogue entries for many examples, where one finds notes such as 'No full stop after …'.

AVEC · LE · TEMPS ·

PAVLATIM ·

Fagel, pamphlets and the STCN file

Jaap Harskamp
CAMBRIDGE UNIVERSITY LIBRARY

THIS SHORT essay deals with three distinct but interrelated aspects of Dutch book history. First of all, attention will be paid to the international character of printing and publishing in the Netherlands. The focus will then shift to the contemporary effort of producing a pre-1800 national bibliography: to what extent is the outward-looking and cosmopolitan nature of Dutch publishing reflected in this retrospective catalogue? Finally, emphasis will be laid upon the Fagel Collection and in particular the substantial number of pamphlets that this collection contains. How relevant is this collection? Would it be a worthwhile undertaking to integrate this collection into the national bibliography?

Publishing, internationalism and the STCN

The Short Title Catalogue Netherlands (STCN) is the Dutch retrospective bibliography for the period 1540–1800. It covers the subject areas of the humanities, sciences and social sciences. Included are descriptions of Dutch post-incunabula, but single sheets have been omitted. By the end of 2013 the STCN database contained more than 200,000 titles and over 500,000 copies of books published in the Netherlands (irrespective of the language) and of books in Dutch published abroad. The STCN has been compiled by the Dutch National Library (Koninklijke Bibliotheek) and includes the collections of the KB itself, the university libraries of Amsterdam, Leiden, Utrecht, Delft and

Groningen, the important city libraries of Haarlem and Deventer, the City Archive of The Hague, the Alkmaar Regional Archive and others. The STCN is of crucial importance to those who study the proud history of printing and publishing in the Low Countries. It was (and remains) an economic activity that from the outset had a strong outward-looking and cosmopolitan dimension.

From its early development, publishing and bookselling in the Low Countries developed into an international business. In 1580 Lowys (Louis) Elzevier, a former apprentice of Christopher Plantin in Antwerp, moved from the southern Netherlands to the northern university town of Leiden where he set up his own bookshop. Six years later, after working mainly as a bookbinder and bookseller, he was appointed beadle of Leiden University. The first Elzevier to run a printing office was Louis's son Isaac (in Leiden from 1617), who also became university printer. Subsequently, the large Elzevier family ran major offices in Leiden and Amsterdam, whilst the houses in Utrecht and The Hague were of less importance. Members of the dynasty were known for their shrewd commercialism in the book business. They were among the foremost European publishers of their time for the variety and number of their publications (over 2000 titles) at low prices.

Their output consists of a wide range of works in theology, philosophy, politics, law and medicine, French plays and *belles-lettres*, not to mention a set of outstanding dictionaries or the large number of dissertations and disputations that were produced within the various faculties of Leiden University. Reissues of the Classics with annotations by contemporary scholars were widely sold. The commercial success of these reissues allowed for the publication of more recent work by various outstanding authors (Erasmus, Descartes, Galileo, Grotius) and for more risky undertakings such as the publication of the philosophical works of Thomas Hobbes in Latin. For example, Hobbes' *Elementa philosophica de cive* was published by Elzevier in three different editions (1647, 1657 and 1669). The 1669 edition is included in the Fagel Collection (see fig. 1). In 1653 the firm published a French translation of this work. The 1675 Dutch translation, entitled *De eerste beginselen van een burger-staat*, does not mention a printer on the title page. This rare work is also part of the Fagel Collection.

The language of publication of the Elzevier output is mostly Latin, but there are also works in Greek, French, Italian, an occasional one in Dutch or German and in a number of Semitic languages – but none in English. Continental Europe during the seventeenth century neither spoke nor read

Fig 1: Thomas Hobbes, *Elementa philosophica de cive*, Amsterdam: Daniel Elzevier, 1669. (Fag. H.16.78)

English and Daniel Elzevier's renowned Amsterdam stock catalogue of 1674 (768 pages, some 20,000 items) lists only nineteen titles in English. The study of Arab language and literature at Leiden flourished thanks to the legacy of Thomas van Erpe (1584–1624), who used the Latinized name of Erpenius. His first book, published when he was twenty-nine years of age, is an Arab grammar that stayed in print until the early nineteenth century. Leiden University stimulated the printing of texts in non-Western languages, particularly in Hebrew, Aramaic and Arabic. In his house, Erpenius used his own eastern printing press, known as the *Typographia Erpeniana linguarum orientalium*, for which he was subsidized by the university. A year after his death his widow sold the whole stock of type to Isaac Elzevier for the colossal amount of 8000 guilders. It allowed the Elzevier dynasty to continue the use of a unique typographical resource that turned out to be of crucial importance to the firm.

The Elzevier family combined the production of quality books with sound business practice. It made its sales catalogues widely available and explored every possible means of selling books. There seemed to be no conflict between considerations of quality in either content or presentation on the one hand and the concept of the book as an economic commodity on the other. By the end of the seventeenth century, their publications were already widely collected. Apart from private collections, major holdings outside the Netherlands are to be found in London, Cambridge, Paris, Brussels, Copenhagen, Stockholm, the Baltic states and even in St Petersburg. The Elzevier dynasty highlights the truly cosmopolitan nature of Dutch publishing and bookselling in the seventeenth century.

During the eighteenth century the nature of publishing in the Netherlands changed from that of the 'Golden Age', but not the activity itself – far from it. Printing, publishing and bookselling remained economically vibrant where other commercial activities were in decline. With the revocation of the Edict of Nantes in 1685, large numbers of Huguenot immigrants had moved from France to both the Netherlands and England. There were many philosophers, writers, publishers and printers amongst these refugees. The number of books translated from English into French and vice versa increased sharply. Dutch printing presses played an important part in this internationalizing process, publishing and distributing works in translation by John Locke, Isaac Newton, David Hume and many others, thus contributing to the migration of ideas, so crucial for the advance and spread of the Enlightenment: one of its essential preconditions was the assimilation of English philosophical and social opinions by Protestant immigrants from the Low Countries and France.

Does the STCN reflect the internationalism of Dutch publishing? Does it give us an insight into the spread and distribution of books produced in the Netherlands? The STCN project has been largely limited to Dutch libraries and institutions and, within a relatively short period of time and with a massive commitment, the outcome has proved to be both significant and relevant. During my years as Curator of the Dutch/Flemish Collections at the British Library, I was able to add the complete collection of some 30,000 pre-1801 Dutch imprints to the STCN, in addition to the extraordinary Elzevier Collection held at Senate House in London. This effort was an exception: if we restrict ourselves to the British Isles then there are many other substantial collections that should be added, such as those at the Bodleian, at the Wellcome Institute, and in Trinity College Dublin, and Cambridge and Edinburgh universities. All of these libraries and institutions hold significant collections of Dutch imprints. The STCN website informs the user that the project was completed in July 2009. It is the word 'completed' that I object to. It gives the false impression that work on the STCN is finished. Why not use the phrase 'scaled down'? Why not add an ambitious statement of intent that large collections held abroad shall be included 'in due course'? The STCN is a valuable tool to the book historian. Yet the task is unfinished. It is a work in progress.

One of the crucial questions for the book historian is the dispersion of Dutch imprints. Where did books go to, for what purposes were they exported, was there a target audience, who ordered the books, who sold them, who transported them, who collected them? Why are so many of the eighteenth-century French titles with Dutch imprints that I have so far located only to be found in London and/or Cambridge and not in the Netherlands? Such questions need to be answered. Of course, a national library has a number of duties and responsibilities that are equally important, time-consuming and costly. If money is scarce, cultural events and activities will suffer. When it comes to cutting costs, culture is a prime target. That seems to be the general rule. Yet the STCN should remain a flagship project, just like the English Short Title Catalogue has always been. After all, it is through the STCN in particular that the Dutch National Library presents itself to researchers worldwide. The history of Dutch printing and publishing is too cosmopolitan to be looked at from a solely national perspective.

The benefits of a wider international approach will be substantial. In September 2009 I started work on the collection of Dutch imprints held at Cambridge University and within a period of two years nearly 600 new titles were added to the STCN. Of the holdings, estimated at 12,000, some 70 per cent had been added by May 2014. The strike rate of unrecorded materials runs at about 13 per cent, partly (but not exclusively) because of the substantial collection of French titles with Dutch imprints. A similar percentage of unrecorded materials was found in the collections of the British Library, but it is interesting to note that the holdings of BL and CUL complement rather than duplicate each other. The fact that so many (potentially unique) copies of books survive only outside the country in which they were printed illustrates the importance of international collaboration in this field of research. It is an exciting prospect that Trinity College Dublin has expressed an eagerness to have its holdings of early Dutch imprints included in the STCN. While the TCD Library has other early Dutch imprints, priority should be given to those in the Fagel Collection, where the great majority is located.

Pamphlet culture

The Elzeviers were first and foremost academic printers and many of their publications are present in the outstanding Fagel Collection. In an age of ever-growing demand for printed materials this left plenty of scope for other publishing firms and individual printers to concentrate on different materials, from fiction, poetry, plays, maps and religious tracts to information sheets on current affairs. Some 2000 printers are known to have worked in Holland during the seventeenth century. There was a 'division of labour' in printing long before Adam Smith introduced the term into economic historiography.

In 1605 Antwerp-based publisher Abraham Verhoeven (c. 1575–1652) produced a periodical news sheet of European events called *Nieuwe Tijdinghen*, the first 'newspaper' in the Low Countries. Soon, however, the centre of news-gathering and information distribution moved to Amsterdam where a number of multilingual *courantoes* were published (Amsterdam has been called the oldest press centre of Europe). The Dutch were made aware of current affairs by the appearance of weekly (sometimes bi- or tri-weekly) newspapers that began to appear in the 1620s. These papers played a key role in disseminating information by using reports from their 'correspondents' in far-flung locations.

One paper even employed war reporters who followed the Republic's army on its various campaigns.

The word *courant*, directly derived from the Dutch, became current in England during the seventeenth and eighteenth centuries. The first serialized *courantoes* to appear in England (1621) were printed in Amsterdam. News 'out of Holland' or 'out of Amsterdam' became the chief source of information for those who wanted to know about political developments. From the outset there was an ambiguous feeling towards newspapers: they were both eagerly awaited and frowned upon with suspicion. Both Charles II and James II objected to the detailed English news that was spread in the Dutch gazettes (especially in the well-informed *Haarlem Gazette*). News publications undertaken by Milton, Defoe, Nathaniel Mist and others, however, were all modelled on Dutch examples.

Such 'newspapers' had been preceded by – and for a considerable time during the seventeenth century ran parallel with – the news pamphlet. *Ad hoc* publications, unbound books, booklets relating the latest news, and other ephemera, were among the most inclusive or democratic aspects of the social life of early modern Europe. Pamphlets were cheap (printed in small numbers, but quickly reprinted if in demand) and within reach of almost everyone. Because they dealt with topical issues, such pamphlets found their way through large segments of society, and their content was widely discussed amongst its readers, thus multiplying their impact. Research into this type of material not only yields rich information about the development of the processes of publishing printed matter, but also about the spread and effect of news stories. Pamphlets participated in the discussion of the political or religious topics of the day. They reported on wars or broadcast calamities (sometimes illustrated with images of the event or explanatory maps) such as the Fire of London.

Clandestine publishing was a booming business in the Netherlands. A climate of relative tolerance towards ideas that clashed with Protestantism, combined with a sharp sense that anti-papist sentiments could be turned into a profitable undertaking, and all this supported by a well-developed national and international commercial infrastructure, made the publishing and selling of books and pamphlets a lucrative business. Pamphlets were certainly not neutral or objective. More often than not, they took the kind of stance that today would be described as 'propaganda' (the word has a religious origin: it was not until the nineteenth century that it acquired political and military connotations). The pamphlet culture of the age reflects not only a growing sense of time and place in the seventeenth century, but also an increased awareness of diplomatic relations and international (European) rivalry. However, like many such publications, pamphlets were 'used', that is to say, read, discussed and subsequently discarded. That is why many pamphlets have become extremely rare and are difficult to trace. In the past, they have all too often been ignored by librarians (not unlike early dissertations and disputations from the various universities). Even now, there are many collections of pamphlets hiding in large libraries that are not catalogued and hence remain irretrievable. A systematic ordering of the pamphlets in the Fagel Collection will undoubtedly add to the large stock of pamphlets that are so far recorded in the STCN.

In a time when the notion of nationhood was as yet a matter of little concern, Holland was effectively made up of cities. This city culture created a society that did not nurture the leading role of an aristocracy, as was the case in Britain. Socio-economic life was dominated by well-to-do burghers who lived and worked in the cities. Equality of opportunity in Dutch economic life gave society a competitive edge that was at the time unrivalled elsewhere in Europe. It was an atmosphere in which the arts, including the art of printing, flourished. There have been rather wild and unsubstantiated suggestions that in the seventeenth century more books were printed in the Netherlands than in the rest of Europe put together. Nevertheless, the output was vast, especially if one takes the large number of pamphlets and news-sheets into account. England's restrictive policies on printing had created an additional – albeit specialist – market opportunity for the Netherlands, where since the 1520s Protestant works were printed in the English language (in spite of regular protests from the English authorities).

The Dutch distribution networks at this time were largely independent and well developed. In England by contrast, the trade was controlled by the Stationers' Company, which in 1557 received a royal charter in order to monitor heretical and seditious writings. In 1586 the Star Chamber decreed that printing would only be allowed in London, with exceptions made for the university presses at Oxford and Cambridge. It was not until 1695 that the Licensing Law was abandoned. Moreover, the Puritan Revolution and two civil wars created an atmosphere of intolerance and a spectrum of religious ideas that were considered dangerous to either Royalists or Parliamentarians. Censorship was a continuous threat to any author at the time. The Netherlands offered an asylum, both physical and intellectual, in body and in print.

The pamphlet stands at the beginning of the age of information. It is this aspect that makes the Fagel Collection a particularly fascinating one. As Timothy Jackson has indicated in his Preface, the Fagel Collection was both a working library with substantial holdings in history, politics and law, and a library of the cultivated mind with an interest in *belles-lettres*, philosophy, travel, maps, etc. However, it may well be that in the end the massive number of pamphlets included in the collection will turn out to be the most interesting aspect for historians and book historians alike. The relevance of this particular aspect of the collection lies in the fact that the pamphlets cover the complete period of intense contacts and hostilities between the Netherlands and England (including Ireland and Scotland), from the early English intervention in the Spanish-Dutch war, to the three major Anglo-Dutch wars, culminating in the Glorious Revolution and the inauguration of William and Mary. To the student of Anglo-Dutch relations this substantial collection is invaluable and deserves the closest possible scrutiny.

Printers and preachers

In 1585, under the Treaty of Nonsuch, Elizabeth I decided to intervene directly in the war between the United Provinces and Spain, agreeing to provide the Dutch with £126,000 a year to pay an English force of 6400 soldiers and 1000 horses. In return, the Dutch were to deliver to her the two 'cautionary' towns of Brill and Flushing as insurance for the repayment of English war expenses. In 1589 Elizabeth named Robert Sidney, 1st Earl of Leicester, the governor of Flushing. The port had strategic military importance and provided a listening post on the continent. During the previous year, the English ambassador in The Hague had been granted the former Roman Catholic Chapel of the Sacrament Hospital (at the Noordeinde) to be used for religious services specifically aimed at the Earl of Leicester's soldiers. By 1595 this privilege was extended to include the entire English community in the city. The building was henceforth known as the English Church. The English presence in the Netherlands was by then well established. It was the beginning of a period of close Anglo-Dutch relationships in which the cities of Flushing (military centre) and Middelburg (administrative centre) played leading roles. These contacts were intensified with the arrival of many English religious refugees who settled in or around Middelburg. With a home audience in mind, they were eager to make their voice heard by using the printing press.

It is remarkable to see how many (and how quickly) pamphlets published in England were translated into Dutch and vice versa, more often than not in multiple translations and in multiple printings. This is an aspect that – as yet – has rarely been considered, but there must have been on both sides of the Channel a veritable translation industry at the time, which further emphasizes close Anglo-Dutch/Flemish relationships. One of the first pamphlets that Jackson mentions in his list of examples taken from the Fagel Collection proves this very point. The pamphlet concerned was issued on 1 October 1585 and is entitled: *Een verclaringhe der oorsaken beweghende de coninghinne van Enghelandt, hulpe te gheuen tot beschermінghe des* [...] *volckes der Nederlanden* (see fig. 2 and p. 194). This pamphlet is a translation of *A declaration of the cavses mooving the qveene of England to give aide to the defence of the people afflicted and oppressed in the lowe countries*, printed in 1585 in London by Christopher Barker. The importance of this pamphlet to the Dutch is reflected in the number of editions of the translation that are recorded. The STCN points to six variant copies, all from 1585. One was printed in Middelburg by Richard Schilders; another in London (in Dutch!) by Barker; two by Aelbrecht Hendrickz in Delft; one by Gillis Rooman in Haarlem; and one by Cornelis Claesz in Amsterdam. All the important cities were well and truly informed about Elizabeth's crucial decision.

The appearance of the name of Christopher Barker in this context is not surprising. Barker was an outstanding figure in the printing trade towards the end of the sixteenth century, a shrewd businessman who managed to acquire the most lucrative of all patents, namely the Bible patent. He is first heard of as a publisher in 1569. Barker acquired the office of Queen's printer in 1577. The title was not a privilege bestowed graciously as a favour, but a business patent bought from the previous holder. The full patent granted to Barker the office of royal printer of all statutes, books, bills, acts of Parliament, proclamations, injunctions, Bibles, all service books to be used in churches, and all other volumes ordered to be printed by the Queen or Parliament.

More intriguing is the fact that the pamphlet mentioned above appeared simultaneously in London and Middelburg. Early contacts between the two cities were numerous. Middelburg, in the southwest of the Low Countries, was in close proximity to the English-governed towns Flushing and Brill. Printer Richard Schilders (c. 1538–1634), born in the Dutch-speaking part of Hainault, had fled to England in 1567 because of his Calvinist beliefs. He worked in London as a printer and became a member of the London Stationers' Company in 1568. In 1579 he was invited to return to the Netherlands to become Middelburg's

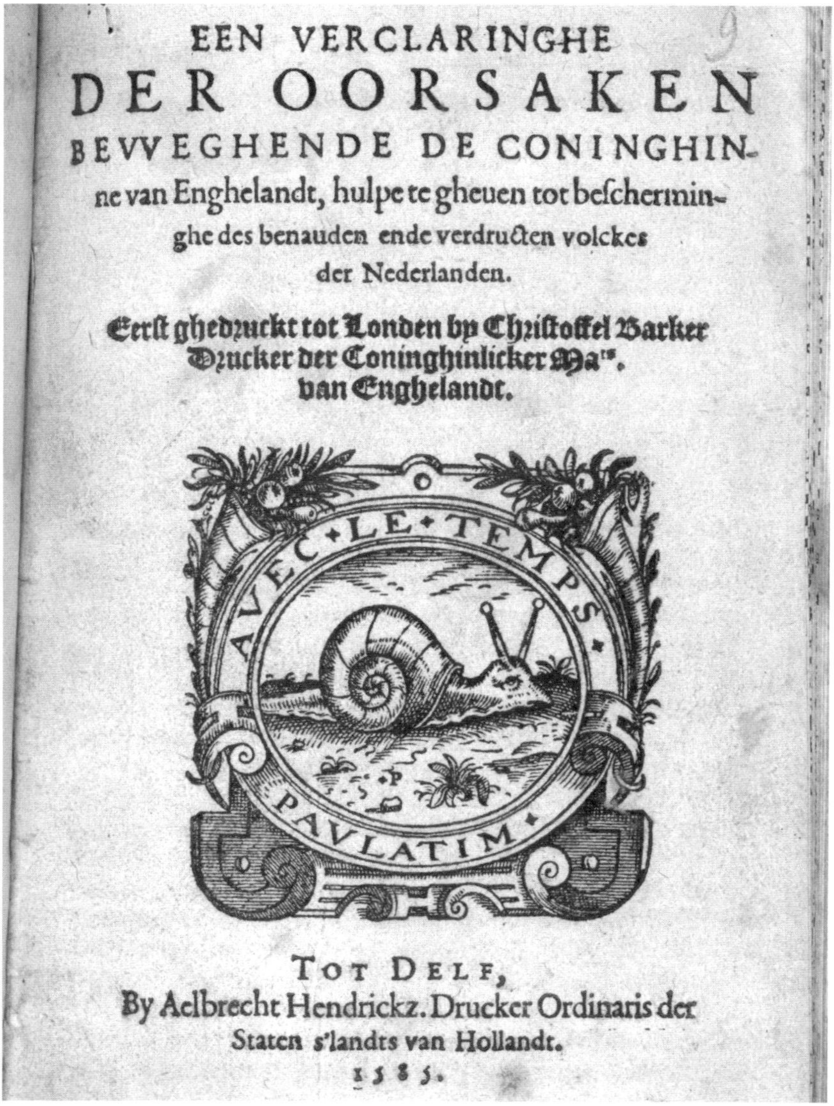

EEN VERCLARINGHE
DER OORSAKEN
BEVVEGHENDE DE CONINGHIN-
ne van Enghelandt, hulpe te gheuen tot beschermin-
ghe des benauden ende verdructen volckes
der Nederlanden.

Eerst ghedruckt tot Londen by Christoffel Barker
Drucker der Coninghinlicker Ma^{ts}.
van Enghelandt.

AVEC LE TEMPS.
PAVLATIM.

TOT DELF,
By Aelbrecht Hendrickz. Drucker Ordinaris der
Staten s'landts van Hollandt.
1585.

Fig 2: *Een verclaringhe der oorsaken beweghende de coninghinne van Enghelandt, hulpe te gheuen tot bescherminghe des* [...] *volckes der Nederlanden*, Delf: Aelbrecht Hendrickz, 1585. (Fag. H.3.8, no. 9)

local government printer. He printed a large number of Puritan tracts there, in both Dutch and English. He often acted as translator himself. It is significant that English Brownists had settled in Middelburg during the period that Schilders was active there. When the exiled Calvinist theologian Dudley Fenner (c. 1558–87), under the protection of the Earl of Leicester, became preacher to the English merchants at Middelburg, he chose a house in the proximity to Schilders. Soon Schilders was busy printing Fenner's prolific output until the latter died in Middelburg at a young age.

Religious contacts remained close throughout the seventeenth century. In 1630, Glasgow-born William Spang (1607–64) was appointed minister of the Scottish church in the staple town of Veere. He did much to promote Presbyterianism in the Netherlands. He publicized the history of the Scottish church with *Brevis et fidelis narratio in regno et ecclesia Scotica* (1640, reprinted as *Rerum nuper in regno Scotiae gestarum historia* in 1641), and published *Motuum Britannicorum verax Cushi ex ipsis Joabi et oculati testis prototypis totus translatus* in 1647 (printed in Rotterdam; both works are listed in the TCD Library's printed catalogue of 1872, available online, though not as part of the Fagel Collection). After serving the congregation of Veere for twenty-three years, Spang was appointed minister at Middelburg in November 1652. He remained at Middelburg until his death there on 17 June 1664. His son William followed in his father's footsteps as minister of Middelburg between 1682 and 1683.

Religious printing was not the only connection between England and Middelburg. Many refugees from the southern Netherlands had settled in Zeeland. They either stayed or crossed from there to England. Those who had settled in England remained in continuous contact with their Dutch/Flemish families and religious friends, and business relations were also close. Hieronimus Willemsen Aschman, for example, served at the Dutch Church in Austin Friars as a deacon for most of the second decade of the seventeenth century and in the 1630s and 1640s as an elder. Later in life he became burgomaster of Middelburg. It is not surprising that Middelburg was given prominence in the paintings decorating the triumphal arch that the London Dutch community erected for the coronation of James I in 1604. To many Dutch immigrant merchants in London, Middelburg was a second home in this period. The inclusion of the large number of pamphlets collected by Fagel in the STCN will undoubtedly extend our knowledge of and stimulate further research into the close political and religious contacts between the English-speaking world and the Low Countries during the late sixteenth and seventeenth centuries.

Outlook

At the invitation of Trinity College Library I have made an attempt to assess the importance of the Fagel collection of pamphlets in relation to the STCN. Due to time limits I had to restrict myself to a statistical analysis and suppress the continuous temptation to study the content. In order to establish a relevant sample of documents I consulted ten randomly chosen volumes of pamphlets covering a period from the 1580s to the 1760s. Again, at random, from each volume I checked ten pamphlets against the holdings recorded in the STCN. These are my findings. In the entire collection there is a small number of pamphlets with German imprints and of French language materials with a (modern-day) Belgian imprint. These materials are not included in the STCN. However, the overwhelming majority of the pamphlets are in Dutch and have either Dutch or Flemish imprints. Of the hundred pamphlets checked against the STCN file, twelve were not recorded (two of which in variant editions) and six would prove to be a second copy (i.e. only one other source mentioned in the STCN). In other words, the predicted strike rate of unrecorded or variant materials runs at 12 per cent.

What can we conclude from this research? From a purely statistical point of view it will be a worthwhile exercise to add the entire Fagel collection of pamphlets to the STCN. The predicted strike rate of new and variant titles is more than sufficient to justify the effort. On the one hand, it will place this specific collection within the sophisticated framework it deserves and, on the other hand, the value of the STCN will be enhanced by the inclusion of a substantial number of (possibly) unique materials. That in turn benefits both the study of Dutch history and that of early Anglo–Low Countries relationships. There is another important reason to consider: it is very rare indeed to find such a comprehensive collection of related materials under one roof. It would most certainly be beneficial to the STCN if these rare 'special' collections were included and, if possible, specially marked or highlighted. This would not only open up the availability of resources, it might also stimulate research into the passion of collecting itself, and with that, into the formation, history and fate of treasured collections.

Biographies

Charles Benson was Keeper of Early Printed Books in Trinity College Library from 1988 until his retirement in 2011. He has contributed to the study of the nineteenth-century book trade. He is currently completing a dictionary of the members of the Dublin book and allied trades 1801–51.

David Brown is completing a Ph.D. on the Adventurers for Irish Land 1641–60, a group of English merchants, privateers and colonial projectionists who managed to acquire, for a time, almost 20 per cent of Ireland. David graduated from Trinity College Dublin in 1987 and has worked in a number of different areas including Historical GIS (Geographical Informations Systems) and digitization projects with an emphasis on large documents. He was involved in a voluntary project to make high-resolution digital images of the maps in the Fagel Library undertaken by Andrew Bonar-Law and Leslie Brown 2009–11 and has worked most recently on the Down Survey of Ireland project that has attracted a global audience since its release in March 2013.

Peter Fox worked for fifteen years in Trinity College Dublin, first as Deputy Librarian and then as Librarian and College Archivist. He subsequently moved to Cambridge as the University Librarian and retired in 2009. In 2011 he held a Visiting Fellowship at the Trinity Long Room Hub. He has edited several books, including the commentary volume to the Book of Kells facsimile (Lucerne 1990), *Treasures of the Library, Trinity College Dublin* (Dublin 1986) and *Cambridge University Library: the Great Collections* (Cambridge 1998). His latest book, *Trinity College Library Dublin: A History*, was published in 2014 by Cambridge University Press. He is a Fellow of Selwyn College Cambridge.

A graduate of Corpus Christi College Oxford, **Clare Guest** has held numerous research fellowships at Trinity, most recently a Long Room Hub Visiting Fellowship. She works principally on art and thought of the Italian Renaissance and her most important publication is *The Understanding of Ornament in the Italian Renaissance* (Leiden 2015). She is currently Visiting Research Fellow in the Department of Italian, TCD.

Jason Harris is Lecturer in Early-Modern History and Director of the Centre for Neo-Latin Studies in University College Cork. His research focuses upon the intellectual culture of early-modern Europe, with particular emphasis upon religious thought, the cultural manifestation of humanist ideas, and Neo-Latin prose stylistics. He has published studies of the friendship circle of the Flemish cartographer Abraham Ortelius and of numerous aspects of the corpus of early-modern Irish writing in Latin.

Jaap Harskamp holds a doctorate in comparative literature from the University of Amsterdam. Until recently he was Curator of the Dutch/Flemish Collections at the British Library. At present he is in the process of adding the pre-1801 holdings in Cambridge University Library to the STCN. He has published on a wide range of subjects, most recently with the substantial study *The Anatomy of Despondency: European Socio-Cultural Criticism 1789–1939* (Leiden and Boston 2011).

Having graduated in German and French from Trinity College Dublin, **Tim Jackson** spent his working life there in the Department of Germanic Studies, retiring as Associate Professor in 2008. His principal area of research has been medieval German literature, in particular spiritual literature and the romance. His most important publication is *Typus und Poetik. Studien zur Bedeutungsvermittlung in der Literatur des deutschen Mittelalters* (Heidelberg 2003).

William Kelly is a graduate of the universities of Glasgow and Strathclyde. A trained librarian, he spent most of his professional life on the staff of the National Library of Scotland. He is now an Honorary Research Fellow in Edinburgh Napier University's Scottish Centre for the Book. He has published widely on German and Low Countries bibliography.

John Loughman is Senior Lecturer in the School of Art History and Cultural Policy, University College Dublin.He specializes in seventeenth-century Dutch art. Among his publications is (with J.M. Montias) *Public and Private Spaces: Works of Art in Seventeenth-Century Dutch Houses* (Zwolle 2000). He is currently preparing a monograph on the landscape painter Aelbert Cuyp.

Helga Robinson-Hammerstein is a Fellow Emerita of Trinity College Dublin, where until 2008 she taught Modern European History to undergraduate and postgraduate students. Her principal interest is in Early Modern Central European History, on which she has published numerous studies. In particular she has explored the rare collection of early sixteenth-century pamphlets among the Early Printed Books in TCD Library and in the Herzog-August-Bibliothek, Wolfenbüttel. She was a member of the International Commission for the History of Universities and its General Secretary from 1995 to 2005.

Theo Thomassen studied history and archivistics and holds the Chair in Archival Science at the Department of Media Studies at the University of Amsterdam. He started his professional career as an archivist at the First Department of the then General State Archives in The Hague. His major objects of research were the archives of the Dutch ambassadors abroad, the States General and the secretaries and chancelleries of the States General, and in particular the documentary collections of the greffiers Fagel. After moving to the Dutch Archives School and Reinwardt Academy he kept this fascination alive. His doctoral dissertation (Amsterdam 2009) has been published as *Instrumenten van de macht. De Staten-Generaal en hun archieven 1576–1796* (Den Haag 2015).

Index of personal names

In general, the Fagels themselves are noted only where there is a reference to an individual member of the family. Page numbers in italics refer to monochrome figures within the text. Plate numbers are at the end of relevant entries.